Clergy Assessment and Career Development

Clergy Assessment and Career Development

Richard A. Hunt
John E. Hinkle, Jr.
H. Newton Malony
Editors

Abingdon Press
Nashville

Clergy Assessment and Career Development

Copyright © 1990 by the General Board of Higher Education and Ministry, The United Methodist Church

This book is printed on acid-free paper.

Library of Congress Cataloging-in-Publication Data

Clergy assessment and careet development / Richard A. Hunt, John E. Hinkle, H. Newton Malony, editors.
   p. cm.
   Includes bibliographical references.
   ISBN 0-687-08653-1 (alk. paper)
   1. Clergy—Rating of. 2. Clergy—Post-ordination training.
3. Career development. I. Hunt, Richard A., 1931- . II. Hinkle, John E. III. Malony, H. Newton.
BV4011.7.C54 1990
253' .2—dc20   89-38791
                                                                              CIP

To the glory of God and the benefit of the church universal in its unending quest to improve its ministry to all persons

CONTENTS

PART ONE

Introduction

1. Overview of Dimensions and Issues—*Richard A. Hunt, John E. Hinkle, Jr., and H. Newton Malony* 13

PART TWO

Church, Career, Family, and Personal Contexts of Assessment

2. Tracking God's Call: Basic Theoretical Issues in Clergy Assessment—*James E. Dittes* 21

3. Spiritual Formation in Theological Education and Psychological Assessment —*Edward Wimberly* 27

4. Lifetime Development of Clergy—*Winston E. Gooden* 32

5. Personal Growth for Clergy—*Richard A. Blackmon and Archibald D. Hart* 36

6. Spouses and Families of Clergy —*Cameron Lee* 43

7. Nurturing Dual Career Couples—*Richard A. Hunt* 48

PART THREE

Research Methodologies and Perspectives

8. Pitfalls and Possibilities in Processing People: A Psychometric Perspective —*Richard L. Gorsuch* 55

9. Issues and Models in Criterion Development—*John E. Hinkle, Jr., and Emily D. Haight* 61

10. Development of an Assessment Instrument—*David A. Hogue* 67

11. Psychometric Characteristics of a Ministerial Assessment Battery—*Michael P. Comer* 72

12. Agency Selection Committees and Evaluation—*Pam Holliman* 78

13. Changing Patterns of People Entering Ministry—*Howard Stone* 82

14. Predicting Ministerial Effectiveness—*Laura F. Majovski and H. Newton Malony* 86

15. Lilly Quality of Ministry Projects—*Joseph P. O'Neill* 90

PART FOUR

Assessment Procedures and Methods

16. ATS Profiles of Ministry Project—*Daniel O. Aleshire* 97

17. The Theological School Inventory (TSI) and the Inventory of Religious Activities and Interests (IRAI)—*Richard A. Hunt* 104

18. A Clergy Personnel Selection Battery—*John E. Hinkle, Jr.* 109

19. Structured Assessment Interviewing—*Charles R. Ridley* 113

20. A Systems Approach to Personnel Development in Church Ministries —*Thomas M. Graham* 119

21. Self-evaluation Through Relational Experience: A C.P.E. Perspective—*John Patton* 123

22. Report Writing for Churches and Candidates —*H. Newton Malony* 129

23. Legal and Ethical Issues in Assessment—*Leila M. Foster* 134

PART FIVE

Gender and Cultural Issues in Assessment

24. Culture Fair and Gender Fair Assessment
—*Harvey Huntley, Jr.*.................140

25. Issues in the Assessment of Women
—*Joan Scanlon*.....................144

26. Black Populations—*Edward Wimberly*.....149

27. Hispanic Populations—*Pablo Polischuk*....154

28. Asian Populations—*Chan-Hie Kim*.......158

29. Native American Populations
—*J. David Pierce*..................163

PART SIX

Applications Among Church Structures

30. Seminary Applications
—*Sue Webb Cardwell*................170

31. Ecumenical Career Development
Centers—*Thomas E. Brown*...........175

32. Alban Institute Approaches to Assessment
—*Roy Oswald*......................179

33. A Protestant Denominational Application
—*Robert F. Kohler*..................184

34. Clergy Assessment in Roman Catholic
Applications—*Brian P. Hall*..........189

PART SEVEN

Conclusions for the Future

35. Assessment in the Future—*Richard A. Hunt, John
E. Hinkle, Jr., and H. Newton Malony*....198

Appendix

References...........................206

Biographical Profiles of Contributors.......215

Index...............................220

ACKNOWLEDGMENTS

A survey of current theories, perspectives, and technologies for doing psychological assessment of candidates for the ordained ministry and of clergy was initially conceived by Richard A. Hunt and John E. Hinkle, Jr., as members of the Advisory Committee on Psychological Assessment, a part of the Division of Ordained Ministry of the Board of Higher Education and Ministry of The United Methodist Church.

Major funding for this volume was provided by the Division of Ordained Ministry, thanks to the vision and encouragement of Robert F. Kohler, a director in the division, and of Don Treese, executive director. The enthusiastic cooperation of Greg Michael, Abingdon editor for this project, has facilitated the preparation of this volume and made such a complex project much more enjoyable.

The editors also want to acknowledge the many helpful suggestions from a wide range of sources in addition to the good work of each contributor to this volume. In addition, James Ashbrook and James Dittes, members of the Bier symposium in 1966, provided important insights for this report on advances since that conference.

We are indebted to Joan Hunt, who did much of the detail work necessary to contact each author and bring chapters to their publishable form. In addition, the Word Processing Office at Fuller Theological Seminary aided in translating files from various program formats to a common word processing form.

We also appreciate the kindness of the American Psychological Association and the Robert E. Krieger Publishing Company for permission to reprint materials as noted in this volume.

Research and development in clergy assessment can progress only as rapidly as funding allows. Across the years, the Lilly Endowment, Inc., has consistently supported major projects in this area, including the Theological School Inventory, the Readiness for Ministry Project, and the Quality of Ministry program. Evidences of this support appear in several chapters in this volume. In addition, other funding sources and the labor (often unpaid) of many researchers have made the advances reported here possible as gifts to the work of the ecumenical church in the world today.

We are indeed thankful to God and to all whose efforts have joined in this continuing work of leadership development and nurture so that the church can do Christ's work in the world.

Introduction

1

Overview of Dimensions and Issues

RICHARD A. HUNT, JOHN E. HINKLE, JR., H. NEWTON MALONY

Defining Clergy Assessment

Clergy development refers most broadly to all the career-related changes a pastor makes across life, from preparation through retirement. Clergy assessment is set in the context of this career development perspective. As used in this volume, clergy assessment includes all standard methods (methodologies) that may be employed in candidly and accurately understanding an individual in relation to a career in the ordained ministry. These characteristics must be identifiable and measurable. The individual's functioning may be actual (current or past) or potential (in the future).

Combining these elements is complicated, as illustrated by this one-sentence formal definition: Clergy assessment refers to the full range of methodologies employed in intentional information gathering, analysis, and reporting about the characteristics of any individual in relation to functioning as an ordained minister in any Christian tradition.

The word *assessment* implies that a comparison is to be made between "what is" and some specified standard or set of criteria. Some type of decision or judgment regarding the substantive aspects of these comparisons will then be made. In the area of clergy career and candidate assessment, four distinguishable, but overlapping, sets of variables are identified that emphasize fitness, competence, readiness, and effectiveness.

These categories of criteria may be related to one another in the following manner:

> Fitness for preparation for and engagement in the practice of effective professional ministry initially means that an individual possesses the potential (capacities and characteristics) to develop competencies (skills needed in ministry) to the point of readiness to begin the practice of effective professional ministry. (Hinkle, 1979, p. 1)

Fitness dimensions usually focus on whether an individual has the potential to become an effective minister. Potential includes all dimensions that contribute to this outcome, such as intellectual ability, personality structure, interpersonal styles, accuracy and appropriateness of self-image, interests, motivations, and uses of social support networks.

Competencies refer specifically to interpersonal, relational dimensions that affect others. Examples of competencies are listening skills, abilities to communicate ideas and feelings accurately, maturity of judgment, and other abilities that enable groups to function effectively.

Readiness suggests that an individual has prepared sufficiently enough to be "ready" to take up the practice and responsibilities of a specified professional ministry. Sufficient preparation includes theory and practice in both basic academic areas and applied situations. An example of readiness is having an adequate knowledge of scriptures, church history, and theology. These and other basic academic disciplines are synthesized with skills (*praxis*) in the application of the gospel to the needs of persons in parish and other professional ministry settings.

Effectiveness emphasizes how well clergy minister in given settings with specific resources and limitations. Effectiveness builds upon fitness, competence, and readiness. Personal functioning (fitness) and social functioning (competence), combined with preparation (readiness), when applied to a given situation, produce greater or lesser degrees of effectiveness.

A significant implication of these interrelated concepts of criteria is that no single category of criteria is sufficient by itself to guide the comparisons necessary for effective clergy assessment. In an oversimplified manner, some may have considered each dimension separate, implying that psychological assessment examined fitness, academic (or seminary) assessment evaluated readiness, and field assessment and feedback by church authorities emphasized effectiveness, with competencies perhaps being involved in all these. By contrast, an integrated view acknowledges that these functionally distinguishable dimensions are also interrelated in very complex ways.

Ashbrook (1970) has carefully identified the limits and possibilities for "testing" (usually paper/pencil instruments) in assessing the "fit" between an individual and education (preparation) for ministry as well as ministry itself. Assessment in the more general sense looks at career patterns, career settings, and career output. These involve interactions between persons, places, purposes, and performances that are constantly repeated across one's lifetime.

The present volume primarily focuses on psychological assessment of candidates and of clergy in terms of fitness, competence, readiness, and effectiveness. This intrapsychic focus emphasizes the psychological requirements—both intrapersonal and interpersonal—of clergy functioning. These are a major, though not exclusive, thrust and do not emphasize the broader aspects of the match between an individual and a specific context for ministry. The context for effectiveness may also be seen as the psychological demands or requirements for effective functioning in a clergy role.

In terms of the foregoing categories of criteria, our focus on psychological fitness, psychological competence, psychological readiness, and psychological effectiveness is a mosaic or grid of assessment points by dimensions. Thus other dimensions of effectiveness in ministry—such as preaching, teaching, administration, and pastoral care—are related to, but not synonymous with, effectiveness from the psychological perspective.

Purposes of Clergy Assessment

Clergy assessment is needed to inform both personal and institutional decision making regarding personnel matters. Committees must select candidates from among applicants, and applicants must make self-reflective career choices. Both of these decisions are usually seen as being in the context of God's will and leadership.

Additional decisions must be made regarding the nurture, development, and formation of persons who are preparing for the ministry or placement in educational field work settings. Assessment must also be used by leaders in making decisions concerning problematic, ineffective, or troubled clergy, as well as for placement of clergy in parish and other work settings. Thus assessment can inform decisions involving selection, development and formation, placement, and remediation of persons in relation to all professional ministries.

Individual and Institutional Clients in Clergy Assessment Procedures

In formal assessment situations, the needs of the institution and the needs of the individual are often complementary, but at times they may be in conflict. Potential conflict may exist when a selection decision must be made. The institution's right to have complete and accurate information may conflict with the candidate's rights to privacy and confidentiality. Contracts and procedures need to protect the rights of each party without infringing on the rights of the other.

Formal Professional Assessment of Candidates and Clergy: Who Does It?

While supervisors, managers, and committees in religious institutional structures frequently have high levels of competence in assessment, the emphasis in this volume is on the professional specialist who functions as an evaluator of candidates and clergy in a more technical and nonadministrative context. Examples of such specialists are clinical psychologists, career counselors, professional pastoral counselors, supervisors of clinical pastoral education, and psychiatrists. These professional evaluators have in common a developed set of procedures, instruments, and theories on the basis of which their assessments are conducted. Here the term *instruments* includes procedures such as structured interviews and simulations as well as questionnaires and paper/pencil inventories.

In selecting an assessment professional, the primary concern is finding that person who can be trusted to deliver the relevant information needed by the client, whether the client is an institution or an individual. Other factors—such as geographical accessibility, cost of services, flexibility of service delivery, and any potential dual role relations between the professional and the client—also bear upon the choice of the professional evaluator.

Psychiatric evaluation is essential in remedial situations. In such cases, an individual's discomfort, distress, and dysfunction in the clergy role, or in preparation for ministry, may have reached crisis proportions. Intensive intervention, including medication, hospitalization, or other procedures may be required.

Clinical psychologists, who are trained and have experience in clinical evaluation and personnel selection, are most likely to apply both structured interviewing techniques and a variety of standardized tests and inventories to evaluate personality. Some psychologists have also had theological training and may be ordained clergy. Some of these may also describe themselves as pastoral psychologists.

Psychologists who have theological training and clinical pastoral education supervisors have the advantage of being familiar with religious language, church settings, and stresses of the ministerial role. Their training in the structured interviewing of clergy and in strategies of intervention often is based on educational models of normal development as well as on clinical models of pathology.

The professional evaluator of clergy and of candidates for the ordained ministry may use various techniques of interviewing and psychometric measurements. Usually a combination of methods yields the benefits of each approach and compensates for the major liabilities of each. The clinician-instrument interaction is fundamental to the reliability and validity of the findings and interpretations in psychological assessment.

Culture, Gender, and Other Biases

Cultural, gender, and age biases may exist in the assessment instruments, in the professionals who do assessment, and in the persons who use assessment information. The skilled clinician who knows assessment instruments well and is aware of these potential sources of bias can correct for them in the interpretations that may be made of the data.

Professionals who create or use assessment procedures for clergy evaluation must also be aware of culture, gender, age, and other biases that may influence the assessment process. In many assessment situations, a panel of female and male professional assessors and interviewers that includes representatives of both sexes and of salient ethnic and cultural groups can attend to these perspectives in the assessment process. Many details of these issues are addressed in the section on gender and cultural issues in assessment, chapters 23–28.

Some Dimensions of Assessment

Assessment of clergy is set in a mosaic of possibilities, some of which can be described by the bipolar end points along the following dimensions.

1. Written responses (essays, paper/pencil inventories) versus oral responses (interviews) or behavioral samples.

2. The subject's (or candidate's) own self-report (self-rating of abilities) versus the report of another person observing the performance of the subject (performance feedback and evaluation).

3. The subject's internal state (perceptions, motives, feelings, intentions) versus the subject's external performance (behaviors, patterns of action, accomplishments).

4. The subject's maximum performance (intelligence and ability tests) versus typical performance (inventories of frequency and preference for specific activities).

5. Presentation of resulting data in a narrative form versus using a structured arrangement of scales and profiles.

6. The purpose of the procedure is to benefit the church needs versus benefiting the needs of the subject.

7. The application of the procedure at the initial steps toward a career (screening and selection of applicants) versus at any stage thereafter (placement in seminary classes, assignment to a parish, promotion, retirement planning).

8. The procedure may collect data only from the subject (the candidate) in contrast with including information from others (spouse, family, congregation).

9. The assessment may be voluntary or may be required by a church or educational authority.

10. The focus of the assessment may be on past events (family experiences, school awards, work accomplishments) instead of on current activities (parish, school activities) as possible predictors of either current or future performance.

This brief outline suggests some of the facets involved in clergy assessment, although this special field is certainly not limited to these dimensions.

Recent Roots of Clergy Assessment

Clergy assessment is set in at least two major contexts. One is the vocational development approach initiated early in this century with the work of Parsons and others. That has become the twentieth-century refinement of centuries of apprenticeships and informal guidance of persons into their adult work as part of a less technical society. Super (1957) brought together many of the pivotal fundamental concepts that have guided these vocational development perspectives. Pietrofesa and Splete (1975) provide a helpful brief survey of contemporary career development concepts.

The more basic context for clergy assessment is the church's preparation throughout the centuries of individuals for clergy roles. Clergy assessment is a modern expression of the efforts of the church to identify, select, and train its clergy and other leaders, as surveyed in considerable detail by Richard Niebuhr (1956) and by Niebuhr, Williams, and Gustafson (1956).

These two roots of clergy assessment were first brought together in the pioneering work of Mark May (1934), which in some ways seemed ahead of its time in its potential for influence on churches and their clergy assessment and selection procedures. In addition to the work of Richard Niebuhr and others in the 1950s, the studies of Blizzard (1958a and 1958b) gave rise to the development of specific instruments and procedures for clergy assessment. By the mid 1960s, studies relating to clergy, including clergy assessment, had accumulated to some 700 that were indexed and summarized by Menges and Dittes (1965), with their supplement appearing in 1969.

Work on clergy assessment issues accelerated in the 1960s and 1970s with the support of the Lilly Endowment, Inc., for the development of the *Theological School Inventory*, the establishment of the Ministry Studies Board, and the development of the *Readiness for Ministry* (now *Profiles of Ministry*) programs. During this time, church related career development centers for clergy were also being established.

In the past thirty years much important work on clergy assessment issues has been done. Many of the writers in this volume have been personally involved in the advances that they discuss. They represent most of the available perspectives on these issues, with roots and indebtedness to many sources that space does not permit describing.

There are, however, at least three major preceding landmarks in clergy assessment that must be acknowledged. First was the early 1950s work on motivation for the ministry that was reported by Samuel Southard (1955). The need for instruments like the *Theological School Inventory* and *Inventory of Religious Activities and Interests* (chap. 16) was first identified in that period.

The second landmark was the symposium on psychological testing for ministerial selection, sponsored in 1966 by the Academy of Religion and Mental Health, and reported under the editorship of William C. Bier (1970). In this conference, a more comprehensive view of clergy assessment from both theological and psychological perspectives was articulated and many recommendations for next steps were offered. Three major recommendations from that conference should be repeated here to remind us all of continuing needs in the areas of clergy assessment (DeWire, 1970).

First, initiative should be taken at the national level to encourage leaders, researchers, and others working with clergy assessment issues to work on specific projects to answer clearly identified needs around clergy assessment. Among these are work on the criterion problem, test development and use, values in relation to assessment, methods other than paper/pencil tests, and linkages with similar career assessment programs in other fields.

Second, better coordination and control of research activities among the many groups and agencies will enable them to relate their projects to the work of others, replicate results, and pool information for the benefit of all denominations and traditions wishing help in these areas.

Third, better communication of research findings to church administrators, candidate committees, and parish ministers and lay leaders is needed. Someone should provide "a clearing house for the purpose of listing and consolidating the gains and knowledge that we have acquired in the use of tests, with a view to" extending research in this area (DeWire, 1970, 261). This agency could provide resources and help to researchers in designing their research.

As will be seen in the chapters that follow, some progress in the directions envisioned by the Bier report has been made, especially by the Lilly Quality of Ministry Project (see chap. 15). Much remains to be accomplished. In many respects, the present volume is a follow-up to the work of Bier and his associates at the 1966 conference.

A third major advance was the development and modifications in the *Readiness for Ministry* project that is reported in Schuller, Strommen, and Brekke (1980) and in chapter 16 by Daniel O. Aleshire. This major research project has created a series of workbook, interview, and field observation methods for measuring these dimensions and placing them in the context of denominational norms.

The present volume brings many of these research perspectives together, partly as the basis for a national ecumenical conference on clergy assessment in 1990. Future directions for clergy assessment research and applications will be presented in chapter 35.

From Past to Present . . . and on to the Future

Most of the basic theoretical issues concerning assessment remain with us, mostly in the form that

James Dittes stated them in his chapter in Bier (1970). For the current volume, Dittes (chap. 2) again relates current issues to those of the past and challenges us to deal with these in improved ways.

Since that important conference of 1966 (reported in Bier [1970]), additional issues in assessment have appeared, some gains have been made, and much yet remains to be done. As shown by the table of contents, we have chosen to arrange current thinking on clergy assessment into five major clusters or parts, as described below.

PART TWO: Church, Career, Family, and Personal Contexts of Assessment links clergy assessment and career paths of clergy with their other personal development across the adult life-span. These chapters by Dittes, Wimberly, Gooden, Blackmon and Hart, Lee, and Hunt place assessment in these larger contexts and systems, interacting with candidates and clergy.

PART THREE: Research Methodologies and Perspectives addresses many of the technical issues that form the scientific bases for valid assessments of all types. From his thorough knowledge of research methodology and multivariate statistical procedures, Richard Gorsuch (chap. 8) addresses some of the same dangers and opportunities regarding clergy assessment as does Dittes.

Central to the improvement of assessment procedures for clergy is the criterion problem. In chapter 9, John E. Hinkle, Jr., and Emily D. Haight describe their efforts to establish reliable criteria with which to validate assessment procedures.

The continuing research on clergy assessment issues at Garrett-Evangelical Theological School has produced several important dissertations. In addition to the Hinkle and Haight chapter, three other chapters report some of these findings. David A. Hogue (chap. 10) describes how he conceptualized and researched an assessment instrument. Michael P. Comer (chap. 11) reports on his matching of assessment data to selected criteria. Pam Holliman (chap. 12) shows how denominational committees use psychological assessment in relation to other sources of information about candidates.

The vision, concern, and commitment of the Lilly Endowment, Inc., to improve the quality of clergy across the years has been the major influence on research and development of clergy assessment for nearly four decades. Lilly Endowment has supported three major research efforts that have had far-reaching effects on clergy assessment. The first was the initial development and production of the Theological School Inventory in the late 1950s and early 1960s. The second was, in cooperation with the Association of Theological

Schools, the development of the *Readiness for Ministry* program.

The third major set of research projects funded by Lilly Endowment focuses on improving the recruitment and selection of ministerial candidates. Joseph P. O'Neill reports on this current research thrust concerning the "Lilly Quality of Ministry Projects" (chap. 15). Howard Stone, in chapter 13, summarizes one of these projects.

PART FOUR: Assessment Procedures and Methods provides many forms of assessment in its eight chapters.

Daniel O. Aleshire (chap. 16) brings us up to date on "The ATS Profiles of Ministry Project," the revised form of the *Readiness for Ministry* project. Richard A. Hunt (chap. 17) reports on "The Theological School Inventory (TSI) and the Inventory of Religious Activities and Interests (IRAI)," instruments that began being used in the late 1960s.

Too often, assessment has been narrowed to depend heavily on paper and pencil instruments. Three chapters address this issue by lifting up assessment methodologies that rely primarily on clinical interview techniques. Charles R. Ridley (chap. 19), coming out of a personnel selection background, has researched and developed "Structured Assessment Interviewing," which has proven especially useful in identifying clergy who will be successful in organizing and planting new churches. Another personnel selection perspective is described by Thomas M. Graham in chapter 20. John Patton, a leader in the clinical pastoral education (CPE) movement for many years, describes some CPE approaches to interviewing in chapter 21.

An example of a clergy personnel selection battery is provided by John E. Hinkle, Jr., (chap. 18), who provides a case study of a denominational structure that supports uniformity of selection criteria and a battery for assessing those criteria. H. Newton Malony (chap. 22) then considers issues that are involved in reporting to clients, both candidates and churches. Leila M. Foster, an attorney and ordained minister, identifies some of the legal and ethical issues that must be answered in relation to clergy assessment (chap. 23).

PART FIVE: Gender and Cultural Issues in Assessment alerts us to the heterogeneity of churches and clergy in society today. In chapter 24, Harvey Huntley, Jr., reports on ways to sensitize leaders and professionals to cultural and gender issues in relation to assessment. Issues in assessing women for the ordained clergy are carefully explored by Joan Scanlon in chapter 25.

Among many possible ethnic and cross-cultural factors that affect assessment, we have selected four populations for detailed treatment of clergy assessment issues in chapters 26–29. Edward Wimberly considers assessment with black American populations; Pablo Polischuk describes Hispanic-American populations; Chan-Hie Kim focuses on value differences between Asian and American populations; and J. David Pierce describes factors at work in Native American (American Indian) populations.

PART SIX: Applications Among Church Structures describes several ways in which clergy assessment is used. Five of these are described in detail. Sue Webb Cardwell, out of her research and experience with TSI and *Readiness for Ministry* in a seminary setting, describes how assessment can be used in seminaries (chap. 30).

Ecumenical Career Development Centers have been a major provider of career and personal assessment for ministers. Thomas E. Brown, a pioneer in this area, describes the history and current status of assessment in these centers (chap. 31). Roy Oswald, an experienced

member of the Alban Institute, gives both cautions about assessment and alternate approaches to providing nurture for clergy in chapter 32.

Career assessment in relation to the broader concerns for ordained ministers in Protestant traditions is the focus of Robert F. Kohler (chap. 33). Brian P. Hall (chap. 34) provides a parallel analysis of assessment among Roman Catholics.

In our attempt to look at selected examples of all the ways that assessment of clergy is currently being researched and provided among all Christian traditions, we have undoubtedly missed some segments or failed to report them adequately for some groups. With this awareness, the editors will attempt the risky task of assessing the future of assessment in the concluding chapter (chap. 35).

Church, Career, Family, and Personal Contexts of Assessment

2

Tracking God's Call:

Basic Theoretical Issues in Clergy Assessment

JAMES E. DITTES

Why Assess?

At least since Moses' astonished stammering at the burning bush (Exodus 31), the encounter with the call of God has been an exhilarating and a tumultuously troublesome adventure. Startled by this intrusion into his quiet life as a shepherd, Moses mistrusted, pondered, and balked, saying: "I am nobody. What can I tell them? Don't send me. I am a poor speaker. Please send someone else." Yet, he then obeyed. Discerning the call rightly and responding fitly are daunting lifelong dilemmas. What is it I am called to do? How? With whom? Will they heed me? Am I adequate? These—Moses' puzzles—are the persistent and urgent questions, never with a finally clear answer, that confront the minister at the outset of his or her career and, not uncommonly, daily thereafter. For even the most faithful and effective minister, what day does not begin and what day does not end with twinges of self-scrutiny? Am I hearing the call rightly? Responding fitly?

To buttress their own self-assessment, ministers have long turned to the church for guidance. This is the community and the hierarchy that has taken the responsibility for confirming the call by their acts of ordination and assignment and who have their own reasons—out of concern for the welfare of the church and its mission—to want to give scrutiny to a minister's sense of calling.

Two kinds of questions have concerned clergy and their churches. These may be called "whether" questions and "how" questions: (1) *whether* a person is called, should be admitted to seminary, should be ordained, should be placed in a particular assignment, and so forth; (2) *how* a person can be assisted (toward making a decision, toward effective ministry) by particular interventions—such as by providing counseling, therapy, and particular kinds of supervision or training.

The first question to be asked of assessment, then, is why it is being used, what kinds of questions is it to help

answer. "Whether" questions, guiding decisions about screening and placement, are largely concerned with prediction (to be discussed at the end of this chapter), with matching a particular person now with the requirements of an anticipated vocational position later. They are concerned with the resources of the person and the needs of the position. This is Moses' questioning of his own fitness for the mission to which he is being called.

"How" questions, leading to decisions about guidance and training, are largely concerned with process and change. They are concerned with matching the resources available (in therapy or in training, for example) with the needs of a person, as well as with the needs of a vocational position. This is God coaching Moses on how to deal with the Hebrew people, how to use his staff and his brother, Aaron. This is a seminary student choosing, or being advised to choose, one course rather than another, or a term of CPE. This is a minister being afforded a study leave or a spiritual retreat or being advised to restructure staff assignments.

Through the centuries, ministers and churches have made such assessments with varying blends of intuition, prayer, tradition, guided by varying theological and psychological principles, implicit or explicit. Since World War II, in the United States, they have turned for assistance to the psychological measuring and diagnostic techniques that have emerged in that period, which this book largely refers to as "assessment." But even as the "science" of assessment supplements or replaces the long practiced arts of assessment, the principal question of the diagnostic assessment and of the research experience that guides it remains the same age-old haunting dilemma: How can one discern the call of God rightly? How can one respond fitly?

On the whole, questions of selection have occupied this new mode of psychometric-assisted assessment and the research supporting it. Hence the prominence in this volume and this chapter: Whose call is to be affirmed? Who gives promise of effective ministry? What did God see in the refugee shepherd named Moses?

Assessing Assessment

The most fundamental and persistently haunting question about assessment, one that has bothered many of its practitioners fully as much as its clients or critics, is about its own adequacy to the task at hand. Is assessment—in terms of the psychometric and clinical procedures discussed in this book—relevant to discerning God's call and the presence or promise of God's saving ministry in and through a person's professional life? Or does God's ministry work through factors quite different from the characteristics discernible to assessment? Could modern psychometricians and diagnosticians ever see what God saw in Moses?

Clergy, clergy candidates, church agencies, and officials experience an urgent need for help and want the assessment to be helpful, and the biases of the twentieth-century mind trust quantifiable, research-based science. But this need and the bias does not establish the validity of assessment. The burden of proof must remain on those who advocate and use it.

Much that is fundamental—theologically and scientifically—argues against the validity of assessment: the sovereignty of a God never to be confined to the ken of his creature; the freedom of a Spirit blowing where it will, a Spirit with a penchant for using stones rejected by builders; the history of a church whose faith has been energized time and again by persons beginning with Peter and Paul who would not obviously pass muster of modern assessment. Traditional ecclesiology separates, ever since Augustine's decisive attack on the Donatists, the effectiveness of the clerical *office* from the human characteristics of the clergy holding that office.

Contemporary understanding about projection, transference, myth making, and social roles emphasizes how a clergy figure plays crucial roles in the lives of people quite independently of any "real" personal characteristics of the actual clergy. Does the effectiveness of God's ministry really depend on any human characteristics discernible to assessment?

How Set Apart Is the Clergy?

In assessing the validity of clergy assessment, a special question arises about the uniqueness of the clergy role. Implicitly or explicitly, assessment tends to make judgments about clergy that are generalized from principles first applied to other non-clergy situations. (This is a natural consequence of clergy and churches turning to "outside" experts as part of the seemingly inevitable process of the assimilation of the church to the "world.") The tendency is to suppose that the "effective clergy" is one who shows characteristics of being "healthy" or "normal" or someone who is a good "student" or an effective "leader" by criteria developed in the academic or commercial worlds, or perhaps someone who resembles a good social worker.

The church, worshiping a God who chose not only radical incarnation, but also drastic rejection and crucifixion as the means of saving, is intended to be in the world but not of it. Its clergy are to serve the world but are also sacramentally set apart from it. Should we expect that effective ministers will resemble successful leaders in the "world"? Instead should we expect that those who participate most effectively in God's ministry to the world should look "different"? Those who assess have the burden of proof of showing that their judgments are appropriate to the very special case of Christian ministers. If notions of what it takes to be a good parent or a good business executive or a good nurse are used to assess what it takes to be a good minister, these judgments must not be smuggled in, but must be made explicitly and intentionally.

The assessor must show that God's ministry does require characteristics that resemble good parenting, good business administration, good nursing, or whatever. More than this, the assessor and the assessor's clients must be constantly suspicious of any such generalizations and be ready to be open to the radical "crucifixion" mode of ministry, in which God's chosen instruments will resemble the "abnormal," the misfits and failures of the world. The assessor must be asked and must be ready to answer the question: What theological and psychological understandings of ministry, and what empirical data support the appropriateness of your judgments specifically to Christian ministry? God's call to ministry may well be a call *out* of the "world" and away from the standards the world uses—a call to those who are "different" and a call to be "different." Who is God calling and to what?

Specifying the Call

If assessment needs to be specific to Christian ministry and not relevant just to psychological health or effective professional functioning in general, perhaps God's call and, hence, the assessor's focus must be still more specific than that. Perhaps the call is not just to a vocation of ministry that is peculiarly different from worldly pursuits. Perhaps the call is to particular forms and settings of ministry that are peculiarly different one from another. Perhaps ministry is just as diverse and just as localized as Paul's hymn (I Corinthians 12) to the diversity of gifts, so that to speak of the characteristics of "ministry" in general is not to speak of the characteristics of any ministry. The Bible's testimony to God's commitment to locating saving acts in radically particular historical events should raise considerable caution about assessment of "ministry" generally. The needs of ministry and God's intentions may be quite different, whether one is talking about the last century or the next, rural or urban, white or black, developed countries or Third World nations, men or women, singles or families, south or north, elderly or children, white collar or blue collar, Baptist or Presbyterian, prophet or priest.

The assessor's image of the ideal ministry, to which candidates are being matched, consciously or unconsciously, may be utterly valid for a congregation of people like the assessor and yet be quite dubious for dissimilar groups. Perhaps the assessing decisions and procedures discussed in this book have to be made separately from different historical and cultural contexts. It is up to the assessor to specify what particular social group and style of ministry is in mind and what its particular requirements are, or else to offer persuasive thinking and evidence for treating "ministry" as an undifferentiated whole.

Predictors, Criteria, and Their Connection

Assessment is a kind of diagnosis, or an unveiling. God's call and the capacity to respond fitly to it cannot be readily seen. It is discovered by clues that can be more easily discerned, such as a person's answers to questionnaire or interview questions. Usually, it is a kind of prediction. Some characteristics of a candidate "now" may predict some characteristics of that person's ministry "later." Usually the "now" characteristics that are measured are called *predictors,* and the "later" characteristics that are predicted are called *criteria.* The difficult, crucial tasks in assessment are to be accurate about identifying the important predictors and criteria and to be thorough about establishing—empirically and conceptually—the connection between them. How sure are we that the predictors really do diagnose, disclose, and predict the criteria?

The development of assessment procedures should start with careful identification of criteria. What image of effective and faithful ministry is to be enhanced and safeguarded? Assessment always has some such image in mind, at least implicitly; to be responsible, the image must be rendered as explicitly and carefully as possible. In particular, the questions about generalization, just discussed in the preceding section, need to be addressed—questions about the distinctiveness of ministry

and about the distinctiveness of diverse ministries. Is the criterion, the image of ministry, borrowed from general and secular notions of effective institutional leadership (what makes a good executive?), for example, or is it carefully derived from some differentiated and focused notions of Christian ministry? Is it targeted on particular needs of ministry in particular settings with particular groups?

Every assessment also chooses to examine particular characteristics of the candidate—the predictors. Of all the characteristics that could be measured, why choose these? The answer to that question should be: Because these predictors accurately predict to the criterion. The answer should not be, as is too often the case: Because these are predictors that can be easily measured.

This accurate prediction—the connection of predictors and criteria—should be established both empirically and conceptually. Empirically, with large enough samples followed up over a long enough time, data should show that there is in fact a close connection between the presumed predictor and the appropriate criterion. For example, is a particular personality trait in a minister, in fact, correlated with a congregation's sense of God's grace and guidance among them? Conceptually, or theoretically, careful reflection on *how* and *why* the predictor leads to the criterion explains the importance of the particular personality trait to God's work and gives some understanding of the nature of ministry. It is being emphasized here that these empirical data and these theoretical reflections need to be specific to ministry (not generalized from non-ministry research) and specific to particular forms and conditions of ministry (not generalized about all ministers). No prediction should seem so obvious or be allowed to be so implicit and buried that the empirical and theoretical validation is not insisted upon.

To emphasize the crucial difference between predictors and criteria and to emphasize that in assessment *someone* is inevitably making predictions that need to be carefully scrutinized, let us consider, stripped down to elementary form, a typical assessment transaction. A bishop employs a psychological consultant to conduct interviews and to psychologically test candidates for ordination. Skipping over the problem of what questions the psychologist chooses to ask and what tests to use, the psychologist faces a more excruciating dilemma: what to say about the candidate. The psychologist feels much more confident and comfortable limiting the report to describing the present personality characteristics of the candidate; for example, "This person is intelligent, introspective, and slightly defensive." But what the bishop most needs is to hear a prediction and evaluation, such as, "This person will function as a minister with sensitivity and effective leadership and should be accepted for ordination." Such prediction, after all, is the urgent purpose of the assessment. But it is the most precarious element, involving huge inferences, very often unacknowledged and untested, so that, properly, neither bishop nor psychologist feels confidence in making the prediction, and we would, properly, tend to mistrust either one if they did advance such prediction with a sureness.

Yet, one way or another, often casually and unscrutinized, the predictions are made. People often take this judgment for granted. Predicting the effective minister seems just as obvious and self-evident as predicting the political office holder's performance on the basis of the campaign performance, or using courtship experience as a basis for expectations in marriage.

The most urgent assistance that can be offered the psychologist or the bishop, or a committee or a board or even the candidate, or any assessor who makes this predictive leap, is to insist on asking the question: Why? What is the assumed connection between description and prediction, and where did this assumption come from? Is the connection derived from something demonstrable in the careers of clergy and in an understanding of God's ways with God's people, or does it perhaps reflect unacknowledged personal and cultural biases about preferences in religious leadership? How did God perceive in the fugitive shepherd a liberating leader that others, even Moses himself, could not see?

There is no test and no other assessment procedure in existence for identifying effective ministers—nothing even approximating the tests that are used for admitting candidates to law and medical schools and for admitting graduates into the profession. Tests and other procedures assess (sometimes reliably) the "now" or "predictor" characteristics—current interest, evaluations by teachers or others, perhaps of intelligence and some personality traits. But there is as yet little established scientific basis for connecting these precisely with the important criteria that candidates and church officials must consider. Prediction remains an art that should be informed by as much explicit theorizing as possible.

Chain of Prediction: "Before" Predictors

As convenient and common as it is to speak of predictors and criteria, assessment is actually far more complicated than that. There is, in fact, a *chain* of very difficult predictions or inferences, a chain that extends at either end, inferences we must make before we establish predictors and inferences we make after we identify criteria.

At the front end, there is huge inference in asserting that the test or interview or rating scale actually measures intelligence or commitment to ministry or personal sensitivity or preaching talent or whatever predictor we routinely claim it measures. All that we really know is that the candidate answers particular questions in particular ways (either in an interview or in writing) or that someone else describes the candidate in particular ways (as by assigning a course grade, or completing a rating scale about the person's performance in a field education setting, or in a psychiatric interview). One end of the chain of inferences is anchored in these data—its only anchor.

How do we reliably move from assembling these answers to claiming we have measured intelligence or preaching talent or any other predictor—even before we make the more audacious move beyond predictor to criterion? The answer to this question lies in the psychometric procedures of establishing *reliability* and *validity*. These techniques, which are discussed in most of the chapters in this volume, are well established and can be safely applied to establish that an interview or test or rating scale measures something (reliability) and that it measures what it says it measures (validity)—*if* they are used. The available techniques are trustworthy, but one cannot be sure that they have been responsibly used with available assessment procedures. The question of reliability and validity needs to be rigorously and vigorously asked of any assessment procedure and should not be assumed.

Chain of Prediction: "Beyond" Criteria

Still more complicated and difficult, and much less well addressed, is the extension of the chain of inference at the "criterion" end. Most of what we usually call criteria—certain behavior of ministers, for example, or "success" measures—are actually only *approximate* criteria and, in this chain, function in fact as predictors of more ultimate criteria. The ultimate criterion of ministry may be regarded as the presence of God's grace and guidance in the life of God's people and their faithful response to that presence. What does such presence and response look like? How can assessment help candidates to recognize and implement God's call so as best to assist their people's life in faith and grace? These are the matters we ultimately would like to know. But no one knows how to know that. We can imagine and even encourage criterion studies that push closer toward this ultimate criterion by devising scales to assess such characteristics as parishioners' growth in Christian faith, awareness of God's grace, graciousness of life-style, sense of citizenship in the kingdom, responsible love for neighbor, and so on. But as of now, such criteria are not available to assessment.

At best, we sometimes try to make inferences about these more ultimate criteria by identifying such more easily measurable parishioner behavior as regularity of church attendance, service activities, prayer, Bible reading, and contribution of time or money. But to use these factors as criteria is to leave begging—as hauntingly for assessors as for clergy—the question about the connection of such activities with the more ultimate criterion of life in God's grace and faith.

We are more often forced to be content with "criteria" that are still much farther removed from the ultimate criteria. We usually do not consider characteristics of parishioners' lives (toward which ministry is directed) but rather characteristics of *ministers*, such as: whether candidates actually proceed to ordination, whether they persist in ministry throughout their career; whether their churches grow in size, budget, and participation in denominationally encouraged programs; whether they are judged by parishioners, peers, or superiors to be good ministers; whether they report themselves to be content in ministry; whether they follow this or that style of counseling or preaching; how they distribute their working time; whether they stay informed in biblical and theological study, in economic and political affairs, active in prayer life; whether they have avoided or controlled conflict in their churches. When these or other characteristics of ministers are used as the criteria, it is often thought self-evident that we are dealing with some aspects of effective ministry. Indeed, such criteria are often prominent among those used by search committees, bishops, and other authorities in identifying effective ministers.

Even if there could be consensus and a rationale for such criteria, and reliable ways to measure them, they are still only approximate criteria. It is at best a good guess—or, perhaps more accurately, a lifelong search—to know what characteristics of ministry, if any, best foster or participate in the Christian life of a faithful community; and what may be true for one community may not be true for another. So the guess must be as informed as possible. There should be unrelenting insistence that use of any ministerial characteristic as a criterion be derived from a thoroughgoing theory of ministry that is rooted in biblical, theological, psychological, and sociological reflection.

Status Quo Criteria

Two procedures promise to avoid some of these more difficult problems about defining effective ministry by trusting and tracking the existing processes by which the church has done its calling. One of these takes as normative those persons who have become and have remained ministers. The reasoning seems to be that the process of call, as it has worked in the past, can be trusted to have placed in ministry those who most fitly belong there. Matching the characteristics of candidates against the characteristics of existing clergy can then become a way of identifying those who more closely (and those who less closely) match the norm of the existing group, presumably giving an empirical assist to a process of selection by modeling what is occurring naturally.

The other "status quo" criterion takes as the norm the composite expectations of members of the Christian community—a procedure best illustrated by the *Readiness for Ministry* project (see chap. 16). Laypersons, bishops, seminary faculties, anyone who can be taken as speaking reliably for God's church, can be asked to articulate the qualities they want in clergy, and the candidates can be matched against this norm of composite expectation. This presumably also gives technical facilitation to a process of selection already occurring naturally.

Both procedures have the technical advantage that they can easily be made specific. The goal of locating distinctive criteria for ministry in different communities can be met by simply canvassing ministers or church representatives in any distinctive identifiable segment of the community. This attempts to solve the problem of generalizing unduly for ministry as a whole.

Both procedures have the technical problem of selecting which characteristics of clergy and which expectations of bishops and search committees are relevant and important. The researcher, by using open-ended questions, can trust the respondents to identify the crucial characteristics. Or the researcher can take the basic conceptual responsibility for defining appropriate characteristics and give respondents, in effect, multiple choices.

Beyond these technical advantages and problems, however, lies the fundamental theoretical question posed by these options: Do we trust the existing processes to be normative? Consider the pool of existing clergy and the articulated preferences of existing church leaders and representatives. Do we regard these as valid indicators of a call process that assessment can facilitate by making it more quantitative and explicit? Or do we regard these as indicators of an all too fallible call process, which assessment is to correct and remedy? That question must not be avoided, though it usually is. But neither can that question be easily answered. My own judgment—to be personal about a question that has little other basis for resolving—is that assessment has produced an inflated "savior" mentality, being perceived as on a mission to correct past errors. This idolatry needs to be transformed by greater appreciation for a wisdom that God has lodged in the church, a wisdom that needs to be made explicit as much as it needs to be improved on.

Summary

Candidates and churches, puzzled or even anguished to discern aright the call of God to Christian ministry, understandably in the twentieth century turn for help to the technical proficiency of assessment procedures. Unfortunately, the main help that assessment can provide is to turn back to the candidates and the churches the same anguished question—the criterion question—now more sharpened: What does God call for in the ministry of those who are called forth? Assessment needs more help from the churches in identifying the contours of faithful and effective ministry before it can help the churches identify those who are called to exercise that ministry.

3

Spiritual Formation in Theological Education and Psychological Assessment

EDWARD WIMBERLY

Few issues raise as much controversy in theological education as spiritual formation. Too often, psychological assessment is not linked directly to spiritual formation, although theological education—whether basic, advanced, or continuing education—is an implicit context for both clergy assessment and spiritual formation.

Several factors contribute to making spiritual formation controversial. The first factor is the many theological orientations in theological education that make for diversity in defining the meaning of spiritual formation. For example, the various labels given to theological orientations—such as Orthodox, neo-Orthodox, liberal, natural, evangelical, liberation, feminist, and others—begin to put in focus how diverse definitions of spiritual formation can be if viewed from each of these perspectives. In assessing clergy and theological students, the great diversity in definitions, theories, and approaches prevents a facile consensus regarding what should be done about and how we should define spiritual formation.

A second factor that makes spiritual formation a difficult issue to address in theological education is its locale in the curriculum. Should the classical fields address this concern, and if so, how? Should the practical fields address this issue solely, or should there be an overall institutional thrust based on a consensus? Some institutions attempt to make an institutional thrust of spiritual formation by designating those faculty who are involved in small group leadership in field education as the institutionally sanctioned leaders to carry out spiritual formation.

A third problem has been the history of theological education itself. A brief understanding of the history of preparation for ministry is instructive. Several models of theological training have characterized theological preparation for ministry up to the present time. These models give some hint about how spiritual formation was conceived and practiced (Hough 1984, 66-78).

The first model of theological training was that of the Master. In this model the minister was viewed as an authoritative teacher rooted in the history of the teaching of the sages. This model dominated the seventeenth and eighteenth centuries. The Master was grounded in an authoritative body of literature and was authorized to teach it. This person was given authority to teach the traditional beliefs of the church. Formation in this master model consisted of the study of ancient languages, Scripture, history, philosophy, and logic. The professional and spiritual formations were conceived of as taking place through the study of the disciplines and in the privacy of one's own devotional life in Protestant traditions.

By the nineteenth century, the science of theology emerged, and there were specialties in sacred literature, dogmatics, ecclesiastical history, and practical theology. The dominant view of theological education was that of the Master, but the new science of theology was an attempt to ground the authority of the Master in the methodology and literature of scientific theory. Formation of the minister, practically and spiritually, was viewed in the context of specialized discreet disciplines. Thus each discipline would have its own view of what practical and spiritual formation would look like. Therefore, the modern diversity preventing consensus regarding spiritual formation was born in the nineteenth century.

With the dawn of the twentieth century, the idea of ministry as a profession emerged. Organizational roles became more important in the life of the church. The idea of the minister as the church builder and manager of organizations developed. Closely related to this professional model was that of the minister as a professional therapist who was seeking the status and credentials of professional counselors and therapists. In the emphasis on the role of the minister as professional manager and therapist, seminaries began to train ministers to respond to the rapid changes taking place in industry and in political, social, and social service organizations, and assessment for these purposes became more important.

Formation in this model professionally and spiritually was thought of in the context of what it meant to be professional. More specifically, formation took place in the context of field supervision in organizations, churches, and social agencies. Spiritual formation was thought of as taking place at the same time as professional formation, particularly in theological reflection on one's work.

In the seventeenth, eighteenth, and nineteenth centuries, the image of the minister as Master and the ideal of formation carried with it an image of a minister whose practical and personal identities were rooted securely in the faith tradition. However, with the emergence of the twentieth century, a conflict emerged concerning the relationship of formation to the faith tradition—that is, formation began to take more seriously scientific bases of professional ministry rooted in professional knowledge and skills of secular professions. This was often done to the neglect of the faith tradition, particularly in liberal institutions. Following this trend, theological formation and assessment of clergy began to take place without much attention to the relationship of faith to the contemporary idea of profession until relatively recently.

This brief history suggests that cultural, intellectual, and historical circumstances greatly shaped the ideas of formation in ministry from professional and spiritual perspectives. The question of how seriously we take our historical faith identity while responding to the needs of a changing world is still one we must wrestle with today. We have experienced the pitfalls of responding to a changing world without an intact historical faith identity, and we must work on our spiritual and faith identities while doing professional formation and assessment.

We are living in a period of history in which contemporary culture and our historical faith are merging to coalesce in a different way than in the past. A new synthesis between the professional and spiritual is being forged. This new synthesis is emerging in a model in which the builder, manager, and therapist images are merging with the critical-historical faith functions of the Judeo-Christian tradition. This new model is taking seriously the need for the scientific base for professional formation and assessment as well as the need for spiritual formation that helps to secure the minister's identity within the faith tradition.

My thesis is that the formation of ministers professionally and spiritually in the future will take seriously the role of the minister as a bearer of faith, both as storyteller and as listener to stories of people attempting to live faithful lives. The overarching need in our culture today is not for healing, identity, or social reform in the minds of some contemporary critics of society and the church, although these dimensions are indispensable. Rather the need of people today is for a plot (or structure of meaning) that provides healing, identity, meaning, and direction in the lives of people (Hillman, 1983).

Once this plot is in place, people will have a framework and a basis for broader participation in society, socially, economically, politically, and religiously. The future of ministry will depend heavily on how well the church and seminaries are able to train ministers to respond to the needs of people in contemporary culture. This means that we must know how to identify the factors and experiences in candidates and clergy that facilitate and/or inhibit the competencies required of these ministers, who both incarnate and elicit faith stories. The minister as storyteller and story-listener as the focus of professional and spiritual formation in theological schools is emerging as an important agenda for theological education and assessment.

For the purposes here, formation in theological education is defined as the arena in which theological students as individuals and as groups gather together to claim the memory of our faith tradition as well as to be claimed by it. This claiming and being claimed are done in such a way that personal, spiritual, and professional transformation take place. Joseph Hough, former Dean of the School of Theology at Claremont, suggests that our task is to enable theological students to engage their faith heritage in theological education in such ways that faith history becomes personal history (Hough 1984, 63). I think that this can be done by focusing our attention on the minister as storyteller and story-listener. Assessment can enable both ministers and mentors to understand the factors that enable us to be both storytellers and story-listeners.

Formation involves an interaction between the faith tradition and professional models of training and education. Personal formation, spiritual formation, and professional formation are interrelated processes within the entire formation process. It would be helpful to make some brief distinctions among these three interrelated and interacting dimensions of the formation process.

Personal formation is making an impact on the growth of the person as a self apart from others as that self interacts with his or her own body, psychic life, family, primary groups, socio-cultural setting, and environment. Spiritual formation involves making an impact on the self as a spiritual entity as well as a minister, as these two dimensions interact with other dimensions of the self, family, primary groups, socio-cultural setting, and environmental factors. Professional formation involves making an impact on the interaction among the self, the spiritual self, and the sense of self as minister on one hand and the correlation of the faith tradition and the knowledge and skills of the professions on the other hand. As indicated, these aspects of formation are relational and have only been distinguished for purposes of definition.

How persons interact with their faith tradition is a crucial issue that clergy assessment must address. Moreover, spiritual formation must not neglect the faith tradition in its work, because such neglect leaves the students with their own stories without roots in the communion of those of our past. How we engage our faith tradition in formation affects how we assist students, both lay and clergy, to become bearers of the story of faith.

Contemporary psychological theories of the formation of self and God images, brain theory, and narrative theology can be windows into the issue of spiritual formation in theological education. The image of the self as minister is rooted fundamentally in symbol and story in our faith tradition. This image has its early beginning in childhood. This early image of self as minister continues to be influenced by theological education and by other current experiences. This "self as minister" image can be influenced by helping the student to engage his or her core image in a critical and participatory curriculum that addresses the core image as the central and primary focus of theological education at some point in the seminary experience. Finally, the implications for assessment of this examining of spiritual formation in theological education will be drawn.

The Emergence of Narrative in Theological Education

The place of story in the development of persons has been appearing frequently in the literature in the last ten years. Much attention has been given to it in theology, biblical studies, ethics, and in the practical fields. I am sure that part of the reason for this new emphasis is the awareness that Paul Ricoeur recounts in his work *The Symbolism of Evil*. He emphasizes that the self is constituted at the basic level through symbolism, and then it works out its abstract language about itself subsequently (Ricoeur 1969, 9). This means that the self, at least initially, grasps hold of symbols and images

from its primary figures (parents) that help the self become rooted and grounded in the world as a self.

Ana-Maria Rizzuto says that a similar symbolic process describes the formation of God images in children (Rizzuto 1979, 183). An important aspect in the formation of God images is the mythology that the child learns about his or her own birth from the parents. The mythology consists of the parents' communication to the child whether the birth was welcomed or whether it was an accident. Often a mythology of being welcome or unwelcome is the basis of the God image in children. This birth mythology, along with good enough parent-child relations, gives shape to the child's self-image.

In the case of ministers, it can be hypothesized that the self as minister is formed by a similar process of interaction between birth and early childhood mythology, good enough parent-child relations, roles that the children learn to play in their families when they have the capacity to learn roles, and the religious stories with which the child learns to identify. The complex interaction among birth mythology, parenting roles, and stories gives rise to the self as minister early in the child's life. This is true even when the child becomes an adult and selects ministry much later in the life cycle.

Mythology and symbolism are important in the self-image as minister not only at the early stages of life of the child, but this symbolism continues to work at a subconscious level as well, feeding and nourishing one's self-image and the image of self as minister throughout life. Moreover, our sense of self as ministers is a result of a long process taking place, beginning with the birth story and continuing to develop as one interacts with significant others, learns roles, and identifies with stories as one proceeds through the life cycle until adulthood. In adolescence, early adulthood, and adulthood, aspects of this unconscious process are made conscious in ways that help the person to be intentional about his or her vocational life. William James called this unconscious process of growth subconscious incubation (James 1961, 186). That is to say, a maturing process of a religious nature is taking place. This process can be tapped by theological education and assessment in order to help the student to be more intentional in professional and spiritual formation.

One of the primary ways to access the subconscious process is through story or narrative. In the subconscious incubation process, the self begins to relate to narrative through identifying with stories. In fact, the self will anchor itself in story as a way to make sense of the self in the world, according to some psychologists of religion (Spilka et al. 1985, 5). This self, God images, and the sense of self as minister are formed early and are usually permanent parts of identity, according to both Rizzuto (Rizzuto 1979, 203) and Vergote (Vergote and Tamayo 1981, 19-23) in their studies of God images.

From a theological and psychological assessment view, the formation of the self as minister is an ongoing process that is affected by and builds upon its early formation. This means that this formation of the self is affected by theological education, mentoring, assessment, and supervision processes. We must intentionally clarify the details of how this happens so that assessment can be in the service of spiritual formation rather than reducing spiritual formation and growth to psychological terms only.

Making an Impact on the Self as Minister

From early childhood and throughout life the self continues to grow and develop as one's inner history takes shape in relationship to interaction with the faith story. A person's faith story takes root when that person participates in the life of the community in which the faith story is told and shared. As the person worships, is nurtured, and cared for in the life of the church, the symbols and stories of the faith tradition begin to affect the person's unconscious and conscious life. The incubation process is being influenced as a result of the person's involvement and participation.

The subconscious incubation process may be affected by church involvement, by theological education, and by the ways assessment is used in these communities. The subconscious incubation process is being formed and reformed each day as the person engages in preparation for ministry. We must be more carefully intentional in terms of how our assessments affect each person's intrapersonal and interpersonal processes in the context of each person's earlier development.

To have an impact on the subconscious incubation process of that student in theological education, the education process must take seriously the work on the study of the brain. James Ashbrook, my colleague at Garrett-Evangelical, has been helpful in describing the affects of the subconscious incubation process (Ashbrook and Walaskay 1979, 93-97).

Ashbrook's work takes seriously the holistic functioning of the brain. The brain has two interrelating and interacting hemispheres that separate distinct brain functioning. One hemisphere of the brain is the arena for cognitive functioning, which analyzes, separates, distinguishes, and manipulates. The other hemisphere focuses the brain on patterns, wholes, and designs and is relational. The relational dimension of the brain responds to immediate experience through nonsensory media, which include dreams, symbols, myths, imagination, prayer, and mysticism.

Given this symbolic relational nature of this dimension of the brain, it is plausible to expect that this dimension is involved in the ministry formation process. As we learn more about the holistic functioning of the brain, we can address spiritual formation in the context of theological education and assessment. More precisely, through imaginative approaches to curriculum and methodology, it is possible to address both dimensions of the brain-mind as they combine in the formation of the self.

The Goals of Spiritual Formation

Theological education has implicit and explicit goals for formation as expressed in each seminary's curriculum. Likewise, clergy assessment and development also has implicit goals concerning formation. Clergy assessment can enable a candidate or clergy to take a critical look at past and present experiences in the context of her or his own faith tradition. What the student learns in this model of theological formation is helpful, but the student must be mentored to engage the faith tradition in ways that are growth producing and growth enhancing.

This next stage beyond is when the formation process helps the student to evaluate critically his or her faith tradition and to reenter this faith tradition in ways that enhance growth. Spiritual formation in assessment and theological education could assist the individual to evaluate the leftover childhood elements of the faith tradition that did not enhance growth and that frustrated the development of the personal self and the self as minister in the student. It could also help the student to reengage the faith tradition in ways that facilitate growth.

Case Study

A very bright student spends inordinate amounts of time in his fantasy life. This student is very much in touch with reality, but he made books his escape early in his life. He has an extremely broad base of knowledge and is well versed in many subjects. However, his studies and reading have not helped him to fit in with the group when group identification would be the normal thing. His fantasies of what it would be like to be involved, particularly with the opposite sex, prevent him from getting involved.

One day, I asked this person what his major self-image was. He pointed to the Greek mythological image of Sisyphus. I asked him to describe this person. He said that Sisyphus was a man who was compelled to roll a stone up a hill. When he would almost get the stone to the top of the hill, the stone would become too heavy to push and would roll over Sisyphus and back down to the bottom of the hill. The student felt that this was the story of his life.

While I helped this student to explore this image so that I could get a better picture of the subconscious incubation process, I discovered a negative story that I didn't want to pursue. However, later in our work together, he introduced a biblical image that had potential growth producing dimensions. He said that he felt like a pilgrim who would never fit in. He expressed this as negative, but I decided to amplify this image. I asked him if he was aware of the pilgrim nature of the book of Hebrews, and he said no. Together we explored some of the meanings of the pilgrim in Hebrews.

This encounter illustrates several elements that are important in considering assessment and spiritual formation. The first is that symbols still have impacts on one's self-image at later stages of growth. Second, it is possible to engage the subconscious growth process through the relational and symbolic dimension of the person. Third, it is possible to use both aspects of the brain, the rational and the relational/symbolic, in helping the student to address the need to grow at a depth level. Fourth, it is possible to use field education, supervision, assessment, and many other experiences for reflections that tap the subconscious incubation process for the professional and spiritual growth of the student. Fifth, it is possible also for the curriculum to have courses in it to help the student to expand personal understanding of self in ministry. In this example, I recommended that this student take a course in Hebrews, which would expose him to the pilgrim image.

Supervisors can help students to tap into the subconscious incubation process taking place within them. Advisors can also help students to find images that lead to these depth processes and can be familiar enough with a theological curriculum and with assessment and supervision opportunities to advise the student about courses and experiences that could help the student expand, modify, or influence the subconscious incubation process.

Not all images are growth producing. However, if a person has been a participant in the faith story, there is at work within the self an image of seeking holistic growth. For example, the person in our case study not only had the negative Sisyphus image, but he also had the pilgrim image, which was positive if it were explored. This image could be explored via imagination and reflection for its growth producing potential for the person. This can indeed be approached in the contexts of theological education and of sensitive discussions of assessment information. Assessment can become more adept at relating to the whole person.

Implications for Psychological Assessment

Serious attention has been given to the way psychological testing could assist professional and personal formation. Normally, psychological assessment does not include assessing the way a person utilizes the faith tradition in his or her formation.

One important area in which spiritual formation can be linked with assessment is the use of the assessment process to look at the ways the individual appropriates the faith tradition in terms of self and professional understanding. For example, does the way the person appropriates the faith tradition facilitate or inhibit growth? Indeed, if narrative anchoring of self and self as minister in the faith tradition is basic to self-development, then this dimension should be part of the assessment task. Such psychological assessment could greatly enhance the spiritual formation process with persons in seminaries and in continuing theological education.

The minister as storyteller and story-listener can be an additional focus for assessment and theological education. This approach can begin with tapping into the student's own subconscious incubation process. Through this holistic process, it is possible to model how the individual is able to listen to others' stories and to influence them. Through the formal study of selected courses, it is also possible to help the student to draw from those courses the things that will help him or her to communicate the gospel story in helpful ways. Indeed, the future belongs to the storyteller and the story-listener, and psychological assessment can assist in the formation of students as storytellers and story-listeners.

31

4

Lifetime Development of Clergy

WINSTON E. GOODEN

Assessment and evaluation of men and women for ministry can benefit from an integration of an adult development perspective with the usual methods of evaluation. This chapter provides a description of some critical stages and tasks during adulthood and draws some implications for the task of the minister.

Entering the Adult World

Those men and women who enter the ministry early—that is, during their twenties—do so at a time in their lives that has its own unique tasks and challenges. The period of the twenties (22-28) is a time that Levinson et al. (1978) describes as requiring the formation of a life structure that enables the young person to enter the adult world. Prior to the twenties, the person is in a pre-adult world that is centered in the family of origin. To enter the adult world more fully, a structure is needed that allows the young person to explore various choices prerequisite to forming commitments. In the broadest sense, the task of the twenties is to enter the world of adulthood. This makes the twenties a season of exploration, a season of beginnings, a time of life typified by tentative and provisional commitments that can facilitate the level of learning and clarity that firmer commitments require. The ethos of the twenties is colored by this task, and for many it is an exciting, yet unstable—even chaotic—time of life.

Other major tasks require attention at this time of life. One task is the formation of an occupation. This task requires that the young adult make a choice that fits with his or her skills, talents, and interests and then pursue the requisite training and education. Persons entering ministry are beyond the stage of choosing and being trained, but they are novices. They have yet to learn through actually working in the area what the extent and limits of their talents are and how appropriate the choice is given their talents.

Another task closely related to that of forming an occupation is forming a Dream. The Dream (capitalized because of its specific use here) involves hopes and plans, but it is more than that. It is the imaginative activity that enables the young person to have a sense of self in the future. The Dream is not simply a fantasy. It is a very personal formation of who one is to be as an adult in the world. The Dream begins as a form of imaginative play that locates the person in some future role that captures the essential motivation and meaning of the person's striving. Formation of a Dream for ministers would seem important. The heroic image involved in the Dream might include being a great preacher, an evangelist of great repute, a moral reformer, a nurturer of the spirit, and so on. A critical issue for the young pastor is the degree to which the Dream can be included in the occupational structure and pursued to its fulfillment.

The Dream provides a sustaining energy during the early professional years, when the young pastor may begin to doubt the feasibility of the Dream. The Dream includes ambitions and ideals that energize the work of the pastor. It may be useful during the evaluation of a pastoral candidate to find out about his or her Dream and how that Dream will fit in with the ethos and vision of the congregation to which the young pastor is called. A mismatch between the young pastor's Dream and the congregation's vision of its own future may lead to difficulties for both the pastor and the congregation.

A third task closely allied with that of forming the Dream is forming a mentor relationship. The mentor is usually a person who is one-half to a full generation older than the person receiving mentoring (the "mentee"). While the mentor guides, counsels, and supports the mentee, the mentor's role goes beyond that of a role model. The critical function of the mentor is to believe in the mentee's Dream and to help the mentee pursue it. Since the Dream begins as an imaginative act—an act of faith about who one will be in the future—the mentor facilitates the Dream by supporting this imaginative quest and exhibiting faith in the mentee. The mentor's support is internalized by the mentee. Now there is someone else who knows that the mentee can make it. This adds to the mentee's confidence and is particularly important in times of doubt and difficulty.

A mentor-mentee relationship requires the availability of mentoring figures and the readiness of the young pastor to be mentored. A critical issue in the potential for a mentor-mentee relationship to develop may be the young pastor's ability to form relations with older pastors and authority figures.

Another task of the twenties is that of forming a relationship that may lead to marriage and a family. The outward aspects of this task involve engaging in relationships with persons of the other gender and learning about them beyond one's personal, family-linked stereotypes. The internal aspects involve dealing with the crisis of intimacy versus isolation. The ability to open oneself to others, to disclose one's thoughts and feelings and to hear those of others without fear of absorption and loss of boundaries, is a prerequisite for healthy and satisfying marriages. It also seems particularly crucial to the functioning of pastors in several areas of their work. The role demands not only an ability to relate to many people at once, but also an ability to be intimate with an individual, a couple, or a family. The capacity for open intimate engagement of others seems a key developmental task for those engaged in ministry. This task interacts with entry into the pastoral role in some important ways. The role of pastor demands large time commitments, which often detract from time spent with one's spouse (or potential spouse), or with one's children. Those who are new parents are learning the role and are involved with the developmental task of becoming a parent at a time when there is a strong demand for heavy investment in the church.

The capacity for self-disclosure, open communication, vulnerability, and risk taking implied by intimacy is developing at this time; yet, the role of pastor requires a high degree of intimacy with persons for whom the pastor must function as a caring authority.

The Age Thirty Transition

As the twenties come to an end, the young person typically has made basic life choices in occupation and marriage. This is still a time of learning and exploring, and there is often a sense that one can still choose differently if things do not work out right.

A new season emerges at the end of the twenties and spans the years from 28-33 approximately. This time, called the age thirty transition, is a time of doubt and questioning, a time of reevaluation. The young person asks whether his or her choices were made with integrity. Many young persons enter professions because of parental expectations, and some marry as a way of leaving home. This is the time when compromises are often questioned, and the possibility of change is explored. The central task of the age thirty transition is to reappraise the life structure built in the twenties, to modify or change it if necessary, or to keep it and enhance life within it. For some young people, the work of the age thirty transition involves moving from a pattern of ceaseless exploration in work and relationships to one of firmer commitment.

Some persons will leave the ministry at this time. Though the reasons may vary, one important cause might be a sense that one's Dream cannot be fully pursued in the context of ministry. Also, many persons may enter the ministry at this time. To them, the ministry may appear as being more in keeping with their Dreams.

Persons being evaluated during the age thirty transition, as during all transitions, may appear uncertain or may shift back and forth between questioning their call to ministry and being very certain. It is important that the questioning and reappraisal be accepted as stage appropriate and be fully understood in terms of their implications for future performance in ministry.

The administrative and executive functions of a pastor require confidence and strength of personality. These attributes are beginning to emerge in the twenties. A young pastor at this stage may be bright, but must yet develop wisdom. The young often pretend to more confident, capable, and committed than is really possible at this stage. For some, this leads to feelings of falseness. A surprising number of young professionals in their late twenties and early thirties confess to feeling fraudulent because of this perceived difference between what is expected and their own sense of where they are.

The person's broad task in the age thirty transition is to terminate the time of being a novice, to end the exploration, to clarify goals and make more firm commitments. The result of this time of questioning and fine-tuning is in the best cases a life structure that is built around key relationships in the areas of occupation, marriage, and family. While there usually are several other important aspects of the life structure, these three are usually central.

Settling Down

The thirties provide a new season with a variety of tasks. The theme of the thirties is one of settling down, of consolidation, and of working toward advancement.

In the early thirties, one pursues the Dream more concretely through work or other channels. The early thirties are often devoted to forming a niche, finding a place, defining an enterprise, and clarifying the steps that lead to fulfillment of the Dream. The remainder of the thirties is often spent single-mindedly climbing the ladder that leads to such fulfillment. Of course, there are many variations on this pattern. Some persons who earlier have stayed with what seemed to be a good occupational or marriage choice may feel trapped in the wrong structure and in the mid-thirties attempt to break out of it. The pattern of settling and working toward advancement, though it seems desirable, is not the only pattern for the thirties.

By the end of the thirties, there is a search for tangible evidence that one's enterprise is a success. There is as well an effort to "speak with one's own voice," to have authority, and to be recognized for what one has accomplished. This wish for authority and greater individuation may be fraught with conflict since one may still need to rely on powerful others to gain the promotions and affirmations one desires. Yet, such reliance may undermine the very sense of independence one seeks.

Persons entering ministry in their thirties may feel that they are behind their peers occupationally. They enter the occupation at a time in life when many of their peers are past the entry phase and are working toward advancement. The late entry will make it difficult to achieve a sense of authority and achievement, which is part of the stage Levinson et al. (1978) call "Becoming One's Own Man or Becoming One's Own Woman."

Mid-life Transition

As the thirties come to an end, early adulthood is ending. The life structure built to pursue early adult Dreams and to provide a context for growth and living may now come into question. As middle adulthood approaches, a time of transition sets in.

The mid-life transition (ages 40-45) is a time to reflect on, to reappraise, and possibly to change the life structure of early adulthood. A brief word about transitions may be helpful here. A *transition* is a time of life that may take up to five years, but may also be of shorter duration. The transition terminates one time of life and initiates the next season. At the beginning, there is a process of termination; in the middle there is a process of separation; and at the end there is a process of initiation into the new phase. Transitions are often painful and difficult times in which one mourns the past and lets go of one's place in it. There is as well the process of reshaping identity to include a new status and the new social, psychological, and existential realities of a new time of life. Transitions, then, are times of questioning, reevaluation, and change.

The mid-life transition is that which terminates early adulthood and initiates middle adulthood. One who confronts the issues of this transition comes to terms with the fact that one has stopped growing up and has started to grow old. One comes to terms with the gap between the aspirations of early adulthood and one's achievements in the light of those aspirations.

The heart of the mid-life transition is the opportunity for working on issues that are both spiritual and psychological. One of the core issues of the mid-life transition, and that which makes it a potentially crisis-filled time, is the issue of death. Ernest Becker (1978) argues persuasively that the denial of death is a basic human motive that organizes character. Death is the basic human anxiety, and to cope with it we fashion character defenses and carve out heroic roles that seemingly protect us from this core anxiety. At mid-life, the early adult heroics and defenses can no longer stave off the awareness of mortality. Even when the Dream is fulfilled, a person realizes that the hero of the Dream is mortal and that fulfillment of the Dream does not bring immortality. This leads to a painful process of "disillusioning," or giving up the illusion that one would live forever or that if one achieves the Dream one would live happily ever after. This disillusioning task is even more painful for those who, in spite of their best efforts, fail to achieve their dreams. Mid-life invites a change in the defense of denial as a way of dealing with death, weakness, failure, and all aspects of human life that point to our basic mortality.

The heroic quest to fulfill the early adult dream is supported by illusions, and in the interest of the Dream and the self-definitions of early adulthood, many aspects of the self are suppressed.

Mid-life provides an opportunity to integrate the great human polarities within the self. One such polarity is the young/old polarity. Young/old polarity involves integrating within the self that which is young, alive, and energetic with that which is wise. It requires as well the integration of those aspects of self that are green, foolish, and uninformed with those that are old, decaying, and dry. A new self-image can be forged that does not split off aspects of experience but that integrates them into a whole. Accepting one's mortality is a major issue here.

McAdams (1988) argues that the crisis of mid-life is a generative crisis. It is so because the realization of one's mortality throws into question the meaning and value of one's life. What does my achievement mean now that I am more clearly aware that I will die? What am I living for? Answers to these questions need to be able to survive the death of the individual. McAdams, drawing on Erikson, points out that generative solutions to mid-life crises demand that individuals create and give the creation as a gift to the next generation. Generativity then involves both creating and caring. It also involves having a life project that is not centered on the self and its survival but is committed to what is beyond the self.

Working through the illusions of one's youth and forging an identity that accepts as part of oneself attributes that were once denied or suppressed set the stage for new and more creative relationships. The Dream of middle adulthood may not be centered on youthful ambitions but now may center on caring and generative service. Persons may now be seen, treated, and valued not primarily because of how they fit one's plans or advance one's Dream but as ends in themselves. The inner work of the mid-life transition opens the way for changes in the key areas of the life structure.

Those who enter ministry during middle adulthood are very likely to be responding to the mid-life themes previously discussed. The pastoral side of ministry demands a high level of caring and generativity. There is in the profession a high need for commitment to the welfare of others. While these attributes are salient requirements for pastors at any age, it is at mid-life in particular, and middle adulthood in general, that the task of integrating within the self the more generative and nurturing attribute is at its peak. Those who enter the ministry at this time of life may be seeking an occupation that allows them to integrate and live out these attributes. The person entering the profession at middle age may then have the advantage of having fewer conflicting thoughts about issues of caring and nurture and find the pastoral role one that uniquely enables the expression of these characteristics.

The formation of a pastor is a lifelong task. The role places on persons requirements that may create stress and conflict when these requirements do not match the developmental level of the candidate. The pastor's performance at the time of evaluation may be affected by the life stage issues the candidate is managing. Overall performance in the role of pastor will be affected by various issues at differing stages of life. For instance, young pastors will have a harder time being empathic with certain issues that older congregation members experience. Being empathic in certain situations may require certain developmental experiences. A congregation may be at a stage in its life that contrasts sharply with where a pastor is in his or her life. The pastor's Dream may not fit with the ethos or plans of the congregation, and this may affect the pastor's performance.

This brief survey emphasizes the need to relate assessment and spiritual formation to the lifetime development of clergy and their families. This adult development perspective can also clarify predictor and criterion relationships, career persistence and change, burnout and renewal, and other clergy issues.

5

Personal Growth for Clergy

RICHARD A. BLACKMON AND ARCHIBALD D. HART

Ministry is a very hazardous profession. "There are few professions that demand as broad a range of different skills and styles of action as the ministry" (Smith, 1973). More than 75 percent of pastors surveyed reported at least one major period of stress in the ministry (Mills and Koval, 1971). Because of pastoral burnout, one third of all pastors reporting found themselves pondering the implications of leaving what they thought would be their life work (Daniel and Rogers, 1982).

Doing professional ministry is especially hard on the "person" of the pastor. The apostle Paul says that we have the treasure of the gospel in "earthen vessels" (II Cor. 4:7), which highlights both the glory of God and the limits and weaknesses of those who serve God. For the pastor, his or her "person" is the key tool for an effective ministry, but this is the aspect that is least trained and equipped for the challenging task of ministry.

In our own research and teaching, we have identified at least five areas of "emotional hazard" that all pastors must uniquely face in their ministry. They include: personal relationships, depression, stress and burnout, sexuality, and assertiveness. Careful attention to assessment, prevention, and treatment (if necessary) of each of these hazardous areas is essential for a long and fruitful ministry. While we are emphasizing the vocational aspects of ministry hazards, there are other dimensions as well (spiritual warfare, the cost of discipleship, and so on).

Ministers can either "waste out" or undergo a "controlled burning out." We assume that pastors prefer to be able to say at the end of their lives that they have given all they had to give—this is a controlled burning out. Unfortunately, we often see the reverse: ministers "wasting out" and leaving the ministry demoralized, depressed, and disillusioned even with the God they so desperately wanted to serve. A pastor who is undergoing a "mid-life crisis" is often one who has "wasted out."

Personal Relationships

The nurturing of a minister's relationships is vital both for ministry effectiveness and for the vocational satisfaction of the minister. A network of personal relationships (people important in the life of the minister, whether or not he or she likes them) helps ministers to survive ministry burnout and stress (Brown, 1985). Ministers need quality relationships in at least two content areas: (1) realistic feedback of their job performance and (2) close confidantes with whom they can share their private feelings.

The work of ministry often lacks adequate success criteria, making ministers insecure about their performance. Having trusted persons to give feedback for each of the dimensions of job performance (teaching, leading meetings, counseling, administrating) is crucial. Brown (1985) found that the more extroverted the minister, the greater dependence he or she had on these support dimensions.

The majority of ministers do not have an adequate support system. Over time, sources of support erode. Ministers may feel "burned" by some of the friendships they form early in their ministry because of charges of favoritism, competition, and the complexity of multiple roles. This makes them more and more cautious, and congregation members are cautious of them. Members often idealize a pastor and project qualities they need onto the pastor, which creates barriers to having equal (supportive) relationships.

Because of role conflict, congregation members can seldom be equal friends who support needs that exist for every pastor. A pastor is set aside for a particular role and purpose. Ministers may try to take themselves out of their role, only to have their congregation put them back!

Role pressures contribute to the loneliness of ministry. Over 70 percent of surveyed ministers report feeling a frequent sense of loneliness (Blackmon, 1984), which puts more pressure on the family of the minister.

While the majority of minister marriages are warm and supportive (Jud et. al., 1966; Blackmon, 1984; Alleman, 1987), a significant percentage feel tremendous pressure in the fish bowl of the pastor's family (Mace and Mace, 1980; Blackmon, 1984).

A minister's time with his or her family is often too little, and availability of time for family commitments is almost always unreliable. It is this unreliability of availability due to frequent emergencies, interruptions, and erratic scheduling that is the most damaging to family life. Inadequate assertiveness, especially in declining requests for special activities, aggravates this unreliability. Countless ministers' children recall childhoods of returning home from vacations early, interrupted meals, and various other thwarted activities with their minister parent or parents. Moreover, the lack of clearly defined days off and the frequently narrow social interests of a pastor often make family time uncreative. Heavy work loads and high self-expectations round out the complex impact of the ministry on family life.

These relationship and support issues can be assessed by administering the Social Network Assessment Profile (Brown, 1985), which quantifies the various dimensions (structural, content, and qualitative) of a pastor's social network and identifies the extent to which these needs are or are not being met. Personality inventories (such as the 16PF) also aid in informing direction and treatment for restoring the balance in a pastor's social network.

Improving a minister's personal functioning involves proactively and strategically finding places in the social support network for sharing private feelings and getting realistic feedback. Implicit in this task is helping pastors to accept the limitations their role as pastors places on meeting their support and friendship needs within or without their congregations. Finding other sources of friendships (other ministers in the community, support groups, clubs, reinvesting in old friends, and so on) is often part of this task.

Another important task in preventing problems in both the support network and the family is to educate the congregation (and sometimes even the denomination) about their role in supporting the pastoral family. Many ministers must educate their church leaders about "normalizing" some of the special pressures their children experience. Sometimes spouses (who have many expectations placed on them) are advised in times of family or marital stress to go to another church (perhaps once a month). It is impossible to experience the same person as both spouse and pastor, and congregations need to be educated about this!

Depression

The incidence of ministers' depression has historically been difficult to assess because of their reluctance to admit to such a problem. As one author notes, "the minister is not supposed to be depressed. He is supposed to help others deal with their depression. It is not only shocking to his church members when they find their minister is fighting depression, it is shocking to the minister himself" (Faulkner, 1981, 41). However, a recent study found that 12 percent of the ministers surveyed "always" or "often" felt depressed in their ministry (Blackmon, 1984). This figure matches earlier estimates of "depression severe enough to warrant professional attention" for the general population (Hart, 1978).

Surviving and thriving in the ministry must involve an ability to manage depression effectively. The very nature of pastoral work creates many conditions leading to depression. These include the demands placed on them and their own erroneous ideas about their calling.

The ministry is an adrenally demanding profession. Pastors must recruit adrenaline constantly to meet the challenges of public visibility, weekly sermons, emergencies, meetings, and the like. Many ministers then have difficulty "switching off" to restore physiological equilibrium and allow for adequate recovery. The net result of this difficulty can be an adrenaline over-demand and eventual shut down that is usually experienced as depression. In the study cited above (Blackmon, 1984), almost 40 percent of ministers surveyed felt significantly more depressed on the day after preaching and worship because their bodies were physiologically reacting to the over-demand of adrenaline for worship performance.

Many ministers have erroneous ideas about their calling to ministry. They exaggerate their own importance, often feeling indispensable to their jobs. This sets up unreasonably high expectations for the minister, which he or she is bound to fail to achieve, setting the stage for depression and burnout.

The ministry is replete with experiences of loss, which is one of the principal dynamics of reactive depression. Inadequate success criteria, the volunteer structure of the church, the lack of clear boundaries between the ministerial role and the minister's self-image, and public visibility and expectations are sources of loss for the minister. The loss experience requires time for grieving. If ministers recoil from this grieving process, then deeper depression may be precipitated. Those with a history of much ungrieved loss may become oversensitive to even the smallest of current losses, thus exaggerating the consequent depression.

The assessment of depression proneness in ministry does not differ significantly from assessing depression in the general population. The MMPI (Hathaway and McKinley, 1965) and Beck's Depression Inventory (Beck, et al., 1979) are excellent devices to identify the presence of significant symptoms of depression. Upon such assessment, a more thorough investigation through a case history of the minister's specific sources of depression is essential. This will provide clear direction for treatment strategies. For example, if endogenous depression is suspected, then the use of psychotropic medication as an adjunct to therapy may be necessary.

Education is the primary vehicle for prevention and treatment of depression in the ministry. Understanding the differences between endogenous, reactive, and neurotic depression is crucial for effective depression management. A thorough understanding of how the ministry is "loss-prone," along with a model of grieving that appropriately helps the pastor adjust to each loss experience, has proven effective with the pastors we have worked with both in classrooms and in psychotherapy. Pastors can be encouraged to set time limits to their grief (depending on the nature of the loss), to identify the loss triggers in their own ministry, to accept the reality of their losses, and to develop a cognitive perspective on their losses.

In most cases, a referral for psychotherapy to a professional is absolutely necessary for those who are suffering from major forms of depression. Pastors often have few safe enclaves to unveil their own suffering and can be helped tremendously by a professional who is sensitive to their unique calling and experience as a minister. Support groups (especially of other ministers) can also be very helpful. Cognitive therapy is often the approach with the most effective results.

Educating ministers about the effects of adrenaline on their body's physiology (Hart, 1987) is also effective. The "post-adrenaline depression" phenomenon, previously described, is poorly understood among pastors. We teach ministers that Monday is likely to be their least effective day because of adrenaline depletion following Sunday worship services, which are often a "peak" experience. Since many ministers take Mondays off, this means that their family probably gets them at their worst! Many have therefore been encouraged to readjust their schedule to make Monday a "light" work day, allowing for slow recovery, and to take Friday off, when they are in a better position to enjoy themselves and their families.

Finally, the issue of over-attachment to the task of ministry can fruitfully be examined with almost every pastor. Every depression-prone minister greatly fuses his or her personal identity with the pastoral role. Little separation of these roles is encouraged. Few outside interests and restricted friendships with nonparishioners insulate many minsters and leave them prey to judging themselves only in the light of what is occurring in their ministry. This leads to a very vulnerable self-esteem, ego insecurity, and dependence on successful job performance for satisfaction. Becoming a well-rounded person with a wide variety of interests can do much to minimize the unique hazards of ministry.

Stress and Burnout

Ministry, in almost every denomination, is a test of one's capacity to manage stress and burnout effectively. Mills and Koval (1971) found that over 75 percent of a large sample of ministers reported at least one major period of stress in their ministry, with 66 percent calling it "severe." One reason for this stress is increased performance expectations, making it easier to feel inadequate. In the Jud et al. (1970) study of male ex-pastors, the dominant reason men left the ministry was a strong sense of personal and professional inadequacy.

Recent years have seen a growing interest in the unique stresses in the pastoral ministry. A careful distinction must be made between burnout and stress in the ministry (Hart, 1984). Burnout is best defined as "emotional overload or exhaustion." Burnout can be understood more as a protective or defensive reaction to emotional overloading and serves as a warning to pastors that they have given too much of themselves to others and too little to themselves. The core symptom is a feeling of demoralization, with consequent disengagement, loss of idealism, a pervasive feeling of defeat, and a blunting of the pastor's emotional life.

Among helping professions, the pastorate is recognized as having a high incidence of burnout (Ellison and Mattila, 1982). A recent study found positive correlations between burnout and conflict avoidance, dependency, shyness, and aggressiveness in pastors (York, 1982). A follow-up study showed negative correlations between burnout and a minister's feeling of control, scheduling freedom, a large salary, more education, and larger churches.

Stress is distinguished from burnout in its previous physiological focus and effects. Stress problems in ministry can most easily be identified by assessing the symptoms of distress (for example, headache frequency, gastrointestinal disturbance, and anxiety symptomology). Blackmon (1984) found that ministers as a group do *not* have an unusually high incidence of symptoms of stress, such as high blood pressure, frequent headaches, stomach problems, muscular problems, and job fatigue. However, those pastors who were identified as having "Type A personalities" (competitive, quick-tempered, ambitious, and always in a hurry) reported significantly more stress symptoms. In addition, Type A ministers worked more hours, slept less, and tended to be younger than Type B pastors (the opposite of Type A—easy going, less frustrated, and more patient). Apparently, Type A pastors don't endure in the ministry as long.

In assessing the issue of leisure and relaxation, Dittes (1970b) suggests that pastors have a "little adult syndrome" because they do not know how to relax. Blackmon's study (1984) found that an overwhelming majority of ministers of four major denominations take less time off than they are given. In addition, two-thirds of all ministers exercise less than once each week, and three-fourths sleep less than seven hours each night. Oswald (1982) notes that ministers are out of touch with their bodies or choose to ignore the signals their bodies send. The root problem, according to Oswald, is that pastors lack an adequate theology of self-care. It is only by protecting the pastor's own personal resources (learning to relax and take care of oneself) that he or she can be empowered to thrive and endure an entire career in the ministry.

We believe the best way to assess for stress and burnout in the ministry is to focus on the above mentioned symptoms. A number of stress symptom checklists are available, and regular physical and psychological examinations are important. The MMPI can be an important indicator of anxiety as well as of some of the emotional factors involved in burnout, such as excessive guilt, low self-esteem, and depression. Burnout can be further assessed with the Maslach Burnout Inventory in conjunction with a clinical interview, focusing on emotional exhaustion, depersonalization, loss of hope, and demoralization.

The primary prevention strategy for avoiding stress and burnout in the ministry is to restructure a minister's beliefs and theological understanding of self-care. Many ministers mistakenly assume that they must sacrifice all personal life and untold numbers of hours to perform their jobs. Because a pastors' work is never completed and the needs are never fully met, they accuse themselves, feeding false guilt, by believing that things would be better if only they worked harder. Disillusionment and burnout easily set in. A more balanced perspective that is developed in the early stages of ministry can be tremendously useful, especially one that differentiates personal life from professional life.

Learning adequate coping skills can enable one to

manage the inevitable stress of ministry. Assertiveness training, time management, developing an adequate support network, avoiding excessive responsibility, learning to define success intrinsically, and learning to slow down all have proven to be effective in both prevention and treatment for pastors. This also involves attention to the typical pastor's overextended life-style. Hart (1985) believes that ministers use adrenaline arousal excessively, which both causes physiological wear and tear and sets up the pastor for depression at the inevitable adrenaline let down (for example, after a preached sermon).

Mastering an effective relaxation technique is also crucial in establishing the correct balance between the demands the pastorate makes on the body and providing appropriate recovery time. A number of resources (tapes and books) are available, and many pastors have successfully worked various relaxation methods into daily devotional or meditation times (see Hart, 1987 for a listing).

Finally, an especially significant issue for burnout is the amount of attachment a pastor feels toward his or her vocation. Over-attachment clearly exacerbates the potential for stress and burnout problems. This is one of the reasons we emphasize the development of a well-rounded personal life for every pastor, including personal and family activities outside of the church.

Sexuality

The topic of how the minister relates to the opposite sex is closely related to the area of personal relationships. This issue was mentioned earlier in this chapter, but because of problems that frequently arise, we believe it warrants separate discussion.

The minister's sexuality has received very little treatment in the literature (except in the media) and is almost never discussed in gatherings of pastors. Our study (Blackmon, 1984) was the first empirical attempt to ascertain statistics for this area, and the numbers were astounding. Among four major denominational groups, 37.15 percent acknowledged they had engaged in what they considered to be "inappropriate sexual behavior for a minister." In addition, 12 percent admitted to having sexual intercourse with a congregation member other than their spouse. This figure exceeds the client-professional rate found for psychologists and physicians (Holroyd and Brodsky, 1977). A follow-up study by *Leadership* magazine conducted in 1987 essentially confirmed these statistics (Hart, 1987).

While these statistics are alarming and surprising to us, clinical experience with ministers confirms the emerging picture and alerts us to the inherent hazard that sexuality creates for ministry. The ministry focuses primarily on relationships, and it is only natural that an affectionate bond would develop between minister and parishioner, especially in the counseling setting. We assume that sexual temptation is a problem for all to overcome; every man and every woman has his or her "weak spot" for compromising the nature of a ministry relationship.

Why is the frequency with which ministers become sexually involved in the ministry context so high? One reason is a misinterpretation of the relationship dynamics in ministry. Ministers become the recipients of a wide range of intense emotions from their congregation, ranging from romantic love to intense hostility. Pastors frequently puzzle over how it is possible that a parishioner who shakes his or her hand with warm, effusive praise on Sunday can be calling with hostile criticism on Tuesday morning. This phenomenon is known as "transference," or the process in which people project their own (often unmet) needs onto an idealized figure. Such transference can be "positive" (affection, warmth, and so on) or "negative" (anger, rejection, and so on), and it most commonly involves dependency, romantic feelings, hostility feelings, and ambivalence about authority.

Many ministers do not understand the concept of transference or how to deal with it. They aren't sure what to make of the intense emotional barrage that comes their way. Many pastors take these projections personally, as if their personality or their performance is attracting the emotional response.

It is crucial to understand that the majority of feelings like this arise because of the pastor's role, not because of inherent personal qualities of the minister. Psychologists and other mental health professionals are trained to identify and conceptualize these intense feelings toward themselves as projection and to use the experience to facilitate the healing process. We believe pastors similarly need to be trained in transference (and countertransference) dynamics. Of those ministers with training in such dynamics, a significantly lower percentage had engaged in sexually inappropriate behavior (Blackmon, 1984).

Countertransference, the tendency for the pastor to project his or her unmet needs on someone in the ministry, also contributes to the frequency of sexual acting out. While marital dissatisfaction does not by itself explain pastors who are sexually inappropriate, it obviously makes a pastor more susceptible. Other common reasons for countertransference are unresolved personal problems (unmet needs), situational pressures in the pastorate, and conflicting values between pastor and church member.

Assessing the likelihood of sexual problems in the ministry is difficult. Clinical experience seems to indicate that pastors who don't know themselves well and the impact that they make on others are the most likely targets. Pastors are often frustrated people who unwittingly attempt to get their own needs met through ministry situations, and this can set the stage for sexual problems. Most pastors who have "fallen" report that they never intended for the relationship to become sexual.

A history of previous sexual impropriety and transference "proneness" can point to personality problems. Poor ego strength and a tendency to find one's identity through the pastoral role are strong indicators of potential conflict. We often ask blunt questions about past flirting behavior, a person's need for attention from the opposite sex, the quality of the marriage relationship (including the sexual component), fantasy life, and sexual history. Bold and open discussion is well tolerated by most ministers, especially younger ones.

Ministers must thoroughly understand the dynamics of transference and receive training in the most appropriate ways to respond to it. In training seminars, we often devise role-play situations in which a pastor is taught to respond in appropriate ways to romantic interest, hostile aggression, and excessive dependency from congregation members. Long-term therapy techniques for resolving transference problems in counselees is not advised. Instead, pastors are trained to receive transference feelings naturally and to work at putting the responsibility for the feelings back onto the parishioner. In addition, helping ministers interpret strong emotions toward themselves as transference is helpful. Excessive transference potential should be referred for professional help.

In a recent article, Hart (1988) has proposed that a more formal code of ethics be established to help regulate ministry relationships. He argues that ministers (unlike mental health professionals) are currently only loosely bound by a moral code that is subject to differing interpretations. To illustrate the difference between ministers and mental health professionals, psychologists in most states are obligated ethically (and in some cases, legally) to refrain from sexual or erotic contact with patients, as well as from other forms of "dual role" relationships. Although ministry roles differ from those of other health professionals, more clearly articulated boundaries for ministry relationships, especially as they relate to dual roles, would help prevent many problem situations from arising.

An effective prevention strategy is to encourage the pastor to set up an accountability system in which he or she can freely discuss ministry relationships, problems that arise, and situations needing outside consultation with a trusted colleague or professional. We have seen some ministers use their spouse for this purpose successfully, but others find that this kind of disclosure is too threatening to the spouse. We encourage pastors to critique their own feelings about a ministry relationship. Sometimes they may need an objective viewpoint. The more a pastor feels the need to keep a relationship secret, the more potentially dangerous it can become. Frankness and honesty with at least one other person helps to diffuse attractiveness and restore objectivity.

An accountability group also addresses the issue of countertransference and prevention of problems. It is very important for a clergy person to know his or her own needs, drives, weaknesses, and stress points. A minister must constantly assess whether he is using his congregation to meet his or her own unmet needs. A pastor who is too enamored of power will not do the necessary work to moderate the inevitable idealization that encourages transference.

Finally, because the pastoral counseling situation is probably the most vulnerable to sexual impropriety, it is very important for the pastor to know his or her limits. Knowing when to refer to a mental health professional is an increasingly important skill to acquire. Often, an experience in psychotherapy will help a pastor to identify those personality areas most susceptible to countertransference issues.

The Minister and Assertiveness

In the personal development of clergy, we have found the issue of assertiveness to be paramount. Each time the topic is broached in a class or seminar by the authors, an exaggerated resistance to the idea of a Christian minister's being assertive emerges. And yet, clinical experience shows us that under-assertive (and excessively over-assertive) ministers are much more likely to suffer from depression in the ministry, burnout, helplessness, and especially problems with anger and resentment.

In working with under-assertive ministers or in assessing ministerial candidates, it is important to define assertiveness, first with the best secular model available (we usually use the passive-assertive-aggressive continuum of Alberti and Emmons, 1970) and then in the context of Christian sacrifice. We usually define assertiveness as the capacity to claim one's rights in the absence of anger. If the pastor is angry, then he or she easily becomes aggressive, which congregations are not quick to forgive. Assertiveness should bind the minister to the congregation over time, not alienate him or her from them.

The Christian modification to the secular definition of assertiveness is to believe also that we have the "freedom" to sacrifice those rights if we so choose. Sacrifice is only meaningful if we have experienced our capacity to claim our rights. Many ministers are confused about this and deem themselves "Christian" because they are constantly feeling forced to sacrifice themselves. Much "sacrifice" is more likely a passive weakness bordering on cowardice.

The best method of distinguishing this difference is to see whether the sacrificial response leaves the minister with anger and resentment. If so, then the sacrifice is probably just passivity. If there is no anger, then the sacrifice is from a position of strength.

Under-assertive ministers (passive) are characterized by a number of factors. They generally find it difficult to set limits; they cannot say no to requests; they are easily manipulated by stronger individuals; and they are unable to express angry feelings constructively. This often builds up to an aggressive expression of angry feelings, which leaves the minister with feelings of guilt for having made emotional outbursts. In addition, under-assertive ministers usually avoid conflict situations, and they are excessively apologetic with people.

Overly assertive ministers (aggressive) usually have an autocratic style of leadership. This style is often efficient, but it suffers in building morale, especially on a church staff. Autocratic ministers are often manipulative and intimidating and are characterized by angry attitudes, and they build buffers around themselves that create distance from members.

Appropriately assertive ministers are free to choose when to sacrifice personal rights without resentment or guilt. They also recognize weakness in others and develop an ability to make mature decisions about protecting themselves in difficult situations. Assertive ministers are also free of hostility, even in its more subtle forms, and are sensitive to the feelings of others as well as of their own.

To assess the degree of assertiveness in minsters, we use a hand-scored assertiveness inventory that includes 30 items (Wolpe and Lazarus, 1966). Each item involves a situation pastors are likely to face that demands choosing between assertion and passivity. The MMPI is a useful tool for discovering passive-aggressive tendencies, and the Novaco Anger Scale helps delineate specific areas in which a pastor is likely to feel hurt and angry.

To treat and/or prevent problems that arise with under-assertive and aggressive ministers, we work to educate ministers about the assertiveness model, and the Christian modification discussed above. It is important to note that every pastoral situation requiring a response involves a decision to be assertive or not. Common pastoral situations are explored (handling unreasonable requests, managing conflict, discussing an excessive workload, receiving criticism, and the like) and passive, aggressive, and assertive options are role-played. A one-page assignment of "Pastor's Rights" is completed and discussed in the classroom format. These interventions have not been empirically tested, but clinical experience and follow-up reports indicate that they are especially significant in preparing ministers with tools for handling the inevitable role conflict and expectations in ministry.

In addition, a minister's support group is encouraged to help ministers practically by sharing problem situations and exchanging feedback from the group. Most likely, a given situation has been experienced (either positively or negatively) by another group member, and strategies and suggestions can be offered.

The problem of anger and its resolution also need to be adequately addressed. Cognitive control, delay, and relaxation techniques are taught both as prevention and as treatment of anger situations in ministry.

Conclusion

The pastoral ministry has increasingly become a difficult and hazardous profession. The impact of the ministry on personal development requires a thorough conceptual model for each particular ministry hazard in order to anticipate and adjust to the exigencies of ministry. This chapter has outlined briefly a model for conceptualizing personal relationships, depression, stress (and burnout), sexuality, and assertiveness. A more detailed analysis would include the minister and guilt, anger, self-esteem, role conflict, and personality differences.

6

Spouses and Families of Clergy

CAMERON LEE

Marital and family relationships are social contexts in which individual spouses and family members interact. These relationships in turn are embedded in still larger social contexts. The clergy family's most immediate social context, of course, is their congregation. The patterns of relationship between the clergy family and the congregation are important correlates of the quality of clergy family life and clergy assessment.

Interest in the marital and family relationships of ministers is not new in itself. Nearly three decades ago, before inclusive language was emphasized, J. C. Wynn wrote:

> The minister's interpersonal difficulties affect his entire parish. . . . When his professional life and his family life are at odds because he has still to come to terms with both, when he suffers from a professional role conflict and is unsure of the expectations of church and community, and when these are compounded by the minister's own immaturity in faith and work, the church membership is certain to feel effects. Paul's salty word to Timothy is apropos: "If a man does not know how to manage his own household, how can he care for God's church?" (Wynn, 1960, p. 10).

Here interest in clergy family life seems secondary to the focus on the ministry. The minister's family problems are of concern because they betray an underlying lack of maturity, which will have a negative impact on the ministry.

Although this is correct to an extent, it reflects a one-sided bias that focuses much more on the ministry than on the minister. Several references are available to clergy on the theology and practice of ministry to families (Hulme, 1962; Stewart, 1961, 1979; Wynn, 1957, 1982), but little substantive literature reflexively applies the same care to the minister's own family.

Numerous studies on ministers and their spouses emphasize individual as opposed to relational issues. For example, several research studies on "the min- isterial personality" focus on correlations between individual personality variables and ministerial adjustment or style (Bier, 1970; Hofmann, 1960; Nauss, 1973; Oates, 1961). Studies of ministers' wives target primarily individual matters as opposed to marital dynamics (Alleman, 1987; Denton, 1962; Douglas, 1965; Ritter, 1982; Wimberly, 1981). While such studies are useful and valid, complementary research on relationships is also needed.

Even studies that purport to focus on clergy marriages may actually fail to assess the marital relationship itself. In one often cited study, for example, fifty-six clergy couples were given 330-item problem checklists, and the responses of the ministers and their spouses were then compared (Presnell, 1977). The bulk of the findings, however, represent parallels drawn between individual responses, rather than an assessment of the marriage itself.

Not only must the family and marital relationships of clergy be directly assessed, but the social context of these relationships should be studied as well. As Douglas has written, "the relationship between husband and wife can only be understood in the context of their individual and joint relationship to a particular local congregation" (Douglas, 1961, 37). Research and theory regarding clergy marriage and family relationships must begin to account for the clergy's social context—namely, the congregation. Indeed, the importance of the clergy family-congregation relationship is often implied, but seldom studied directly. For example, David and Vera Mace (1980) asked ministry couples to list the advantages and disadvantages of clergy marriage. These couples' responses have more to do with the quality of their relationship to the congregation than with the quality of their marriage.

Sociologists of religion have long studied the interaction of clergy and congregation, largely through the lenses of role conflict (Anderson, 1971; Blizzard, 1956, 1958a, 1958b, 1959; Glock and Roos, 1961;

Ingram, 1981; Maddock, Kinney, and Middleton, 1973; Perry and Hoge, 1981; Smith, 1973). Few studies, however, directly relate the study of congregational contexts to the assessment of clergy marriages and families.

Marital and family relationships cannot be fully assessed by focusing only on the individual spouses or family members. Furthermore, these relationships must also be taken in their social context, the most immediate level of which is the clergy family's relationship to the congregation. Warner and Carter (1984), for example, use the Dyadic Adjustment Scale (Spanier, 1976) to assess the quality of clergy marriages, using lay couples as controls. They found that the clergy marriages in the sample fared significantly more poorly than did their lay counterparts. Such descriptive information, however, has little explanatory power. The question is not simply whether clergy marriages and families are doing better or worse than others, but what environmental factors contribute to the variance.

Although the range of methods and instruments for assessing relationships lags far behind that for individuals, research into clergy marriage and family relationships requires both mid-range theories and an overarching epistemology that will allow for both the generation and the coordination of hypotheses and research data. The epistemological perspective that I call a *social ecology* (Lee, 1987, 1988; Lee and Balswick, 1989) can be "loaded" with different mid-range theoretical perspectives, which are then interpreted as necessarily partial explanations of a more complex whole.

The Perspective of a Social Ecology

Webster's Third New International Dictionary defines *ecology* as "the totality or pattern of relations between organisms and their environment." The epistemological perspective of a *social ecology*, therefore, assumes that the clergy family is embedded in a more comprehensive social and emotional network and that the relation of the clergy family to these contexts must be studied in order to understand the family itself.

The ecological approach is not in itself an explanatory theory, but "a way of thinking and an operational style" (Auerswald, 1968), which shares the holistic emphasis of General Systems Theory (Bertalanffy, 1968). As John Sutherland has written:

Behavioral properties of any real significance are generally dependent upon a context for their viability. From the system perspective, this means that the search for the whole cannot end simply with an inventory of parts analyzed in effective isolation or with partitioned

expressions of their interrelationships. Rather, the *field* must also be defined. And it is the system as a whole, not the isolated parts, which is significant when we move to the ecological dimension of socio-cultural or behavioral phenomena (Sutherland, 1973, p. 37).

An ecological orientation begins with the assumption of *non-summativity* (Speer, 1970), or the principle that "the whole is greater than the sum of its parts." This means that the phenomenon we call "family" cannot be fully explained by individual factors. The approach then adds that the behavior of both individuals and groups should be understood in the context that gives it meaning: its physical and social environment. A *social ecology*, then, applies this holistic epistemology to the study of social factors.

Although any social group can be considered a "whole" in its own right, an ecological perspective will not partition off groups from one another. Social ecology has both *horizontal* and *vertical* dimensions. Not only are there numerous coexisting groups, but also each group is embedded in a hierarchy of larger and more complex social organizations (Lee and Balswick, 1989; Watzlawick, Beavin, and Jackson, 1967). The social ecology, then, is a network of reciprocally interacting and nested social groups. A determinedly ecological approach can be extremely complex, continually expanding the boundaries of its investigation into all levels of the social environment.

To simplify and organize such an investigation by delineating the various levels of analysis, Urie Bronfenbrenner describes the essence of an ecological approach:

The ecology of human development involves the scientific study of the progressive, mutual accommodation between an active growing human being and the changing properties of the immediate settings in which the developing person lives, as this process is affected by relations between these settings, and by the larger contexts in which the settings are embedded. (Bronfenbrenner, 1979, p. 21)

For Bronfenbrenner, the connections between the various levels and settings of the total ecology are subtly but effectively intertwined, so that events in one part of the social environment may trigger adaptive changes in other parts, even those that appear unrelated or remote.

To help organize analysis, Bronfenbrenner (1979, pp. 22-26) distinguishes between four levels of the ecological field. The four levels, in order of increasing generality and complexity, are the *microsystem*, the *mesosystem*, the *exosystem*, and the *macrosystem*.

The most basic level of analysis is the *microsystem*, a

complex but relatively persistent pattern of ongoing activities, roles, and interpersonal relationships in a face-to-face social setting. The microsystem is more than simply a collection of individuals and their characteristics, or the place where they interact; it also includes the patterns of interaction and the individuals' experience of them.

Treating the clergy family as a microsystem implies that assessment of clergy marriage and family life should intentionally focus on interactional variables in addition to individual adjustment. Research at this level would stay within the boundaries of the clergy family, using marital and family inventories and observational methods to assess relationship patterns.

Individual family members, however, also participate in other settings; the children may go to school, or the spouse may work. The totality of the interaction between a family member's face-to-face settings is that person's *mesosystem*, or a "system of microsystems."

Work and family roles of clergy overlap, making boundaries and distinctions unclear. The family life of clergy must be understood in the context of the interaction of the minister's microsystems of family and church with the mesosystems of the other members of the clergy family.

The *exosystem* refers to a social setting that does not directly involve an individual, but in which events affect or are affected by what happens in the settings that *do* contain that individual. The effect is due to another person, who at the same time shares a microsystem with the individual and is also a member of the exosystem.

The exosystem concept highlights the interconnectedness of various microsystems. We need not be members of a social system for that system to have an impact on our lives. This essential insight, taken in broad perspective, allows us to visualize a chain of exosystemic influences that may connect seemingly unrelated events in the social ecology. It is at this level in particular that researchers need to broaden their empirical horizons and see beyond the family to the immediate social environment in which the family is embedded.

The final level of analysis is the *macrosystem,* where cultural and subcultural beliefs and role prescriptions come into play. For clergy, this may include expectations of family and marital roles, deriving from the local community, the denomination, and the normative values of the society as a whole. There are differences between denominations and congregations in such areas as role involvement and the relationship of theological orientation to institutional structure (Alleman, 1987; Moberg, 1970; Schuller, Strommen, and Brekke, 1980). Another study examines how social class

differences may affect clergy-parish relationships (Mitchell, 1965).

At the macrosystem level, ecological analysis extends beyond the confines of the local church body. A particularly important area for study is how denominations differ in the type and frequency of stress placed on clergy marriages and families. For example, three of the most common stresses faced by clergy are (a) inadequate finances, (b) living in a parsonage on or near the church grounds, and (c) frequently or unexpectedly moving their families to a new community (Lee, 1987; Lee and Balswick, 1989). Ministers, denominational authorities, and those involved in research and assessment alike should seek ways of enhancing the quality of clergy marital and family life by becoming proactive at this level of the social ecology.

Toward Ecological Assessment

The logic of an ecological approach challenges traditional research wisdom. The experimental ideal in psychological research is *control*, eliminating the effect of environmental factors by either holding them constant or reducing them to the level of chance. Where human social behavior is concerned, however, this ideal tends to run aground on the problem of external validity.

The difficulty is implicitly ecological. If one assumes that human behavior (or at least the behavior that is of interest to psychologists and sociologists) is intrinsically social, then experimental designs that abstract behavior from its meaning-giving social context may be moving away from, rather than toward, the understanding of human nature. For this reason, some family researchers have attempted to study family interaction in its natural environment—the home, using participant observation and other data-gathering techniques (Kantor and Lehr, 1975; Vetere and Gale, 1987).

Rather than abandon the classical experimental model, we must keep its results in context (Bronfenbrenner, 1979, pp. 36-37). Ideally, ecological experimentation, instead of controlling out environmental variance, would "control it in" by systematically manipulating contextual variables and observing the results. Clergy assessment can become more conscientiously ecological in its orientation. Survey research, for example, which cannot manipulate variables, can still seek out systematic covariance between environmental factors and clergy marriage and family life.

We have found that relationships between clergy families and their congregations are strongly and significantly correlated with such variables as clergy marital happiness and family stress (Lee, 1987; Lee and

Balswick, 1989).* In these studies, each spouse was asked to rate his or her degree of marital happiness, using a single seven-point Likert-type item adapted from Spanier's Dyadic Adjustment Scale (Spanier, 1976). A second, similar item also asked spouses to rate their degree of happiness in their present ministry environment on the same seven-point scale.

Our surveys also assessed three variables related to the interaction between the congregation and the clergy family. Each item was presented as a four-point Likert-type scale, ranging from "mostly false" to "mostly true." The first, *intrusion,* measured each spouse's perception of the degree to which the congregation intruded on their family life, or otherwise took advantage of family members. The second variable, *integration,* assessed to what extent the clergy family felt a positive relationship to the congregation, much as a nuclear family might feel toward a benevolent extended family. Scores on both variables were computed separately for each spouse and were then combined into total intrusion and integration scores for each couple. The critical items for the two scales are presented in Table 1 below.

Table 1

Items for Ministers' Intrusion and Integration Scales

Intrusion:
1. I am frustrated by the number of unnecessary phone calls I receive at home from church members.
2. Our family has all the privacy it needs.
3. My ministry allows me enough time for my family.
4. I feel that my salary is fair.
5. My ministry allows me enough time for myself.

Integration:
1. Our family experiences the congregation as a loving and caring community.
2. I feel accepted by the congregation as their authoritative leader.
3. Family members find it easier to discuss things with people outside the church.
4. Family members have a need for friends outside the church.
5. Our family feels a sense of unity with the members of the congregation.

☆ ☆ ☆

I gratefully acknowledge the contributions of Dr. Bill Hogue, executive director, and the Reverend Michael Carlisle of the Southern Baptist General Convention of California, whose technical and financial support made the study possible. Further details of the study can be obtained by writing to: Cameron Lee, Graduate School of Psychology, Division of Marriage and Family, Fuller Theological Seminary, 180 N. Oakland, Pasadena, CA, 91182.

A third interaction variable, *overlap,* parallels Kieren and Munro's notions of the absorptiveness and enmeshment of clergy roles (Kieren and Munro, 1988). The pastors and their wives were asked to use a six-point Likert-type scale to rate: (a) the degree of perceived overlap between church/congregational life and family life and (b) the degree of overlap that they would like to have. The difference between the two was computed for each spouse and then combined into a single discrepancy score for the couple. Table 2 gives a brief summary of the findings.

Table 2

Correlations of Interaction Variables with Happiness in Marriage and Ministry for Southern Baptist Clergy Couples (N = 150)

	Correlation (r) with Happiness in:	
Interaction Variable	Marriage	Ministry
Intrusion	−.21[b]	−.33[c]
Integration	.24[b]	.68[c]
Overlap (Discrepancy score)[d]	−.17[a]	−.24[b]

[a] $p < .05$
[b] $p < .01$
[c] $p < .001$
[d] Intrusion and overlap were correlated at r = .52, $p < .001$.

All three interaction variables were significantly correlated to the clergy couple's marital happiness score. Thus on the one hand the greater the congregational intrusiveness perceived by the couple, or the greater the discrepancy between perceived and desired overlap, the lower their marital happiness. On the other hand, the greater the integration of the couple into the congregational family, the higher their reported marital happiness.

There is, of course, no basis for inferring the direction of causality. In an ecological model, it is assumed that the interaction is reciprocal, not unidirectional, and thus the degree of correlation is itself of interest.

Conclusion

The language of the church as family is not simply a poetic metaphor, but a social reality. Edwin Friedman has written that of all work systems, "the one that functions most like a family is the church or synagogue" (Friedman, 1985, 197). The clergy family, then, is a *family in a family,* subject to the same joys and sorrows that any nuclear family faces in relation to its extended family. Research and assessment of the marriage and family relationships of ministers should attempt to understand these relationships in their social context. The social ecological perspective is one way to envision the epistemological and empirical task.

7

Nurturing Dual Career Couples

RICHARD A. HUNT

For denominations that allow ordained ministers to marry, at the beginning of the twentieth century the dominant, almost exclusive, model of marriage in relation to ordained ministers was the "male pastor and wife." Often the wife was assumed to be an unpaid helper to her clergy husband, with some women feeling specifically called to the vocation of "pastor's wife." When the pastor's wife did work outside the home, it most likely was as a teacher in the community school or perhaps in nursing.

Across the decades, many factors have combined to produce multiple models of minister and spouse (wife or husband). Women have moved from having no vote to being elected to major political offices and from not being eligible for ordination to being elected bishop. In the population of the United States, the percentage of homes with only one spouse having paid employment approaches only 10 to 15 percent of all households.

Examples of the shifts in the treatment of ordained ministers and spouses can be found in the writings of Bader (1942), Blackwood (1951), Denton (1962), and Douglas (1961). Alleman (1987) has compared recent changes to the Douglas study of 1961.

Our increasing understanding of the complex network of relationships between an individual's family of origin, career and occupation, marriage, and family of procreation means that clergy career and marriage issues are increasingly important. Although terms are not precise, the "dual income" couple refers to any couple in which both spouses earn income, although one or neither spouse may think of his or her work as a "career." Within this broad range are "dual career" couples, in which both spouses intentionally prepare for and work in occupations that are part of their lifetime career path commitments. Careers in medicine, law, education, and ministry are now expanded to additional career options in dozens of fields that were not even created a few years ago.

When both spouses commit themselves to careers, additional issues and potential problems must be resolved. Among these are child care, work location, time priorities, household management, and personal identity as being in a career and/or being a spouse. Many of these general issues of dual career couples are addressed by sources such as Hall and Hall (1977) and Heckman, Bryson, and Bryson (1977). A helpful overview of dual career couples and families is available in Pepitone-Rockwell (1980).

The title *clergy couple* may mean only that one of the spouses is a cleric, regardless of what the other spouse is doing. Within the dual career couple context, the recent phenomenon of "clergy couples" (dual career couples in which both spouses are ordained ministers) can be more precisely described as "dual clergy career couples." Perhaps the most extensive research on these couples has been done by Robinson (1988).

Dual Clergy Career Couples

Dual career marriage and ministry issues were first directly addressed in the work of Hunt and Hunt (1976) and of Mace and Mace (1980). Rallings and Pratto (1984) more recently have focused on what they see as the special issues for dual clergy career couples.

Kieren and Munro (1988) describe absorptiveness and enmeshment as major role demands of dual clergy couples. Enmeshment, then, suggests that the boundaries between one's employment or profession versus one's private, family, and leisure life become very blurred, with the profession tending to control all of one's life (Kieren and Munro, 1988, p. 240). From their framework, the clergy role is highly absorptive, demanding a high investment of the person's energy and resources, involving the whole person, and intruding on all aspects of the person's life. As one bishop's wife lamented, "If my husband were merely having an affair with another woman, I could cope with that. But when his love affair is with God and the entire church, I sometimes feel overwhelmed and forgotten!"

In a study of 988 respondents, Robinson (1988)

compared dual clergy couples (in which both spouses are ordained clergy), female clergy with career spouses, male clergy with career spouses, and male clergy with non-career spouses. Generally, clergy couples do not differ in their marriages from other married clergy. Within this context, however, 40 percent of dual clergy couples—as compared to 25 percent of other married clergy—experience competition with their spouses on an "occasionally, often, or very often" frequency. Fifty percent of dual clergy couples and 31 percent of other married clergy are positively motivated by competition with their spouses.

Pragmatic concerns, competition, enmeshment, conflation (intrusion of work into couple and family areas), and sex role expectations were studied by Robinson (1988). Dual clergy couples are neither more nor less enmeshed than are other married clergy. Dual clergy couples do differ from others in the other four dimensions studied, but, except for conflation, the differences are not great.

Nearly all married clergy report that work and ministry concerns are brought into their time as a couple or family (higher conflation). However, this happens more often for dual clergy couples who also find more understanding about these work concerns from their clergy spouse than ministers married to a non-clergy spouse.

Women in dual clergy couples report experiencing more criticism from others about their career-marriage combination than do women in other couple arrangements. More than other clergy, dual clergy couples experience criticism from church members and from colleagues more than other couples.

Issues and experiences are not related to the ages or number of years of experience in ministry of dual clergy couples. The number of problems and issues neither decreases nor increases across time. Where problems do occur, it seems that they are much more the result of more basic psychological factors, such as self-esteem, envy, personal boundaries, and gender identity. Rather than producing problems, it seems likely that the dual clergy career marriage situation may intensify these deeper issues for a minority of these couples.

Perhaps the major issue for dual clergy couples is to work actively to protect their time together as a couple from intrusions of church concerns. With two busy schedules, dual clergy spouses may utilize personal time together for "business" meetings concerning the pragmatics of their respective professional ministries. This is perhaps more tempting for these couples because both spouses are trained in the same profession. Almost half of all dual clergy couples plan and strategize with their spouses regarding work or ministry issues during their time off (Robinson, 1988).

Two Examples of Ways to Nurture Couples

The United Methodist Candidacy Studies

In The United Methodist Church, initial assessment of candidates for the ordained or diaconal ministries is set in the larger context of the Candidacy Process (Hunt and Kohler, 1988). There are four major stages in this process.

First, the "inquiring candidate" studies a basic resource, *The Christian as Minister* (1988), and consults with his or her pastor and/or other ministers about the ministry as a calling and profession. This step is intended to invite many persons to consider the ordained or diaconal ministries as possible career options. A brief description of this program will provide a perspective for seeing how the candidate's spouse (or spouse to be, if any) can be involved.

Second, the "exploring candidate" is assigned to a trained supervising pastor as a mentor and guide to a cafeteria of twelve "exploratory studies." In the initial study, the supervising pastor and the candidate meet and plan the process to fit the needs and goals of the candidate. Studies two, three, and four consider God's calling and vocation as seen in the Bible, in the ecumenical church and its models for ministries, and in the traditions of The United Methodist Church.

Study five invites the candidate to relate personal spiritual formation and vocational decisions. In study six, on "self inventory," the candidate participates in the United Methodist assessment program (see chaps. 17 and 18 of this volume) with an approved "pastoral evaluation specialist."

In studies seven through ten, the candidate consults with others to obtain their feedback and perspectives; explores single, marriage, and family life-styles in relation to potential ministries the candidate is considering; considers ministries in relation to his or her own age, sex, and ethnic, cultural, and other personal characteristics; and "second career" and other career decisions across one's lifetime. Study eleven addresses educational preparation for professional ministries. The final review study enables the candidate, on the basis of these explorations, to shape personal career decisions.

Third, the "declared candidate" is the time when the candidate "goes public" in saying that he or she understands God's leading to be toward a professional ministry as a career. In this stage, the candidate meets with local church and district committees for official certification as a candidate for the ordained or diaconal ministry.

Fourth, the "certified candidate" stage continues the candidate's relationship with church representatives and the supervising pastor until the candidate is ordained or certified for the ministry.

In this process, married candidates have opportunities to include their spouses as much as the candidate and spouse desire. Exploratory studies five through eleven are especially open to these possibilities. The supervising pastor (and spouse, if any) may meet with the candidate and spouse (and family, if they choose) as these meetings seem desirable. Candidates also have the option of including their spouses in parts of the assessment process.

In attending to marriage and family dimensions in relation to career and assessment decisions about the ministry, two contrasting principles must be held in appropriate balance. One is the "career" principle that the candidacy process, including its assessment components, is specifically for the candidate. The church is not "hiring" the spouse as an "unpaid associate minister" so the married candidate's spouse and family (or single candidate's lack of marriage) should not be included in any selection decisions.

In contrast is the "network" principle that, from a systems perspective, the candidate's life situation and support systems (such as spouse or dating patterns, family of origin, children, and other personal factors) do indeed make an impact on his or her fitness, preparation, and performance as a professional person. If the spouse is also employed or is a career person (now the majority of couple situations), and even if the spouse is a homemaker and/or an unpaid volunteer worker, variations of these "career" and "network" principles also apply to the spouse.

One of the major goals of the Candidacy Process is to mentor the candidate in coping with these contrasting principles in relation to his or her career and life decisions. Thus the exact process will vary according to the candidate's situation; yet, at a deeper level the process encourages the candidate to begin to deal with relationship issues that will be with the individual throughout life.

A Five-year Retreat Plan

Expressing nurturing care for clergy, candidates, and their spouses is an essential parallel to clergy assessment. In addition to the possibilities that are available in the United Methodist Candidacy Process, more recently the *Marriage in Ministry* program of The United Methodist Church (Walker and Sherman, 1988) has been developed to focus specifically on couples.

The rationale of this program is to provide confidential counseling to clergy candidates and spouses that is administratively separate from the assessment process. It also seeks to assist couples to distinguish personal, couple, and contextual (church and/or seminary) problems from one another, with appropriate assistance for each area. In addition, it alerts couples to potential stresses in ministry (see chaps. 4–6 of this volume) and seeks to foster self-reliance and spiritual formation resources through ongoing contact with counselors and spiritual directors.

This *Marriage in Ministry* program assumes that the candidate and spouse will begin the "first year" during the year in which the candidate is in the United Methodist Candidacy Studies program (Hunt, 1987). It begins with a weekend candidacy retreat for candidates and spouses, during which couples identify the systems in which they operate (couple, family, families of origin, church, community, and so on), identify areas for growth, and increase their positive resources for coping.

During the second year, the couple complete two marital questionnaires and meet with a therapist for a three-hour history gathering session. After this session, the therapist, the spiritual director, and another colleague discuss implications and recommendations, after which the couple receives feedback. If appropriate, therapy may be recommended as part of the follow-up to this conference. In the third year of the program, a couples' "seminary retreat" provides a series of group and couple experiences in which spouses can identify patterns of relating and affirm them as positive or replace them with other more satisfying patterns.

By the fourth year of the program, it is anticipated that the candidate will be in full-time parish work. Written resource materials will be sent quarterly to each couple. As in previous years, couples may have additional private consultations with the therapists.

A "parish retreat" is planned for the fifth year. The couple focus on time management, ways to develop support systems outside the parish, views of parish dynamics, and further examination of how the couple's own needs interface with parish, denominational, and other contextual systems. This program is now being instituted in some of the annual conferences of The United Methodist Church.

Summary

Marriage issues make an impact on all clergy, whether married or single. For those who are married (or plan to be), their spouses directly affect their work and career through the husband-wife interactions around time, schedules, planning, money, energy, sex, extended families, location, and the many emotional needs and strengths of each partner. For those who choose not to marry or whose church does not permit marriage or who are divorced, the minister must still deal with being single in the context of a "marrying and divorcing" society.

In many ways, one's clergy career is greatly affected, for better or worse, by personal relationships around marriage. In addition, if one's spouse is also a career person, whether clergy or another profession, then the management of two careers, at least one home, and perhaps children and other relatives and in-laws, is compounded. At every step, assessment and related nurturing programs must enable candidates, partners, and churches to cope in healthy ways with these lifelong relationships.

Research Methodologies
and Perspectives

8

Pitfalls and Possibilities in Processing People:

A Psychometric Perspective

RICHARD L. GORSUCH

The purpose of this chapter is to consider clergy assessment from a psychometric perspective. This is, please note, only one perspective for the review of such procedures, since a theological perspective is also needed (see section II of this volume). But the psychometric perspective does provide the unique focus from which we shall approach the task in this chapter. Psychometrics is the distillation of experience and empirical research on using data in processing people.

This chapter can only highlight principles that might be applicable to a particular situation. Utilization of the principles will be enhanced by using additional technical sources, including books on psychometrics such as Anastasi (1982) and Nunnally (1978), *Standards for Educational and Psychological Testing* (AERA/APA/ NCME Joint Committee, 1985), and the *Uniform Guidelines on Employment Selection Procedures* (U.S. Equal Employment Opportunity Commission et al., 1978). Nathan and Cascio (1986) place these materials into the context of court decisions in this area. To use the recommendations below, a person is assumed to be knowledgeable of the theology, polity, and common practices of the religious setting for the ministry for which assessment is done. Indeed, this is sufficiently important that I would only recommend as a consultant someone with in-depth experience with ministry in that setting, regardless of the person's psychological or psychometric qualifications. Generally it is easier to add the psychometric understandings to a person knowledgeable about a ministry setting than vice versa.

The Importance of Empirical Evidence

Basic research on the human condition suggests that we must begin our task by learning two rules.

Rule 1: Do no harm. It seems to be a general assumption that assessment procedures can only do good and not harm. But Oswald (chap. 29) reports

clergy damage done through clergy assessment. My experience confirms his analysis, for sometimes the result of my empirical work has been unwarranted early retirement or other relocation of personnel.

As we collect more data, we find more instances of doing harm than those of doing good. We should indeed take seriously the anxieties that are raised in clergy by assessment and selection procedures. All assessment procedures—including interviews and what are generally deemed non-psychometric approaches— do have substantial costs and so must produce substantial benefits in order to be helpful. For example, in one master's project I directed, we found that providing social support for individuals actually led to a negative change in their behavior. Sometimes well-intentioned programs like "Big Brothers" have negative side effects, such as producing more runaways (Institute for Social Research, 1976).

Rule 2: Remember our limits. Gorsuch and Malony (1976) reviewed literature dealing with this rule. The temptation to "play God" can only be countered when we recognize that our human judgments are fallible indeed. We cannot with certainty identify a ministerial candidate who will fail at ministry, nor can we guarantee success to another candidate. At best we can only increase the odds.

Psychometrics as a field of study starts from fallibilities of human judgment. It is a result of research and studies since the early 1900s on how to improve human judgment. The conclusions are very clear: Sawyer (1966) notes that *every single study* he reviewed that compared empirically based procedures against human judgment found that the empirically based procedures do as well as or better than the human judgment. Hence each chapter's author as well as the readers of this book may occasionally do as well on appropriate psychological batteries, but generally they will do worse.

The reason psychometrics do as well as or better than human judgment is that psychometrics is not counter to or in opposition to human judgment, but has carefully built the best from human judgment into the questionnaires or other approaches. Thus if we want to evaluate a person's anxiety, we use exactly those questions that clinicians over the years have found to identify anxiety.

One of the more deceptive problems in human judgment is that we are inclined to trust our own experience rather than research data. That is illogical because the research data combine the experiences from many individuals. Each one of those persons is almost as likely to be as valid as is our own judgment, but the average of many individuals is much more likely to be accurate than any single person—including you or me.

Courts also have noted the fallibilities of human judgment. They indicate that the guidelines noted at the beginning of this chapter apply to any and every type of assessment technique (Bersoff, 1988; Nathan and Cascio, 1986, p. 12). These include casual interviews, application forms that have no formal scoring, and reports from probationary periods. This is consistent with those standards. All human judgment is subject to the same qualifications and requirements as formal psychometric procedures. That is appropriate, since psychometric procedures are only extensions of normal human judgment.

The more empirical we become, the more we find limitations on our judgments. Utilizing empirical and psychometric approaches does indeed provide us, at times, discouraging data. But the wrong approach is to turn back to doing only theology or to drop psychometric procedures for unnamed or casual procedures. In doing so, we go from the known limitations of procedures that are far from perfect to procedures that have been found time and time again to be even worse.

There are corollaries to Rule 2. One is the fact that as we obtain more information, we are more likely to make a mistake rather than to make an accurate judgment. People have the unfortunate tendency to make sense out of nonsense and to find patterns in unpatterned data (see Armstrong and Soelberg, 1968). Hence the common procedure of giving large batteries of tests for assessment and then evaluating the results—whether by one psychologist or a committee—intensifies the problem rather than reducing it.

As an example of what can be done using human judgment and more sophisticated psychometric procedures, consider Comer's report (chap. 11). Letters of recommendation have seldom been found to provide useful data; yet, Comer reports some value. Comer used a clear coding system set up to evaluate the letters, thus using known psychometric principles to improve the yield from the letters.

Note in the example from Comer that data were used to judge the procedure, not human judgment. Using human judgment to pick the "best" procedure is again utilizing a known fallible technique for which statistical analysis has been developed as an appropriate corrective. For that reason, we should never pick instruments by majority vote, rather than the existing data. The likely result will be that the instrument that most people have been trained on is the one selected, as in the case of Hinkle's report in chapter 18 of this volume, when the MMPI was selected.

Psychologists are no more infallible than ministers or laypeople. But psychologists are scientists and, therefore, they have the criterion of data on which to base their judgment. Thus the only time a psychologist can claim to be an expert is when the psychologist notes supporting data; otherwise the "expertise" is based on an *argumentum ad hominum*. Consultants in clergy assessment should know appropriate empirical data bases. Potential consultants should be closely interviewed to assure appropriate knowledge about the ministerial situation and relevant research. If they cannot reference supporting empirical studies and share some of the details, then they are not appropriate consultants.

The Importance of the Situation

Selection is one possible reason for clergy assessment, but the usefulness of data depends on the amount of selection. For example, if every candidate goes on to be ordained, then the ministerial selection process involves no selection. No data, despite its origin, will then be of help.

A major problem that Comer (chap. 11 of this volume) and Malony and Majovski (1986; see also chap. 14 of this volume) confronted is the fact at least 90 percent of clergy candidates were selected. With such a high selection rate, it is hard to justify using any procedure unless it has high validity. No procedure involving interviews or letters of recommendation could help much in this situation. The few candidates that are dropped have such an overwhelming mass of negative information that any formal evaluation procedure probably could add little except to assure due process.

Those involved in clergy assessment may see their function in terms of counseling and placement. Cardwell (chap. 30) notes that there are many seminary applications of clergy assessment for counseling. The rationale, of course, is that the persons themselves will aid in the selection task and that, even if all are selected, they will be better pastors for that.

Unfortunately I know of no data that document this

hope. Those involved in such tasks should note studies of negative side effects from interventions in other areas. Check Joan McCord's study (1978), in which she discusses a strong mentoring program for teenagers that failed to reduce delinquency as intended. Instead the mentoring led to the participating subjects' dying at a younger age and being more dissatisfied with life than a random control group who were not mentored. Until we have studied the effects of such mentoring on clergy, the past literature has identified enough negative side effects so that we cannot assume a positive impact.

If assessment of clergy is deemed appropriate either for selection or counseling, the reader must also be warned that it should be legal. Foster's study, in chapter 23 of this volume, is essential as a starting place with further reading, such as Nathan and Cascio (1986). I strongly suspect that clergy assessment that uses a battery of tests like the MMPI by clinical psychologists who have little experience with the setting of the ministry or with personnel procedures as in industrial or social psychology would be judged illegal by the courts unless there were specific data showing the battery's effectiveness.

Validity: The Major Psychometric Requirement

An assessment procedure, whether casual interview or sophisticated test, is valid to the degree to which it provides accurate information that is necessary to reach an appropriate decision in that setting. No procedure is assumed to provide accurate and useful information unless that procedure is documented empirically.

Conditions Producing Poor Validity

One condition that has historically led to poor validity is when the assessment technique and the criterion are of different levels of breadth or depth. For example, if the criterion is how powerful the sermons of the candidate are, then a psychological test of the preacher's personal feelings or an interview that explores his or her relationship with his or her spouse will show poor validity. Those techniques are not at the same breadth and depth as the criterion. Instead one would need to examine, possibly, the background of the candidate in public speaking, his or her theology of preaching, and the effect of past preaching in similar situations.

Most procedures for clergy assessment are broad, and that is appropriate since the ministry itself is a broad endeavor. Thus a psychological test—such as the 16PF, which asks about many different areas of life—separates out many occupations from the test's norm group (Mershon and Gorsuch, 1988). Assessment procedures will be ineffective if the critera are defined more broadly or more narrowly than the assessment procedure.

Another condition under which no increase in validity can be found is when the new assessment procedure essentially covers material that is included in assessment procedures already in use. For example, a limit in Comer's chapter 11 is that an excellent study identifies a model but provides no information on whether the information so obtained adds something new to information already available. Such studies can be more useful if they identify ways to gain the information more accurately and more easily than current procedures.

A condition under which a valid assessment procedure will *look* invalid, even if it is valid, is when the research is conducted in a sample of those whom it was used to select. For example, assume that the assessment procedure eliminated 100 percent of the candidates with a long-term neurotic problem and kept 100 percent of the normals. Then assume that the assessment was correlated with indexes of neuroticism collected twenty years later within only that sample that it helped select. Since these are people without long-term neurotic problems, the only neuroticism noted would be that which developed at a later time. Hence the test would correlate zero within the sample when it was doing its work with 100 percent success rate. If an assessment procedure is used for its full predictive power, that assessment procedure will correlate zero with success when evaluated only with those selected by the procedure. Hence any validation technique can be made to look bad by simply running a correlation between its results and an outcome measure from people who were selected by that procedure.

Predictive and Content Validity

While there are several types of validity, the most relevant ones are predictive and content validation. Predictive validation involves correlating the information from the assessment technique with an appropriate criterion at a later date in a sample that was not selected by that technique. The problem is developing and measuring an appropriate criterion (see Hinkle and Haight, chap. 9 of this volume). The problem is similar for content analysis. Content analysis judges the validity of the assessment procedure on the similarity between its content and the content of the task for which the assessment is being made.

All guidelines and standards require a careful analysis of the appropriateness of the criteria or content. The best evidence is that which is closest to what people actually do. Thus conclusions of an informed committee are deemed to have considerably less value than an actual job analysis, using formal time sampling or critical incident methodologies. All guidelines strongly recommend an empirical job analysis.

Fortunately for many Protestant denominations, such a job analysis has been the focus of the *Readiness for Ministry* (now POM) project (Aleshire, chap. 16 of this volume) and the Theological School Inventory (Hunt, chap. 17 of this volume). Given the sophistication of those studies, they are the essential bases to begin in ministerial assessment. To do otherwise would be unethical under American psychological ethics and would, given the court decisions, place those establishing the assessment procedure in legal jeopardy. One way of evaluating a consultant would be to see whether he or she were knowledgeable about the details—actual instruments used and outcomes—of the TSI and *POM* studies.

Sometimes other criteria are used in the short-term that are useful, provided their limitations are considered. Comer (chap. 11) finds that the MMPI does predict judgments of one clinical psychologist. This is theoretically appropriate because the clinical psychologist had probably been trained on the MMPI and used the MMPI in developing those judgments.

However, it may be that the judgments of the clinical psychologist were in part based on MMPI results. If so, then a correlation between MMPI and clinical judgments would capitalize on both true and error score information from the MMPI and inflate the correlation.

The higher the relationship between MMPI data and clinical judgment, the more it is possible that a computerized report based on the MMPI might be a replacement for clinical psychologists at a considerable savings in cost, which is, of course, a prime reason for developing psychometric procedures. But that criterion should not be confused with the long-term one of ordination or of success in ministry. As Comer notes, the MMPI had no such validity, a finding already replicated (Malony and Majovski, 1986). The lack of positive results for the MMPI is in keeping with our general knowledge of it. It was, of course, developed for a totally different purpose: diagnostic classification of people already judged abnormal.

Reliability

Reliability is technically defined as the proportion of the variance that is "true score" or generalizable variance. Since validity is the variance generalizable to the desired target, reliability, although essential, is less important than validity.

Reliability is highly useful with the interpretation of scores from an assessment procedure, since the standard error of measurement is computed from the reliability. When individual scores per se—such as an MMPI score of 71 on scale 3—are reported, those receiving such scores should know that the standard error of measurement is such that the 71 could have occurred if the person's underlying true score on that scale were, for example, between 67 and 74.

Fair Use

Even though positive evidence exists for an assessment procedure, there remains the question of fair use. Fair use of a test means that it is appropriate to use the information in making the decision and it is not an infringement of civil rights or other ethics. For example, the MMPI contains several religious items that, if answered in a pro-religious direction, add to the person's being seen as disturbed. Bier (1971) has proposed modifications to reduce this bias to make the MMPI more appropriate for clergy.

Besides simple examples, "fair use" is difficult to define and is defined by different people in incompatible ways. For example, many in our culture deem any difference in means between two ethnic groups as biased against the group that scores lower on that measure. Other definitions would say a test is biased only if it predicts an outcome for one ethnic group well but, when applied in the same manner, predicts it poorly for the other ethnic group. Even here there is considerable difference because of how "poor" is defined. Statistically it is generally impossible to meet all of the different definitions of fair use at the same time, due to the complexities in those definitions.

The area of fair use is not one in which the courts have a good record. They have been inclined to follow simplistic definitions and to evaluate only one assessment procedure. However, while one device may have some bias, an assessment committee has to be careful not to replace it with another assessment device that is even more biased. For example, when the courts have thrown out intelligence tests for assignment to classrooms in favor of unnamed, but more subjective, procedures—such as teachers' estimations—I, as a psychologist, would be unable to participate ethically in that process unless data on the objectivity of those other procedures were provided. Given the history of human judgment in our culture over the past two hundred years, I suspect that many teachers' judgments would be more ethnically biased than the better psychological tests.

Several conditions must be met to use the same assessment techniques with multiethnic clergy. These are (a) the ministerial candidates will be working in the same setting; (b) the assessment procedure has been shown to have validity for that setting; and (c) any differences between ethnic groups on the assessment procedure follow the differences in performance in that setting. Notice here that the emphasis is on validity regarding the setting, in keeping with the emphasis noted above on job analysis as a basis for empirical or content validity. For example, if pastors are being assessed for working in a Spanish-speaking congregation, all assessment interviews and instruments should be given to them in Spanish regardless of whether or not the pastors were raised to speak English. If they are being interviewed by a psychologist, the selection committee should require that interview to be conducted in Spanish only. The assessment procedure must match with the characteristics of the setting in which the ministry is to be carried out.

Sample Tests of Possible Use in Ministerial Assessment

Given the above discussion, assessment procedures from the *Readiness for Ministry* project and the *Theological School Inventory* should always be considered. These have been developed especially for this task by those conducting job analyses, and they have known psychometric properties.

A screening device may be used to determine whether a more extensive evaluation should be made. If the screening test indicates that there may be a problem, then an appropriate evaluation would be made to see whether there is a problem. Use of a screening test instead of the full battery of tests is desirable for several reasons. First, unless there is evidence to indicate further need, it is a waste of time and resources for a battery to be given (unless you are doing long-term research in which the battery is not scored until the long-term criteria are available). Second, remember Rule 2, noted above, and its implication for multiple pieces of information. If an entire test battery is always given, then, unless sophisticated statistical techniques are used rather than human judgment, there is a distinct possibility that decisions will be made from random patterns in the data.

The Tennessee Self-concept Scale (Fitts and Roid, 1988) has two special scales that could be of use for screening purposes in ministerial assessment. These scales screen for neuroticism or psychoticism. They were developed by empirically comparing responses of those clearly neurotic or psychotic with those who were clearly normal. Those above a particular point on each scale have been found, in cross-validation of the scale, to

be more likely to be judged neurotic or psychotic. Since it seems that one goal of most ministerial assessment procedures is to eliminate someone who is obviously neurotic or psychotic, this test can serve to select those for a clinical psychological assessment to determine if either condition exists.

The 16PF (Cattell, Eber, and Tatsuoka, 1970) can be used for screening and for comparison with occupational groups. Since the items on the 16PF cover a wide variety of situations, many of which do occur in ministry, it can be expected that it would relate in a global manner to occupations, including ministry. The expectation of a strong relationship to occupations has been confirmed empirically in the comparison of profiles of occupations to the general population profiles (Mershon and Gorsuch, 1988). Because it does have sixteen different scales, it has been found to predict twice as much of the variance as would a personality scale with only six to eight scores covering the major accepted personality dimensions (Mershon and Gorsuch, 1988).

When one goes beyond simple screening tests, like the Tennessee Self-concept Scale, then consultants who thoroughly know the instruments to be used are needed. For example, with the 16PF, some counter-intuitive results on success in ministry and other occupations have been found. Brown (1985) replicated the finding that extroverts—particularly 16PF scale H—will feel quite successful in ministry if their social support is positive, but they will be "burned out" if their social support is negative. Introverts, on the other hand, function more independently of social support systems than do extroverts. Hence if it is necessary to place a minister into a difficult, chaotic situation in which there would be little firm social support—such as a church with major internal conflicts—the introvert as defined by the 16PF is the one to place in that situation rather than the extrovert. (The interpretation is that the introvert who is in ministry has successfully established a set of defences against other people's judgments, which allows them to keep operating even in awkward situations.)

Appropriate expertise is also necessary to generalize results of even some fairly common scales. While intelligence is one of the best predictors of employment success (Gottfredson, 1986), social psychologists are hesitant to suggest that brighter is better in all social situations. Evidence also suggests that leaders are most effective when they are only somewhat brighter than the group they are leading. This also leads to somewhat counter-intuitive ministerial selection, for it suggests that people at both ends of the range of intelligence might be undesirable as ministers. Please note that there are no direct data on this topic with ministers per se and so we cannot come to a conclusion yet. But this does serve to underscore the need for moving cautiously in our assessment procedures and supporting research.

Concluding Comments

A major purpose of this chapter has been to introduce some basic psychometric thinking and to encourage reliance on psychometric data. It has also been to discourage the sophomoric error of, when finding that psychological assessment devices have numerous sources of error and bias, going to procedures for which no such empirical information exists. What we know about human judgment suggests that unvalidated interviews will do no better—and generally will do worse—than psychometric devices.

While there are many pitfalls in clergy assessment, the greatest pitfall is to ignore the knowledge that we already have. These knowledge bases concern what ministry is and does—as found in the *Readiness for Ministry* and the Theological School Inventory projects—and the psychometric principles of validity of tests and human judgment. A further conclusion is that any psychological consultant will improve assessment procedures only if the consultant is knowledgeable about (a) ministry in the focal setting, (b) the technical job analysis data of ministry from the *Readiness for Ministry* and TSI projects, and (c) assessment approaches for which the consultant can reference supporting empirical data.

9

Issues and Models in Criterion Development

JOHN E. HINKLE, JR., AND EMILY D. HAIGHT

When pastoral evaluation specialists move beyond simple psychological description into the realm of prediction or selection, they will be faced with "the criterion problem."

The criterion is, of course, that aspect of human performance which we wish to predict in a given assessment problem. Although such a concept may appear obvious on first consideration, criterion analysis has proved to be the most recondite and vexing issue confronting personality assessment today. In fact, criterion analysis is typically referred to as "the criterion problem" in much the same manner as we speak of "the racial problem" or other complex issues defying easy solution. Basically, the "problem" resides in the considerable discrepancy that typically exists between our intuitive standards of what criteria of performance should entail and the measures that are currently employed for evaluating such criteria. (Wiggins, 1973)*

Many complex issues arise in the criterion definition phase of personnel selection, including what methods to use (consensual or empirical) in developing criteria and how to verify or validate the effectiveness of the criteria once they are applied. This chapter will discuss a few illustrative theoretical and practical issues involved in criteria development, and then present three models for criteria development with brief case vignettes as an illustration of each. These models are (1) the Consensual Model, (2) the Theoretical/Empirical Model, and (3) the Combined Model. Before moving to the description, discussion, and illustration of each of these three models, we address general issues in criterion development.

General Issues in Criterion Development

The Impact of Individual, Institutional, and Socio-cultural Frames on Selection Criteria

Any discussion of selection criteria is set within a framework of socio-cultural assumptions. These assumptions are largely unarticulated, or if articulated are not viewed as problematic, in most conversations about selection criteria. Failure to take proper account of cultural assumptions in considerations of criteria identification and development is here seen as extremely problematic. One result of such failures is an unconscious ethnocentrically encapsulated approach to criteria identification and development. This culturally encapsulated approach can eventuate in a construing of criteria which then have the effect of excluding from participation in ministry those from other cultural realities than that of the majority or dominant cultural group. Hence the broader socio-cultural and cross-cultural frame of reference pointed to here is intended as one important antidote to cultural or social sources of exclusion.

Awareness and application of multiple frames of reference can provide a basis for appropriate approaches to culture and gender differences in the construal and application of selection criteria (see Wimberly, chap. 26 of this volume). Awareness and intentionality in these matters can enhance fairness and justice to those applicants from alternate or variant cultures or cultural groups.

Culture and Gender Fairness in Selection Procedures

Fairness in selection processes at the level of culture and gender require attention to these and related factors in the identification, development, measurement, and interpretation of selection criteria (Huntley, chap. 24 of this volume). This perspective suggests that values (forces) bearing on selection criteria may emerge from socio-cultural definitions at a variety of levels. It asserts that such values or forces from any of these levels will affect all other values in the process in significant ways. Like a "Rubic's cube," if one significant value is changed at any level, the configuration of values will change at other levels. If the central cultural value(s) defining personhood changes, other parameters are affected. If values in the role are redefined, then other values are affected. If institutional values are different and institutional functioning is imaged in an alternative perspective, then role and personal values will also be changed.

Exceptions to the foregoing model of integrated personal, social, and cultural systems may occur in cultures that manifest less valuational and structural integration. Nevertheless, the examination of socio-cultural assumptions can contribute to the reduction of monocultural ethnocentric biases and introduce a greater degree of flexibility with reference to the "real world" (multicultural) variance in any population being assessed. With these general, but essential, issues in mind, the discussion turns now to the matter of method by setting forth three models of criterion development.

The Consensual Model of Criterion Development

The first of the three models of criterion development to be discussed is the consensus model. This model of criterion development fits into the "situational analysis" component of the Wiggins personnel selection model (Wiggins, 1973). Three distinctions are crucial to understanding this stage of the selection process: criterion definition by "significant others," the distinction between explicit and implicit criteria, and a differentiation between standards of performance and psychological criteria.

The first distinction involves the discovery or designation of who within the structure has the authority, expertise, or obligation to determine selection criteria (judicatory boards, bishops, seminary faculties, congregational committees, the clergy, the laity). The second issue is comparing any discrepancies between formalized, verbalized, or explicit criteria with the actual results of the application of these standards. Are there in fact implicit criteria that a selection procedure modeled on the explicit criteria would not account for? Third, are there psychological job requirements that are not specified in performance-oriented selection criteria or procedures (for example, fitness criteria)?

The consensus model is probably best understood by illustration. Space limitations preclude a full case presentation here; therefore, an illustrative case will be summarized by date, event, and action. A full description of the application of this model in a denomination would show the intricate and meticulous administrative steps that were followed in reaching consensus on the criteria for clergy assessment and devising a method for operationalizing those criteria within that denomination.

The following is an outline of the flow of events and actions in The United Methodist Church that illustrate this model.

Phase I - Regional Denominational Judicatory Activity

Date	Event	Action
1972-74	Regional Workshops to discuss issues in psychological assessment	Identified need for criteria
1975-Feb	Workshop on standards for ordained ministry	Initiated work on criteria
1975-May	Workshop on standards for ordained ministry	Stated categories of criteria needed. Established on-going committee
1975-Fall	Committee on Nurture & Assessment	Organized N & A committee. Received/discussed criteria paper
1976-Feb	CNA - Task Force on Criteria	Formalized criteria document by categories and specified stages of application

Phase II - Seminary Activity

Date	Event	Action
1976-Nov	Faculty (GETS) adopts criteria for "preparation for ministry"	Criteria for evaluation of student tenure adopted
1976-77	Seminary Assessment Service (Garrett-Evangelical Theol. Sem.)	Operationalized criteria for student placement

Phase III - National Level Denominational Activity

1978-Feb	National Consultation on Psychological Assessment	Identified issues Elected National Task Force
1978-May	National Task Force on Psychological Assessment	Organized activities and commissioned study of current practices
1978-79	Regional Workshops (5) with active Pastoral Evaluation Specialists (Chicago, Atlanta, Dallas, San Francisco, Philadelphia)	Standard core test battery adopted and PES criteria orient

Phase IV - Activities of the Task Force

In 1981, the National Task Force on Psychological Assessment was succeeded by the Advisory Committee on Psychological Assessment of the Division of Ordained Ministry. This committee has been engaged in the following activities:

1. Developing and researching a standard core test battery.

2. Recommending policy and procedure for psychological assessment, with particular concern for confidentiality, informed consent, and the ethics of file handling and management.

3. Establishing a national level program of psychological assessment at the entry level as part of the United Methodist Candidacy guidance process.

4. Consulting with and training selection officers and others in the proper use of psychological reports.

5. Carrying out major research projects (six to date) on the program and test battery.

6. Developing criteria for the selection of evaluators and preparing a national directory.

7. Establishing a research archive for data collection and authorized research.

8. Conducting a regular schedule of training events for all categories of persons involved in the process.

9. Developing a manual of procedures for judicatory officials and for pastoral evaluation specialists/psychological consultants.

10. Establishing a regular newsletter for the further dissemination of information concerning psychological assessment in terms of the identified criteria.

The foregoing list of dates, activities, and results may serve to give the reader a sense of the extensive nature of this consensual and democratic administrative process, with reference not only to criteria, but also to program development, implementation, and evaluation. The significance of achieving and articulating a consensus on criteria for personnel selection is not to be underestimated. But standing alone, consensus-based criteria are not enough. A further movement from consensual to empirical processes is essential to the further refinement, specification, and implementation of criteria relevant to the development of effectiveness in ministry. The movement from consensual to empirical considerations of criteria development is treated more specifically in the next section of the chapter.

The Theoretical/Empirical Model of Criterion Development

In the "theoretical/empirical" model, one uses previously selected groups to determine what criteria were used in that selecting procedure and how consistently they were applied, so that the identified criteria can be evaluated, modified, or intentionally continued as is.

Unlike the consensual model, which begins with abstract considerations of "what should be" the criteria in selecting clergy, the empirical model begins with the selections that have already taken place and demonstrates from "what is" what the operative criteria are. The consensual model deals directly with explicit criteria, while the empirical model deals with both "explicit" (intentional) and "implicit" (unstated or unintentional, yet still operative) criteria.

Empirical methods—such as factor analysis or multiple regression—allow researchers to find patterns in the quantitative data that illustrate common elements within groups or dissimilarities between different groups. From these patterns, one can determine how the groups were originally selected and thus what criteria appear to have been used in the selection process.

Practical considerations often determine when the empirical model can be used. A long enough history must exist in a large enough population in which consistent selection criteria and procedures have been used in order to generate the data necessary for the statistical analysis. This usually means having empirical data available from a uniform selection procedure using a standard measurement battery and the same (or highly similar) evaluators over several years. And this data must be collected in computer compatible forms and made available by the evaluators for such research. These conditions were met in the foregoing illustration of the consensus model.

Case Illustration

The use of the theoretical/empirical model for criterion development is described in detail by Haight (1980). Candidate data were collected from seven years of blinded pastoral assessment files of the evaluators used by two annual conferences of The United Methodist Church. This data included the pastoral evaluation team's rating of fitness for a candidate (a six-point scale, from highly recommended to reject) and the board's subsequent decision about the candidate (accept or reject). The analysis began by using only the Minnesota Multiphasic Personality Inventory (MMPI) from the multi-measure assessment battery. The pastoral evaluation team was asked to study their own procedures for clinically evaluating a 129-scale profile, categorizing their concerns about candidates into eight general components and listing the specific scale combinations they used to evaluate each concern. By combining the standardized scale scores for each component, a single component score was obtained. A multiple regression analysis provided strong evidence as to the relative emphasis being placed on each component as well as the good general predictive ability of such a model in subsequent validation groups.

The most predictive indicator from the MMPI scale scores was a measure of the "severity of record" based on the number of times a candidate had selected scale scores that were outside the normative range for clergy. This indicated that no particular personality style was

being overly prized or unduly eliminated, but that personality extremes of any nature would cause the evaluators to caution the board about the candidate's psychological fitness for ministry.

Comer (1983) extended Haight's study both in time and in scope by adding two additional years of candidate data on which the Haight results were again cross-validated and by adding several additional components from the battery into the study. From these combined studies, it was clear that consistent patterns were being followed in how candidate assessment data was being evaluated to generate fitness-for-ministry recommendations and which components of the battery were being most heavily weighted in the assessment decision. Thus through such empirical studies, the operative criteria in this one assessment process are gradually being revealed so that the evaluators and the boards (selectors) can make informed decisions about whether to continue or alter the assessment procedures to conform to the explicit (consensually derived) criteria.

The Combined Consensual/Empirical Model of Criteria Development

In the above examples, the consensual model was used by the judiciary to derive its explicit criteria, and the theoretical/empirical model was used by a pastoral evaluation team to study its own psychological assessment procedures. In the following case illustration, both the consensual and the theoretical/empirical models were used by the same group of people: a seminary assessment service staff. The assessment service staff utilized the consensual model to determine the explicit criteria they believed they were using, and then they tested the accuracy of their conclusions through a statistical analysis of their assessment decisions over a several year period. Thus both models were combined in an effort to delineate clergy assessment criteria.

Case Illustration

A detailed description of this model is found in Means (1980a). Within the Assessment Services of Garrett-Evangelical Seminary, there had been some twenty years of experience in making a particular kind of clergy assessment decision—namely, whether or not a student was personally and professionally ready to utilize the particular learning context of Clinical Pastoral Education to a high enough degree to warrant academic credit for the experience. The staff began to ask itself whether they could specify more precisely on what basis they were making these decisions and whether, by having such criteria spelled out, they could increase their own accuracy and consistency in making such decisions.

First, the staff employed the consensual model and reflected together on their own clinical processes and decision-making criteria. After many hours of discussion and detailed self-observation of written clinical reports and staffings of those reports, they developed successive drafts of a paper delineating the criteria they identified: (1) the ability to integrate cognitive and experiential learning, (2) the ability to form empathic relationships, and (3) the ability to accept and carry out the role of student chaplain.

Having now conceptually identified these criteria, their task still remained to determine whether or not these were indeed the criteria being applied, and if so, were they being applied consistently enough to be a valid representation of the decision-making process. Means (1980a) undertook the task of doing the empirical analysis necessary to answer these questions.

Using a criterion sample of sixty-seven students who had been assessed for CPE over a two-year period and who had been placed into accept or reject categories, Dr. Means conducted a discriminate analysis of selected psychometric data generated by these students. The Minnesota Multiphasic Personality Inventory (MMPI) and the Shipley Institute for Living Scale (Shipley) were chosen. A team of three independent psychologists specified scales and scale scores relevant to the measurement of each of the three criteria identified by the staff earlier. These variables do discriminate students into accept or reject categories for two of the three criteria; only predicting the criterion related to the ability to carry out the ministerial role failed.

The combined consensual/empirical approach utilized the advantages of deriving criteria from the consensus view of "experts" and then subjecting the criteria identified to empirical procedures designed to measure whether the consensus criteria were in fact the operational criteria. Results indicated that two of the three consensus criteria were appropriately conceptualized, operationalized, and measured for use in empirical analysis.

The third criterion was not properly operationalized or measured by the MMPI and Shipley. Speculation is that the Leadership Scale on the Theological School Inventory would have provided a more appropriate and accurate measure. Empirical tests of this speculation could help determine its feasibility. Nor is the present criterion study complete without an additional empirical investigation of the long range criterion—that is, would students who are selected for the CPE experience be more effective learners in that experience than students who are deselected?

Criteria Development as Process

The foregoing consideration of three models of criteria development needs to be seen as part of a single process, rather than simply as three separate projects, for purposes of understanding the nature of criterion development. To this point, the discussion has focused on the important task of criteria development (establishing the criteria). An equally important insight is the understanding that criteria are fluid rather than static, and criteria must be updated on a recurring basis.

Given the metaphorical nature of definitions of the self-in-culture, the impact of socio-cultural change on role definition (and hence the changing nature of the self-in-role), the relationship between the descriptive and the normative in criterion development, the changing interaction between the individual and the institutional, and related variables, criteria are not and cannot be static, fixed once and for all in the socio-cultural structures. Criteria identified at a given point in history are more like a snapshot than a movie. Hence, the identification of criteria through consensual and empirical means should be seen as an ongoing process.

In terms of the future, the cutting-edge in the personnel selection field (see chaps. 15-20 of this volume), and in pastoral evaluation, is the development of ultimate criteria and long-range studies showing the predictive validity of assessment/selection strategies. Of particular difficulty is the task of carefully defining the ultimate criteria and its measurement appropriately and specifically enough to determine whether the selection procedure was successful. This also implies that those rejected by the selection process are still available for study, or were allowed to practice in some other context, so that long-range comparisons can be made.

The multi-trait, multi-method research design can be very useful at this point. For example, if one wants to evaluate the accuracy of a pastoral evaluation process, one begins looking at whether the earlier measures predicted later performance in ministry. The researcher faces not only the difficult task of measuring performance, but also the prospect of specifying what aspects of that performance were indeed predictable from the earlier measurements. Generic or global definitions of performance will be misleading, and they combine many similar, but different, traits or variables within them. Is the performance measure really measuring "success," "satisfaction," "survival" (continuance in the practice), "effectiveness," or "fitness"? Do these variables behave differently depending on what method is used to measure them (self-ratings, performance observations by peers or parishioners, quantified data like size of church or church growth)?

By using multiple methods to measure multiple variables related to the ultimate criterion, one learns much more about the accuracy of the original selection strategy and how it should be modified for future use. Though the difficulties encountered in the specification and measurement of ultimate criteria are great, efforts to do so are mandatory. As Wiggins (1973) notes,

> Although psychologists are continually berated for their present inability to cope with the almost insurmountable criterion "problem" in most areas (Roman and Prien, 1966), they must also be admired for their courage in taking this first and most difficult step in the prediction process. Positions must be filled, decisions must be made, and society must somehow go on in the absence of final

solutions to the problems posed by ultimate criteria. At best, the assessment psychologist can develop an informed awareness of and sensitivity to the pitfalls of criterion analysis and supplement this by common sense. Criterion measures should be selected with respect to their relevance to both intermediate and ultimate criteria. Careful attention should be given to the likely multidimensional nature of any criterion, and global measures should be developed with extreme caution. Criterion measures should be reliable and should be evaluated by the same psychometric standards applied to predictor measures. Finally, criterion measures must be practical in the sense that they must become available in time to be used in the evaluation of an ongoing assessment program.

It is our hope that the reader will gain some additional understandings of both the significance and the operation of processes of criteria development, whether in the form of the consensual, empirical, or combined consensual/empirical approaches.

10

Development of an Assessment Instrument

DAVID A. HOGUE

A major problem in the assessment of clergy candidates has been the selection of criteria that could be currently assessed and those that could be predicted in the future. While the assessment of current criteria has its own significance (for instance, current level of mental health), assessors of candidates for ministry are charged with the task of making predictions about future functioning. Most research has understandably concluded that assessment of current functioning has been more reliable and valid than attempts to predict those same or similar criteria in the future.

Two dimensions of future functioning in ministry have attracted interest from researchers over the past years. Effectiveness in ministry has been a significant criterion for a number of years and a major interest of church judicatories in the selection of candidates for ministry. Of more recent interest has been the job satisfaction of persons in ministry, both from the economic standpoint of the years of training invested in those candidates and from a genuine interest in the welfare of clergy.

While a number of instruments have been developed to measure job satisfaction in corporate and other settings, no instrument has been published that is designed to assess the specific job satisfactions of clergy. The study reported below in this chapter was developed to be such an instrument to measure the satisfactions of persons currently functioning in ministry, rather than those being considered for candidacy. Its purpose was to develop a reliable and valid instrument for clergy that may later point to other potential variables assessable at the point of candidacy. In that sense, it is not a predictive instrument, but a measure of current attitudes that may later be predictable from other measurable criteria, such as MMPI variables, seminary records, and recommendations.

Job satisfaction in itself is not necessarily directly correlated to effectiveness. A number of persons function for some time in a variety of careers independent of their success, or for that matter independent of their satisfaction. Therefore, job satisfaction must be defined in such a way that one does not confuse it with other variables, such as effectiveness, endurance, hours per week worked, or many of the other assumed indicators of job satisfaction.

It is important that any instrument be related to current theory and practice. Therefore, the first section of this chapter will briefly outline theoretical issues in job satisfaction studies, with particular attention to the theory underlying the *Satisfaction in Ministry* (SIM) instrument. Following that will be a description of the development of one instrument to measure job satisfaction—a predicted criterion variable.

Theory

Job satisfaction measures have appropriately followed from the theoretical understanding of the construct. A brief review of theoretical approaches will be considered here. For a more complete review of theories of job satisfaction, see Lawler (1973) and Hogue (1985).

Lawler outlines three categories of theory in job satisfaction studies. *Fulfillment* theories depend on the concept that individuals bring with them to job settings a configuration of needs and values seeking gratification. Satisfaction depends on the degree to which these needs are gratified by the characteristics or context of the work. *Discrepancy* theories define job satisfaction as the difference between the expected or desired rewards from a job and the actual rewards. *Equity* theory suggests that a person's expectations about what should be received from his or her job are largely determined by what he or she thinks others receive from their jobs.

This study conceived of job satisfaction as being dependent on four major factors in the interaction between the minister and the work environment: (1) needs, motivations, and values of the minister; (2) roles and tasks that the minister plays in order to express those needs in the work environment; (3) working conditions, including institutional setting and values of the particular agency; and (4) rewards, including pay, recognition, and the like.

Job satisfaction, then, was conceived as an attitude resulting from an optimum interaction between the worker/minister and the total environment (French et al., 1974; Harrison, 1978). Satisfaction was understood as occurring to the extent that the individual and organization can maximize the "fit" between the individual's needs and professional roles within which he or she must function and further between those roles and the conditions and rewards that are extrinsically related.

Job Involvement and Life Satisfaction

Two other theoretical issues were covered and correlations were examined with job satisfaction in this study. Job involvement was defined as "the extent to which the individual identifies with the job" (Gruneberg, 1979) and as "the internalization of values about the goodness of work or the importance of work in the worth of the person" (Lodahl and Kejner, 1965). Life satisfaction was measured by an instrument adapted from McHolland (1966) and was an attempt to understand the relationship between satisfaction with career and satisfaction with life in general.

Method

A. Scale Development

In order to generate a pool of items for the Satisfaction in Ministry scale, a theoretical structure was necessary. It was unique to the work of ministry, and it was deemed important to focus on the career of ministry as a whole, rather than on a particular work setting, thus focusing this study more particularly on "occupational satisfaction."

Research completed in the late 1950s by a task force of the National Council of Churches of Christ surveyed over 800 ministers from a variety of denominations and employed an open-ended question format from which they performed a content analysis of motivational components (Dittes, 1964). From this study, the Theological School Inventory was developed and has become a basic assessment tool in many seminaries across the country (see chap. 17 of this volume).

Seven motivational components were extracted and designated as Acceptance by Others, Intellectual Pursuits, Self-fulfillment, Leadership Success, Evangelistic Witness, Social Reform, and Service to Persons.

This study assumed those components to constitute the basic work-related needs of clergy. Four items for each of these dimensions were written for the original instrument. In addition, individual items dealt with standard of living, family life, perceived effectiveness, and subject's reported satisfaction with the job. Subjects were instructed to indicate the way they usually or generally felt. A Likert response format was used, indicating levels of agreement with the statement.

B. Pilot Studies

An initial pilot study was administered to United Methodist clergy in attendance at a required administrative meeting in May of 1980. From these clergy, 156 marked questionnaires were collected that yielded 142 usable questionnaires. An SPSS reliability program produced fairly encouraging results, including Cronbach's coefficient alpha of .89 and Guttman's lower bound of reliability of .92.

A Spearman-Brown prophecy formula was applied to the .89 coefficient alpha. It suggested that 10 parallel items would increase alpha to .94, an increase deemed unjustified by the increased length. The Very Simple Structure program revealed a one-factor solution, achieving a .913 score. Eigen values also supported the one-factor solution with a value of 6.8, accounting for 34.1 percent of the variance.

A second pilot study turned to validity issues. Free Methodist clergy, attending a voluntary workshop, completed the SIM questionnaire in addition to a widely recognized industrial job satisfaction instrument, the Job Descriptive Index (JDI) (Smith, Kendall, and Hulin, 1969). The latter instrument includes sub-scales dealing with work, pay, promotions, supervision, and co-workers. In addition, scales were included to measure satisfaction with life in general (McHolland, 1966) and job involvement (Lodahl and Kejner, 1965). Items were added to measure sense of call, support for a conference/denominational personnel, and relationships with co-workers. Respondents were asked to register choice of work setting and geographical location and to supply information about time allotment.

While a composite criterion measure did not achieve satisfactory reliability, a multiple regression analysis was performed on each of the independent variables to predict the criterion. A multiple correlation of .517 was achieved by the SIM, life satisfaction, job involvement, and concept of call scales. The five JDI sub-scales produced a multiple correlation of .532. All scales were, therefore, included in the final instrument prepared for the primary study.

C. Primary Study

The primary study involved all male students in professional degree programs from a Midwestern seminary from 1965 to 1982, when the Minnesota Multiphasic Personality Inventory and the Theological School Inventory were first administered. Too few female graduates were included in the group to draw adequate conclusions from any data that would have been collected.

In addition to the data collected in the last pilot study, data was collected on location of current employment, size of current or last congregation served, number of parishes served since graduation from seminary, number of non-ordained positions held since graduation from seminary, years in the current parish, annual income needed and income realized, denomination, marital status, happiness of marriage, and spouse's attitude toward ministry. Also, permission was obtained from subjects to copy answer sheets from their MMPI and TSI data collected at the time of entry into seminary. These data were collected for later analysis of correlations with job satisfaction in ministry.

A total of 353 questionnaires were mailed, and 217 responses were received, producing a 61.5 percent return rate. Reliability data were calculated by the McTEST program at Northwestern University. Job Descriptive Index (JDI) forms were scored by hand.

The procedure in this study involved comparing the performances of the SIM questionnaire with the JDI against three different criteria. The first criterion was the Kunin "Faces" scale, developed in 1955 for the General Motors Corporation (Kunin, 1955). A second criterion, desire to stay in their present jobs, was calculated from respondents. In order to increase the reliability of this criterion, it was combined with the "Faces" scale, resulting in a score range of 1 to 9, with 9 indicating the most highly satisfied. Finally, the Job-in-General scale from the Job Descriptive Index was utilized as a third criterion.

Table 1.

Predictor Variables	Criteria
1. SIM questionnaire	"Faces" Scale
2. Satisfaction with Life	"Faces" plus Choice
3. Job Involvement	Job-in-General Scale
4. Work	
5. Pay (Job Descriptive Index Scales)	
6. Promotions	
7. Co-workers	
8. Supervision	

Results

The total sample was originally and randomly divided into two sub-samples. A first sample (or "calibrating sample," N = 108) was utilized in the first stepwise forward multiple regression analysis. A second cross-validation (or "validating sample," N = 109) was utilized for cross-validation of results.

Table 2 (p. 70) presents the results of the initial study of the multiple regression correlations. It will be noted that for the first two criteria, the SIM questionnaire demonstrated the highest correlation, and in the third, the Satisfaction with Life scale produced the highest correlation. It was concluded from these results that the SIM and Satisfaction with Life scales produced strong predictive correlations with all three job satisfaction criterion measures.

The second set of analyses attempted to predict the criterion measures with the five sub-scales of the JDI. The work sub-scale (the only intrinsic measure in the JDI) was the most highly correlated predictor variable for all three criterion measures, and the only one to demonstrate significant correlations across all three criteria. A combined analysis of all eight predictor variables is shown in Table 3 (p. 70).

The SIM items were written with parish clergy specifically in mind. Since the sample included graduates in specialized ministry settings and some functioning in non-clergy settings, it was speculated that correlations would be stronger if only the parish clergy were included in the analysis. Table 4 (p. 71) presents the results of that analysis, and it does in fact confirm strengthened correlations, especially where the ministry scales themselves are utilized.

Cross-Validation

In order to check the validity of the multiple correlations calculated in the initial sample, scores in the validation sample were predicted by use of the equation provided by the last analysis (parish only). Values of the constants and beta-weights were used from Sample 1 (parish only) and applied to the predictor variable values in Sample 2 (the validating sample, this time including all subjects) to predict criterion scores on each of the three criterion measures. Predicted scores were compared to actual scores. Differences between predicted and observed scores were computed and examined to determine whether they fell within the 95 percent confidence interval of prediction. The results demonstrated that the equation held up quite strongly (Hogue, 1985).

Table 2.

Stepwise Forward Multiple Regression Analysis:
A Comparison of Two Job Satisfaction Measurement Instruments

Calibrating Sample   N = 108

Criterion:	Faces	Faces + Choice	Job-in-General
Predictors (Ministry Scales)			
Satisfaction in Ministry	.626* (1)	.692* (1)	.662* (2)
Satisfaction with Life	.644* (2)	.708 (2)	.640* (1)
Job Involvement	.655 (3)	.716 (3)	.675 (3)
Predictors (Job Descriptive Inventory)			
Work	.446* (1)	.500* (1)	.799* (1)
Pay	.507 (4)	.549 (3)	.831* (2)
Promotions	.479* (2)	.559 (4)	.840* (5)
Supervision	.507 (5)	.560 (5)	.838* (3)
Co-Workers	.499 (3)	.529* (2)	.840 (4)

For all values, $p < .05$
(Numbers in parentheses indicate order of steps in regression equation.)
* Indicates that the addition of this variable results in an increment in the multiple regression that achieves significance at the .05 level.

Table 3.

Stepwise Forward Multiple Regression Analysis
A Comparison of Eight Variables Predicting Job Satisfaction

Calibrating Sample   N = 108

Criterion:	Faces	Faces + Choice	Job-in-General
Predictors (All eight variables)			
Satisfaction in Ministry	.626* (1)	.692* (1)	.871 (6)
Life Satisfaction	.657 (3)	.725 (3)	.851* (2)
Involvement	.666 (4)	.730 (4)	.871 (5)
Work	.644* (2)	.714* (2)	.799* (1)
Pay	.671 (7)	--- (0)**	.866* (3)
Promotions	.668 (5)	.733 (6)	.871 (7)
Supervision	.671 (8)	.733 (7)	.870 (4)
Co-workers	.670 (6)	.733 (5)	.871 (8)

For all values, $p < .05$
(Numbers in parentheses indicate order of steps in regression equation.)
* Indicates that the addition of this variable results in an increment in the multiple regression that achieves significance at the .05 level.
** F-level insufficient for further computation.

Table 4.

Stepwise Forward Multiple Regression Analysis
A Comparison of Two Job Satisfaction Measurement Instruments

Calibrating Sample   N = 80

Criterion:	Faces	Faces + Choice	Job-in-General
Predictors (Ministry Scales)			
Satisfaction in Ministry	.674 (2)	.737* (2)	.683* (2)
Satisfaction with Life	.655* (1)	.699* (1)	.710* (1)
Job Involvement	.684 (3)	.751 (3)	.734* (3)
Predictors (Job Descriptive Inventory)			
Work	.525* (1)	.565* (1)	.767* (1)
Pay	.594 (4)	.624* (2)	.806* (2)
Promotions	.588 (2)	.658 (4)	.824 (5)
Supervision	--- (0)**	.659 (5)	.823 (4)
Co-Workers	.566* (2)	.650* (3)	.819* (3)

For all values, $p < .05$
(Numbers in parentheses indicate order of steps in regression equation.)
* Indicates that the addition of this variable results in an increment in the multiple regression that achieves significance at the .05 level.

Conclusion

This study demonstrated the development of an assessment instrument developed to measure the job satisfaction of clergy, particularly those serving in parishes. Reliability coefficients scored regularly in the high .80s and low .90s. Validity studies that sought to compare the performance of this instrument with recognized industrial job satisfaction instruments suggested that the instrument performed well in comparison.

It is suggested that an assessor wishing to measure the job satisfaction of clergy must determine several things before selecting an instrument for a particular setting. The general psychometric properties of reliability and validity should, of course, be adequate. An assessor wishing to measure job satisfaction as compared to other clergy, might well select a vocation-specific instrument, with the advantage of tapping dimensions unique to that vocation. Those wishing to compare the satisfaction levels of clergy with other occupations must utilize an instrument that is applicable across vocations, such as the Job Descriptive Index.

The Satisfaction in Ministry scale should be useful to both clinicians and researchers. As normative data are collected, the instrument could provide valuable information for active clergy undergoing vocational counseling or assessment. Clinicians may be able to compare an individual minister's level of job satisfaction with that of others, as part of a larger battery of assessment instruments. Denominational and seminary officials may be able to use the instrument to determine the levels and dimensions of job satisfaction among their constituents in ministry, and perhaps to promote remedial action where indicated.

Researchers may be able to determine correlates with current related variables, such as satisfaction with life, marital status, and conditions of church setting. Ultimately, the prediction of satisfied ministers may be made possible, as correlations are explored with MMPI variables and other measures made at the time of candidacy or seminary entry. It is hoped that this instrument might contribute to our knowledge of what promotes effective and fulfilling ministry.

11

Psychometric Characteristics of a Ministerial Assessment Battery

Michael P. Comer

Since its beginnings, the Christian church has had procedures to select its leaders. From Jesus' choosing the disciples (Mark 1:16-20), the selection of Matthias (Acts 1:23-26), and standards for bishops (Titus 1:5-9) to the present assessment of aspiring clergy, the church has had established assessment procedures. Evidence of the aspirant's faith theology, abilities, and personal character has been regularly examined. In the Methodist tradition, there are questions from the "Historic Examination" (see *The Book of Discipline* of the United Methodist Church, 1980, paragraph 425). These are questions originally used by John Wesley to examine the faith, theology, ability, and character of prospective clergy. Every Methodist minister since Wesley has had to answer these questions.

The present United Methodist clergy assessment procedure has eight steps (partly described in chaps. 9 and 18 of this volume). It can be considered a multistage personnel decision strategy (Cronbach and Gleser 1957; Wiggins 1973). Since The United Methodist Church guarantees its full member clergy employment for the duration of their careers, which is often forty or more years, the procedure is intentionally designed to be thorough. Several Annual Conferences have used consulting psychologists to adjunct their screening process (DeWire, 1979; Jones, 1981). Haight (1979) makes helpful distinctions between description, prediction, and selection as psychologists augment the selection process. Description involves a clinical summary, gathered from various methods and measures of personality, vocational interests, intelligence, and so on. Prediction, on the other hand, involves the psychologist's best estimate of how the applicant will actually perform as a professional pastor. Prediction must be supported with empirical evidence of predictive validity.

Within the United Methodist ordination process, selection decisions are the final responsibility of ecclesiastical groups that consider evidence of the applicants' call to ministry, faith, theology, personal character, and other data. A psychologist can function only as a consultant, providing additional descriptive and perhaps predictive information. The decision making group then considers the latter information with the former. Consulting psychologists will not make selection decisions.

Psychological assessment can be considered as providing a nurturing as well as a screening function. Nurture begins with a thorough and professional clinical assessment of the applicant's assets and areas for growth. Recommendations and guidance can be offered.

Two Midwestern United Methodist Annual Conferences have used the consultive services of the same psychologist for the past ten years. One has used the consultant at three levels: the District Committee, probationary member, and full member levels. The other conference used the consultant at the latter two levels. The consultant administered a battery of tests to measure personality, vocational interest, intelligence, thought processes, and self-concept, and the consultant conducted clinical interviews. Descriptive as well as predictive information has been reported to the appropriate ecclesiastical groups and to the applicant. Haight (1980) studied this assessment procedure using archived data from probationary and full member level assessments.

The study reported here expands upon Haight. Her MMPI data is used, and added to it is data garnered from four additional sources: (1) the Strong Vocational Interest Blank, or Strong-Campbell Interest Inventory; (2) the Shipley Institute of Living Scale; (3) the Adjective Check List; and (4) letters of recommendation. The five components of data were combined via multiple regression, attempting to predict Haight's original two criteria: (1) the psychologist's rating of the applicant on the basis of scores on these instruments and other clinical data, and (2) the church's ordination decision. Haight's study sought to make explicit the nature of the present psychological assessment procedure. The

Instruments Used for Data Collection

Haight found a cluster of twenty-seven MMPI scales labelled "severity of record" that highly predicted the psychologist's level of recommendations ($p = .001$). No MMPI data predicted ordination decision. As noted above, her MMPI data is used in the present study. This consists of the number of scales with T scores exceeding critical levels. The MMPI data component was coded and entered with a range from 0 to 27.

During the ten-year history of the present assessment procedure, two versions of the Strong Vocational Interest Inventory have been used (1969 and 1974; see Campbell, 1971). Scales from these instruments were selected intuitively by the psychologist and his associates to represent the variety of occupational activities routinely encountered by local parish clergy, scales that are ordinarily elevated, and whether the elevations are favorable evidence for the applicant's finding satisfaction in the work of local parish clergy. Standard scores from these scales were recorded for use in a sub-analysis described below.

Based on this clinical experience, the psychologist and associates judged how typical the applicant's vocational interest profile was compared to those of other applicants. Key phrases were used in the final written report that are easily translated into quantitative values. These phrases and their values were: (1) very typical or close fit; (2) typical, conforms, or predicts; (3) roughly typical or loose fit; (4) mixed (some typical and some atypical); (5) undifferentiated or diffuse; and (6) not typical. These values were added to the multiple regression formula as the vocational interest component.

The Shipley Institute of Living Scale was used as a convenient IQ test. There are three numerical scores: verbal, abstract, and combined IQ equivalency scores. In addition, the magnitude of difference between the verbal and abstract scores was noted. Should the abstract score be substantially larger than the verbal score (A greater than V by 15 or more), the psychologist would interpret that the applicant has intellectual ability that is not being used. Conversely, should the verbal score be substantially larger than the abstract (V at least 15 greater than A), the interpretation was made that the applicant is using all of his or her ability and is now at full intellectual potential. The three scores plus the numerical difference between abstract and verbal scores are used as the multiple regression IQ component.

The Adjective Check List was used as an indication of the applicant's self-image. The particular constellation of the ACL's 24 scale scores is taken as an indicator of how aware the applicant is of his or her needs and other ACL measures. The psychologist made a judgment as to how closely the self-image presented on the ACL corresponds to the personality profile of the MMPI. The latter is the standard to which to former is compared. The consultant used key phrases indicating the degree of correspondence between the two measures. These phrases are easily quantified: (1) very accurate or very realistic self-image; (2) accurate or realistic self-image; (3) reasonably, roughly, or fairly accurate self-image; (4) bad, neutral, average, undifferentiated, or nondescript self-image; and (5) not accurate, not realistic, or very inaccurate self-image. These five numbers constitute the ACL self-image component of the data.

Letters of reference are the final data component. Each applicant submitted the names of four references: a pastor, a colleague, a parishioner (if the applicant is serving a church), and a fourth person of the applicant's choice. These persons, who were contacted directly by the psychologist, completed a standardized reference form. This reference form covers how long they have known the applicant; the nature of their relationship; the applicant's honesty, character, personal appearance, and industry; the applicant's aptitude for ministry and for forming relationships; and any other questions or concerns regarding the applicant.

Letters of reference are notoriously lenient. Nevertheless, they do provide an indication of how the applicant is experienced by other persons, which can be useful convergent data. The author developed a six-point rating scale to rate the approximately 1,800 letters in this study. A sample of all letters were read and frequently used phrases were recorded and became the base of the scale. Care was taken not to contaminate this rating. Thus letters were read and rated before any other of the applicant's data was examined. An overall judgment was made, weighing comments from the various parts of the reference form. The arithmetic mean of rated letters for each applicant was used as the final letter's component of data. The rating format used is noted on Table 1.

The distribution of the six-point scale did approximate a normal distribution. A 10 percent sample of letters was rated by an outside person with only the Table 1 scale available to him. A Pearson Product Manual was used as a measure of interrater reliability. It was .68.

Further data from the letters was also recorded. These were who wrote the letter (pastor, professor, or friend); how many years this person had known the applicant; and how well this person knew the applicant. These, too, were encoded numerically as shown in Table 1. In his final written report to the Annual Conference, the psychologist used key phrases that constitute his overall level of recommendation. These phrases are easily quantifiable, which is what Haight did for her study. Her format was used in the study reported here.

The letter of reference form asks the referee to comment on several specific areas—such as character, integrity, personal appearance, work habits—and it leaves room for general comments and areas of concern. In rating these letters, phrases from all areas will be considered with particular attention given to the general comments and/or concerns.

Table 1.

Rating Codes for Letters of Recommendation

Rating	Term	Phrases used
1	Outstanding	truly exceptional, truly superior, outstanding, brilliant, best in years, a rare find, (this category for the few very best)
2	Excellent	excellent candidate, gifted, above reproach, held in the highest esteem, remarkable, one of the finest, can't say enough
3	Highly Competent	recommendation without qualification or reserve, highly respected, a natural, held in high regard, very effective, highly recommended
4	Well Qualified	much above average, well thought of, most capable, above average, appreciated by all, perceptive most of the time, many signs of maturity, sufficiently endowed with gifts, no reason to doubt, effective, recommended
5	Average	average, see how he/she progresses, no questions at this time, generally good, has potential but needs to grow, fair, needs experience, some questions
6	Poor	turns others off, abrasive, manipulative, opinionated, alienates others, needs a lot of growing, can't recommend, needs counseling, serious questions

Haight used MMPI data from the years 1972 to 1978. The present study added MMPI data from 1979 to 1982 and the other four components of data from 1972 to 1982. Beginning with 1978, one Annual Conference requested that the psychologist no longer make an overall rating of the applicant. Thus no key phrases were available for applicants in this one conference from 1978 to 1982. The consultant, therefore, rated these applicants on a post-hoc basis to increase the overall N of Haight's and the present study. One hundred thirteen applicants from a total of 450 were rated post-hoc. The psychologist reported that such a rating was not at all difficult, since all information used for the overall rating was available in a copy of the final report. Such ratings, based on identical information, was still being done for the other conference.

Methodology

The present research used a passive observational correlation method (Cook and Campbell, 1979). Data was combined via multiple regression using the SPSS program to predict the psychologist's ratings. Haight's original severity of record 1, which counted how many scales exceeded a critical level, and severity record 2, which used actual T scores from these various scales, were each used in a multiple regression formula to see which contributed most. Further, each of Haight's formulas was revalidated on 1979 to 1982 applicants.

Due to changes from the SVIB to the SCII and different norms for the male and female scores (Campbell, 1974), vocational interest scores were converted to Z scores before a separate vocational data analysis. Scale scores from the selected scales were combined via multiple regression in an attempt to predict the psychologist's rating of vocational fit. This was to explore which scales empirically seem most influential on the psychologist's decisions.

After the final multiple regression formula was calculated using all data, unit weights were substituted for beta weights, and a comparison of predictability was observed. The psychologist's rating was again the criterion.

Cross-validation procedures were conducted using two different formats. Initially, Conference 1 was used as the derivation group and Conference 2 as the validation group. Second, subjects from 1972 to 1979 were used as the derivation group, and those from 1980 to 1981 were used as the validation group. A one-way analysis of variance (ANOVA) was used with the psychologist's ratings by years to investigate differences in the ratings across years. Finally, SPSS discriminate analysis rather than multiple regression was used to predict the dichotomous yes/no ordination decisions.

Results

Of the 450 subjects, not all had complete data for each measure studied. The reason for such incomplete files was not clear. Subjects were overwhelmingly male; most were evaluated for deacon's level; approximately half were for each conference. They were roughly evenly distributed across years. The vast majority of subjects were rated as either recommended or recommended with qualifications by the psychologist with approximately equal numbers in each category. ANOVA of the psychologist's ratings by years showed no significant differences.

The decision to ordain in an overwhelming number of cases was positive. Of all subjects in which the ordination decision was known (318) only 25 or 9.8 percent were turned down. It is not known how many of these subjects later reapplied or whether they were eventually ordained as clergy.

Haight found that severity of record 1, which is the number of scales exceeding a predetermined critical value, was more predictive than severity of record 2. She later used T scores. In the present revalidation, severity of record 2 was more predictive, a reverse of her findings. Haight found formula 1 to correlate .32 (p = .002) cross validated. Revalidated formula 1 correlates only .18 (p = .018). She found formula 2 to correlate .03 (p = .336), cross validated, while revalidated it correlated .33 (p = .001).

Measures of central tendency were calculated separately for the various forms of the Strong vocational instrument. This norm data is available elsewhere (Comer, 1989). The separate multiple regression sub-analysis using vocational scale scores to predict the psychologist's vocational interest rating yielded interesting results. Only the SVIB male form T399 had sufficient N to give meaningful results, N = 355. Seven scales of the nineteen studied accounted for 39.5 percent of the variances. These results are summarized in Table 2.

Table 2.

Multiple Regression of Strong Vocational Interest Blank Data for Males to Predict Rating of Fit

1969 SVIB-M form T399   N = 355

Scale	multiple R	R2	R2 change
minister	.486	.236	.236
law/politics	.555	.308	.072
percent occupations liked	.586	.343	.034
religious activities	.604	.365	.021
writing	.615	.379	.014
music	.621	.385	.006
teaching	.628	.395	.009

A number of scales reported by the psychologist to be useful empirically did not appear to be so. These were social service, psychiatrist, psychologist, and sales manager.

A summary of the five-term multiple regression analysis of data is presented in Table 3 (not cross validated).

Table 3.

Summary of Multiple Regression Prediction of Psychologists' Rating Using Haight's Severity of Record 2 MMPI Formula

Variable	Simple R	Multiple R	R2	R2 Change
ACL rating of fit	.359	.359	.129	.129
Severity of record 2	.296	.452	.205	.075
Letters of recommendation average rating	.329	.518	.269	.063
Vocational data rating of fit	.290	.548	.301	.031
Shipley equivalency IQ	− .112	.549	.302	.001

As can be seen, the psychologist's judgment of ACL to MMPI correspondence is most predictive of his final overall rating. This alone accounts for 12.9 percent of the total variance. The MMPI data alone in the form of reference letters is the second most predictive, adding another 7.5 percent of variance. Letters of recommendation were third most predictive, accounting for another 6.3 percent of variance. Vocational data added only 3.1 percent of variance, and IQ data was nearly useless, accounting for only another 0.1 percent of variance.

Intercorrelations of the five terms can be seen in Table 4.

Table 4.

Five-term Intercorrelation Matrix

ACL Rating	ACL	Severity	Letters	Vocational	Shipley
Severity of record 2	.034				
Letters, average rating	.170	.077			
Vocational rating	-.023	.613	.072		
Shipley equivalency IQ	-.076	-.183	-.057	-.013	

As noted above, cross-validation procedures were conducted across conferences and across years. A summary of cross-validation results is in Table 5.

Table 5.

Cross-validation of Multiple Regression Formula

Derivation group   Conference 1, Years 1972-1979
   N = 160: R^2 = .3771   N = 258: R^2 = .3714

Validation group   Conference 2, Years 1980-1981
   N = 178: R^2 = .2954   N = 80: R^2 = .2355

Shrinkage   .0817   .1359

Across conferences, the five-term multiple regression formula holds up remarkably well. Shrinkage was only .0817. Across years, the formula did not hold up as well. Shrinkage increased to .1359.

When unit weights were substituted for the traditional beta weights, the multiple regression formula held up quite well cross-validated. Corresponding values for R (the multiple correlation) differed by .03 or less. The unit weighting procedure actually out performed beta weighting cross-validated across years.

Haight's MMPI multiple regression formulas could not significantly predict ordination decisions. The present research used discriminate analysis that is more robust for dichotomous decisions. The results are presented in Table 6.

The present study's five terms, four more than Haight

used, predict ordination decisions with only mediocre success, since 61.63 percent of the cases were correctly

Table 6.

Discriminant Analysis of Board Decisions, Classification Results Using Severity of Record 2

Decision	Predicted group membership		Total N
	Yes	No	
Yes	146 (61.9%)	90 (38.1%)	236
No	9 (40.9%)	13 (59.1%)	22

61.63% cases correctly predicted

predicted. This is only slightly better than chance for dichotomous decisions.

Discussion

This study can be seen as one model to study empirically an assessment program. The study further makes empirically explicit essentially implicit clinical judgments.

Much of the data involved subjective judgments. The most predictive fit of the ACL to the MMPI was a subjective judgment, as was the judgment of vocational fit. The criterion of final rating was likewise a subjective judgment. All were made by the same individual. Thus this can be seen as the psychologist predicting the psychologist. Letters of reference were surprisingly predictive, and while their ratings were certainly subjective, they reflect how the applicants appear to others. As has been demonstrated, they can be more predictive than the present use of vocational interest and intelligence tests.

While this study accounted for nearly 30 percent of the total variance, 70 percent remains unaccounted for. This is a substantial amount, considering that only a proverbs test, incomplete sentence blank, autobiographical statement, and personal data questionnaire of the battery remain instituted. The post-hoc ratings may have yielded recommendations that were less consistent. The amount of resulting rating inconsistency, if any, and its effect on the results is unknown. Further, the weaker cross-validation across years may indicate that the psychologist varied ratings over the years studied.

The psychologist purported to be strongly influenced by the MMPI. This is confirmed by the results. The ACL to MMPI fit and MMPI severity of record are, by far, the two strongest predictors of the psychologist's decision. Interestingly, patterns of vocational interest, which the psychologist purported to be less important for selection, were empirically sustained. Applicants apparently have settled their vocational interest by the time of Deacon and Elder evaluations.

Shipley IQ data made only a minuscule numerical difference between abstract and verbal scores—.1 percent to the total variance—and did not significantly correlate with final rating contributions. This IQ data hardly seems worth the time and expense involved. The applicants had completed bachelor degrees and were in or had completed graduate school by the time they were evaluated. The academic requirements would thus seem to have previously screened out persons with deficient intellectual abilities.

Each of the five terms seem to be tapping its own factor, as they are not highly intercorrelated, with the exception of vocational interest and reference letters (see Table 4). The latter two terms have a substantial positive correlation of .613.

Ordination decisions were largely unpredictable. There were simply too few no decisions to allow for a robust discriminate analysis. Also, the selection rate for both conferences is nearly 92 percent. With nine out of ten applicants being ordained once they reach deacon or elder levels, an evaluation's impact on quality of choice is minimal at best. Conferences with high selection rates will have to decide intentionally whether an evaluation is cost effective.

Results of the unit weighing approach in the five-term formula indicate that it is as predictive as the traditional beta weight approach. This confirms evidence in the literature (Dawes, 1979). Despite the elegance of traditional beta weight multiple regression, the unsophisticated unit weighing is as predictive. Psychologists, therefore, need not be concerned with a complicated scale of variably weighing data.

Conclusions

This study is one more of many that indicate that clinicians are very good at discerning which data to consider. However, clinicians are notoriously inconsistent with clinical judgments (Dawes, 1979; Goldberg, 1970, 1976). It may well be that the clinical incon- sistency is the major factor in the 70 percent unaccounted variance.

Further, assessments completed to enhance ordination decisions are of questionable predictive validity in the absence of criteria-based validity data. Clearly such evidence is very difficult. Not the least of such difficulties is the criteria problem of defining effective clergy. Yet, ethical and legal considerations would preclude using invalidated evidence in selection decisions (Albright, 1976; APA, 1975; Miner and Miner, 1973; Peterson, 1974).

Approximately 40 percent of United Methodist seminarians are female. Assessment models based on traditional male clergy and/or male normal objective measures may be particularly unfair to these women. Further research on female clergy incorporated into assessment procedures is needed. Afro-Americans, Hispanics, Asian-Americans, and Native Americans are all minority groups whose presence is felt within The United Methodist Church and other denominational groups. Fair assessment of these people likewise necessitates the addressing of issues noted above for women.

Objective measures that lessen the magnitude of clinical judgment would certainly be beneficial. However, traditional clinical instruments, such as the MMPI and the ACL, have been notoriously poor for predictive purposes. Instruments with demonstrated validity for predictive purposes could appropriately become a part of the assessment battery.

Surprisingly, letters of recommendation can be very useful. This is particularly so if the applicant does not select all references and the recommendation form is quite specific, including defined numerical ratings in addition to prose comments.

Finally, psychological assessment has its place, augmenting selection decisions and/or for the applicant's personal information. However, procedures are designed and structured and the instrument is chosen, according to its primary purpose. Traditional clinical instruments may be very valuable for nurturing assessments for personal information. Any procedure, however, with a selection component must be supported with validity evidence.

12

Agency Selection Committees and Evaluation

PAM HOLLIMAN

The concern for effective psychological assessment plus the need for information to initiate change and develop resources for agency selection committees has resulted in the need for the evaluation of clergy assessment procedures. Evaluation can be utilized to review assessment programs as part of a committee's process to orient new members, to respond to specific criticisms of program procedures, and to improve member understanding and use of assessment processes.

Evaluation is defined in terms of a variety of purposes:

> Evaluations may be undertaken for management and administrative purposes, to assess the appropriateness of program shifts, to identify ways to improve the delivery of interventions, and to meet requirements of funding groups who have fiscal responsibility for allocating of program monies. They may be undertaken for planning and policy purposes, to help decide on either expansion or curtailment. . . . Finally they may be undertaken to test a particular social science hypothesis or a professional practice principle. (Rossi, Freeman, Wright, 1979, p. 21)

Rossi, Freeman, Wright stress establishing rigorous experimental designs to determine the effectiveness of a program. Program planning and monitoring of ongoing programs, as well as impact assessments to assess change from an intervention, are all aimed at reaching conclusive cause and effect statements. They state that for all of the above purposes:

> The key is to plan and implement an evaluation that is as objective as possible; that is, to provide a *firm assessment,* an assessment where the results would be unchanged if done by another group or replicated by the same evaluators. (p. 21)

Thus Rossi, Freeman, and Wright understand evaluation research in the framework of rigorous or quasi-experimental research. Further, these authors see that this research occurs in the context of political and social realities that include some limitations of time, money, and human resources.

Mason and Bramble (1978) define evaluation research similarly to Rossi, Freeman, Wright's stress on effectiveness as "the process of determining the adequacy of a product, process, procedure, program, approach, function or functionary" (p.111). They emphasize determining the *worth* of a particular phenomenon, rather than generalizable knowledge or theory about a whole class of phenomena or focus on the development of certain products or materials or the promotion of certain products (p. 112)

Mason and Bramble outline three perspectives that have been developed for designing and conducting evaluation research. Each tends to broaden the above definition due to the considerations and concerns each theorist brings to the research field.

The perspective developed by Tyler and Bloom in educational evaluations focuses on defining specific goals as behavioral objectives in the development of educational curricula, products, or materials. Scriven, focusing more on programming, makes a distinction between evaluation during program development and evaluation of the final program model. Finally, Stufflebeam considers evaluation an ongoing process at the decision making level (Mason and Bramble, 1978, pp. 113, 121).

Within the above theories and models is an assumption that objectives and expected outcomes are clearly identified and articulated before evaluation for effectiveness, adequacy, or worth is attempted. The models, however, include few guidelines for determining goals and expected outcomes, particularly in a setting where these are not clear. Likewise, there is the assumption in the models that these objectives and expected outcomes are linked to the program to be evaluated and that this connection can be stated. The primary focus, then, in these models is to test that rationale, to determine how effectively and efficiently the program accomplished those goals.

Agency selection committees interested in evaluating their clergy assessment procedures may not have such clarity. At best, objectives and expected outcomes may be only generally conceived or assumed by committee members. Lack of a shared understanding of goals may be pervasive. Further, one impetus to conduct an evaluation is to clarify the relationship between perceived selection needs and ongoing assessment programs. In these instances, much prior work is necessary before more rigorous research designs can be applied to clergy assessment programs.

Rutman (1977) developed a theoretical model that provides a structure and specific guidelines for conducting the beginning work of evaluating clergy assessment programs. Rutman, in agreement with other theorists, stresses rigorous methodology for evaluation research. However, Rutman also emphasizes the "evaluability" of a program and suggests a methodology for determining that evaluability. Rutman states three preconditions for evaluating a program's effectiveness and efficiency:

1. a clearly articulated program;

2. clearly specified goals and expected effects;

3. a rationale linking the program to the goals and expected effects.

If these preconditions are absent and the program is nevertheless evaluated, then it is likely that the study will be inappropriate and largely irrelevant for the purposes of planning, budgeting, and managing programs. In these instances, there may be doubts and questions about what took place when the program was implemented. Data may be collected on goals or expected effects that are so vague that the data have little meaning. Finally, there may be a failure to recognize the weakness of the rationale linking the program to the goals and expected effects so that the pitfalls of the evaluation could have been avoided through prior analysis (Rutman, 1977).

Determining evaluability is often, thus, a prior step to more rigorous research. Rutman suggest two steps for determining the evaluability of a program and for determining the preconditions for an evaluation study: (1) an evaluability assessment and (2) formative research.

An evaluability assessment focuses on evaluating the three preconditions for developing and realizing a comprehensive evaluation study. This assessment indicates what aspects can be evaluated and offers suggestions as to questions to be answered before an evaluation study is begun. Further, an evaluability assessment can be used to generate hypotheses for an evaluation study.

Formative research, the second phase for determining the evaluability of a program is focused on collecting data on the program's operation. Rutman cites three reasons for supplementing evaluability assessment with formative research. These reasons are quite relevant and appropriate for evaluation with agency selection committees' programs of clergy assessment.

The first reason is to provide a check on the accuracy of the user's understanding of the program, its goals and outcomes, and its linking rationale (Rutman, 1977). Given the reality of changing committee membership and the attendant differing levels of understanding about clergy assessment that probably exist on any committee, formative research can serve as a check on what is conceptualized by committee members regarding these programs.

Second, Rutman states that the evaluability assessment is likely to reveal difficulties the managers face in actually conceptualizing the preconditions. Changes in committee membership, different ideas about assessment, the interplay of theology and psychology, uses of assessment, and experience with assessment contribute to difficulties in conceptualizing the preconditions. Formative research can provide some basis for changing the process of assessment as well as informing and/or revising expectations by users.

Third, formative research can provide data as to latent goals and side effects that may not have been identified in an evaluability assessment. Committees may be unaware of particular effects on candidates and on committee functioning by the use of psychological assessment processes. With formative research effects can be identified in order to provide a more detailed and complete understanding of the program.

Finally, Rutman focuses the purposes of formative research not only in terms of determining evaluability, but as a means to increase the evaluability of a program. The evaluator collects data related to program personnel, organizational structure and climate, policy, and the context in which the program operates. For agency committees, these aspects would include an understanding of agency theology, polity, demographics of the selection area, committee organizational functioning, and the political and social factors relevant to committee decision making.

To illustrate the viability of Rutman's research process for agency selection committees, a summary of the author's study of representative decision making groups (Annual Conference Boards of Ordained Ministry) in The United Methodist Church follows.

Involved in the study were groups from seven geographical governance areas, or Annual Conferences, of the denomination. Both an evaluability assessment and formative research were conducted.

An *evaluability assessment* essentially focuses on the decision making system served by an evaluation study and determining the questions to be asked in an evaluation. This assessment involves a series of steps that bound and define the program from the perspectives of the user and of the evaluator. The sequential steps as outlined by Rutman are as follows.

1. Identify the primary users of the planned evaluation, and from their point of view, determine what activities and objectives constitute the program.

2. Collect information on the intended program activities, goals, objectives, and the assumed causal relationships.

3. Synthesize the information collected, resulting in the development of a *rhetorical program model* which is a flow model or models depicting intended program activities, intended impacts, and the assumed causal links.

4. Attempt to determine the extent to which the program, as represented by the rhetorical model, is sufficiently unambiguous that evaluation is feasible and potentially useful. Two (2) criteria are applied: (A) Have the intended users of the evaluation agreed on a set of measures of program activities ties and program objectives? (B) Have the intended users of the evaluation agreed on a set of plausible, testable assumptions linking program activities to program outcomes and impacts? The purpose is to evaluate only those aspects where there exists agreed upon measures of success and testable causal relationships.

5. Provide feedback of the results of the analysis to the program managers/intended users and the identification of program components and objectives that are amenable to evaluation. (See Rutman, pp. 23-24.)

Meetings were held with the selection committees or their representatives. The purposes of the meetings with the committees were (1) to explain the purpose of the study; (2) to outline and develop a relationship between the board and the researcher; (3) to determine the purpose and process of psychological assessment as understood by the committee; and (4) to explore the total context of a committee's selection process (Holliman, 1985).

Following each of the meetings, the data gathered through interviews and group discussion were organized, summarized, and sent to the participants for clarification and review. Linking rationale as outlined in Rutman's steps three and four was developed for each selection group involved in the study. This rationale was further tested through the *formative research* and was included in the final report of the study.

The methodology of formative research focused on a program's operation should produce new information and relies largely on an inductive approach. Thus formative research focuses on the search for causal relationships and differs from evaluation research aimed at testing hypotheses. The methodology of formative research is not a form of social research, but it aims at establishing the preconditions for an evaluation study. The methodology useful in pursuing this purpose is commonly accepted research methodology, including participant observation, program documents and records, questionnaires, unstructured interviews, and analysis of literature. Data can be collected from clients and users through interviews, records and/or observations of program personnel, and monitoring the operation of the program.

The intent of the methodology is to try to articulate a program, its goals and effects, and the relationship between program and outcomes. Consequently, the data are equivocal and suggestive, rather than definitive. Data are focused more on subjective than on objective measures of effects in order to attempt to refine the understanding and expectations of users of a program. Likewise, in order to clarify, develop, and operationalize a program and its goals, the emphasis is less on holding a program constant and more to provide information on a program that is ongoing—that is, how the program works (Rutman, 1977).

Based on the meetings and interviews with the selection committees, written materials from these committees, and national materials developed to guide the assessment process, two questionnaires were developed and mailed: one to persons who had been members of the selection committees over a four-year period and the other to persons who were clergy applicants interviewed by those committees. Questionnaires were numbered and personal identifying information removed (blinded) upon their return.

The goal of this research is to generate hypotheses to develop an evaluation study of a program. Thus analysis of the data implies rather subjective criteria. The analysis is focused first on the descriptive, on how actual programs of psychological assessment are working as defined and as perceived by the users (selection committee members and the evaluated clergy applicants). A second goal is to determine the rationale linking the goals and objective of the programs to the outcomes, identifying side issues as well as latent goals and unexpected outcomes.

Descriptive analysis was conducted by tabulating all responses to the questionnaires by the geographical area of each selection committee in two groups: selection committee members and clergy applicants. The data from these two groups were also tabulated across the seven geographical areas.

While all the data are analyzed to discover the presence or absence of linking rationale and thus to ascertain the feasibility of an evaluation study, the answers to the free response questions may provide crucial data pertinent to these goals as well as indicating unexpected outcomes and latent objectives. Answers to questions were rated by two readers, based on scales developed by the researcher. Interrater reliability was determined for each of the questions based on comparison of the ratings given by each reader. A subjective report was also written by a third reader, based on guidelines written by the researcher. A final report was mailed to each participating selection committee.

The results of this study across the seven geographical areas and various programs indicated strong agreement among selection committees and applicants as to selection criteria and the high priority of psychological assessment in the selection process. Committee members expressed agreement as to the purposes of psychological assessment. Applicants expressed high satisfaction with feedback received from the process. Both committees and applicants expressed similar concerns and questions regarding the process of assessment.

The criteria stressed in the literature for conducting evaluation research are (1) clearly identified and articulated goals and expected outcomes, which are (2) linked to a program by (3) clearly stated connections. If any of these are lacking or unclear, then a pre-evaluation study of the kind described here is recommended.

A pre-evaluation study can be enhanced considerably if clear written records of correspondence, orientation material, and assessment program processes are maintained over the years by selection committees. Use of an outside, but knowledgeable, research consultant to plan and conduct the study is recommended. The consultant needs some familiarity, if not experience, with the denomination and its expectations for clergy and selection.

The pre-evaluation study should involve as many persons as possible who are a part of the selection process, particularly to determine unexpected outcomes. Access to clergy applicants who were not accepted is crucial to a complete picture of the outcomes of an assessment program. An attempt to articulate *subjective,* as well as objective, selection criteria is important. Attention by committee members to their own subjectivity can help clarify linking rationale as well as why the psychological assessment program functions as it does.

Finally, it is recommended that selection committee members and the committee's psychological consultant or pastoral evaluation specialist meet annually to discuss and clarify the goals and procedures of psychological assessment. Articulating assumptions, differences, and questions can only enhance the process and provide an ongoing basis for more formal evaluation.

13

Changing Patterns of People Entering Ministry*

HOWARD STONE

Clustered together off in the corner at almost any gathering of ministers, you may find a group talking about how people now entering the ministry are not the same as those in years past. The tone of such conversation usually involves a mixture of nostalgia for the past, recognition of the changing of the guard, and scorn for the "newer generation" as lacking what the older one had.

One might wonder if there is truth to such claims. Are individuals entering the seminary and ministry really different from what they used to be? Is a new breed of student coming to seminary? If people who are attracted to ministry today are different from their colleagues of the past, in what ways have they changed?

The Purpose of the Study

This chapter will describe some of the findings of a longitudinal study that undertook to determine whether, in fact, there have been changes among entering seminary students at a mainline Protestant seminary. It examined psychological tests and demographic data covering a twenty-five-year span (1962–1986). Statistical procedures were performed to ascertain whether any such changes were evident, whether existent changes indicated linear or nonlinear trends, and whether they were statistically significant. Readers who wish more detailed information concerning the study or the statistical procedures used may refer to a series of published articles reporting the data (Stone, 1989a, 1989b, 1990a, and 1990b).

Data garnered from 1,139 first-year students from the years 1962 through 1986 were included. All were enrolled for the M.Div. degree; special students and candidates for other degree programs were excluded. The mean number of students per year was 45.56. These numbers ranged from a low of 21 in 1967 to a high of 78 in 1978. Eighty-five percent of the students were male, 15 percent female. Sixty-five percent were Disciples of Christ students, 18 percent were Methodist, and 17 percent represented other denominations.

Entering students took a battery of tests during their first week of school. (These instruments are used for guidance purposes while individuals are in seminary.) The tests used were: The Minnesota Multiphasic Personality Inventory (MMPI), probably the most frequently used psychological test of personality; the Theological School Inventory (TSI), a self-report inventory designed to evaluate seminarians' decisions for the ministry; the Otis Self-Administering Test of Mental Ability—Higher Examination, a self-report IQ test; the Diagnostic Reading Tests—Survey Section; and either the Miller Analogies or the Concept Mastery.

The study of ministerial students by the use of psychological tests is not new. For over fifty years, numerous studies have tried to describe components of the ministerial personality. Researchers, such as Jack Bloom (1971) and Allen Nauss (1973) have summarized a number of the studies and have attempted to draw schemas of what such a personality is like.

Little research, however, has attempted to note changes over time in the character of those who choose the ministry, the primary focus of this present study. Since one of the major changes is the influx of women and second career individuals, these two groups will receive special review. Finally, the prediction of future ministerial effectiveness using entrance tests will be discussed.

It is difficult to generalize from the study of one seminary to other seminaries and to all people entering ministry, to cross denominational lines or regional borders. All results have to be treated tentatively. Nevertheless conclusions can be drawn about one particular Disciples of Christ seminary, and it may be that the findings will apply to other mainline Protestant seminaries and denominations as well.

Changes in Those Entering Ministry over Time

At the beginning of the period studied, 1962, the effect of social activism in ministry upon seminarians'

*This research project was made possible in part by grants from Lilly Endowment, Inc., and the Research Fund, Brite Divinity School, Texas Christian University. Statistical consultation was provided by Richard Hall and Rick Clubb.

motivation to bring about change to social structures and address social problems was strong. This influence, though, did not reach its peak until near the end of that decade. A factor might be that the seminary also was a haven where people opposed to the war in Vietnam could avoid being drafted. The years 1967 through 1971 were the peak period when alternatives to the military draft were being sought. They also were a time of heightened idealism, and the church was seen as a vehicle for altering the ills of society.

Those years of social activism had a profound effect on the church in the second half of this century, and those who were attracted to the seminary at that time were somewhat different from persons who preceded or followed them. Theologically, they were less conservative than their predecessors, and no group of seminarians since has been as theologically liberal as they were. What is interesting is that the level of theological conservatism of present seminarians is approaching a return to that found prior to the late 1960s.

During the period of heightened social activism, those attending seminary felt less certain of their vocation, less definite in their decision about entering ordained ministry, than at any period prior or since. The level of definiteness dropped from 1967 to 1971, but has since returned to levels that existed prior to the late 1960s. The research findings also suggest that the call to ministry in entering seminarians between 1967 and 1971 was motivated relatively less by both natural and special leading. Students during that period considered an immediate and compellingly direct intervention by God to be relatively less crucial to their vocation. This was a distinctive break from those who had come to seminary before them.

The motivation to bring reform to the structures of society, as one might predict, was highest during the 1967 to 1971 period. (This motivation was also reasonably high in the early 1960s and in the five-year period after the late 1960s.) Since that time, however, the image of ministry as an important way in which people can remediate social problems has continued to decline. It is presently at its lowest point in twenty-five years. The impetus for social reform is higher for theologically liberal students than for conservative ones.

It was predicted that of the various motivations for ministry, the evangelistic drive would be lowest among people entering seminary from 1967 to 1971, but would increase again, if not to previous levels. As it turned out, of the twenty-five years studied, the early 1960s found students more strongly motivated by a desire to evangelize than at any other time; evangelism reached a low during the late 1960s and has rebounded somewhat since then.

Although the entering grade point averages of college graduates going to seminary increases with each succeeding year, their academic abilities (measured by IQ, reading ability, and Concept Mastery or Miller Analogies) are steadily decreasing and are now at an all-time low for the twenty-five- year period. This is the bad news of the research. At this seminary, students cognitively cannot stand shoulder to shoulder with their peers from the past. The lower academic abilities of recent seminarians is suggested by other indices. For example, the percent of college graduates later going into ministry who were Phi Beta Kappa members in 1945 to 1949 was 3.9 percent, while in 1980 to 1983 it was 0.8 percent (*Key Reporter*, p. 2). Now more than ever before, top college students are choosing professions other than ministry.

Women and Second Career Students

It seems unlikely that the church will ever be the same after the influx of women entering ordained ministry. Although women have been pastors in the Christian Church (Disciples of Christ) for over a hundred years, only the last fifteen years have seen them entering seminary in any numbers. Three hundred thirty-nine first year regularly enrolled students from the years 1980 through 1986 were included in one particular statistical procedure. Two hundred thirty-eight of the students were male, while 101 were female.

Men and women entering the ministry are similar in a number of ways—sometimes, in fact, more alike than they are in the general population. There are crucial differences between the sexes, however. These differences shape the way each ministers. Women are more theologically liberal than men, and younger students are more liberal than older ones. (For the research, an "older student" was defined as over being over the age of thirty and a "younger student" as entering seminary immediately after high school or college, age twenty-three or less.) The inclusion of the age factor helps us to understand the theological gap between the sexes. One reason women appear more theologically liberal than men is that older men are significantly more conservative than either of their younger counterparts—male or female—as well as older women. Younger men and women, however, do not differ significantly on theological stance.

The motivation for evangelistic witness was also different for the older male. Although older students in general are more motivated to ministry by a desire for evangelism, it is the older male who is significantly different from the other three groups in that respect. These results give credence to the complaint sometimes heard in counseling from older male seminary students that they feel "out of sync" theologically with the rest of their colleagues. In fact, they are. It appears that the influx of older men entering ministry will require seminaries to consider how to address such students theologically. And, in counseling, greater sensitivity to the legitimacy of such students' theological concerns will be needed.

The TSI flexibility scale (TSI-FL, see chap. 17 of this volume) measures the "open, probing, tentative attitude toward beliefs and ideas. . . . The high *FL* scorer is much more likely than the low scorer to welcome the analytic, searching enterprise of theological education" (Dittes, 1964, p. 54). High TSI-FL scores are negatively correlated with interest in parish ministry. Women score higher on the TSI-FL scale than men do. Women score as being more flexible. This is especially true when comparing older men and women. There is a significant difference between these two groups. Of the four groups, older women have the highest TSI-FL scores, and older men the lowest. This suggests that older women are more open, inquiring, and flexible in their beliefs, which is especially helpful in attending seminary, but the low TSI-FL score of older men suggests that they will find the parish ministry more congenial to their interests.

Women also have greater interest and motivation for the intellectual aspects of the study of theology and preparation for ministry than men do. This is indicated by higher TSI-I scores. (In this study, younger students and theologically liberal students also have higher TSI-I scores than do older and more conservative students.) Hunt, Cardwell, and Dittes (1976) describe seminarians with high TSI-I scores as people whose "major concern and experience is with abstract issues rather than involvement and commitment to the reality of parish work in a church" (1976, p.33). Such people tend to be less convinced about the viability of day-to-day parish ministry. Women's higher TSI-I scores also may indicate greater uncertainty or even disillusionment with the parish ministry and perhaps with the church as a whole.

In addition to the TSI-FL (flexibility) scores of women—which make them more congenial to the study of theology at a seminary—and their TSI-I scores—which indicate greater intellectual interest in the theological quest—women seminarians also have superior academic abilities. The scores on the Otis IQ, the Diagnostic Reading Test, and the Concept Mastery all loaded a factor analysis into one category, Academic Ability. Women scored higher on this factor than did men and, in the present sample, are better equipped cognitively to do the seminary work.

Two additional results from the study bear not on gender issues but on older or "second career" students. Older seminarians in this sample have higher TSI-F and TSI-D scores. Both results help us understand something about the decision to go into ministry at a later time in one's life. Older students have a greater sense of self-fulfillment (TSI-F) as a motivation for ministry. However, Hunt, Cardwell, and Dittes caution: "This change of careers may cause these persons to claim an ease in making sacrifices or conceal inner uncertainties with an overstated sense of fulfillment that the ministry is perceived to offer. If this career change is motivated by a search for individualistic contentment, high *F* may be disillusioned in some seminary or denominational traditions" (1976, p. 37). Such concerns certainly are something the pastoral counselor must consider when giving care to second career seminarians and ministers.

In addition to a greater self-fulfillment motivation, older seminarians are more definite and clear about their decision to enter the ministry (TSI-D). Many describe having received the call earlier in life, but sought to evade it until they could do so no longer. As they entered seminary, they were quite certain of their vocation. Older students also tend to have had more parish experience as well as a background in other careers.

Predicting Effectiveness

It would be useful for denominational church occupations committees, as well as for seminary advisement counselors, to be able to predict from entrance test scores which students might be effective ministers in the future. However, one might question whether such factors as personality and motivation to ministry are sufficiently stable at entrance to seminary for predictions for future performance in ministry to be made with any certainty.

One hundred sixty-three of the 1,139 subjects in this research project were rated by judicatory supervisors (typically after 3½ years of seminary and 2 to 4 years of ministry). There can be considerable disagreement about what defines an "effective minister"; in this study, the rating of a judicatory executive familiar with each minister's performance was used. Supervisors' ratings on the question of the "overall appraisal of the minister" were grouped into "above average" and "average" ministers.

While results have provided statistically significant findings, they fail to discriminate the above average and average minister to a degree that would be useful for advisement. A correct classification of 68 percent of ministers into one of the two groups was achieved. However, the classification accounted for only 12 percent of the variation.

While such results may not support the ability of present tests to provide sufficient discrimination of future effectiveness, they offer some interesting findings. Measures of academic ability—such as IQ, Concept Mastery, or Miller Analogies—and reading ability fail to predict which ministers will be effective. This insignificant result seems to suggest that something other than the academic or cognitive skills people bring to seminary are determinants of their future effectiveness. The MMPI and especially the Mf, Pa, Pt, K, Sc, Ma, and Si scales are the best predictors of effectiveness of the test and demographic data available for the study. It is more useful than a series of demographic variables, the TSI or the classic measures of academic ability.

Some General Thoughts

Some of the results of this longitudinal study have been surprises, others predictable. Some results verified hunches. A picture of the changing seminarian has begun to emerge, much like a picture of a changing landscape. The person who walks into the theological school today is not the same person who entered the ministry a quarter-century ago.

Critical changes in the character of those who are entering ministry appear to reflect some of the changes in our society, but they also may reflect the view of academically superior young college students who see ministry as a less viable career option than in the past. Although these trends show up in one particular study at one particular seminary, there is reason to believe that they may echo the situations of mainline Protestant seminaries across the country. Longitudinal research on changes among incoming seminarians is presently going on at other schools and in other denominations; from such research we will be able to gain an even clearer and more detailed picture. Only as a more complete image of these changes has been formed will it be possible to consider strategies for improving the overall quality of ministry in the 1990s and beyond.

14

Predicting Ministerial Effectiveness

LAURA F. MAJOVSKI AND H. NEWTON MALONY

The research reported in this chapter was an extension of the Haight (1980) design (see chap. 9 of this volume) to address the larger issue of the role of psychological assessment in predicting ministerial effectiveness. The major contribution of the Haight (1980) research is that it demonstrated a moderate relationship between psychological assessment and ordination decisions.

The design of the present research investigated the predictive relationship of psychological recommendations to actual measures of both primary and secondary criteria of ministerial effectiveness.

Results from Two Studies

Three studies were originally conducted (Majovski and Malony, 1985), with the first two reported here: Ordination Study; Effectiveness Study; and Prediction Study. The purpose of the Ordination Study was to investigate the determinants of the psychological assessment recommendations and the relationship of both the determinants and recommendations to ordination decisions. The purpose of the Effectiveness Study was to investigate the relationship of psychological assessment recommendations to measures of ministerial effectiveness. The purpose of the Prediction Study was to investigate the relationship of overt predictions of ministerial effectiveness from psychological assessments to actual measures of effectiveness.

Ordination Study

The Ordination Study included eighty-four males and three females as participants. The mean age was thirty-one-years old, with a range from twenty-five- to fifty-six-years old. All participants were referred for psychological assessment by the Board of Ordained Ministry (BOM) of the Southern California-Arizona Conference of The United Methodist Church (UMC). At the time of the psychological assessment, all participants were candidates for the final level of ordination within the UMC—that is, elder. All psychological assessments were conducted over a five-year period (1973–1977) by the same psychological evaluator (PE).

Three questions were investigated by the Ordination Study: (1) What are the determinants of the clinical decisions of the PE? (2) What is the relationship of those same determinants to the BOM ordination decisions? (3) What is the relationship between the PE and BOM decisions? Assessment tools included the MMPI and IRAI (see chap. 17 of this volume).

Each original recommendation was transformed into a descriptive code as follows:

8 = Accept (without condition)
7 = Accept (with counseling for spouse)
6 = Accept (with counseling for self)
5 = Accept (with counseling for both)
4 = Defer (with counseling for spouse)
3 = Defer (with counseling for self)
2 = Defer (with counseling for both)
1 = Reject (without condition)

Correlational analysis of the MMPI scale determinants and PE recommendations revealed significant correlations. The following individual scales were negatively correlated with PE recommendations: D ($r = -.21$); Hy ($r = -.21$); Mf ($r = -.23$); and Pt ($r = -.22$), all significant at $p<.05$. No other MMPI scales were significantly correlated with PE recommendations.

The correlational analysis of the MMPI configural profiles with PE recommendations revealed negative correlations with both profiles: Invalid ($r = -.23$) and Unhealthy ($r = -.39$). Both were significant at $p<.05$. Thus the MMPI data contributed as determinants of PE recommendations both by individual scale and by configural profile.

Analyses of IRAI scales and configural profile results

revealed that no significant correlations were found between PE recommendations and the individual IRAI scales.

The relationships of the MMPI and IRAI scale and profile data were found to have no significant relationship to BOM ordination decisions.

When the MMPI and IRAI individual scales were considered together in relationship to PE recommendations, only two MMPI scales accounted for significant variance in PE recommendations: D (R = −.24; F = 5.62; df = 1.91; $p<.05$) and Ma (R = −.39; F = 9.84; df = 1.91; $p<.01$). Together, the two scales accounted for 15 percent of the variance: D = 6 percent and Ma = an additional 9 percent. No other scales accounted for additional variance.

The PE decisions were then analyzed with the combined configural profiles of the MMPI and the IRAI. Two profiles accounted for a total of 19.5 percent of the variance: 15 percent by Unhealthy MMPI profile (R = −.39; r = 16.71, df = 1.91; $p<.05$); and an additional 4 percent by the Unsuitable IRAI profile (R = −.44; F = 4.51; df = 1.91; $p<.05$).

Similar analyses were conducted with BOM decisions and the combined MMPI and IRAI data. No combination of MMPI or IRAI individual scales or configural profiles accounted for any variance in BOM decisions.

When all eight levels of PE decisions were compared to the binomial BOM ordination decisions, no significant relationship was found. The BOM decisions and the PE decisions had three levels: accept, defer, and reject. A 3x3 Chi-square analysis showed a significant relationship between the BOM and PE decisions (X^2 = 19.58; df = 4; $p<.05$).

Effectiveness Study

At the time of the Effectiveness Study (between three and eight years after ordination), seventy-one of the original subjects were available for participation. Inclusion in the Effectiveness Study depended on a participant's having a current assignment to a parish setting. The remaining sixteen subjects were excluded from the Study because they were not employed in a parish setting during the year of the Effectiveness Study (1980–1981).

Two questions were investigated in the Effectiveness Study: (1) What is the relationship between the PE recommendations and actual ministerial effectiveness? (2) What is the interrelationship of the primary and secondary measures of effectiveness?

Measures of effectiveness in this study included both primary and secondary criteria. The Ministerial Effectiveness Inventory (MEI) was developed by this researcher to gather primary measures of ministerial effectiveness (specific observable behaviors). The MEI is a fifty-nine-item Likert-type questionnaire derived from the comprehensive study of the characteristics of effective ministry in the United States, conducted by Schuller et al. (1980). The MEI items are descriptors of the eight main characteristics of effective ministry that were rated as "quite" or "highly important" or as "quite" or "highly detrimental" in the Schuller et al. research (1980).

The eight areas include the following: (1) having an open, affirming style; (2) caring for persons under stress; (3) evidencing congregational leadership; (4) being theologian in life and thought; (5) undertaking ministry from a personal commitment of faith; (6) developing fellowship and worship; (7) having denominational awareness; and (8) not having disqualifying personal and behavioral characteristics.

A total of twenty-four MEI items were developed from these eight areas with an additional thirty-five items from the important determinants of effectiveness identified by UMC participants in the Schuller et al. research (Trotter, 1980). Only those items that met the same criteria of being rated as "quite" or "highly" either important or detrimental were included. Thus a fifty-nine-item questionnaire was developed, which asked the rater: "How characteristic is this *item* of your minister?"

The MEI questionnaires were mailed to three types of raters for each of the seventy-one subjects (Ss) included in the Effectiveness Study. Each S was asked to complete the MEI questionnaire. In addition, MEI questionnaires were mailed to the District Superintendents of all Ss. In the UMC structure, each minister is assigned to a local geographic district, which operates under the direct supervision of the District Superintendent (DS). MEI questionnaires were also sent to the members of the Pastor-Parish Relations Committee (PPRC) of the 1980–1981 church of each participant. Members of this committee are from the local congregation and work closely with the pastor in all matters concerning the functioning of the church.

The following return rates were obtained (N = 71): Self = 93 percent; DS = 93 percent; and PPRC = 83 percent. The split-half reliability of the MEI questionnaire was evaluated by the rating group and found to be: Self = .82; DS = .96; and PPRC = .99. The possible range of MEI scores is 59 to 354, with 148 as the median score.

Secondary measures of ministerial effectiveness—that is, consequences of leadership—included the following variables: membership (of total church); attendance (main weekly worship service); church school (weekly attendance, all ages); salary (including allowances); and giving (annual total, by congregation). The data for each of the measures were obtained from the statistical record in the annual journal published by each Conference of the UMC. Secondary measures of effectiveness were incomplete for several participants due to omissions in published data and inaccessible conference journals. For comparative purposes, the values of the secondary measures of effectiveness were computed as percent-change for the length of current parish assignment, divided by the number of years in the current parish assignment. No significant correlations were found between the PE recommendations and either primary or secondary measures of effectiveness.

The same statistical procedures were used to investigate the relationship between the measures of effectiveness and the configural profiles of the MMPI and IRAI data. No significant correlations were found between the measures and the profiles.

Multiple regression analysis was conducted to investigate further the relationship of the MMPI data and the measures of effectiveness. Several of the primary measures were negatively correlated with the MMPI scales. Results revealed that 8 percent of the variance of PPRC ratings was accounted for by the scale Ma ($R = -.29$, $F = 4.00$, df $= 1.91$; $p<.05$). In addition, 11 percent of the variance of Self ratings was accounted for by the scale Pd ($R = -.33$, $F = 7.87$, df $= 1.91$; $p<.01$). No variables accounted for variance in the DS ratings.

Only one secondary measure of effectiveness had a significant relationship with the MMPI data. The attendance variable had 7 percent of its variance accounted for by the Si scale ($R = .27$, $F = 4.81$, df $= 1.91$; $p<.05$).

An additional analysis was conducted to investigate the role of the length of time since original psychological assessment and the measures of effectiveness. Results from the one-way ANOVA revealed only one significant difference between the evaluation groups. The most recent group of participants, those assessed in 1977, were evaluated by the DS raters as significantly lower than the groups assessed between 1973 and 1976.

Correlational analysis of the primary measures of effectiveness indicated a significant relationship between PPRC and DS ratings of Ss ($r = .59$, $p< .01$). Self ratings were not significantly correlated with either DS or PPRC ratings.

Correlational analysis of the secondary measures of effectiveness indicated high intercorrelations among membership, attendance, and church school. Membership and giving were also significantly correlated. Salary was significantly related only to church school.

Significant correlations were also found in the analysis of the interrelationships of primary and secondary measures of effectiveness. DS and PPRC ratings were significantly related to three secondary measures: membership, attendance, and church school. Self ratings bore no significant relationship to any secondary measures of effectiveness.

The results of the Effectiveness Study reveals the following: (1) no significant relationship was found between the recommendations of the PE and the measures of effectiveness and (2) significant interrelationships were found between the various measures of effectiveness.

Discussion

Results from the Ordination Study indicated that psychological recommendations depended largely on personality data and, to a lesser degree, interest data. The significant use of MMPI configural profiles in determining these recommendations confirmed the previous findings of Haight (1980). In addition, several individual MMPI scales were significantly related to these recommendations. The negative relationship of certain elevated profiles to psychological recommendations was consistent with previously cited research, relating various MMPI scale elevations to lack of perseverance in seminary (Godfrey, 1955; Aloyse, 1961; Vaugh, 1963; and Weisgerber, 1962).

The investigation of the predictive validity of psychological recommendations to ordination decisions was the primary purpose of the Ordination Study. Results indicated a significant relationship between the recommendations and ordination decisions confirming the Haight research (1980). However, this relationship was only significant when the recommendations and decisions were compared in general categories—namely, accept, defer, and reject.

Despite the demonstration of a significant relationship between psychological recommendations and ordination decisions, the value of the contribution of these psychological assessments is questionable. The psychological evaluator found little overall variance among the participants and recommended 90 percent for ordination. The significant relationship between recommendations and ordination decisions resides in the fact that 74 percent of those recommended for ordination were ordained. However, for the remaining 26 percent of those recommended, other data outweighed the psychological recommendations. Furthermore, 71 percent of those recommended for deferral by the psychological evaluator were accepted for ordination. Only 67 percent of those who were recommended to be rejected without any reconsideration were actually deferred or rejected. One subject was ordained counter to the psychological recommendation not to be ordained under any conditions. No significant determinants of ordination decisions were found in any of the psychological assessment data.

One possible explanation of the above finding would be the constricted range of variables. The psychological recommendation data were positively skewed. Even when data from psychological prediction scores were forced into a normal distribution, no significant relationship to any measures of effectiveness was found with either distribution.

However, a wide range of scores was found on both primary and secondary measures of effectiveness. Furthermore, significant positive intercorrelations were found between the measures of effectiveness and several raters. On the basis of these findings, the measures of effectiveness are assumed to be valid.

Regarding the measurement of ministerial effectiveness, several research notes need to be highlighted. Pastors' self-ratings of effectiveness were unrelated to any other measures of effectiveness used in the present study. This suggests that pastors respond to different indicators of personal ministerial effectiveness than do their supervisors or their members. Therefore, future research would need to explore these differences as well.

15

Lilly Quality of Ministry Projects

JOSEPH P. O'NEILL

For the past thirty-five years, the Lilly Endowment, Inc., has made several significant investments in developing instruments for the selection of candidates for the ministry. Beginning with support for the Theological School Inventory in 1953, the Endowment showed its steadiness of purpose by underwriting the development of *Readiness for Ministry* in the late 1960s and has continued to support that endeavor through several revisions over a twenty-year period.

The Endowment's newest investment, indeed the largest single program the religion division has ever funded, is again targeted at the recruitment and selection of candidates for the ministry. Unlike previous programs, which supported the efforts of a single team, the new "Quality in Ministry" program is a constellation of more than fifty individual projects in three tiers of activities.

The Endowment, in its prospectus, proposed to cooperate with and assist those institutions and agencies that are responsible for recruitment and selection of theological students to: (a) attract more able candidates to the ministry; (b) identify more clearly the characteristics of successful candidates; and (c) identify barriers that may prevent potentially successful candidates from considering the ministry as a form of service.

The three-tier program rested on two assumptions. First, it reflected the Endowment's judgment and that of many church leaders that improving the quality of future candidates to the ministry is crucial to the effectiveness of the church's moral and religious leadership. Yet, the Endowment also acknowledged that defining standards for the selection of candidates is a thorny issue indeed. The term *quality* will necessarily represent a complex of factors that will differ from denomination to denomination.

The plan also reflected a second assumption: that a convergence exists among church leaders in their descriptions of the qualities of character and intellect they are searching for. While the needs of each religious body are not identical, there does seem to be some consensus about a broad common ground that merits exploration. Consequently, the program calls for a major research effort to clarify issues related to the quality of candidates for the ministry.

In the fall of 1987, the Endowment received 204 proposals in its first round of competitive grants; of them, 40 projects were funded. The proposals themselves, even when not funded, were of great interest. Coming from a broad range of institutions, they represented, in effect, the best thinking the field had to offer. As we began to analyze their content, we found a clustering of themes in five broad categories: the discernment of a call, recruitment of minorities, mentoring, the character of nontraditional seminarians, and the demographic analysis of changes in seminary student bodies over time.

Discernment of a Call

The religious ethos in many denominations tends to define a call to ministry as an experience similar to that of Saul's on the road to Damascus. This narrowly subjective definition of "the call" may exclude many who could engage in fruitful ministry but have not experienced such an invitation. Winebrenner Seminary, for example, has undertaken a program that would allow the denomination to broaden its definition of "calling" to include other biblical types of call that relied more on objective characteristics than on a subjective experience. The seminary proposes to construct a set of profiles that would allow them to encourage persons with the necessary objective qualities for ministry to recognize their call.

Moravian Theological Seminary is addressing a similar problem. Many Moravians are uncomfortable with the idea of recruiting for ministry, seeing it as a loss of faith in the workings of the Holy Spirit. Indeed, any formal discussion of what qualities a good minister should have is almost taboo in many Moravian circles. Like Winebrenner, Moravian Seminary is conducting a systematic study of Moravian ministers to construct a profile of the characteristics of successful ministry.

In these two proposals and similar ones from the Mennonites and the Church of the Brethren, we find that both the description of the problem and the methodology to deal with it have a number of common elements. One is the use of "profiles." It would seem that the methodology of *Profiles in Ministry* is being adapted to local circumstances. Another common feature is mention of an increasing rate of involuntary terminations. There is some evidence that congregations are less willing to tolerate a minister's inadequate performance. For example, according to a 1988 report commissioned by the Southern Baptist Convention, an average of 116 of the denomination's 37,000 churches dismiss their pastors each month. This figure is sharply higher from the average of 88 dismissals a month noted in a 1984 survey.

The Church of the Brethren, in its proposals, notes that the denomination has, without much theological reflection, begun to think of ministry as one of the "helping professions." Historically this is not the way the Brethren have defined ministerial leadership. Theirs was a "ministry with" all the other members of the congregation, not a "ministry for" them. As the original meaning of the ministry grows dim, congregations no longer call out one of their own members and ordain him or her for leadership. Instead they have increasingly turned to the outside for a full-time professional pastor. As a result of these changes, the Church of the Brethren perceives itself to be in the midst of a leadership crisis. The denomination's smaller congregations insist on a full-time minister, even though their meager resources often allow them to retain only people of marginal quality who are unfamiliar with Brethren traditions.

Mennonites, too, have noticed that changes in the common culture have outdistanced theological reflection. As Mennonites moved increasingly from rural occupations into business and the professions, their patterns of ministerial leadership have changed. The "bench"—a plural ministry of gifted members recognized for their leadership in the community—has given way, generally, to a single-pastor-plus-lay board model. The change in structure has outdistanced the change in culture. And the Mennonite Church is experiencing increased stress in the relationship between pastors and congregations as measured by an abnormal rate of involuntary terminations.

The Mennonite Church, in its proposal to the Lilly Endowment, is mounting an effort to clarify the pastor's role by examining why so many gifted young people in the church are not interested in positions of congregational leadership.

The Mennonite church proposes to establish reference groups that would prepare alternative models for ministry: two for congregations of 300 and 150 members—that is, able to support a full-time salaried pastor; and a third for congregations too small for a full-time pastor. These models would examine problems that make impacts on church leadership and will act as barriers to recruiting gifted young people into the pastorate.

What becomes clear from the proposals clustered under a rubric of "discernment of a call" is that many Protestant denominations have not actively recruited candidates for the ministry, in part because they have not had to and in part because they felt they should not. The call to Christian ministry is a matter of grace, not merely human choice. These churches have experienced no lack of candidates responding to that call. However, many denominations are now rethinking both their theology of "the call" and their lack of intentionality in building up the church's future leadership.

Recruitment of Minorities

The pattern of proposals dealing with the recruitment of minorities varies sharply according to denominational polity. By and large, in those denominations where the authority to ordain rests with the congregation, there is no question about the recruitment of minority candidates but how to provide them with an appropriate education. New York Theological Seminary, for example, enrolls a large number of black and Hispanic pastors of inner-city churches. While a good number belong to mainline Protestant denominations, the majority are leaders of small, storefront Pentecostal and evangelical congregations made up of the city's poorest residents. The seminary has made its programs accessible to the non-English speakers among these ministers by establishing a bilingual M. Div. program in Spanish and Korean.

The seminary proposes to survey their M. Div. graduates over the past five years to determine the characteristics essential to success in urban ministry. After gathering information from clergy and lay leaders through questionnaires and face-to-face interviews, NYST will evaluate its admissions criteria, curriculum, and recruitment procedures.

Golden Gate Baptist Seminary in the San Francisco Bay area has mounted a similar effort. California is a major gateway for immigrants from Asia and Latin

America. The seminary has begun to meet the need for theological education in the language of the immigrant by opening centers that teach theology in Spanish, Chinese, Korean, Tagalog, Thai-Loatian, and Samoan. These centers currently serve 250 students, many of whom are already pastors of storefront churches.

The seminary proposes to recruit more qualified candidates by holding colloquia for prospective clergy. Everyone currently studying at one of the Ethnic Leadership Development Centers will be invited to identify two or three outstanding members of his or her congregation for inclusion in the colloquium program. Guests will be surveyed for interest and ability in the ministry. Follow-up activities will include assessment and opportunities for further education.

The ease with which congregationally based denominations incorporate minority clergy into their ranks is not so readily matched by denominations that are more hierarchically organized. According to a 1987 survey conducted by the National Conference of Religious Vocation Directors, less than 10 percent of the Roman Catholic religious communities who responded accepted both "Anglo" and ethnic (black and Hispanic) candidates over the past six years. The usual pattern is that a community will accept either one or the other, but not both, despite universal policies about openness. The resistance to "social minorities"—widowed, divorced, disabled, alcohol dependent—is even greater.

The National Black Catholic Congress, under the leadership of Bishop John Ricard, proposes to bring together priests—black and white—with a proven track record in recruiting high quality black candidates for the priesthood. They would especially draw on the experience of two religious orders—the Divine Word Missionaries and the Josephite Fathers—who have been especially successful in nurturing black priests. The proceedings of a two-day conference would be edited and published so that its finding would be helpful to other religious orders and dioceses.

Mentoring

One of the more intriguing sets of issues that has surfaced in the Quality of Ministry program is that of imagining or modeling. Before one makes a choice of profession, one must, in some sense, imagine oneself in the role of a minister or priest. The objective correlative to that subjective imagining may be a concrete person, a composite, or indeed a congregation that one might be leading. Research into the subjective process of modeling will be undertaken by Vanderbilt Divinity School.

The perception at Vanderbilt is that theological education has been fragmented into a series of academic and practical competencies and has lost a unifying focus. In this functionalist approach, preparation for ordained ministry has been reduced to the sum of the tasks ministers perform. Vanderbilt Divinity School has sought to restore theology—as a habit, not just as a discipline—to the core of seminary education. The habit of theology is a way of thinking, acting, and interpreting that allows Christian persons to live faithfully in a pluralistic world.

Vanderbilt's experience is that many exceptional candidates for the ordained ministry have an aversion to the functionalist approach to ministry. They are unable to imagine themselves as functionaries (preachers, evangelists, counselors, or religious educators), but have instead imagined themselves as persons genuinely interested in pursuing truth.

Vanderbilt Divinity School proposes to undertake a reimaging of the ministry based on theology as a habit. The aim is not to replace such functions as preaching and pastoral care with functions more enticing. The proposal is to foster a wide-reaching discussion of ordained ministry from which a new set of images of ministry will emerge.

Looking more to the objective correlative, Colgate Rochester Divinity School will examine the role of the congregation both as model and as nurturer. Colgate Rochester has found that its best students—those who make the fullest use of educational resources and go on to exceptionally effective ministries—come from vital congregations. A review of the 346 recent admissions applications shows that with the exception of four students, all applicants cited the important role a local congregation played in their decision to attend seminary. Of the four who did not acknowledge the role of their local congregation, none is currently in ministry.

The Divinity School has identified a number of quality congregations whose vitality has inspired highly qualified candidates over the years. The school proposes to study the characteristics of these exemplary congregations and disseminate its findings to its two sponsoring denominations, the American Baptist Churches and the Episcopal Church.

In contrast to the congregational focus at Colgate Rochester, the project at Fuller Theological Seminary centers on the person of the individual pastor or dedicated lay mentor. Based on experience with a variety of screening devices including—*Readiness for Ministry,* the Theological School Inventory, MMPI, and others—the Fuller project assumes that the most important element in the recruitment and selection process is the personal relationship between the student and a mature Christian person who encourages the student's progress toward ministry.

Fuller proposes to study this mentoring process to identify the characteristics of a successful mentor; what successful mentors look for in a candidate; why the candidate is influenced by the mentor; and whether age, gender, or denominational affiliation affect the relationship. Outcomes include programs to train clergy and laity in the mentoring process.

Several of the Roman Catholic proposals also focused on the importance of mentoring as a way of counteracting the decline in vocations. In the twenty years between 1966 and 1986, the number of candidates preparing for the priesthood in the American Roman Catholic Church has dropped by more than half, from 8,325 in 1966 to 3,853 in 1986. A disproportionate share of this decline has been borne by the religious orders whose candidates now make up only 30 percent of the pool, compared to 40 percent in 1967 and 1968.

In its proposal, the Archdiocese of Minneapolis stated that many priests seem to be reluctant to encourage young men to enter the priesthood. Those who do refer candidates to the seminary often have a different definition of quality from that of the seminary. Indeed, most priests lack the experience to evaluate the quality of potential candidates.

The Archdiocese proposes to establish a Leadership Interview training workshop in which five priests from each of the Archdiocesan deaneries will participate. Once trained, these priests will be given the opportunity to use their new skills in interviewing candidates, and they will be evaluated by an experienced panel.

In an approach taken by several Roman Catholic proposals, the Archdiocese of Detroit has initiated an intensive campaign to build a systematic approach to promote vocations to the priesthood. Realizing that personal encouragement is the "secret" to a successful program, the vocation office has begun a program to nurture the idea of service to the church in the middle grade school and high school years. This program, entitled *Focus Eleven*, targets those who are eleven years old and those who are in the eleventh grade. The vocation office proposes to use the *Story of My Life* as a discernment tool and then personal follow-ups and mailing to nurture the idea of service.

The Catholic diocese of Evansville, Indiana, also plans to administer *The Story of My Life* to some 900 Roman Catholic high school students. From this number, it hopes to identify some twenty to thirty students who may have the qualities for church leadership. These students will be interviewed by the project team to identify those who have not only the talent, but also the interest in a church leadership role.

As a follow-up, those interested will be invited to take a closer look at the meaning of ministry. The young men will be invited to spend a day at St. Meinrad's seminary, interacting with candidates for the ministry and experiencing seminary life. Young women will be invited to a one-day retreat on church leadership opportunities for women, supplemented by several evening discussions of the same topic.

The process of mentoring/modeling is a complex one in which the attitudes toward the role of the clergy are as much shaped by the general culture and mass media as by the church itself. In an effort to deal with the cultural definition of the clergy's role, Harvard Divinity School will examine the ministry as a public profession. Harvard's perception is that since the beginning of this century mainline Protestant denominations have experienced a steady decline in their ability to influence American public life. As a consequence, the ministry has suffered an erosion of its public dimension, and its image as a profession has been fundamentally altered. Today the ministry is less able to compete successfully with other professions in attracting both adequate talent and numbers. The ministry has become a marginalized profession and theological education increasingly separate from fields that provide technical expertise in addressing the problems of contemporary public life.

Harvard Divinity School proposes to mount a major innovative program aimed at addressing this crisis in the image of contemporary religious leadership. The program will also address the recruitment of nontraditional students whose convictions, experience, and informed perceptions would raise the standards of excellence in the profession.

The Divinity School's effort to revitalize the public competence of ordained ministry coincides with a growing university-wide concern with ethics and the professions. The climate within the university has become increasingly open to the investigation of ethical, and even explicitly religious, issues in such fields as medicine, law, government, education, and business. The school proposes to stimulate collaboration and discussion across professional boundaries and to seek to redress the marginalization of the ministry in society and to renew its public role and authority.

Recruitment Among Nontraditional Population

One of the common experiences of university-based divinity schools is that many of their gifted students do not see ordained ministry as a viable way "to make a difference in the world." Though they are persons committed to social justice and exhibit strong personal values, they do not see the church as a vehicle of social and cultural change. Such students are often called "seekers" or searchers.

By definition, searchers are very bright, usually under the age of thirty, interested in theology as a discipline, and are very committed to social concerns. But searchers differ from other candidates with similar qualities in that they exhibit a high degree of tentativeness about their call to ministry.

Vanderbilt Divinity School, for example, reviewed the files of 393 M.Div. graduates from 1977 to 1987. Of that number, 113—a little more than a quarter—fit the profile of a searcher. All 113 subjects included in their admissions essays a negative critique of American society and prevailing social norms.

As you might expect, they are individuals who, if they cannot reform the world, will try to reform the seminary. Life would be easier without them, but it would also be duller. We find fewer and fewer searchers among candidates as they move into their early and upper thirties. Indeed, the most distinguishing characteristics of older candidates from all our studies is the certainty they have about their vocation.

Longitudinal Studies

To probe and test the issue of the quality of candidates over time, the Endowment has funded a series of longitudinal studies at both the seminary and the denominational level.

Brite Divinity School at Texas Christian University has collected and put into machine-readable form twenty-five years worth of entrance tests—IQ, Miller Analogies, MMPI raw scores—on 1,140 Brite M.Div. students. They propose to analyze this data to determine how Brite students have changed over the past twenty-five years. Special attention will be given to the ways that women and the influx of older candidates have changed the characteristics of the pool.

Saint Francis Seminary in Milwaukee and the Episcopal Diocese of Chicago have collected similar material. For the past eighteen years, the Diocese of Chicago has used a battery of tests to measure a variety of personal qualities and gifts. These measures have proven to be highly predictive of certain types of performance—for example, persistence in ministry. The diocese would now like to broaden the scope of its criteria to include certain areas of leadership.

The diocese proposes to interview fifty incumbent Episcopal priests, their superiors, and members of their congregations to elicit criteria indicative of leadership qualities. Draft performance reviews would be formulated and tested on a second group of fifty to validate their usefulness.

An effort will be made by Educational Testing Service, the recipient of a grant to coordinate the entire Quality of Ministry program, to put these various individual data bases into a common format. While keeping strict confidentiality, records for *Readiness for Ministry*, the Theological School Inventory, and files from individual seminaries will be welded onto a data base of some 50,000 individual cases spanning twenty-five years or more.

Conclusion

The Lilly Endowment's "Quality in Ministry" program supports a variety of interesting research and action projects through academic year 1991. For the most part, the benefits will be specific to a particular seminary or denomination. No new broad-based instruments—such as the Theological School Inventory or *Profiles of Ministry*—are contemplated. It should be noted, however, that much of the useful information and models for new research are based on these two instruments. Thus the new Lilly initiative builds on the firm foundation of past research.

Assessment Procedures
and Methods

16

ATS Profiles of Ministry Project

DANIEL O. ALESHIRE

rofiles of Ministry (POM) is a program of clergy assessment begun in 1973 as the *Readiness for Ministry* program. It was developed at the request of the Association of Theological Schools in the United States and Canada (ATS), which maintains program ownership and management.

Profiles of Ministry includes: (1) an extensive, empirically derived summary of criteria; (2) assessment instruments for entering seminary students and necessary interpretive resources for evaluating student scores (POM Stage 1); and (3) a group of instruments for graduating seminary students and career ministers, along with interpretative resources appropriate for these individuals (POM Stage 2).

Two Questions for Clergy Assessment

The information and resources that are part of the *Profiles of Ministry* program reflect an ongoing response to two fundamental questions regarding assessment: (1) What should be assessed? (2) How should the assessment be made? While these are simple questions, they can require surprisingly complex answers—at least in the context of clergy assessment.

The first question forces the investigator to determine which criteria are important, even crucial, for the practice of ministry. The difficulty in defining meaningful criteria sometimes contributes to a reductionistic error. Since measurement is most reliably made by discrete, univariate scales, the criteria are sometimes artificially reduced to measurable proportions. The result can be good measurement of criteria that are so limited in their focus that the resulting assessment still provides little valuable information about an individual practice of ministry.

The second question points to the need to determine effective methods of measurement that are congruent with the content of the criteria to be assessed. It requires both empirical and theological sensitivities, and the response to this question sometimes leads to an obscurantist error. Since the criteria are many and complex, it can be argued that methods do not exist to assess them reliably. The result of this reasoning can be that a good perception of important criteria is obscured by subjective and idiosyncratic assessment approaches.

Profiles of Ministry can best be described by the responses it has made to these questions. The two major research agenda in the POM program have involved: (1) the identification of criteria and determination of importance assigned to them and (2) the development and subsequent revision of assessment instruments to measure important criterion characteristics.

Defining Criteria for Clergy Assessment

The process of identifying appropriate criteria may be the most distinctive feature of the *Profiles of Ministry* program. The beginning of the program involved an extensive, interactive search to define criterion areas and to assess the degree of importance assigned to each. As the research began, two major assumptions were made about areas of exploration and the proper use of criteria identified by the process.

It was first of all considered important to address the theological and theoretical concerns of ministry, in addition to psychological and professional skill concerns. This assumption was alluded to in the first major report of the early research to ATS:

> From the beginning of the project's design, the research team has been sensitive to this danger of reducing ministry to its human dimension, of highlighting sociological and psychological issues while slighting the more elusive theological dimensions. Therefore, while deliberately pressing to describe the work of the ministry as concretely and specifically as possible, we eagerly invited biblical, theological, and historical input to assure the description of contemporary ministries that would stand the test of theological critique (Schuller, Strommen, Brekke, 1975, pp. 1-2).

The second major assumption was to identify significant criteria while avoiding an imposed prescription of what constituted "good" ministry. Since ATS member schools relate to no fewer than forty-nine different denominations, and since these denominations differ from one another in their perceptions of desirable and detrimental ministry practice, the criterion identification phase sought to provide *descriptive* information about criteria. Individual church bodies or seminaries would thus have a resource—a vocabulary or taxonomy of criteria—that they could use for more *prescriptive* concepts of ministry.

POM decided early that it would attempt to define characteristics in an inclusive and nonreductionist perspective. It sought to identify the theological, psychological, spiritual, and professional skill criteria that could provide both an inclusive perspective of ministry and multiple characteristics for assessment. It also attempted to avoid the determinations that translate descriptive information about ministry practice into prescriptive definitions of positive and negative ministry.

The process of identifying and monitoring criteria can be divided into two major research efforts. The first was the more extensive, and it involved two years of work in the early 1970s. The second effort was conducted in the late 1980s, and it involved the readministration of the criterion survey originally administered in 1974 in order to assess possible changes in the ratings of importance in criteria.

The 1973–1974 Research to Identify Criterion Characteristics

Given the range of concerns and issues underlying the research, it was hypothesized that criteria could best be identified through a major survey of constituencies related to ATS member schools.

Initial Survey Development

Since the survey was to be the primary means by which criteria would be determined, the procedure for its development was gradual, inclusive, and deliberate. An initial pool of 2,000 potential items was generated from two sources: the existing literature on ministry and a rather extensive process of evaluating accounts of critical incidents in ministry practice (see Schuller, Strommen, and Brekke, 1980, pp. 14ff).

The 2000 items were evaluated, edited, and reduced to a set of 834 that were used in a field test version of the survey. This preliminary version was completed by over 2,000 clergy and laity who were drawn from one of five evaluator groups: seminary professors, seminary seniors, alumnae, denominational executives, and laity. The resulting data were used to test the analytic strategies intended for the final survey data and to revise the survey into its final form (see Brekke, in Schuller, Strommen, and Brekke, 1980, pp. 529-37).

1974 Survey Sample and Administration

The revised version of the criterion identification instrument consisted of 440 items, each a statement of a ministry behavior, attitude, skill, or sensitivity. The sample was drawn using a stratified random stage sampling procedure in which: (1) ATS member schools were drawn, (2) who then randomly selected faculty, seniors, and recent alumnae according to sampling instructions for each group; finally (3) the alumnae were given instructions for sampling members of the congregations or persons serving in the ministry settings in which the alumnae were working.

Denominational executives were drawn into the sample by a separate process. A total of 5,169 people responded to the survey, representing 45 percent of the number drawn into the sample. This response rate was not as high as desirable, but for several reasons multiple stage samples may not yield the same response rate as single stage samples (see Brekke, in Schuller, Strommen, and Brekke, 1975, pp. 111-13; see also Brekke, in Schuller, Strommen, and Brekke, 1980, pp. 537-40).

Analysis and Findings of the 1974 Survey

The first, and most crucial, analytic task was the identification of criteria. Once criteria were empirically identified, subsequent analyses explored the variations in criteria ratings by laity and clergy respondents across the various denominational families.

Criterion characteristics were derived from a series of factor and cluster analyses, performed separately on laity and clergy responses. These analyses resulted in the identification of sixty-four criterion characteristics. The most highly rated characteristic consists of the following items: "Serves others willingly with or without public acclaim"; "Recognizes own emotional and physical limitations"; "Laughs easily even at self"; and "Believes the gospel she/he preaches." Criteria are comprised of empirically derived sets of survey items. They convey a logic of perception about either persons who minister or the nature of ministry, and they reflect the variety of theological, psychological, spiritual, and professional criteria the project had hoped to identify.

As the POM program has emerged over time, the focus has been on thirty-six criterion characteristics for which assessment scales have been developed. These scales (as distinguished from the criteria themselves) have been factored, and the resulting factor structure provided a pattern for grouping the criterion characteristics (Aleshire, 1985). The titles and descriptions of the thirty-six criterion characteristics assessed in POM instrumentation are shown in Table 1.

Table 1.

Profiles of Ministry

Ratings of Criteria 1974 and 1987

Cluster		1974	1987
Responsible and Caring			
43	FIDL Fidelity to Tasks and Persons (showing competence, responsibility, skill, and warmth in completing tasks)	6.29 (d,s)	6.30* ( )
42	RESP Personal Responsibility (honoring commitments by carrying out promises despite pressures to compromise)	6.42 (d,s)	6.48 (d,s)
36	LIMT Acknowledgement of Limitations (recognizing limitations, mistakes, and the need for continued growth and learning)	6.35 (d,)	6.44 (d,s)
45	FLEX Flexibility of Spirit (adaptability, balance, free sharing of views, and welcoming of new possibilities)	6.11 (,s)	6.14 ( )
25	ICAR Involvement in Caring (personally involved in mutual exchange among persons learning through suffering)	5.73 (d,s)	5.81 (d,s)
21	PRCO Perceptive Counseling (reaching persons under stress with sensitivity that is freeing and supportive)	6.26 (d,s)	6.35 (d,)
Family Perspective			
48	FAML Mutual Family Commitment (agreement in the minister's deep commitment to family and family's commitment to his/her vocation)	5.83 (d,)	5.98 (d,)
Personal Faith			
37	PIET Commitment Reflecting Piety (consciousness of God's redeeming activity in living a	6.20 (d,)	6.42 (d,)

sense of call to Christ's mission with freedom and courage)

		1974	1987
34	ACLM Service W/o Regard for Acclaim (relying on God's grace, serves without seeking personal reputation for success)	6.52 (d,s)	6.53 (d,)
Potential Negative			
54	SELF Self-Serving Behavior (avoiding intimacy, repelling people by critical, demeaning, insensitive attitude)	6.02 (d,s)	6.16 ( )
63	PADV Pursuit of Personal Advantage (personal insecurity expressed in efforts to gain or to keep personal advantage)	5.59 (d,s)	5.83 ( )
52	PRTC Self-Protecting Behavior (immaturity, insecurity; being buffeted by the pressures of the profession)	5.89 (d,s)	6.09 ( )
60	DMNA Domination of Decision Making (bypassing disciplined task of planning, usurping congregation's decisions)	3.68 (d,s)	3.62 ( )
Ecclesial Ministry			
49	DNOM Denominational Collegiality (acceptance of denomination's directives while maintaining a collegial relationship with superiors and staff)	5.76 (d,s)	5.89 (d,s)
09	LITG Sacramental-Liturgical Ministry (stressing worship, sacramental, and liturgical aspects of the faith)	4.87 (d,s)	5.00 (d,s)
01	RELT Relating Faith to Modern World (sensitive interpretation, teaching of the gospel in contemporary life)	6.20 (d,)	6.10 ( )
02	TBIB Theocentric-Biblical Ministry (attention to God's Word and Person in preaching, teaching, and leading worship)	6.24 (d,)	6.35 (d,)
05	PRCH Preaching and Worship Leading (holding attention while preaching, doing all aspects of a service well)	5.87 (d,s)	5.89 (d,)
28	CLAR Clear Thought and Communication (demonstrates careful thought, communicates understandably, learns from experience)	6.18 (d,s)	6.19 (d,)

---

* For all criteria except 54, 63, and 52, the higher the value, the more important the characteristic rated. For 54, 63, and 52, the higher the value, the more negative the rating. All ratings reflect a scale of 1–7.

Conversionist Ministry

17	EVAN Assertive Individual Evangelism (aggressive approach to the unchurched, hoping to convert them to Christianity)	5.03 (d,s)	5.08 (d,)
19	GOAL Precedence of Evangelistic Goals (believes efforts for bettering society are less important than the evangelization of all humankind)	4.03 (d,s)	3.99 (d,s)
20	CONG Concentration on Congre. Concerns (a ministry that avoids directly confronting social change)	3.58 (d,s)	3.67 (d,)
27	LAW Law Orientation to Ethical Issues (emphasis on God's demands and condemnation as basis for solving personal problems)	4.00 (d,s)	3.85 (d,s)
24	THCO Theologically Oriented Counseling (using theologically sound counseling to help people cope with personal problems)	6.17 (d,)	6.25 (d,)

Social Justice Ministry

18	PLIT Aggressive Political Leadership (working actively, sometimes with pressure groups, to protest and change social wrongs)	4.34 (d,s)	4.42 (d,s)
50	CAUS Support of Unpopular Causes (vigorous participation in community affairs, willing to risk to support a cause)	5.74 (d,s)	5.63 (d,)
08	OPEN Openness to Pluralism (open to cooperation with people whose theology, culture, or methods are different)	5.57 (d,s)	5.61 (d,)
16	OPRS Active Concern for the	5.12	5.22

	Oppressed (knowledgeably, earnestly working in behalf of minority, oppressed peoples)	(d,s)	(d,s)
33	IDEA Interest in New Ideas (involvement with current thinking, openness to testing new or current ideas)	4.75 (d,s)	4.83 (d,s)

Community and Congregational Ministry

11	SERV Pastoral Service to All (reaching out to persons of all classes, whether members or not)	5.92 (d,s)	5.98 (d,)
03	YUTH Relating Well to Children, Youth (sensitivity and skill in ministering to children and youth)	6.04 (d,s)	5.92 (d,s)
12	MISN Encouragement of World Mission (stimulating congregation response to world need that is theologically based and sacrificial)	5.95 (d,s)	6.08 (d,s)
55	BLDG Building Congregational Community (actions that may build a strong sense of community within a congregation)	6.34 (d,s)	6.32 ( )
56	CNFL Conflict Utilization (understanding conflict theologically, using it positively to stress understanding)	6.11 (d,s)	6.11 (d,s)
57	LEAD Sharing Congregational Leadership (active use of lay leadership—regardless of gender—in executing parish strategy)	6.07 (d,s)	6.12 (d,s)
14	UNDR Promoting Understanding of Issues (using theological, sociological, psychological understanding in ministry)	5.39 (d,s)	5.53 (d,s)

d = significant overall variation across *denominational* families, $p<.001$
s = significant overall variation across laity/clergy *status*, $p<.001$

The ratings of importance of the characteristics obtained in the 1974 survey were derived from the responses of the entire ecumenical sample. The data were weighted so that each denominational family had equal voice, as did laity and clergy. The data indicate a significant overall variation across North American denominational families on virtually every criterion characteristic. Laity and clergy were observed to agree with one another on some areas but not others.

The various analyses to identify sources of variance in these data showed that denominational and laity/clergy differences accounted for virtually all of the non-error variance. Little additional explanation came from comparisons of ministry context that raters had in mind, the region of country in which they lived, their gender, their level of education, the frequency of their church attendance, the size of the parish they attended, their age, or their income (Aleshire, in Schuller, Strommen, and Brekke, 1980).

The 1987 Criterion Survey

As the program of assessment was used through the late 1970s and the early 1980s, the question was

ATS Profiles of Ministry Project

Analysis and Findings

increasingly being raised about the possible datedness of the criterion ratings. In response to this question, a shorter version of the criterion rating survey plus a few new items was readministered in 1987.

The method for the survey readministration replicated the sampling frame and administration procedures employed in 1974. The 1987 survey drew a sample of 5,776 individuals, of whom 2,607 returned answer sheets. This represents a 45 percent rate of response, almost identical to the 1974 survey.

The data were analyzed in ways to provide answers for four questions: (1) How stable are the criteria themselves? (2) How have ratings of importance of criteria changed from 1974 to 1987? (3) How do denominational families vary in their ratings of criteria? (4) What new criterion areas appear to be a part of thinking about ministry in the late 1980s?

To explore the issue of stability, each criterion characteristic was evaluated in terms of its internal consistency reliability and the replicability of the factor structure that led to the initial identification of criteria. Preliminary analyses suggested: (1) that the factor structure of items was relatively stable across the two survey administrations and (2) that the criteria defined as sets of individual items in 1974 could be reliably defined by the same item sets in the 1987 data.

The most consistent finding about the ratings of importance was that little change was evident between the 1974 and 1987 ratings. The criterion rating scales have a range of 1.00 to 7.00. Of 36 criteria surveyed in both studies, 20 had variations from 1974 to 1987 of less than 0.10. Of the 15 that varied by more than 0.10, none varied by more than 0.24, or 2 percent to 5 percent of the logical scale range. The 1987 ratings are also shown in Table 1. These criteria appear not to be trendy, time-bound perceptions of ministry. They point to enduring perceptions of ministers/priests and of ministry itself.

When responses were compared by clergy/laity status and by denominational family, the findings approximated the same patterns of variance that occurred in the 1974 data (Strommen, in Schuller, Strommen, and Brekke, 1980, pp. 79-87). The variance in the 1987 responses suggests that North American denominations have considerable agreement about personal characteristics that are judged negatively, some agreement about personal characteristics that are judged to be important for ministry, and minimal agreement about the importance of different approaches to ministry. Agreement on criteria that define the kind of person doing minis-

try is more evident than agreement about the tasks of ministry that person should be doing (see Table 1).

The 1987 survey included over forty new items intended to relate to ministry issues emerging since the early 1970s. Seven criterion areas were identified from these items, dealing with such issues as women and the church, peace and justice, and moral-political concerns, like abortion.

This process of criterion identification underscores the importance ascribed to the definition and monitoring of criteria in the POM program. A characteristic could be considered a criterion only when (1) it reflects an empirically derived structure, suggesting a common image among denominational constituencies; (2) it is rated as important or detrimental to ministry, suggesting that it deals with something crucial to the understanding and practice of ministry; and (3) it has a biblical and theological basis in addition to its empirical one.

Profiles of Ministry Assessment Instruments

The POM assessment instruments and interpretative resources exist in two stages: for entering seminary students, and for graduating seminarians or ministers/priests in practice. The most unique feature of these assessment instruments is their criterion referencing.

Criterion Referencing

The POM clergy assessment resources have been developed as criterion-referenced instruments. Their intent is to focus a student's or minister's attention on the criteria that have been rated as important or detrimental to ministry. The POM profile of scores presents no average scores; and while it is derived from numerical scores, it does not emphasize them. These assessment instruments report the degree of evidence or likelihood with which an individual exhibits some attitude, sensitivity, or skill in ministry. Then, the individual is referred to the relative importance ascribed to each criterion characteristic. By contrast, most instruments are referenced to some comparison group. An individual's numeric score is typically compared to the average score of some defined group. The individual is able to interpret his or her score by noting whether it is higher, lower, or the same as the average score of the group. POM instruments are not designed this way.

This criterion referencing feature creates a different interpretive frame. Instead of statements like "I am higher than average on 'Fidelity to Tasks and Persons,' " the POM instrumentation leads to statements like "I am very likely to exhibit 'Fidelity to Tasks and Persons' (determined from assessment instruments), and this criterion characteristic is considered highly important (determined from the criterion characteristics survey)." The results may confront an individual by suggesting that he or she is unlikely to do something considered absolutely essential, or very likely to minister in a way judged to be detrimental. The individual is referenced not to a group of peers, but to a best estimate of the criteria that exist in the context of ministry.

While the instruments do not reflect all that is sometimes assumed by criterion-referenced instruments, they represent an intentional effort to provide assessment instrumentation anchored to criteria judged important to the practice of ministry (Brekke, 1984).

Profiles of Ministry—Stage I Assessment for Entering Students. *Profiles of Ministry* uses two instruments with entering students that measure twenty-nine characteristics. The *casebook* (Brekke, Schuller, Williams, Aleshire, 1986) consists of twenty-four brief cases that present a problem, issue, or circumstance that calls for a ministry response. The case is followed by questions that ask respondents what they would do and what rationale undergirds their choice of action. The focus questions are followed by statements that reflect various options and reasons. Students are requested to respond to each statement in terms of how likely or unlikely they would be to act or think in the manner described by the statement. An individual responds to 484 of these statements for the twenty-four cases. Casebook items are combined into scales, producing scores for twenty-two different criterion characteristics.

The *interview* (Brekke and Williams, 1986), consisting of a series of questions that are both asked and responded to orally. The interviewer is required to use scripted questions and to tape-record the responses. These responses are later scored by trained coders according to established decision rules. The interview provides scores for nine ministry characteristics.

The Stage I Profile and Interpretative Manual. A computer-generated profile summarizes the scores from both instruments. The Profile groups scores into two broad categories (Aleshire, 1985).

The left side of the profile reports scores that relate to personal characteristics. These are not so much personality or psychological characteristics as they are ways in which personal tendencies manifest themselves in ministry practice. While these are not personality traits, they do identify areas where personal tendencies to keep commitments, care for others, act responsibly, make adjustments as necessary, and exhibit flexibility can influence one's practice of ministry. The left side

also includes scores related to the individual's perceptions of faith and family. The final group of scores on this side of the profile provides indicators about the presence or absence of characteristics that have been judged negatively by virtually all of the rating groups in both the 1974 and the 1987 survey studies: "Pursuit of Personal Advantage," "Self-Serving Ministry," and "Self-Protecting Behavior."

The right side of the profile reports scores related to the individual's perceptions of ministry. Each of these four groups of scores reflects a particular vision or perception of ministry. For some, the focus of ministry efforts is on converting people to Christian faith; for others, the focus is more directly related to changing social structures according to a Christian understanding of justice. Other perceptions of ministry focus on ecclesial life and on ministry as effective service to the community and to the people of a congregation. Since the instruments do not force respondents to choose one over the other, variations in scores can be helpful indicators of the vision of ministry a student would seek to implement in ministry practice.

The *Interpretative Manual* (Aleshire, Brekke, and Williams, 1986) includes introductory material about the *Profiles of Ministry* program, instructions for reading the profile, and a careful description of the meaning of each of the scales. The manual also suggests ways in which combinations of scores characterize approaches or attitudes about ministry. The manual tries to avoid prescriptive definitions of "good" and "bad" ministry. Rather, it provides necessary resources for the individual, with the help of an interpreter, to evaluate his or her own perceptions of ministry and to construct a prescription for good ministry practice that is reflective of the practice and theology of the student's own tradition.

Uses of Scores. POM Stage I scores have been used in several ways. The most frequent pattern of use involves individual or group interpretation sessions with entering seminary students. Students have an opportunity to evaluate themselves seriously in the context of ministry. The practice of ministry has been an abstract goal for many first-year students, and the POM assessment approach confronts them with concrete realities. A profile of an entering class can help seminary faculty to assess the ministry perceptions and sensitivities that class members bring to their seminary studies. POM scores and interpretive resources provide for disciplined discourse about the practice of ministry as well as evaluation of attitudes, tendencies, or sensitivities in students that should either be reinforced or changed during seminary study.

Profiles of Ministry—Stage II Stage II assessment involves three instruments: the *casebook*, (Brekke, Williams, Schuller, and Aleshire, 1988) the *interview*, (Brekke and Williams, 1986) and the *field observation form* (Aleshire, Brekke, and Schuller, 1988). The interview for Stage II is identical to the one administered in Stage I. The other two instruments, however, are different. The *casebook* includes some of the cases and response possibilities that are used in the Stage I instrument, but it uses several different cases and measures several different characteristics. The Stage II *casebook* has a total of 23 cases with 529 items to which the individual responds. The *casebook* for Stage II, like Stage I, includes cases identifying some problem or issue in ministry, followed by several focus questions, which are then followed by statements describing possible actions and reasons for those actions. It provides scores for 23 different criterion characteristics.

The *field observation form*, unique to Stage II, is completed by persons who have had opportunity to observe an individual function in some ministry setting. The observer rates the student or minister on 116 statements, such as: "In leading worship, helps people to experience a sense of God's presence"; "Evidences a clear vision of what spirituality involves"; and "Involves laypeople in making decisions about the long-term future of the congregation." Observers rate individuals in terms of how likely or unlikely they think the individual would be to exhibit the kinds of attitudes or behaviors described by the items. The ratings for items are grouped into fifteen different scale scores. The scoring process allows for as many as five observers to rate the individual, and these multiple ratings are then averaged together for the profile score.

The three instruments used for Stage II assessment provide a rather comprehensive measurement package. They reflect variety in measurement strategy—one is a paper and pencil, closed-ended, self-administered instrument; another is a structured interview that elicits open-ended responses that can be coded and reported as scores; and another instrument asks observers to rate the student or clergy. They provide comprehensive assessment of forty-one different characteristics. They have been designed so that both graduating students and in-career ministers/priests can obtain meaningful information about perceptions of and characteristic approaches toward the practice of ministry.

Profile and Interpretative Resources. The Stage II profile is designed in basically the same way as the Stage I profile, but because of additional information, two profile polls are required. The first page includes scores related to personal characteristics—both those valued as positive and necessary and those seen as potentially negative. The second page reports scores related to perceptions of ministry. The ministry perception scores are grouped into the four categories that are used in the Stage I profile. An *interpretative manual* provides an introduction to the *Profiles of Ministry* program, instructions for reading the profile, separate descriptions for the forty-three scale scores, an explanation of differences among the three Stage II instruments, and information about how best to interpret the scores.

Uses of Scores. Stage II is designed so that it can be used either with seminary students preparing for graduation or ministers/priests already in ministry. The results provide an extensive summary of attitudes and behaviors related to ministry practice and the occasion for serious reflection about individual commitments in the context of congregational and churchly expectations. They can help individuals assess likely areas of tension, appropriate areas for personal and professional growth, and areas of strength. The nature and number of scores provide the opportunity for a comprehensive evaluation of an individual's practice of ministry.

17

The Theological School Inventory (TSI) and the Inventory of Religious Activities and Interests (IRAI)

RICHARD A. HUNT

The Theological School Inventory (TSI) and the Inventory of Religious Activities and Interests (IRAI) are both designed specifically for persons who are considering some type of professional ministry. Historically they were the first instruments specifically designed for clergy and clergy candidate populations. These inventories share a common root in the work of Sam C. Webb and others in the late 1950s.

Theological School Inventory

General Description of the TSI

The Theological School Inventory (TSI) provides a description of the background, motives, and abilities that are important in the vocational development of persons who are preparing for the ministry as a career. The TSI is a self-report inventory designed specifically for the guidance and growth of persons who are at any stage in their professional ministry or who are in the process of preparing for the ordained ministry.

Intended to encourage open and candid self-exploration, the TSI draws no explicit attention to processes of personality dynamics or to such criteria as "mental health." TSI is a highly sophisticated instrument, designed to help a person to articulate many of the subtle queries and concerns about vocational decisions. It assists others to explore these concerns through a mentoring process that includes elements of vocational development and spiritual formation.

The TSI is designed as an inventory of a person's motivations, interests, self-reported skills, and biographical characteristics as related to the ministry as a career and to seminary as preparation for a variety of parish and specialized ministries. Information from the inventory is intended to be used by the student in exploring personal and career concerns in relation to the ministry and preparation for it.

Motives, as measured by the TSI, refer to the rationale a person consciously constructs for deciding on and pursuing a course of action. The items and names of the scales can be openly recognized and acknowledged by students as familiar and non-threatening, and the TSI Guide (Hunt, Cardwell, and Dittes, 1976) encourages this candid exploration. While deeper, unacknowledged psychological processes and motives need not be ignored, the TSI is designed specifically to enable a person to discuss openly the issues involved in decisions about the ordained ministry.

The TSI CC, NL, SL, D, and F Scales

The Call Concept (CC) scale describes the possible range of understandings of the call to the ministry, from immanent, "this world," "natural leading" (NL) to transcendental, "other world," "special leading" (SL). On this scale the respondent can describe what he or she considers to be the expected or normative call to the ministry. Then on the NL (Natural Leading) and SL (Special Leading) scales, the respondent can indicate how much of each of these types of calls are personally experienced.

The Definiteness (D) scale measures how strong one's decision about ministry currently is. Flexibility (FL) explores one's intellectual, emotional, and decision life-style of welcoming or avoiding ambiguity, dogmatism, change, and complexity.

The TSI AIFLERP Scales

The AIFLERP scales constitute an ipsative set of seven specific components of motivation from which the respondent must choose which elements are stronger and which are less personally important. These scales are:

A - Acceptance by Others	Influence of family and friends on decisions
I - Intellectual Concern	Study of theological issues and academic pursuits
F - Self-fulfillment	Expecting the ministry to provide personal fulfillment
L - Leadership Success	Previous successes in leading church and other groups
E - Evangelistic Witness	Desire to proclaim the gospel to reach all persons
R - Social Reform	Concern about social injustice and improving society
P - Service to Persons	Giving individual help to persons in need and stress

Other Scales on TSI

An additional set of nineteen items measure the respondent's self-rated abilities, which are clustered into four areas: social services, patient nurture, persuasive leadership, and teaching proficiency. Several items provide feedback from the respondent about the process of answering the inventory.

Guide to Interpreting the TSI

The Guide to Interpreting the TSI (Hunt, Cardwell, and Dittes, 1976) provides a general description of the TSI and many alternate interpretations of scales. This is to encourage the respondent to engage in exploration and dialogue about the fundamental motivational issues addressed by the TSI.

The guide is designed to be a part of the feedback and counseling interview process to aid the respondent in understanding TSI results. The guide should never be used in place of personal or group sessions.

History and Background Development of the TSI

Now in use for some thirty years, TSI is designed to give guidance to individuals who are considering the ministry as a profession, and to assist in counseling theological students and clergy in the field.

In 1954, the Department of the Ministry of the National Council of Churches and Educational Testing Service submitted a proposal for developing measures for theological school students to Lilly Endowment, Inc., which agreed to support the initial project and continued its support through succeeding stages of the instrument's development. Nearly a decade of research went into the development of the TSI, from the first plans for research to the publication of the first full edition of the manual.

After initial leadership from David R. Saunders and Sam C. Webb, in 1957 Frederick R. Kling became director of the Ministry Study program at Educational Testing Service (ETS) and continued throughout the years in which the TSI was designed and developed. In the context of the collaborative research staff of ETS and of the Ministry Studies Board, Kling may be regarded as the primary creator of the TSI. The strengths of the TSI are due originally to Kling, especially its psychometric rigor, conceptual soundness, practical utility, and its deep sensitivity to actual vocational dilemmas of ministerial candidates.

Ministry Studies Board

As early development ended and the TSI neared readiness for general use, the Ministry Studies Board was formed in 1960 to supervise its distribution and use and to continue study on the instrument. The Lilly Endowment continued to support the initial work of the Board. The Board's original trustees represented in equal numbers the Department of the Ministry of the National Council of Churches and the American Association of Theological Schools with additional members elected at large.

The 1964 edition of the TSI Manual, written by James E. Dittes, implemented Kling's earlier work on the instrument. The publication of the first edition of the TSI completed the transition of the responsibility for the TSI from the Educational Testing Service to the Ministry Studies Board. ETS generously released its rights in the TSI to the Ministry Studies Board at that time.

Harry A. DeWire of United Theological Seminary, Dayton, Ohio, became the first Executive Director of the Ministry Studies Board, after having worked closely with Kling as a consultant and collaborator. Edgar W. Mills, Jr., succeeded DeWire as Director of the Ministry Studies Board in 1965, and the office was moved from Dayton, Ohio, to Washington, D.C. In 1966, Mills formed a committee to assume responsibility and oversight of the TSI.

Computer scoring for the TSI was developed by Richard A. Hunt in 1967 in order to provide scoring services to TSI users and to accomplish research support for the instrument. When Mills left his position at the Ministry Studies Board in 1972, the TSI Committee created Ministry Inventories, Inc., and became its Board of Directors to oversee all sales and support services for the TSI. Hunt became the executive director for Ministry Inventories, and the office was moved from Washington, D.C., to Dallas, Texas. In 1985, these services were relocated to Pasadena, California.

Assistance in the development of the TSI has come from many sources. Ever since the stages of early planning, the project has drawn heavily on the resources of the Department of the Ministry (now the Professional Church Leadership unit of the Division of Education and Ministry) of the National Council of Churches, the Association of Theological Schools, and scores of persons active in the areas of counseling and research from various denominations and seminaries.

Development of TSI Scales

Initial work of the Ministry Study analyzed the work of the parish minister. Data were obtained through questionnaire responses from large samples of ministers and laypersons and from lengthy interviews with smaller samples.

Part of the research questionnaire asked open-ended questions about the personal experiences of pastors in deciding to enter the ministry. The two questions to which ministers responded were:

1. Please describe your own decision to enter the ministry, as you experienced it at the time. Indicate what you thought about the "call" at the time and why you felt you should be a minister.
2. Please give your present evaluation of this experience. Point out any changes that have occurred in your thinking about the call or in your understanding of your own motivation in entering the ministry.

This research questionnaire was sent to about 800 ministers from eight representative denominations—Assemblies of God, American Baptist, Southern Baptist, United Lutheran, Lutheran Church Missouri Synod, United Methodist, Presbyterian U.S., and Presbyterian U.S.A. Although the entire questionnaire required several hours, returns were received from about 500 ordained clergy.

The statements by the ministers were studied to discover the prominent types of motivation stated or implied by them. Once the types were identified, the ministers' statements were reliably sorted into several categories. The TSI items were adapted from these statements. The categories yielded by this content analysis are discussed in a major report (Kling, 1959) and became the initial scales of Form A of the Theological School Inventory.

The First Three Revisions of TSI

Form A also included several other intended scales thought to be of importance in assessing ministerial candidates, and it attempted to measure the relevant "knowledge" on the religious topics a candidate had. The only one of these to survive further empirical screening and refinement is the Flexibility scale (FL).

Form A was administered in the fall of 1958 to the entering classes of twenty-one representative seminaries. Correlational and factor analyses confirmed the NL, SL, CC, AIFLERP, and FL scales as being internally reliable and adequately distinguishable from other scales. Other intended scales did not pass this test. Further statistical and content analyses suggested revision of the wording of some items to balance more adequately the "social desirability" of forced choice items and to reduce ambiguity.

Form B, incorporating these changes, was administered to the entering classes of twenty-eight different seminaries in 1959, 1960, and 1961. Factor analysis of the results (1) confirmed the reliability of the CC and AIFLERP scales as written; (2) suggested the elimination of some of the intended items from the NL, SL, and FL scales; and (3) generated a new scale—the Definiteness (D) scale—mostly from items intended for the NL and SL scales.

Form C as scored retained exactly the same scales, items, and wordings as the revised Form B, although they appear in a slightly different context. Form C was released for general use in seminaries in the fall of 1962 and was administered then to the entering classes of sixty-seven seminaries, almost all of whom cooperated in supplying data that became the basis for the norms reported in the first edition of the TSI Manual.

The Feedback Study of 1970

During the years of ferment and unrest of the late 1960s, the TSI Committee considered whether the TSI was still relevant, accurate, and helpful for seminary students of those times. This concern was especially focused on women and minority students and on those entering newer forms of ministry.

In the 1970 feedback study, 315 students from nine seminaries evaluated the accuracy and usefulness of their own TSI scores. In this representative sample, 10 percent were women and 12 percent were black. Complete details of the study are available in Cardwell (1974).

The students considered all of the TSI scales to be accurate and useful. Nearly half of the respondents thought that all twelve of the TSI scales reflected issues that needed to be considered in thinking about the ministry. The remaining students discriminated between the AIFLERP and the CC, NL, SL, D, and FL sets of scales, reporting that the issues elicited by the AIFLERP scales were especially important in their vocational development.

Most students found that the TSI continued to be relevant to their current vocational thinking. The few negative evaluations tended to come from students who described their theological position as more radical or a combination of positions. There were no significant differences between the TSI evaluations by men and women, but 32 percent of the blacks felt that the TSI had no particular pertinence for them, as compared to 7 percent of whites who thought so.

In addition to confirming the relevance of the TSI, the feedback studies showed that many students were struggling in major ways with many concerns related to their vocational decisions.

The Fourth Revision, 1972: Form D72

On the basis of the feedback study, Form D72 retained the same TSI scales with the same items so that scale scores between Forms C and D are compatible. The only changes in the scored items were an attempt to eliminate sex bias in wording without changing the original meanings of the items.

In Form D72 some changes were made in the instructions to clarify the "timeframe" intended, and the autobiographical information in Section I was revised. Most of the unscored experimental items of Section II were eliminated, and the two NL items from Section III of Form C were included in Section II.

Section III was completely changed and expanded from ten to nineteen items that are designed to allow the student to make a self-evaluation of potential effectiveness of abilities in relation to general and specialized settings for ministry. Some clusters of these items form brief scales to facilitate assessment of skills.

The unscored experimental items in Section IV were replaced by a new set of seven items that seemed to have promise of greater usefulness. An optional Section V was added to provide three essay questions to encourage the student to reflect further on experiences in seminary and the ministry. Several new questions to encourage feedback from respondents about the TSI were included in Form D72. Form D72 also provided a new answer sheet that could be scored by either computer or hand, with a new set of templates and profiles for hand-scoring the form.

The computer scoring services available from Ministry Inventories were expanded to include on the individual profile a printout of the responses in Sections I and III, and group data for an individual seminary became available. This summary includes means, standard deviations, comparisons with other groups as requested, and tabulations of data from Sections I and III. For certain comparisons, t-tests are provided. This has enabled local seminaries to maintain annual monitoring of TSI scores and group profiles.

The 1990 Revision—Form E

In 1988 the fifth revision and update of the TSI was begun with the support of a Lilly Endowment grant for updating the TSI. Revised materials will initially be available in 1990. There were two major purposes of this revision. First, the wording of the TSI items was modified so that they can be answered by persons at any stage of career development, from pre-seminary through seminary, through any time during the lifetime career path. At the same time, wording of the items on Form E was matched carefully with the Form D version so that the TSI scale scores could be matched to scores from earlier years, thus maintaining the continuity of scale meanings and interpretations.

Second, relationships between the TSI and the revised *Profiles of Ministry* (POM) were researched. The primary finding of this research is that these two instruments measure different and complementary aspects of clergy candidates in relation to the ordained ministry. TSI focuses primarily on self-perceptions of motivations and interests in various ministries, while POM focuses more on how a candidate is perceived by others and how a candidate responds to a variety of situations that pastors frequently encounter.

With the 1990 Form E revision, local computer scoring and interpretation aids were made possible. To do this requires guaranteed arrangements that will encourage continuing research on the TSI. Under certain conditions seminaries and career development centers may contract on an annual basis to score and interpret TSI on their own computer equipment, provided that seminarians send copies of raw TSI data to the national TSI office, Ministry Inventories, now located at Pasadena, California.

Inventory of Religious Activities and Interests (IRAI)

General Description

The Inventory of Religious Activities and Interests (IRAI) is a paper/pencil self-report inventory designed to measure interest in activities performed by persons employed in a variety of church-related occupations.

The inventory as a measure of interest is unique in that the items describe activities that persons in church-related occupations perform. Respondents indicate their degree of interest in performing each activity.

For purposes of scoring, items are classified by factor analytic procedures into scales that describe selected roles of the occupations of concern. Thus the instrument can be used as both a job description of various church-related occupations and a psychometric device for measuring and comparing interests in performing various occupational roles.

The IRAI is not intended to measure "religiosity," religious attitudes, beliefs, or values. It is religiously oriented in that it measures interest in a variety of occupational behaviors performed within a church-related frame of reference. It does not measure one's skill in doing these activities, although there probably are complex relationships between skills and interests in doing specific tasks.

While the performance of the activities listed in the IRAI may possibly have various theological implications, or while interest in performing them may be suggestive of various theological presuppositions or bases from which behavior may emanate, the inventory is not primarily concerned with identifying or measuring these implications or presuppositions. It is concerned with identifying and measuring what the person likes and does with satisfaction and enjoyment, which constitutes a basic definition of interest.

Scales of the IRAI

The IRAI contains ten role scales composed of twenty items each that measure interest in performing activities in occupational roles or role segments found in a variety of church-related occupations. A separate check scale measures the tendency of a person to endorse many items that are typically disliked. The content of each of the scales is briefly described as follows:

1. **Counselor.** Bringing comfort and encouragement to lonely, troubled, and sick persons and working with people to help them resolve problems primarily of a personal or family nature.
2. **Administrator.** Planning, promoting, and executing various church-related programs.
3. **Teacher.** Administration of and teaching in the religious education program of a church.
4. **Scholar.** Teaching at the college or theological school, and engaging in scholarly research or writing.
5. **Evangelist.** Evangelism and evangelistic work.
6. **Spiritual Guide.** Assisting people to develop a deeper and more mature faith, talking with others about their faith using biblical and religious terms.
7. **Preacher.** Developing speaking skills, preparing and delivering sermons, and making talks and addresses before various groups.
8. **Reformer.** Speaking out against evil and social injustice and participating in programs of community betterment.
9. **Priest.** Liturgical interests, conducting programs of worship, and performing sacred rites and rituals.
10. **Musician.** Conducting a music program for a church, performing as a musician.
11. **Check Scale.** A variety of activities that are likely to be unpleasant to perform or that are fairly routine clerical tasks. The score on this scale in intended for use in estimating whether the subject's scores on the remaining scales are invalid because of responding to the items incorrectly or in a careless manner.

The individual scale scores provide summary expressions of interest in performing a cluster of generally similar activities that comprise a role segment of various church-related occupations. When compared with appropriate norms, these scores provide the client with some understanding of the relative strengths of personal interests and the interests of various comparison groups.

IRAI and United Methodist Candidacy Studies

In 1977 the IRAI was revised to be part of the United Methodist Candidacy program (see chap. 7 of this volume). Sections containing extensive biographical questions were added to the standard set of 240 IRAI items. Designated as Form M (and revised in 1986 as Form M86), all candidates for the United Methodist ordained ministry were asked to answer the IRAI.

The IRAI profile and narrative display of information provides the candidate and supervising pastor with a range of topics to explore. These include family of origin information, educational and local church experiences, social support network information, and other personal data relevant to decisions about church-related careers.

Summary

TSI and IRAI measure motivations and interests as related to professional ministries. Because they capture important biographical data, they encourage a candidate or clergyperson to explore relationships between these areas and their current decisions and goals for their lives and careers.

Since 1985, the address for information about both the TSI and IRAI has been: Ministry Inventories, c/o R. A. Hunt, 180 N. Oakland, Pasadena, CA 91182. Telephone: (818) 584-5553.

18

A Clergy Personnel Selection Battery

JOHN E. HINKLE, JR.

The discussion in this chapter focuses on the rationale for selecting a national core battery of psychometric instruments and inventories designed to provide information for use in selection and nurture processes in a particular denominational context. A description of the foreground, context, feasibility, and decision making process is included. A "real world" case study approach to the selection of the test battery, in contrast to "arm chair" or theoretical approaches, will be used, though theory is of considerable interest as the discussion sets forth an analysis of the context and provides a rationale for the decisions.

Foreground

Need for the identification and development of the specific test battery in focus here occurred in the context of personnel selection and nurture decisions in a major mainline Protestant denomination (The United Methodist Church). The denomination under scrutiny has an ecclesiology and consequent polity that involve clergy in a personnel management system that is itinerant, appointed, and tenured.

Denominational clergy must be prepared to itinerate in this personnel system. That is, clergy must be prepared to move from one location to another, to serve a variety of congregations in a variety of communities. Clergy are directed to engage in these moves by and through the episcopal supervisory structure in response to the pastoral needs of congregations. Clergy in this system of itineration and appointment are tenured in that the denomination obligates itself to provide a clergy member in good standing with a minimum salary (at least) appointment throughout his or her ministerial career. These three characteristics of the denominational polity (itineracy, appointment, and tenure) affect the clergy role in direct ways and provide a frame of reference for selection decisions. These three characteristics of the clergy role also give rise to strong pressures on the denomination to make accurate selection decisions.

The Criterion Door: Initial and Continuing "Appointability"

Selection decisions are affected by the structures and personnel involved in the decision making process. For example, those who make the selections are themselves clergy from within the system—that is, selection decisions are made by authorized clergy through a majority vote in a committee and board structure within the basic administrative unit in the larger denominational system. Selection decisions apply only to application to the denomination through the particular administrative unit within which the application is lodged. Candidates not accepted in one unit may move to another administrative unit within the denomination and make a second application. Thus the selection decision is made by clergy from within the system concerning clergy candidates who are making application for ministry within their particular administrative unit.

The criterion "door" thus involves the assumption that a candidate will be able to "do" parish ministry with sufficient flexibility and effectiveness in that administrative unit. Having flexibility and effectiveness typically means that selectors who are themselves clergy in the same administrative unit would be comfortable with the prospect of "following the candidate" in a parish, working with her or him as a colleague, or supervising his or her parish work in managerial structures. Additionally, the selection decision relates not only to the perceived characteristics and competencies of the candidate, and the "goodness of fit" with "appointability over time" in that administrative unit, but also to the perceived needs for clergy personnel in the unit in which the application is lodged as perceived by the selectors.

The National Level

The articulation of this general frame of reference provides a context within which psychological assessment of applicants for clergy careers in this denomination takes on a particular, as well as a general, significance. In terms of the particular frame of reference, as noted above, a given selection decision is made not so much with regard to ministry in general. It is, rather, a decision based on estimates of the candidate's capacity for functioning in parish ministry in a particular administrative unit in the company of a particular group of clergy in a particular denomination on the basis of perceived personnel needs at any given time. Nevertheless the underlying general frame of reference, involving considerations of appointability, itineracy, and tenure, is in focus with minor variation throughout the denomination. Hence a coherent and relevant set of criteria (the "criterion door") for selection decisions would appear to be feasible at the national level, based on these structural and functional commonalities (see chap. 12), with variations occurring across units in terms of personnel needs in the unit, the "fit" or match between applicants' gifts and skills and the context of need, and the particular set of applicants available at a given point in time.

Beyond the essential feasibility of a "criterion door" at the national level, with variations at the level of local administrative units, is the fact that this particular set of circumstances puts pressure on those who make the selections. This pressure is felt in terms of (1) the length of time the person may be in ministry—tenure, persistence, and survival—(2) variable placement needs—itineracy and the need for flexibility—and (3) a willingness to go where one is sent—appointment and the need for commitment to the system. These three notions are typically summed up in the phrase "appointability over time." Given these factors, it is not surprising to discover that the denomination has developed a set of criteria for ordination to full time professional ministry (*Handbook*, 1988).

Given the "weightiness" of the selection decision as a consequence of the foregoing factors, the pressure (anxiety) experienced by selection committee members on a recurring (at least annual) basis, along with both the emphasis on selection by majority vote and the "lay" status of clergy as personnel officers, expert consultation is frequently sought and is often needed. Since psychologists are perceived as experts in the assessment of human personality, they are frequently retained as consultants in the personnel selection processes within the denominational structures.

Denominational Utilization

Personnel selection and nurture decisions are being made on an annual basis in each of the seventy-four administrative units of the denomination. Well over two-thirds of those units currently use psychological consultation in their selection decisions on either a regular or an occasional basis. The foregoing discussion has presented the factors that make such an effort feasible.

Rationale for a National Standard Core Battery

The possibility of establishing a national standard core battery for this denomination existed due to structural and functional commonalities, as noted above. Several additional reasons for establishing a national standard core battery of instruments may be articulated. Foremost among those is the issue of quality control. Psychological consultants come in a variety of shapes and sizes, professionally speaking. Since each administrative unit in the denomination is free to select whomever it will as a psychological consultant, the psychologist who is selected to be the consultant in a given instance is typically known to some of the selection committee members through prior contacts. Relationships of trust are essential to such choices, and the choice from among available consultants is frequently made on the basis of prior relationship rather than in terms of an objective comparative review of credentials, education, and current skill level. One consequence of this situation is the need for quality control of psychological consultation and the standardization of procedures that would contribute to that end.

The concern for a high standard of quality in psychological assessment procedures and the consequent reports to selectors, and feedback interviews to candidates arise from a number of factors in addition to those inherent in the tendency to choose a psychologist known to the board. One of those factors is the variability of training among psychologists, many of whom have not been specifically trained in personnel selection. Psychologists contribute to the dilemma of marginal quality when they have not bothered to become expert in personnel selection, but simply transpose assessment of psychopathology from the clinic model onto a personnel selection process.

Another threat to quality is the reality that religious judicatories typically underestimate the complexity and cost of such assessments. Hence judicatories often get little by way of psychological assessment because they are willing to pay so little. On the other hand, the psychological consultant often faces the dilemma of having to volunteer time if the assessment is to be adequate, or do a "quick and dirty" assessment that may (or may not) be better than no assessment at all due to limited budgets. These and other such dilemmas point to the need for quality control of psychological assessment and consultation in personnel selection decisions for clergy candidates.

This chapter focuses on the identification and use of a standard core battery of assessment instruments, with training and orientation in the use of such instruments, as one approach to quality control. Additional features of such a program are the development of role appropriate criteria; population appropriate norms; the identification of professional training and credentials for consultants; and clear specification regarding program, procedure, and policy. Each plays a part in a comprehensive program of quality control and standardization.

The National Process

An event that marks the beginning of efforts to obtain a clear view of the larger (national) picture of psychological assessment within the denomination occurred in 1978 (Jones, 1980). The denomination sponsored a national-level consultation consisting of eighty judicatory officials and psychological, as well as clinical pastoral, consultants to identify and discuss problems and concerns in obtaining and providing expert consultation for the selection process. This consultation identified a set of specific problems to be addressed and elected a national task force to develop potential solutions to those problems. One of the problems to be addressed was the standardization of psychological assessment instruments and procedures.

Surveying Instrument Utilization

The national task force conducted a survey of current practice among psychological consultants within the denominational system in late 1978 (DeWire, 1978). Results indicated that thirty-nine of the fifty-two reporting administrative units were using psychological testing as a part of the selection process. Findings from the 1978 survey, specific to psychological instruments, indicated that certain instruments were being used more frequently than others. Adjustment inventories, interest inventories, and measures of intelligence or academic performance comprised the types of instruments being used in the thirty-nine units using psychological testing.

The breakdown of most used instruments from survey results is as follows. Thirty of the thirty-nine

psychological consultants were using the Minnesota Multiphasic Personality Inventory (MMPI). Fifteen were employing the Edwards Personal Preference Inventory, and a few were using either the Myers-Briggs (6) or the 16PF (5). Given these results from the initial survey of current practice (circa 1978), the hypothesis was developed that identification of a national standard core battery of instruments would be feasible from the perspective of current use.

Feasibility

The potential feasibility of establishing a national standard core battery of instruments from the perspective of the psychological pastoral evaluators was based on the following assumptions and conclusions. First, as the survey results indicated, numbers of psychological consultants had demonstrated a high degree of consistency of choice in their independently chosen set of instruments (DeWire, 1978). For example, thirty out of thirty-nine clinicians were using the MMPI, and half (19) were employing the Strong Campbell Interest Inventory. Second, the assumption was made that the psychological assessors who had made these choices of instruments did so on the basis of a perceived relevance between the data generated by these instruments and the selection decisions to be made—that is, the instruments were perceived to be criteria relevant. Third, while instruments themselves may (should and do) have a demonstrated validity, a major variable in enhancing or decreasing that validity is the instrument-clinician interaction, hence the need to respect prior instrumentation choices by the psychologists for technical, as well as practical, reasons.

Instrument-Clinician Interaction

Many factors are contained within the instrument-clinician interaction variable. Among them are the clinician's training and orientation with reference to a specific instrument, level of experience in using the instrument, familiarity with the instrument's application to a particular population, biases and problems present in the instrument, and the like. These and other such factors suggest that the validity of the instrument needs to be supplemented with the notion of validating the instrument in the hands of a specific clinician. A clinician needs to validate his or her skill with each instrument and with a battery of instruments. Given the fact that these instruments were already in use by the psychologists, it was assumed that the instrument-clinician variable would produce higher validities with some of the instruments currently in use than would be the case if the clinician had little or no previous experience with or interest in an alternate set of instruments.

Finally, it was concluded that the likelihood of being able to convince psychologists to use a different set of instruments than those already chosen was rather limited. At the same time, it was recognized that those consultants not already employing the instruments to be included in a national standard core battery would need to begin the task of learning to work with new instruments.

Strategy

In view of the need to address the foregoing issues, a decision was made by the national task force to invite psychological assessment professionals who were already working within the denominational system to participate in regional workshops in which their views could be heard as input into the final decisions about the core battery and where they could become better informed about the dialogue that was taking place. The thought was that face-to-face interaction among professionals, using a consensus decision model on matters related to the national standard core battery, would be a more effective course of action than decision making by the task force in the absence of such conversations. As a consequence of this judgment, the national task force decided to conduct regional workshops for psychological assessors, designed to provide dialogue about and orientation to the concept of a national standard core battery of assessment instruments (see chap. 9 of this volume).

Additionally, since the results of the DeWire study (1978) had indicated that the MMPI was the leading candidate for a personality inventory to be included in a standard battery, it was decided to retain a consultant for the workshop process who had expertise in the use of the MMPI for personnel selection. In addition to the introduction of a specialized scoring system for the MMPI, the consultant led discussions on the identification of criterion related traits. Thirty-six such traits were identified. Subsequently, an MMPI scoring system that rates candidates on those thirty-six traits was produced by using clusters of MMPI scales that measure the traits, normed to the population (Connolly and Hinkle, 1979). The list of traits so measured was first developed in these workshops by the psychologists who were present and participating.

Regional Workshops for Assessment Professionals

Regional workshops were conducted by the national task force in 1978 through 1979, as is detailed in chapter 9 of this volume. Meetings were held in Chicago, Atlanta, Dallas, San Francisco, and Philadelphia. Psychological and clinical pastoral assessors met in sessions designed to explore the feasibility of identifying a national standard core battery of instruments in a face-to-face dialogical format. Approximately fifty psychological and pastoral evaluators participated in these workshops.

Results of the workshops included articulation of contextual concerns as well as identification of a standard core battery of instruments. For example, participants worked on the development of a philosophy of psychological assessment as related to the denominational personnel selection process, establishment of minimum requirements for programs of psychological assessment in the denomination, identification of areas to be assessed, definition of minimum requirements for a data collection packet, and the specification of instruments to be included in a national core battery (see chap. 9; Hinkle, 1988).

Time Lines

The decisions summarized and recorded in the text above concerning the national standard core test battery were made over a period of three years (1978–81) in a dialogical process involving both the vast majority of assessment professionals who were delivering consulting services and reports in this system and the members of the national task force who were working on this project. But a thoroughgoing implementation of the national standard core battery of instrumentation awaited the development of a central office for the administration and scoring of the inventories.

A National System of Psychological Assessment

The implementation of a national system of psychological assessment of candidates for ordained ministry within the denomination occurred in 1986. The program was first piloted in one administrative unit (Spring 1986) and was then made available to all units on a first-come-first-served basis in June of 1987. During the first program year, over 25 percent of the basic administrative units in the denomination began using the national system, including the use of the standard core battery of inventories. During the second year of operation, additional units were added. Estimates are that 50 percent of the denomination's basic administrative units will be using the system by 1990, with most of the remainder joining in by 1992.

19

Structured Assessment Interviewing

CHARLES R. RIDLEY

There are a variety of procedures and methods that can be used in selection decision making. Interviewing is one method that is employed almost universally. Interviews often provide information that otherwise is inaccessible by other methods. In fact, interview data are the most commonly used predictors in selection decision making (Wexley and Yukl, 1984).

Despite the wide use of interviewing, its actual usefulness is limited for the following reasons. Interview content rarely matches job specifications. Interviewers have personal biases and stereotypes. Interviewers differentially evaluate biographical data. Interviewers are more influenced by negative information than by positive information. Evaluations of interviewees can be affected by evaluations of prior interviewees. Ethnic and cultural differences influence evaluations. More favorable evaluations are typically given to men than to women (unless it is a "female job"), younger than to older, attractive than to unattractive, taller than to shorter, non-handicapped than to handicapped, and verbal than less verbal interviewees.

In the light of these seemingly endless forms of bias, there is a need to maximize the quality of interviews. Generally, the research supports structured interviewing as being more helpful than unstructured interviewing (Arvey and Campion, 1982). In this chapter, I will discuss structured assessment interviewing with a view toward clarifying its role in selection, its basic characteristics, and its essential techniques.

The Role of the Selection Interview

The word *interview* is derived from the French word *entrevoir,* meaning to glimpse or see imperfectly. Every interview, regardless of the interviewer's competence, involves a perception of the candidate that is less than perfect. There are many obstacles that could make the view of the candidate hazy and imperfect. Essentially, the odds are stacked against effective interviewing unless an informed and skilled approach is undertaken.

Despite the potential pitfalls and hazards, effective interviewing is still possible. Effective interviews, though imperfect, minimize evaluation bias and maximize the opportunities to select good candidates. The interview glimpse of the candidate may not be perfect, but the glimpse can be considerably more clear than the view observed in the typical interview. How? First, have a clear purpose in mind for interviewing, and second, use the appropriate techniques to fulfill that purpose.

The primary purpose of the structured assessment interview is to obtain *reliable* and *valid* information from which to predict the future performance of an interviewee. Reliable information is both accurate and dependable. Structured interviewing is based on the theory of behavioral consistency: the best predictor of future behavior is past behavior. Therefore, the focus of interviewing should be on obtaining information about behavior that occurs repeatedly.

Consider punctuality as a critical behavior for a job. Predictably, the person who is consistently tardy will not be successful in that job. Thus the interviewer should gather the necessary information to make a judgment about the candidate's punctuality behavior. The interest of the interviewer is on ascertaining the consistency and repeatability of the candidate's punctuality. Reliable information answers the question: "Is the candidate typically on time, early, or late?"

Valid information, on the other hand, is useful. It concerns the relevance of behavior to the nature of the job. Irrelevant behavior is not useful and, therefore, invalid for this purpose. Using the previous example, punctuality may be useful (valid) to the work of fire fighters. It may be unimportant (invalid) to the work of door-to-door salespersons for whom pressured deadlines are not critical for success on the job. Valid information answers the question: "Will punctuality bear any significance on the candidate's success or failure on the job?"

The interviewer obviously will want to obtain

behavioral data that is both reliable and valid. However, it is possible to obtain information that is reliable but not valid. Why? Reliability, or confidence that one is measuring behavior that persists over time, is a necessary condition for validity. Valid information is always reliable. A skilled interviewer understands the difference between reliability and validity. The primary goal of interviewing, then, is to gather behavioral information that is predictive and relevant to the job under consideration.

In addition to information gathering, the selection interview has a secondary function. The interview should lay a foundation for a continued relationship beyond the interview (Bassett, 1965). In many cases, the candidate may work directly under the interviewer, such as in a supervisor-supervisee relationship. In other cases, the candidate may have an indirect reporting relationship with the interviewer. Both types of relationships would fit within the larger denominational or organizational structure. Even in cases where a no-hire decision is made, the interviewer should usually follow up with the candidate, providing feedback regarding the results of the interview process.

Characteristics of Effective Interviews

Effective interviews have seven essential characteristics (Ridley, 1988). These characteristics are present in every quality interview and operate similarly to the various instruments in an orchestra. Singularly, each instrument produces a unique sound and makes a contribution that is different from the other instruments. Collectively, the sounds of the different instruments blend together to make a harmonious whole.

Like an orchestra, each characteristic of an interview plays a special role in achieving the purpose of good information gathering. One characteristic cannot be a substitute for others. At the same time, the ultimate purpose of the interview can only be achieved if all of these characteristics blend together.

1. Control. The word *control* often takes on a negative connotation. It is often used to mean manipulation, domination or Machiavellianism. Yet, the use of the term *control* also has a positive meaning. This is clearly its connotation in interviewing. Control is actually the most important interview characteristic. All other characteristics depend on it.

To control is to direct or guide the course of discussion between interviewer and interviewee. The interviewer should know in advance the type of information needed to make an informed decision about the candidate. Then, the interviewer directs or orchestrates the interview to obtain that information. Used in this manner, control is similar to the actions of a captain who navigates a ship in the open waters. Without the captain's control, the course of the ship would easily veer off course and fail to reach its destination. Similarly, uncontrolled interviews do not reach their destination in terms of the type of information gathered. Control ensures that all important areas of the applicant's background are covered systematically.

Control is maintained in a couple of ways. First, the interviewer prevents the candidate from rambling. A great deal of information about the candidate must be gathered in a relatively short period of time. The interview should be approached as though this will be the only opportunity to "size up" the candidate. Even when follow-up interviews are scheduled, the interviewer should use time efficiently.

Second, the interviewer encourages the candidate to provide adequate behavioral descriptions. This is the opposite problem of rambling. Some people are reticent in temperament, while other people become intimidated in the interview. In either case, the interviewer needs to draw out the candidate.

2. Completeness. This means that the interview covers all of the relevant behavioral dimensions. Behaviors predicted for successful job performance should be predetermined, usually through a job analysis (Cascio, 1982). For example, Ridley (1988) determined thirteen necessary behaviors.

The complete interview obtains behavioral data about the candidate in each relevant performance area without exception. It is not good enough to cover only one-half or even three-fourths of the dimensions. A candidate could get high ratings on many dimensions, yet make a poor choice for selection. Initially, the candidate may appear attractive, but a low rating on one or two critical dimensions would disqualify the candidate.

Consider a candidate for the job of college basketball coach. The candidate rates high on motivating players, teaching fundamental skills, creating a cooperative team attitude, and having a good won/lost record. But the coach should be rated low on integrity because of a tendency to violate collegiate recruiting regulations. The coach should be an unacceptable hire, despite high performance on many dimensions.

Incomplete interviews fail to gather information across all relevant performance dimensions. One reason is that interviewers sometimes become intrigued with a candidate in one or two areas. As a result, they prematurely arrive at a decision about the candidate based on limited data. This error in evaluation is the "halo effect."

Another reason for incomplete data gathering is the interviewer's lack of control. The interviewee may ramble at length, leaving little time to explore the remaining behavioral categories. Skillful interviewers pace the interview.

A third reason for incompleteness is an emphasis on gathering useless (invalid) information. There are two types. One is superfluous information, which is obtained when the interviewee is encouraged to provide more than enough behavioral descriptions needed to rate adequately the candidate on a performance dimension. The candidate goes beyond reasonable descriptions, despite the relevance of the behavioral data.

The other type is irrelevant information. This is information that is unrelated to the performance dimension. An interviewer may gather reliable (predictive) behavior information that is nevertheless useless. The information is useless because it does not predict performance from one of the predetermined behavior categories. For example, the interviewer may discover that a candidate has excellent ability to write Christian poetry. Writing poetry, however, is not predictive of success as a founding pastor where strong leadership and a vision for the future are critical performance dimensions.

3. Depth. Effective interviewers have depth. While completeness refers to the gathering of information across all relevant dimensions, depth refers to the quantity and quality of the information within each category. Deep interviews obtain the right kind and amount of information to rate each dimension fairly.

Interviewing should establish the candidate's pattern of behavior in each behavior category. An adequate threshold of information serves as the basis for a realistic rating of specific dimensions. Although too much information is unnecessary, the more usual problem is inadequate information gathering. Unskilled interviewers typically fail to get enough useful information.

Assume that leadership is an important dimension. In response to the interviewer's inquiry, the candidate reveals a long history of having leadership roles. The candidate was captain of the soccer team, student body vice-president, chair of the youth delegation at church, and president of the college fraternity. The shallow interview stops at that level of information gathering. The interviewer surmises, usually erroneously, that occupying leadership positions is equivalent to leadership effectiveness.

In the deep interview, the interviewer probes for more information in an attempt to understand the quality of leadership performance. The interviewer elicits such information as the candidate's ability to work through groups, to set realistic goals, to motivate people, to monitor delegated assignments, to develop the skills of subordinates, to handle group conflict, and to achieve group goals.

If inquiry is limited to the quantity of leadership positions held, the interviewer does not have adequate information to rate the dimension of leadership. Possibly, the candidate has an impressive personality that wins the popular vote. Upon closer examination of actual leadership behavior, the candidate is found to (1) hold onto responsibility rather than to provide opportunities for subordinates to develop themselves, (2) block creative thinking, and (3) avoid conflicts or cover them up with superficial solutions.

Depending on the depth of the interview, different ratings could be made of a candidate on the same dimension. Shallow interviews fail in obtaining enough quality data to make adequate ratings on each performance dimension. Conversely, deep interviews provide a solid foundation for the rating of performance dimensions. For the novice interviewer, it is better to obtain too much, rather than too little, data to rate candidates.

4. Flexibility. Effective interviews are flexible. This may sound like a contradiction to control, but it is not. Neither is it an endorsement of haphazard and free flowing conversation. Like any functional system, the interview must have a basic pattern and structure. Yet, the interview must be flexible enough to handle deviations from the basic pattern when in doing so the goals of interviewing are accomplished.

Although there should be a logical pattern, interviewers must avoid conducting rigid and mechanical interviews. Candidates will feel needlessly anxious and stressed. They may experience the process as impersonal without appreciation for their uniqueness. Interviewer sensitivity and spontaneity will furnish the interview with needed flexibility.

Candidates should be encouraged to tell their own stories spontaneously and fully within each behavioral category. Interviewers should interpret comments only to obtain more specific information or to guide the sequence according to the general interview plan. The most successful interviews are those in which the interviewer has little to do in maintaining the pattern. According to Fear (1978), competent interviewers do only 10 to 15 percent of the talking. Fear contends that this allows the candidate to take the center of the stage and the interviewer to analyze the import of the candidate's comments.

5. Low Threat. Effective interviews are characterized by low threat. Getting the candidate to talk during the interview is not enough. To make an accurate evaluation, candidates need to talk about their liabilities as well as their assets. This means getting candidates to discuss topics they would prefer to avoid. An interview climate is needed in which candidates feel free to discuss potentially threatening information about themselves.

A number of techniques are useful in minimizing the threat of disclosure during the interview. Appropriately applied, they can help to achieve openness and frankness. Several of these tips have been suggested by Drake (1972). Show sincere interest in the candidate's personal comfort. Ensure the confidential nature of the discussion. Engage in minimal small talk. Always respond in a nonjudgmental manner. Recognize the power of nonverbal behavior. Verbally encourage the candidate.

6. Retention. Effective interviews have a method for retaining information once it is gathered. The best interview in the world is absolutely useless unless the information gathered is retrievable after the interview for the purpose of evaluating the candidate. Retention in the interview is like having a memory bank in a computer. The information is stored up for future use.

A well-executed interview captures and retains a tremendous amount of information. Most people, though, remember a limited amount of what they hear. Psychological research has shown that information stored in short-term memory begins to fade within thirty seconds. Forgetting is a fact of life. Because of our human limitations, a system of information retention is essential to the interview process. Note-taking is a proven method of data retention. Good interviews are characterized by detailed note-taking. Interviewers should be prepared with writing utensils and paper, preferably a legal pad. They will record quantitative and qualitative behavior descriptions that help paint a rich picture of the interviewee.

7. Informative. Effective interviews are informative. Undoubtedly, the major focus of the interview should be on fact finding about the candidate. However, reasonable opportunity should be provided to address the candidate's concerns. The selection process is, or should be, a two-way decision making endeavor. While interviewers determine the candidates' suitability for a job, candidates determine their interests in the job. Both participants need vital information for sound decision making.

Candidates need information in three areas. First, they need information about job responsibilities and expectations. Included in this category are denominational and organizational matters as well. In every job, there are positive and negative features. For example, the intrinsic rewards for the entry level clergy may be

gratifying, but the extrinsic rewards may be nominal. Effective interviews present a balanced picture. Mistakenly, some interviewers overemphasize the more desirable features in an attempt to sell the candidate on the position. Other interviewers overemphasize less desirable features in an attempt to shield themselves from the later recriminations of an irate employee. Neither approach is acceptable. In either case, the candidate is presented a one-sided picture. Candidates cannot make realistic decisions on the basis of incomplete information.

Second, candidates need information about the living conditions. This area covers such concerns as cost of living, residential conditions, transportation, schooling, and recreation and cultural opportunities. The appropriate matching of these concerns often spells success or failure, regardless of the fit of the candidate with the job.

Third, candidates need to be informed about the details of the selection process. Unlike the interviewer, the candidate comes to the interview without knowing what to expect. Considerable anxiety is associated with the unknown. As a matter of courtesy, the candidate would benefit from knowing the sequencing and timing of the various phases of selection.

Interviewing Techniques

1. Prepare adequately to interview. Effective interviewing relies heavily on what the interviewer does before the interview. Preparation includes familiarizing yourself with the candidate, eliminating the possibility of interruptions, removing physical and psychological barriers, allocating enough time, and being on time for the interview.

2. Initiate and open the interview. The opening of the interview sets the stage for the ensuing discussion. During the first few moments, a relaxed climate and plan for the interview should be established. This is achieved through several steps. Greet the candidate in a friendly manner. Demonstrate interest in the candidate's personal comfort. Structure the interview with comments that outline the discussion.

3. Gather information through appropriate inquiry techniques. Begin inquiries into behavioral domains with open-ended questions or comments. Open-ended inquiry provides an opportunity for candidates to respond as fully as possible. The candidate's responses begin to paint a picture about his or her behavior. By contrast, closed-ended inquiry usually leads to a simple yes or no answer. It does not provide information about the behavior of the interviewee. In an open-ended inquiry, the interviewer might ask: "Describe a time when members of your church were divided over a sensitive issue. I want to know how you went about resolving the division." In a closed-ended inquiry, the interviewer would instead ask: "Have you ever resolved a major dispute or conflict during your ministry?"

4. Use follow-up probes to elicit further information. Follow-up probes, or exploratory questions, keep an interview on track. They also help to paint a more detailed picture of the candidate's behavior. The effective use of this technique depends on an understanding of the basic interviewing principle: The best predictor of future behavior is past behavior.

Interviewers should remember several facts in using follow-up probes. Do not ask leading questions that "telegraph" the right answer. Ask questions with a clear purpose in mind. If necessary, allow candidates to ask questions for clarification of the probe. The interviewer might ask: "How did you get the two groups to begin talking to each other? What did you say when the discussion got heated? How did you get the most vocal persons to take a more conciliatory posture?"

5. Use positive reinforcement. Positive reinforcement rewards a candidate for useful elaboration. It is a form of motivation. Reinforcement increases the probability that the interviewee will continue to provide the type of responses that are helpful for the interviewer to understand better the interviewee's behavior. To give positive reinforcement, the interviewer may say: "That's the kind of information that helps me to get a better picture of you."

6. Use minimal encouragers. Minimal encouragers are prompts to encourage candidates to talk. They share a common feature with positive reinforcement in that they can be rewarding. They are different from positive reinforcement in that (1) they often precede rather than follow the candidate's verbalization, and (2) they tend to be short phrases or behaviors. Among the common minimal encouragers are um-hmmmm, oh?, so, then, and?, for example, repetition of one or two of the client's words, one-word questions, nods of the head, and a variety of gestures and body postures (leaning forward, moving closer, and so on).

7. Use nonjudgmental reactions. To get a balanced picture, the candidates must be encouraged to reveal unfavorable as well as favorable information. Therefore, interviewers must make it as easy as possible for negative information to be discussed. If candidates have

even the slightest perception of judgmental attitudes, they are likely to turn off and avoid discussion of negative information.

Negative information must be accepted without surprise or disapproval. This includes both verbal and nonverbal reactions. At the same time, the interviewer must avoid going overboard in playing down unfavorable information. This will only show hollow insincerity. The interviewer may say something like "Most people have run into a conflict with their superior at some point during their career. I'm interested in knowing your contribution to both creating and resolving the conflict."

8. Use calculated pauses. Experienced interviewers purposely allow occasional pauses. They recognize when candidates need time to reflect before elaborating. Behaviorally-based interviewing is an atypical experience for most people. Much of the information requested has not been previously considered by the candidate. Another benefit of the pause is that it is a powerful *silent* command to continue elaboration.

Calculated pauses also assist the interviewer in listening. There are two cautions in the use of pauses: Do not use them too frequently, and do not allow them to be too lengthy. Basically, the interviewer must exercise prudence and sense the chemistry of the moment. For example, the interviewer should say: "I realize how uncommon most of my questions are, and its perfectly okay for you to take a moment to think of a good example."

9. Interject humor. Interviewing is a serious endeavor. However, a little humor can add spice to the mood. Otherwise, the candidate may experience the interview as dry and sterile. Humor should never be time consuming. It should never place the interviewer on center stage. The constant focus should be on the candidate's story. Therefore, it is probably best to create humor related to the candidate's story. The important factors are to use humor naturally and in good taste, and to use it minimally. The interviewer might say: "When you forgot to show up to make your presentation, that was one time you needed no introduction."

10. Use summary probes and pushes. One method of controlling the interview and eliciting further behavioral descriptions is to use summary probes and pushes. Sometimes, candidates are very descriptive about a situation, but minimally descriptive about their actual behavior in that situation. They elaborate more about the behavior setting than about their behavior or performance. One evidence of this is whether or not the candidate speaks in the first personal singular ("I"). The interviewer should respond by saying something like "The church, as you say, was taken off guard by the influx of Southeast Asians into the community. But it was the general consensus to help them get settled and minister to them. It was an all out team effort of the church. Tell me about your specific contributions and efforts to minister to these people."

11. Use restatements and reflections. Even when candidates describe their behavior, their descriptions may be overly vague. Vague behavioral descriptions are not helpful because interpretation of them is meaningless. By restating a candidate's comments and then using a follow-up probe, the interviewer may demonstrate the inherent vagueness of the candidate's comments. For instance, the candidate may say: "I practically ran the whole show." The interviewer should respond by saying: "You ran the show? Running the show could mean you were the boss and assigned responsibility to other people. It could also mean you did all the work without much support. Tell me what you mean by running the show."

12. Pace the interview. Effective interviews are characterized by completeness, as previously mentioned. Complete interviews cover all of the relevant performance dimensions. Incomplete interviews do not. To assure completeness, interviewers need to pace the interview. They must be constantly aware of the flow of information gathering relative to the time constraints. If they sense that the interview is falling behind, they make appropriate adjustments to accommodate gathering the full range of information. For instance, the interviewer would say: "We've used up about a third of our time. However, I sense that we are falling a little behind where we need to be. I'm going to ask that we go through our questions and answers a little more quickly."

13. Use attending behavior. Attending means to have an attentive physical and psychological presence. Attentiveness on the part of interviewers helps them to learn about the candidate. It also can contribute to the self-respect and sense of security a candidate experiences during the interview. Furthermore, attentiveness facilitates and reinforces communication. To show good attending behavior, the interviewer can do several things, such as relax physically, use varied postures, use good facial animation, and establish good eye contact.

14. Take detailed notes. Considerable controversy exists over the role of note taking in selection interviewing. Opinions range from no note taking to extensive note taking. The former argument claims that taking notes results in loss of rapport. The latter argument claims that good note taking informs decision making.

Note taking is essential. Effective interviews capture a tremendous amount of information. By not taking notes, interviewers run the risk of (1) losing information, (2) distorting information, and (3) confusing behavioral data among candidates. All of these are real threats to fair evaluation.

As mentioned earlier, retention is one of the seven key characteristics of effective interviews. Retention prevents memory loss and is best achieved through descriptive note taking.

15. Close the interview. Concluding the interview involves more than winding down the information gathering stage. It also concludes information giving. Interviews often end on a vague note, creating an uncertainty in the interviewee about the next stages in the selection process. To improve the quality of interview termination, the following suggestions are offered. Be specific in describing job expectations. Do not oversell the position. Maintain rapport with the interviewee. Inform the candidate about the next steps in the process. Follow through as promised.

A carefully structured interview procedure needs to be a major component of clergy assessment. The suggestions described in this chapter will greatly improve assessment of clergy.

20

A Systems Approach to Personnel Development in Church Ministries

THOMAS M. GRAHAM

How well an organization achieves its objectives depends, to a large extent, on the character and qualifications of its personnel. However, it is essential that the nature of the job is well defined before we can begin to assess and select candidates. Recently many church and parachurch organizations have begun to look more closely at their procedures for deployment of human resources.

The purpose of this chapter is twofold. First, the purpose is to define a systems approach to personnel deployment that is based on the organization's stated objectives and goals. Second, the purpose is to describe briefly procedures for conducting a job analysis, which is a key to effective personnel deployment.

To improve performance, reduce attrition, and meet organizational objectives, a holistic approach must be used. Assessment and selection of candidates are only one part of the whole and can only be effective as they relate to other system components. The selection of personnel, whether in North America or in another culture, can only be undertaken in the context of the objectives and goals of the organization in question. Each of these components of the system is described briefly in the paragraphs that follow.

The Organization's Mission

First, an organization must have a clear statement of its purpose and mission, defining what the organization is, what it does and does not do, and why it does what it does. The mission statement is usually broken down into several major objectives that the organization hopes to achieve. These objectives must be reduced to operational goals before an effective action plan can be developed.

Developing Goals

It has been said that "goals begin behaviors; consequences maintain behaviors." The combined goals of the organization should constitute a strategic plan from which fundamental strategic decisions, specific actions, and allocation of resources will be carried out to achieve the mission of the organization. To be responsive, organizations must develop what Blanchard (1985) has called "SMART" goals that are Specific, Measurable, Attainable, Relevant, and Trackable.

Designing the Job

Plans, programs, and systems for advancing the kingdom are not self-activating. They only become actualized by people. The organization must design jobs and tasks to fulfill the action plan. The agency should be able to evaluate every job and task against clearly defined criteria to determine whether that task or job moves the church or agency toward the fulfillment of its mandate. The relationship of how one job complements another should be clear. This will help the organization in anticipating how vacancies can be filled from within the organization.

Job Analysis

Arising out of its mission statement and goals, the organization must define the jobs and tasks that must be accomplished to fulfill the mission by performing a job analysis. A job analysis provides explicit descriptions concerned with various aspects of the job. Four of these factors are described below.

The job context. What are the environmental, cross-cultural, temporal, and resource factors that have an impact on getting the job accomplished? How does one job relate to the other? To have a fully functioning team, for example, how many jobs need to be accomplished? How do they need to be performed? In what order? Are some crucial and others optional?

Job elements. What are the components of each job? For example, what are the various tasks that a church planter must do before it can be said that a church has been planted? These tasks will usually fall into groupings of related tasks, called job elements or job domains. A careful task analysis is the most crucial aspect of a job analysis. Much more will be said about this later.

Job competencies. What skills, knowledge, abilities, and gifts (SKAGs) are necessary to accomplish the job successfully? Without a clear definition of the competencies required, the qualifications tend to be too general. Usually defining job competencies is best accomplished by subject matter specialists—that is, people who know the job well.

Job specifications. What are the qualifications a person must have to perform the job effectively? Some qualifications will be directly derived from job competencies. However, other qualifications are not of the same sort. For example, requiring that a person subscribe to a particular creed or doctrinal statement might be a requirement, but it is not competency. It should also be determined whether there are entry level jobs that will allow a person to develop within the organization without being fully qualified to be selected.

Recruiting

After conducting a careful job analysis, the organization can develop a strategy for recruiting the kind of people it needs to carry out its work. There are several steps to effective recruiting.

Identify appropriate recruiting sources. Once the jobs have been defined and the qualifications candidates must possess have been identified, the organization can develop recruiting strategies. This really asks the question: Where will we find the kind of people the organization needs to perform its tasks? Developing a recruiting strategy includes publicizing the vision, its mandate, and its core values. It also means building relationships with training institutions that are likely to produce the kind of people the organization requires. It may also mean building relationships with candidates well before they are qualified and staying in touch with them during the qualification process.

Prepare realistic job previews for applicants. Traditional recruiting procedures often set initial job expectations too high. The *realistic* job preview sets expectations more accurately by clearly defining both positive and negative aspects of the job. Because candidates can more realistically assess their own capabilities, some will accept the job and some will reject it, based on this realism. When work experience tends to confirm expectations, satisfaction will be higher and attrition will be reduced.

Selection and Staffing

Having defined tasks and competencies, and having attracted a pool of candidates, selection and staffing can be meaningfully addressed. Several questions will help to structure this step. What information do we need about candidates? How can we collect reliable data in the most effective manner? How can we make decisions that have a high probability of predicting success in the most cost effective manner? Some of the important considerations in selection are discussed below.

Identify minimum qualifications. The first step is to determine the characteristics and qualifications that an individual must have to successfully perform the tasks defined in the task analysis. To do this, paramount importance will be given to the job competencies required to perform tasks.

Remove barriers to deployment of special groups. Occasionally organizations exclude qualified or qualifiable candidates because of stereotyped thinking. For example, a church organization might require a seminary education because it has been traditional to assume that it is necessary. In many cases, that is appropriate; perhaps in others it is a tradition that does not have much justification. Clearly identifying the job competencies should remove artificial restrictions on candidates.

Develop valid selection instruments and procedures. The next step is to develop procedures and instruments for collecting applicant data that accurately represent their qualifications. A process for evaluating the assessment data must also be developed that will aid placement personnel in making predictions regarding which applicants are best suited for jobs. Every hiring and placement decision is a prediction—based on prior data—that the individual will perform a task adequately. Without clearly specified criteria for effective performance, predictions can not be validated.

Performance standards and performance indicators must be identified before the validation process can be completed. Without validation, the selection process remains no more than an unconfirmed guess, even though it might be a well educated guess. To conduct validation of the selection process will require a commitment on the part of the agency that it is going to systematically collect performance data and statistically correlate it with selection variables. Even though this is difficult, it is the only way in the long run to improve continually the selection process.

Only after an organization has carefully defined the job elements, job qualifications, and performance standards can an effective and valid selection procedure be established. A continuing review of job requirements must be undertaken periodically to ensure that the organization remains responsive to its mission and to the people it serves.

Appraising Performance

Identify critical job elements. While there are many tasks to perform, those that are more crucial need to be identified and the tasks prioritized.

Develop performance standards and identify performance indicators. Performance standards have to do with the level of excellence with which the job elements are performed. Members of the agency need to know what a job well done looks like if they are to emulate it. Training programs should be constructed to develop specific skill levels in various competencies. The selection qualifications must be validated against performance standards.

Managing Performance

Establish procedures for regular feedback on performance to everyone in the agency. Accountability is essential. We need to be accountable in doing the work of the ministry as well as in the conduct of our daily lives. There have been untold casualties because accountability was too loosely observed. Further, we sometimes assume that those in ministry receive all of the affirmation they need simply because they are doing the Lord's work. Although the ministry carries its own intrinsic reward, all persons profit from being positively affirmed by others when we have done a good job. Develop effective, constructive procedures for affirmation, discipline, and termination.

Get everyone involved in goal setting and thinking innovatively. Build in a provision for added training and restructure the job as needed. Keep the organization horizontal and lean. Create an environment for empowering people.

Measuring Results

The totality of the goals of the organization should constitute a plan that provides the framework from which fundamental strategic decisions, specific actions, and allocation of resources will be carried out to achieve the mission of the organization. Periodic evaluation of how well goals are being attained allows the organization to increase system proficiency at whatever point it might be necessary. This might be revision, clarification, or improvement of any of the system components.

Conducting a Job Analysis

Conducting job analyses is a crucial step for an organization to perform as it seeks to translate its vision or objectives into a realistic action plan for meeting its goals. In conducting a job analysis, Gael (1983) notes that a distinction must be made between (1) information pertaining to the work itself and (2) information associated with, but not directly involved in, the work itself.

Gael (1983, pp. 9-10) distinguishes among tasks, functions, and jobs. A *task* is a discrete organized unit of work. Terry and Evans (1973) provide itemized definitions of the term *task*. A *function* (or domain) is a broad subdivision of a job composed of a group of tasks that are somewhat related because of the nature of the work or the behavior involved. The two types of functions are supervisory (organizing, planning, directing, developing, and so on) and direct work (maintaining, repairing, operating, and so on). The *job* is an amalgam of functions performed by individual employees.

The task is the fundamental unit in conducting a job analysis. Job analyses are generally conducted by observing individuals on the job, by doing a content analysis of written materials about a job (job descriptions, training materials, and so on), by interviewing persons who hold the job or by using questionnaires given to job incumbents and supervisors.

The primary requirement is that all of the tasks that are integral to a particular job must be identified and assigned to job functions. In our work we have generally used experts to generate the tasks and functions involved in the job. Subject matter experts (SMEs) include those performing the job, those who supervise the job, and others who have direct knowledge of how the job should be performed and what the performance standards are.

Writing Task Statements

Following Gael's approach, a task statement contains these four elements: (1) A unit of work, (2) performed by a specific individual, (3) with a definite beginning and end, (4) which results in a product or service. A task statement is a simple sentence with an action verb, an immediate object, and any qualifying information needed (how, why, where, when, how much). Passive and "process" verbs should be avoided.

Next Steps

Based on the job analysis, written descriptions of job content and requirements should be prepared. In particular, the job requirements will focus on minimum qualifications as well as the identification of competencies needed for successful performance in the job. Performance standards and performance indicators must then be identified and valid selection procedures must be established. In addition, training modules can be more specifically defined, performance evaluation more constructively devised, and measurable outcomes determined.

Whether applied to established parish ministries, planters of new churches, or missionary settings, a systems approach to the personnel selection issues raised by clergy and clergy candidate assessment is essential.

21

Self-evaluation Through Relational Experience:

A C.P.E. Perspective*

JOHN PATTON

In order to apply a Clinical Pastoral Education (C.P.E.) perspective on the issue of clergy assessment, I will begin with a somewhat detailed presentation of the assumptions and methods of the clinical pastoral process and then move to their implications for assessment apart from C.P.E. The thesis of the chapter is that a clergy candidate's self-assessment in the context of a relationship to a skilled pastoral interviewer provides the most useful type of data for the assessment process.

Clinical Pastoral Education is both as an assessment process itself and a contributor to the philosophy and method of pastoral assessment. As such, it can best be understood as the gathering and interpreting of data from three primary relationships: those with authorities, those with peers, and those with persons for whom one is functioning in an authority role. The assessment process takes place within these relationships and in reflection upon them. The most significant part of the process is the candidate's or student's own self-assessment made in the light of consultation from the supervisor, from peers, and from those who have experienced the candidate's attempts to minister to them. The primary focus of a C.P.E. model of assessment, then, is self-evaluation based on relational experience.

C.P.E. Structure and Assumption

In this context, the essential difference between consultation and supervision is an administrative one. In pastoral *supervision*, the supervisor has ultimate responsibility for the ministry being performed and, as part of his or her professional function, is required to oversee the work of the supervisee. Thus the successful performance of the supervisee reflects upon the supervisor. In pastoral *consultation*, the consultant may be overseeing the same type of ministry—that is, chaplaincy, pastoral counseling, and so on—but he or she has no responsibility for it. The person seeking

consultation has freely chosen it and may accept or reject the consultation that has been offered. In supervision, once the supervisor and supervisee are in the supervisory structure together, supervision is not voluntary. Whereas the need for supervision is associated with the early stages of ministry or other professions, the need for consultation, both professional and personal, is lifelong.

Although it is not always recognized as such, C.P.E. is a consultative process that takes place within a supervisory structure. It is consultative because it is entered into freely by the student. This freedom of entry is an essential assumption of the process even when C.P.E. is "required" by a seminary, judicatory, or other church structure. Students who deny this assumption of free entry for themselves can abort the whole educational process. Learning from the C.P.E. experience is predicated upon the student's responsibility for choosing to be there and all the subsequent choices related to that initial one. C.P.E. attempts to encourage self-evaluation in the light of the consultation of significant others. But essential to the process is the fact that whatever consultation is offered may be rejected by the students in the process of their self-evaluation.

The administrative distinction between *consultation* and *supervision* is important both for the C.P.E. process itself and for any assessment methodology informed by it. The C.P.E. context takes place in a structure that is primarily concerned with service rather than education. The training institution's concern for education stops when education appears to conflict with service or, in the case of a for-profit corporation, when education conflicts with profitability.

C.P.E. as an educational process is ultimately consultative, dependent on the assumption of students' choosing to be there and their subsequent choices about what they will do with the consultation they receive from

*I am indebted to C.P.E. supervisors Jasper N. Keith, Jr., S.T.D., and Steven S. Ivy, Ph.D., for their valuable consultation on this article.

123

others. The tension between the supervisor/authority structure and the consultative educational process provides some of the most important learning for the student. The student is free to choose what he or she hears or learns, but at the same time, with the same persons, is required to perform certain functions and to fulfill a particular role. The way this often contradictory experience is worked out within the relational structure is the heart of the C.P.E. experience.

Self-evaluation

Methodologically, clinical pastoral education affirms the value and importance of what has happened to the student and requires him or her to recall a variety of experiences of functioning in a pastoral role and share them with supervisors and peers. Following the lead of Paul Ricoeur (1970) and in the light of recent writing in the pastoral care field (Patton, 1981; Gerkin, 1984), one could say that it is a hermeneutical process that requires the student to weigh the value of particular experiences and interpret their meaning. It is a sophisticated reenactment of the old kindergarten experience of "Show and Tell," where the child brings in something symbolic of an experience that he or she has had—such as a rock or a butterfly—shows it to the class, and tells about it.

C.P.E. offers something like that at a later period of development. After going through a formal educational experience in which authorities in the form of teachers and books are the interpreters of the way things are, the students are asked to make their own experience primary—to start with it and then look at the books. In the early 1960s, the Dutch pastoral theologian, Heija Faber (1961), viewing American C.P.E. from his European perspective, identified the following as C.P.E.'s distinctive feature:

> American clinical education tends to send students to work among the patients *without thorough training before hand* and often even without much information or preparation. This happens not only because of the belief in learning by doing, but also because the minister in his profession is not supposed to work according to the system taught him by his teacher but in line with his own personality. Being a minister does not mean applying certain techniques in certain situations, but building up relationship with people.

It is important to note Faber's emphasis on the student's learning to minister to people in line with her or his own personality. C.P.E. today, as well as in the 1950s and 1960s, calls on the student to an evaluation of his or her own work, but not as an objective phenomenon that can be examined apart from the student's own person. To be sure, other persons involved in the training process also evaluate and interpret what the student has done, but the student's self-evaluation comes first and remains the primary part of the process. Thus C.P.E. is a mode of assessment that assumes that the student's self-evaluation is more useful and important than the evaluations of others.

A Relational Model of Assessment

Assessment is relational in that it intentionally examines the student's involvement in what may be thought of as the three primary human relationships: those with authorities; those with peers; and those with persons with whom the student is functioning in an authority role. Students bring with them prior experience in dealing with these relationships, but C.P.E. examines them as they appear in the student's experience in the training center and challenges the student to relate them to the way they appeared in the previous experience.

Relationships with authority were experienced in the student's history with his or her parents and with other parent-like authorities. In the course of a student's experience in ministry within the training institution, there are relationships with doctors, nurses, administrators, and the like. How the student deals with persons in such authority positions provides valuable data for the student to examine with his or her training supervisor. How, for example, does the "put down" the student experienced from the head nurse on Unit A relate to previous experiences with women in authority or with authorities of either sex? What are the implications of the answers to these questions for the student's further ministry in dealing with senior pastors, bishops, or presbytery executives? The clinical supervisor's skill may most clearly be seen in his or her ability to engage the student in self-assessment vis-à-vis these questions.

The student has previous experience in peer relationships with siblings, school friends, other members of his or her athletic teams, and so on. They are also very much present in the training center, primarily in the form of other students in the pastoral training program. They may also be present, however, in the person of students in other training programs and other institutional staff members. How does the student work out these peer relationships and the affection, competitiveness, and cooperation that goes with them?

The student who experiences clinical pastoral education early in his or her career in ministry has less experience in being an authority for others than in being a peer and in dealing with authorities. C.P.E. can provide this experience in a relatively "safe" environment. In a typical C.P.E. experience, the student is designated as a chaplain assigned to particular units in a hospital. The need for service rendered allows the institution to give genuine responsibility to relatively untrained staff, such as student chaplains.

The Focus of C.P.E. Supervision and Consultation

The focus of individual and group supervision in clinical pastoral education is the relationship between the student's performance as a minister and the understanding of the student's person as it is emerging in the interaction of his or her role, function, and identity. This is the quest for unity between action and being, between what one is and what one does (Patton, 1983). The process goes something like the following.

The student brings into individual or group supervision a description of his or her ministry. Other students and the supervisor respond to the description of the pastoral event with comments that compare what the presenter has done with the way the group has experienced the student. How is the action in ministry consistent or inconsistent with who the student is? Certainly, there are other types of responses, such as evaluations of "how good" the act of ministry was, discussion of the psychological dynamics of the patient or student, and suggestions of better ways to minister in this kind of situation. The focus, however, as it has been indirectly taught and modeled by the supervisor, is on the relationship between what the student has revealed about himself or herself to the group and how that seems related to the pastoral event the student has shared.

That is the focus of the supervision. The way the supervisory or consultative remarks (here I am using the terms *supervision* and *consultation* synonymously and not distinguishing between them) are interpreted, however, is within the context of the three primary relationships that the group has experienced with the student or heard about as the student has shared part of his or her life story.

The event, as it was shown and told about, may have revealed the student struggling with an authority within the institutional structure. The training group members may have seen a parallel of that struggle with authority in the way the student relates to the pastoral supervisor. They will also have experienced the student's competitiveness or attempts at negotiation and cooperation with peers in the training group and compare that to something that appears in the report of the pastoral event. What the other students and the supervisor see in the student's relationships is important for the student only to the extent that he or she can use what has been

said in the process of self-evaluation. There is a an obvious analogy here to the process of psychotherapy.

C.P.E. is an ongoing process of self-assessment in relationship. The data for this assessment emerge from the observed interaction of the student's role, function, and identity in relationships with authorities and with peers, and when he or she is functioning as an authority. It is a consultative, educational process superimposed on an institutional, supervisory structure. The focus of supervision and consultation is the student's performance as minister and the understanding the student has of himself or herself as a person.

Assessment Structures Used in C.P.E. Process

The assessment structures are intended to facilitate these goals of the C.P.E. process. Some of the structures that are most commonly used are the admission interview, the contract for learning, and the midterm and final evaluations. In the early days of C.P.E., what is now called the admission interview was called the screening interview. One of the primary assumptions of the screening interview was that the C.P.E. operated on an illness and health model. Students who were too sick to benefit from it were to be screened out, and those who were judged to be good candidates were assumed to move toward greater psychological health through the process. The assumption revealed some of C.P.E.'s psychoanalytic background and bias.

The different assumptions of the admission interview, in contrast to the screening interview, grow out of C.P.E.'s being accepted as a useful part of theological education for ministry with the criteria for its success viewed more in terms of experiential knowledge than improved psychological health. Since the late 1960s, student rights have been taken more seriously, and the competence of a C.P.E. supervisor to make psychological diagnostic judgments has been appropriately questioned and restricted. The judgments may, in fact, be made but not put in writing and made a part of the student's record. Changes across time are also taken much more seriously. Written evaluations that are more than three years old are routinely destroyed because the interpretations in them are unlikely to be accurate appraisals of where the student is at the present time.

In the current C.P.E. process, the admission interview, which is based on the student's application and the interview process, is intended to be a "base line" assessment that is used to communicate to the student how the supervisor understands him or her as a person and what some of the issues relevant for becoming a minister may be. The supervisor is required by the Association for Clinical Pastoral Education (A.C.P.E.)

standards to distinguish "between factual information and the interviewer's observations, conclusions, interpretations and recommendations," and the applicant is invited "to seek clarification, make a written response, or request a new interview with another interviewer" if he or she wishes to do so. Most important in the standards for this process is the reminder to the interviewer that "written and verbal feedback by the interviewer to the applicant should be given with pastoral discretion since no contract for an ongoing relationship necessarily exists between the interviewer and applicant" (Association for Clinical Pastoral Education, 1987).

The contract for learning has become an important tool in facilitating the student's self-evaluation and total educational process. Most important to remember is that the contract assumes that the student has freely chosen to become involved in the training process. It has a variety of forms, but a typical "contract" might look like the following:

1. Objectives (hopes, goals, dreams, needs).
2. How do you want to utilize peers, supervisor, staff, your history, development, and education?
3. What other resources might you employ?
4. How do you want to discipline yourself, be held accountable, evaluate/assess your learning?
5. To whom/where is a report of your C.P.E. to be filed?

Note that the student's responsibility for self-evaluation is specifically stated at the beginning of the training process.

The structure for the midterm and final evaluations is similar. At midterm, students are asked to restate their learning contract, evaluate their use of it, and reflect upon their growth or lack of it in their practice of ministry, in pastoral identity, and in personal identity in the light of the learning contract. They are asked, further, to evaluate the ways they have interacted with their peers and their supervisor.

In the final evaluation, the students are asked to repeat what they have done at midterm and in addition to describe the attitudes, values, and conceptions they carry that are most important for their ministry. They are also asked for a general statement on how they see themselves in relationship as well as giving, as they did before, specific descriptions of their relationships to the significant persons in the training process.

There are other important dimensions of the final evaluation, having to do with the learning of pastoral care and pastoral theology, relation to the training institution, and so on. My concern here, however, has been to illustrate these evaluation structures as facilita-

tive of the C.P.E. process of student self-evaluation in relationship and in consultation with peers, patients, and supervisor.

The Pastoral Dimension of the C.P.E. Process

A final part of this description of Clinical Pastoral Education as an assessment process has to do with its pastoral dimension. Although there have been different meanings of the term *pastoral* in different religious traditions, two have been primary. The first is the administrative, or social, meaning. As in the Old Testament image of the shepherd, further developed with respect to ministry in the New Testament, it involves the shepherd's responsibility for the whole flock of sheep. Pastoral care is the oversight of all in the flock or fold and all that is done to strengthen that group. Thus the pastor of the church or parish in some traditions has been only the senior pastor, the one who was over all.

The more familiar meaning of the term *pastoral* has to do with the lost sheep. Jesus' call to his disciples in Matthew 10 to minister to the "lost sheep of Israel" and the affirmation of his own vocation in terms of the words of Isaiah, "to proclaim release to the captives" express this more familiar meaning. Within the C.P.E. context, both meanings are important. Because the training supervisor also has important administrative duties, individual students cannot claim the supervisor's primary attention. They must place their wants and needs in relation to the supervisor's institutional responsibilities.

Given that important limit, however, they can expect to learn something of the meaning of the term *pastoral* from their relationship to the supervisor. The relationship is not just a teaching-learning relationship. It is a caring one, and one of the most important models students may use in discerning which relationships can be trusted in their ministries.

From the pastoral dimension of the C.P.E. experience, the student can learn the importance of both being a pastor and having one. A C.P.E. supervisor colleague of mine has insisted over the years that the most important thing we can help students to learn is that they are hungry and will be hungry (for relationship) the rest of their lives. It is within the context of a trusting relationship that the students can begin to give honest self-evaluations of themselves to themselves and others.

The C.P.E. Perspective on Clergy Assessment in Other Contexts

In the light of this somewhat lengthy description of clinical pastoral education, its process, focus, and relationships, there are implications of this perspective for assessment in contexts other than C.P.E. The most significant part of the assessment process is the candidate's self-assessment informed by data from three primary relationships: with authorities, with peers, and with those for whom one is an authority. C.P.E. provides contemporary examples of such data from the training experience. An assessment apart from the C.P.E. context must gather similar data from the candidate's reporting and self-evaluation in these relationships.

The first four narrative questions on the standard application for Clinical Pastoral Education give an example of the type of data gathered for use in a clinical interview. Applicants are asked to provide:

1. A reasonably full account of your life, including important events, relationships with people who have been significant to you, and the impact these events and relationships have had on your development. Describe your family of origin, your current family relationships and your educational growth dynamics.

2. A description of the development of your religious life, including events and relationships that affected your faith and currently inform your belief systems.

3. A description of the development of your work (vocation) history, including a chronological list of positions and dates.

4. An account of an incident in which you were called to help someone, including the nature of the request, your assessment of the "problem," what you did, and a summary evaluation. If you have had previous C.P.E. include this information in verbatim form.

The responses to the application questions provide a good deal of information about a student's willingness and ability to assess himself or herself. Perhaps more important, it suggests the individual's level of trust in persons with authority, the degree of positive evaluation applicants have of themselves, and the potential for learning from one's own experience. All of this is appropriate for discussion and for use in the written evaluation of the interview and application materials, with the consultation of the applicant emphasized as a key feature.

In conducting clinical interviews to assess clergy and missionary candidates, our pastoral counseling and C.P.E. center has developed a variation of the C.P.E. admission questions by asking specifically for a narra-tive or story response. For example, we have asked candidates to write a story about one or both of their parents that presents something typical of the family life they experienced in growing up, or about a situation of being called on to help in giving ministry to another and a story about being the recipient of ministry. Another variation is to ask the candidate to write a story about succeeding in ministry and one about a failure in ministry. A third question involves asking candidates to risk placing themselves ten years in the future by writing a story about themselves at that time.

Obviously, these questions are themselves "tests." They are like projective responses to pictures of standardized life situations in that they are ambiguous and call both for the use of the candidate's imagination in constructing a narrative and for commitment to a concrete meaning.

The way the narratives are used, however, is closer to what Ricoeur has called a "hermeneutic of restoration of meaning" rather than a "hermeneutic of suspicion." The candidate's own interpretation of the story is the evaluative focus rather than assuming that the interviewer's wisdom allows for him or her to give the *real* meaning. Moreover, the purpose of the evaluation, as stated in the written materials the candidate receives, is twofold: (1) to provide to the Board of Ordained Ministry (or comparable group) data about the candidate's relational strengths and weaknesses with respect to potential performance as an ordained minister, and (2) experience with a pastoral evaluator skilled in encouraging the candidate's self-evaluation in the context of a caring relationship. The relationship has both the administrative and the caring dimension of the pastoral role, although in just two sessions it has a limited opportunity to develop. Even with its limits, however, the relationship offers a model that the candidate may choose to experience and use in the future.

In emphasizing the importance of the candidate's self-evaluation, this interview model attempts to deemphasize the subject-object dichotomy and to emphasize peership—or at least potential peership—between the candidate and the evaluator. It emphasizes the interpersonal skills of the evaluator and deemphasizes any so-called objective knowledge of the candidate that the evaluator may gain and withhold from the candidate.

With respect to the anthropological assumptions, values, and authority dynamics that were identified earlier as a part of the assessment process, this perspective on evaluation emphasizes choice and responsibility as the central features of our humanity. It recognizes, however, a radical limitation to that humanity and a tendency to relate to others "objectively," in the sense of, "as objects." Recognizing that limit, it insists that the evaluator surrender, insofar as possible, his or her authority position and depend, as a consultant—not as a supervisor—on the candidate's self-evaluation as the primary data to be used in the evaluation. It sees the authority structure of the relationship between candidate and evaluator as inescapable because of the institutional structures within which the evaluator exists and to which the candidate petitions for status. Nevertheless, this process of evaluation values consultation over supervision and views both evaluator and candidate as being in search of a consultative or peer relationship in this and in other contexts in life.

Summary

Clinical Pastoral Education is a process that demonstrates the human need for relationship and consulta-tion, which facilitates one's evaluation and understanding of oneself and one's potential for ministry. Human beings seek to be above or below one another and tend to deny the possibility of the consultative relationship of peers. The C.P.E. experience, within the context of a service institution not too unlike the church, reveals this human tendency to deny peership—even the potential for peership—and to avoid the consultative experience either by subservience to an authority or by being one. Authority structures and supervisory relationships are a necessary part of life as it is. They cannot be avoided. The C.P.E. process and the assessment process informed by it witness to the importance of peership and self-evaluation supported by consultative relationships. Perhaps this discussion of clergy assessment and the possibility of peership can contribute to a hermeneutic of the restoration of meaning rather than a hermeneutic of suspicion in the evaluation process.

22

Report Writing for Churches and Candidates

H. Newton Malony

Report "writing" could better be called report "giving." The basic issue is whether evaluators can communicate what they know about a candidate in a manner that will be useful for the effectiveness of the church's ministry and the fulfillment of the individual. Sometimes this is done in a verbal form and sometimes in a written form, but the form of the report is less important than its content and style. Much can be lost through a confused report; much can be gained through one that is clear and understandable.

While the emphasis in this chapter will be on the written report, the importance of report "giving" in general should not be forgotten. Many written reports are accompanied by dialogue and discussion. Feedback must be judged by its effect, not its format. Walter Klopfer probably underestimated the importance of reporting when he reminded readers of "the complex interprofessional and interpersonal issues that are involved in psychological reporting. The report has been described as an important document that may be influenced by and, in turn, influences the examiner submitting the report, the referror requesting the report, and the client concerning whom the report has been written" (Klopfer, 1983, p. 501).

Keeping the complexity and importance of feedback in mind, the following aspects of giving reports will be considered: (1) why reports are needed; (2) to whom reports are directed; (3) how reports are used; (4) what data reports should include; (5) how reports should be written; and (6) what should be done with reports after decisions are made.

Why Reports Are Needed

It has been said that psychology is "organized common sense." If this is true, why are reports needed? Would it not simply suffice to observe a ministerial candidate or to discuss one's observations over a cup of coffee as one might also talk about the weather and the weekend football scores?

The answer lies in the word *organized*. While many of psychology's observations are "common sensical" and, thus, are recognizable and sharable by observant laypersons, the report of the pastoral evaluation specialist organizes them in a manner that undisciplined common sense can never do. Furthermore, because the observations of psychology are themselves "organized" in the sense that they are systematic and controlled, the report summarizes them in a manner that is not contaminated by extraneous environmental factors or personal prejudgments. Reports are necessities.

The evaluation of clergy candidates should be communicated in a fashion that facilitates meaningful decisions by both the candidate and the church. This is what reports do. Without the organized framework of psychological reports, such decisions would be significantly handicapped.

What types of decisions do reports facilitate? They are of four kinds: screening, selection, confirmation, and guidance. Typically, screening and selection have been the concerns of the church, while confirmation and guidance have been the concerns of the candidate.

The church is interested in excluding those who are unfit for ministry. This is the task of screening. The church is also interested in finding the best persons for its positions. This is selection. Candidates want to know whether they have made the right choice to enter ministry. This is confirmation. If they are not suited for ministry, candidates want advice on what career direction to take. This is guidance.

Thus any report should address these four basic concerns, and it should answer the following questions:

1. Does this candidate possess characteristics that would *disqualify* her or him from entering or remaining in ministry? (screening)
2. Does this candidate possess positive characteristics that would make him or her a good minister? (selection)

3. Can the desire of this person to enter or remain in ministry be supported? (confirmation)
4. If this person's interest cannot be confirmed, toward what career direction should he or she be encouraged? (guidance)

Although psychological reports should never be the only basis on which such questions as these are answered, such reports are integral to the process and should be done in a way that significantly influences the ways in which these decisions are made.

To Whom Reports Are Directed

When I stated that psychological reports meet screening, selection, confirmation, and guidance needs, I anticipated the answer to the question of to whom such reports are directed. They usually should be directed toward both candidates and churches.

Frequently in the past, psychological reports have been directed solely to churches. Because evaluators have considered themselves responsible only to the churches who hired them to undertake the evaluation, they have conceived of themselves as facilitating only screening and selection. Confirmation and guidance have not been routinely considered. Thus they have neglected directing their reports to the candidates themselves.

This inclination to direct reports only to those requesting the evaluation is a default decision not limited to clergy evaluators. Many personnel psychologists working in the nonreligious world have made the same mistake.

While writing reports only for employers may have been legitimate in business and industry, it has never been acceptable in the church. In the church, jobs are expendable; people are not. In the secular world, the reverse may be true. Here people may be expendable, but jobs are not. The theology of church life assumes that every person is valuable. While the talents and traits of certain persons may not suit them for pastoral work, it is the belief of the church that God intends everyone to be in ministry. Helping persons find their ministry by directing the psychological reports toward them is an essential and necessary facet of the examiner's task. Pastoral evaluation specialists should never enter into contracts in which the future ministry of individuals being evaluated does not assume equal importance with assisting the church in screening and selection.

The time has passed when reports of psychological evaluations of clergy candidates can legitimately be directed only to the churches. Candidates themselves must be included. Although such a mandate is obvious when the report is of a mid-career evaluation, it should also become the norm when a candidate is being evaluated in the beginning stages of ministry.

One would hope that directing reports toward both the organization hiring the evaluator *and* the person applying for the job would become the norm in business and industry as well as in the church. Increasingly it is becoming accepted that no adult should be evaluated without receiving feedback. All candidates should be provided a written report and afforded an interview to discuss the findings and conclusions.

How Reports Are Used

The specific ways reports are utilized in the screening, selection, confirmation, and guidance process is yet another critical concern. Reports have been used in a variety of ways.

Some church bodies have provided each member of their candidacy committee with a copy of the report. In these cases, committee members have been asked to read the report along with recommendations, supervisor critiques, background reviews, sermons, and other materials. It has been assumed that the committee members would consider the report as one of the pieces of information they used in making their decisions.

Other denominations have assigned one committee member to read the report and present a summary of it to the committee as a whole. At times, this committee member has had sole responsibility for such reports, while other committee members have assumed responsibility for summarizing other specific material on a given candidate. The committee responsible for summarizing the psychological report often consults with the pastoral evaluation specialist to clarify certain aspects of the written report. Yet another variation of this model has been for one subcommittee to take the total responsibility for submitting a complete report on all material for a given candidate.

Feedback to the candidate has also followed a variety of practices. As I noted earlier, in some cases candidates have not seen the report at all, nor have they been given any type of feedback about the evaluation. Fortunately, this practice is diminishing. In other cases, candidates have been shown the report only when the committee was seeking to justify its rejection or when it was recommending an alternative career. This practice, too, would seem to be inappropriate in the light of the concern of the church to guide its members toward compatible careers in ways that communicate respect, dignity, and affirmation of the "priesthood of all believers."

Contrary to the aforementioned practices, some

committees have two copies of the report sent to the person assigned the task of presenting the candidate to the larger committee. The report is then shared with the candidate and an agreement is reached between the committee member and the candidate regarding the conclusions to be shared. Obviously, this procedure allows the candidate to read and react to the report before she or he appears before the committee.

Another alternative has been for the evaluator to mail a copy of the report to both the candidate and the committee simultaneously. When this practice is followed, the candidate knows as much as the committee and is able to react to the report at an early stage in the process. The candidate also has the option of contacting the evaluator for further elaboration.

The ideal approach is illustrated in yet another practice. This is the practice of having the candidate interviewed by the evaluator, at which time a draft of the report is perused by both of them together prior to the report's being sent to the committee. This alternative provides for a feedback interview, plus it allows for candidate corrections and reactions to be included in the final draft of the report.

Where the evaluation is a mid-career evaluation, the above practice is always followed. Pastoral evaluation specialists of the future, it is hoped, will routinely assume some responsibility for confirmation and guidance. Where this happens, they will always share the report with the candidate. The goals of such procedures assure that candidates are able to use the report for their own development at the same time that committees are able to utilize the report in making screening and selection decisions.

Two cautions about the use of reports should be added. First, both committees and candidates should be encouraged not to overvalue the importance of reports. No evaluation is a perfect assessment of a person's total self, and all evaluations are to be reflected upon and responded to.

Second, reports differ in their value as a function of content and style. Ideally reports should be written in a manner that covers the important areas of concern and communicates findings in a manner that avoids over generalizations and jargon. Pastoral evaluation specialists should always remember that they are not evaluating mental patients. Candidates come for evaluations in relation to career decisions. They do not come for psychotherapy, nor have they agreed to a psychiatric evaluation. Candidacy evaluation is a subset of personnel and career counseling—not psychopathological assessment. Sometimes pastoral evaluators forget this distinction and give into the temptation to overpathologize the situation. It is possible for serious screening to be undertaken without overwhelming the candidate with anxiety or flooding committees with psychiatric and psychological jargon.

What a Written Report Should Include

There is a great need for evaluators to agree on the content of a written report. In reaching a consensus on this matter, a distinction should be made between manifest and latent content. The latent content of a written report is that group of concerns that the evaluator and the committee have agreed should be examined. These concerns include such areas as:

natural ministerial talents or gifts;

graces or personal pastoral style;

interests and preferences for religious activities;

motivations for a religious career;

positive past experiences in which the candidate has learned and been effective;

skills that are compatible with the task demands and stresses of pastoral work;

background knowledge of the substance of the faith.

This is a non-exhaustive list of the *latent* variables that many evaluators and committees expect to be assessed in a report. As opposed to this list of latent variables, the *manifest* content of the report includes a summary of the ways in which the latent variables have been assessed. These manifest variables include:

the interview the evaluator has had with the candidate;

the rating scales completed by persons who know the candidate;

the psychological tests administered by the evaluator;

the task demands of the role/job being evaluated;

the background history and training of the candidate;

the reaction of the candidate to simulation exercises and probing questions;

self-ratings of personality traits, personal habits, related interests, skills, and so on.

This, too, is an inexhaustive list of the means by which the evaluator attempts to assess the underlying areas of concern. They are the manifest variables that are considered in psychological reports.

The report should address the latent concerns through an assessment of the manifest procedures. It should clearly state for the reader the way the two are related. So, for example, a report might say something like "In order to assess the personality structure of the candidate, the Sixteen Personality Factor Test was administered." Such statements as this will communicate to the reader the way the means are related to ends and will diffuse the written report from an excess emphasis on such procedures as psychological tests. Tests should never be reported as ends in themselves, but should be reported as indices of more basic, latent processes. Where reports follow this pattern, readers will avoid becoming overawed by excess jargon and will be able to relate examiner procedures to more basic concerns.

Having noted that reports should address latent concerns through reports of manifest measures, evaluators should be reminded of the audience to which reports are written. As has been noted, jargon should be avoided at all cost in spite of the perennial temptation that plagues evaluators to demonstrate their prowess in these areas.

Second, reporting of "test numbers" should also be avoided. IQ scores, which have often appeared in psychological evaluations, have been overinterpreted as exact measures of ability. Errors of measurement and testing conditions have been frequently ignored, and such scores have often been accepted as concrete facts. While intelligence tests will rarely be included in candidacy evaluations, the above example is but one of the ways that test scores can be falsely interpreted. Evaluators should use their clinical skill and report "tendencies tempered by unique conditions." They should never forget the psychometric properties of their scales and their readers' persistent temptation to overly rely on scores.

How Reports Should Be Written

Prime rules for writing reports are (1) address the questions being asked by the church and the candidate; (2) tell the reader on what type of data the report is based; (3) contextualize the report within personal impressions of the candidate and special conditions of the evaluation situation; (4) integrate all data in summary statements that address screening, selection, confirmation, and guidance concerns; and (5) communicate all of this in a clear and usable style.

A model that has been found to be helpful by many evaluators follows the following outline.

1. Identifying data includes the name, address, phone number, birth date, referring agency, contact person, date of evaluation(s), and evaluative procedures utilized.

2. Background information includes a summary of personal and social history, self reports of motivations for ministry, family background, recommendation reports, work records, and support networks.

3. Test results includes conclusions gleaned from all standardized procedures used in the evaluation. While evaluators do much more than test candidates, the word *test* is an appropriate term for the part of the evaluation that is based on psychometrically standardized scales that have been demonstrated to assess important latent constructs. As noted earlier, while these conclusions should be tied to specific measures, the report should address the underlying dynamics in general terms and should not directly tie a conclusion to a test score.

4. Integrated conclusions consists of summary statements that bring together all of the observations, the intuitions from the clinical interview, the test results, the self reports, the personal history, and the recommendations of others. The evaluator should integrate the material in a way that addresses screening, selection, confirmation, and guidance questions. While evaluators should not predetermine committee decisions, they should not shy away from being firm and clear in their recommendations.

What Should Be Done with Reports After Decisions Are Made?

The final issue in report writing concerns the disposal of reports after decisions are made. Several recommendations are appropriate.

First, reports are confidential materials and should be treated as such. The rights of the candidates should not be violated, and reports should never be used in ways that have not been agreed upon by candidates before they were evaluated. While in the past persons applying for jobs were persuaded to sign away their rights as a condition for being considered, churches should be vigilant about not letting this happen in their candidacy procedures. Churches should bend over backwards in protecting the dignity and the privacy of those they evaluate for ministry. Thus it should be emphasized that it is the privilege and responsibility of the candidate to determine how the report will be disclosed and disposed of.

All candidates should sign a consent form before engaging in the evaluation. Such a form should state (a) the type of evaluation to which they are agreeing; (b) the procedures to be followed; (c) the type of report that will be made and to whom; (d) the persons who will have access to the report; (e) the obligations of the evaluator to candidates and the church; (f) the way in which the report will be duplicated, stored, disposed of, and protected; (g) the length of time covered by the consent form; and (h) the way in which candidates can stop and withdraw from the process, gain possession of all records, and, thus, guarantee their rights to privacy and confidentiality. Where these conditions are not made clear and are rigidly followed, the basic rights of persons are violated, and the church functions at a standard less than that of its secular counterparts.

Much effort should be exerted in safeguarding written reports from becoming public knowledge. This is true apart from whether the report itself was positive or negative. In every case, the report is ultimately the property of the candidate and should be treated with great care. After the Second World War, it was discovered that much intimate test material used to evaluate personnel was left in open files where anyone could access it. The standard for protection of these types of reports is much higher now than it has been in the past.

There is the possibility that church committees will be less vigilant than they should be because their membership changes and because few church bodies have established strict procedures for the storage of such sensitive material. Where, for how long, and to what possible future use these reports will be made are issues that should be made clear to candidates and strictly followed and monitored by church bodies. In cases where the reports are to be used in research, candidates should give their permission, and it should be stated how and whether identifying information is to be included. Yet, in no case should such be allowed unless the candidate agreed to it beforehand.

23

Legal and Ethical Issues in Assessment

Leila M. Foster

Potential legal liability exists in failure to conduct assessments and in improperly conducting assessments of clergy. Lawsuits against churches and church agencies were rare in the past, but now are increasing (Bassett, 1986; Brooks, 1986; Esbeck, 1986; Grissum, 1986; Malony, Needham, and Southard, 1986; and Danchi, 1987). Professional ethical responsibility also attaches to those responsible for personnel and treatment decisions involving clergy. Some of the situations in which assessment may be needed are:

1. Approving candidates for ordination or other entry into the profession.
2. Selecting employees for an entry level position in a specific organization.
3. Assigning a person to a specific kind of work.
4. Selecting a person for advancement.
5. Determining eligibility for further training.
6. Assisting a person in career development.
7. Evaluating performance on the job.
8. Deciding on fitness to remain in the profession or to return to the profession.
9. Evaluating treatment options.

Moreover, assessments may take many forms—interviews, performance evaluations, credential checking, and test batteries. A professional in charge of conducting assessments must be skilled in the selection and use of these methods. The professional must be aware of the legal and ethical duties owed to the person being evaluated as well as the person for whom the evaluation is done and the general public.

This chapter will sketch some of the broad outlines of the legal and ethical duties. Special problems involving drugs (Neal, 1988; Rothstein, 1987) and AIDS (Perkins, 1988; Pabst, 1987) testing will not be covered in order to give more attention to general principles and because the law regarding these problems is in flux. However, both types of testing have potential application in clergy assessments, and professionals in this field should be alert to the issues involved.

Liability from Failure to Conduct an Assessment

Pastor Smith was very successful with his youth program, until some of the boys complained of sexual abuse. Then it was discovered that Smith had been involved in similar activities before entering the ministry. In fact, he had a criminal record.

Reverend Doe was a great administrator. She kept the books of the church as no other minister had done. However, she was embezzling funds as she had done in secular employment as well.

Father Jones was a great hit with the youth of the church. He always planned a lot of events that young people liked—many at a distance from the church. Unfortunately, one evening the car he was driving skidded off the road, and he and some of the young people were killed. Then it was discovered that he had many driving violations in his previous assignment.

When Professor Henry was first hired by the small church college, he was well liked but seemed to be unacquainted with academic ways. When one of his colleagues became suspicious, Henry's educational history was checked. His "degree" was from a diploma mill, and his other credentials were fictional.

Would these cases involve liability of the professional responsible for checking the credentials of these clergy? It is entirely possible they would. Persons injured by the clergy employee might sue the employer, the church hierarchy, and the person responsible for assessments (Cogan, 1986; Frohlich, 1987; Silver, 1987). Could these incidents have been avoided? Possibly they could with a thorough screening program.

As a general rule, effective pre-employment screening programs should involve a review of employment

134

performance, educational history, credit and financial history, criminal history, driving history, in addition to possible screening of worker's compensation history, civil litigation, references, positive identification, residence verification, drug use, and psychological effectiveness (Baley, 1985). If an undesirable employee is not hired through the screening process, the program probably has been cost effective. Failure to make adequate assessment decisions in other contexts, such as evaluating treatment options, also has potential liability consequences.

Liability from Conducting an Assessment

That liability can arise from the way an assessment is conducted can be illustrated in this hypothetical case. Dr. Hotshot has just developed a new assessment instrument that is based on the way football games are played. He thinks that his test will be a great way to evaluate candidates for ordination, since he can then tell which persons will be competitive in seeking to win new converts. Although he has given the test to a number of his clergy friends, he has not had time to do any wide-scale evaluation of the reliability or validity of the instrument on any sample of persons seeking admission to clergy status. He sells the idea of an assessment using the Hotshot Clergy Football Inventory to the bishops of his church on the grounds that the new instrument should help them in increasing church membership. However, the bishops also are interested in good ecumenical relationships, and they find clergy who are docile easier to manage. The bishops hire Dr. Hotshot to do all their screening of candidates. Dr. Hotshot plays football fight songs during some of the testing sessions, but not in others.

When the first round of evaluations are made, it appears that the inventory has screened out a large percentage of women who have not played football and candidates from the South Pacific mission field, where American-style football is not played. Even more surprising is the failing score of Joe Touchdown, a former National Football League player, who claims that the inventory answers to questions about football strategy are all wrong.

Dr. Hotshot tells the Admissions Committee of the bishops that Sue Smith, Aku Aku, and Joe Touchdown should not be accepted for ordination. He tells the administrators of seminaries where these three are students that their scholarships should be discontinued. He also releases this information to the press in a feature article about his new inventory. He suggests that all clergy in his denomination, especially clergy employed in "for profit" operations, should be given this test. He

recommends that those failing to meet a score slightly lower than that of candidates for admission should be referred to him for therapy. He will teach them to be more combative until they are able to pass his test. Dr. Hotshot anticipates that he will have more of the older clergy referred to him for therapy since the older ones will have slowed down and lost enthusiasm for the winning of new members. Unfortunately, Dr. Hotshot did not warn anyone about M.V.P. Super, the highest scorer on his inventory, who beat up Peter Paul, the layperson responsible for evangelism in Super's church.

Dr. Hotshot finds that he is being attacked by the bishops, Sue Smith, Aku Aku, Joe Touchdown, Peter Paul, the Women's Caucus, the South Pacific Caucus, and the Senior Pastors' Association. Also, the State Licensing Commission is investigating whether Dr. Hotshot has engaged in the practice of psychology as defined by state law without being properly licensed.

In our example, Dr. Hotshot clearly violated ethical principles (American Psychological Association, 1981a, 1981b, 1981c; American Educational Research Association et al., 1985; Butcher, 1987; Joint Committee on Testing Practices, 1988). He also violated some of the legal rights of others (Byham and Spitzer, 1971; Schwitzgebel and Schwitzgebel, 1980; Bersoff, 1981; and Pope, 1988).

Has Dr. Hotshot met the obligations of a Test Developer in obtaining reliability and validity measures and in properly identifying the appropriate use of his instrument? Should Dr. Hotshot select only his own untried inventory for the assessment process? Is his scoring system appropriate? Why has he administered the test under different conditions? Should Dr. Hotshot tell the Admitting Committee and the seminary what to do? Has he breached confidentiality and defamed the failing candidates? Has he failed to warn about the dangerous potential of M.V.P. Super? Is it wise for the professional in charge of assessments to become the therapist to persons failing the assessment? Does Dr. Hotshot have the credentials needed under state law for his practice?

Care must be exercised in a discussion of the legal rights involved in clergy assessment. Legal challenges to licensing examinations in other professions may rest on attacks under Title VII of the Civil Rights Act of 1964, under the Equal Protection or Due Process clauses of the Constitution, or under the Antitrust laws (Pyburn, 1988). However, religious institutions have certain protections under the First Amendment of the Constitution and under exemptions in Title VII of the Civil Rights Act.

The extent of the Title VII exemption was recently tested in the Supreme Court case of Amos vs. Presiding

Bishops of the Church of Latter Day Saints (1987). The Civil Rights Act (1964) exemption provides:

> This subchapter shall not apply . . . to a religious corporation, association, educational institution, or society with respect to the employment of individuals of a particular religion to perform work connected with the carrying on by such corporation, association, educational institution, or society of its activities.

Until the Amos case, there was considerable uncertainty as to what activities were exempt and what was a religious and what was a secular purpose (Hill and Li, 1988; Okamoto, 1987; Lupa, 1987; Meltzer, 1986; and Taghvai, 1986). The Amos case involved employees who worked in nonprofit operations of the Mormon Church—a gymnasium and a church garment factory. The employees were fired for failure to adhere to church doctrine and codes of behavior. The Supreme Court rejected the attempt to apply the test of distinguishing religious from secular purpose in nonprofit activities of the church. However, two of the justices stated that they considered the application of the exemption to profit activities of a religious institution still open to question.

While this exemption gives considerable latitude to religious institutions to discriminate in employment matters, it does not relieve them of all liability. Improper release of confidential information, libel or defamation of character, negligence or malicious harm, or malpractice are just some of the potential situations in which suits could be filed against churches and religious personnel.

For anyone involved in assessment, it is essential to engage only in sound ethical practices. Because assessment can be practiced in so many different situations, a number of different ethical codes and guidelines apply. The "Ethical Principles of Psychologists" of the American Psychological Association (1981) cover standards of responsibility, competence, moral and legal standards, public statements, confidentiality, welfare of the consumer, professional relationships, research with human participants, and care and use of animals in addition to the following statement of Principle 8,* applicable to assessment techniques:

> In the development, publication, and utilization of psychological assessment techniques, psychologists make every effort to promote the welfare and best interests of

the client. They guard against the misuse of assessment results. They respect the client's right to know the results, the interpretations made, and the bases for their conclusions and recommendations. Psychologists make every effort to maintain the security of tests and other assessment techniques within limits of legal mandates. They strive to ensure the appropriate use of assessment techniques by others.

a. In using assessment techniques, psychologists respect the right of clients to have full explanations of the nature and purpose of the techniques in language the clients can understand, unless an explicit exception to this right has been agreed upon in advance. When the explanations are to be provided by others, psychologists establish procedures for ensuring the adequacy of these explanations.

b. Psychologists responsible for the development and standardization of psychological tests and other assessment techniques utilize established scientific procedures and observe the relevant APA standards.

c. In reporting assessment results, psychologists indicate any reservations that exist regarding validity or reliability because of the circumstances of the assessment or the inappropriateness of the norms for the person tested. Psychologists strive to ensure that the results of assessments and their interpretations are not misused by others.

d. Psychologists recognize that assessment results may become obsolete. They make every effort to avoid and prevent the misuse of obsolete measures.

e. Psychologists offering scoring and interpretation services are able to produce appropriate evidence for the validity of the programs and procedures used in arriving at interpretations. The public offering of an automated interpretation service is considered a professional-to-professional consultation. Psychologists make every effort to avoid misuse of assessment reports.

f. Psychologists do not encourage or promote the use of psychological assessment techniques by inappropriately trained or otherwise unqualified persons through teaching, sponsorship, or supervision.

The *Casebook on Ethical Principles of Psychologists* (American Psychological Association, 1987) illustrates common violations of these principles. Since inadequate or inappropriate diagnosis, testing, and assessment are a major cause of successful malpractice suits, the American Psychological Association publications contain frequent articles about issues in these areas.

Kenneth S. Pope (1988), in an article addressed to individual practitioners, emphasized the following considerations for avoiding malpractice in areas of diagnosis, assessment, and testing:

1. Awareness of Standards and Guidelines

2. Staying Within Areas of Competence

3. Understanding Measurement, Validation, and Research

---

* "Ethical Principles of Psychologists," Principle 8. *American Psychologist* 36 (June 1981): 633-38. Copyright © 1981 by the American Psychological Association. Reprinted by permission of the publisher.

4. Making Sure That the Client Understands and Consents to Testing

5. Clarifying Access to the Test Report and Raw Data

6. Following Standard Procedures for Administering Tests

7. Awareness of Basic Assumptions

8. Awareness of Assumptions in Specialty Areas

9. Awareness of Personal Factors Leading to Misusing Diagnosis

10. Awareness of Financial Factors Leading to Misusing Diagnosis

11. Awareness of Gender Effects and Cultural Influences

12. Acknowledging the Low Base Rate Phenomenon

13. Awareness of Forensic Issues

14. Attention to Potential Medical Causes

15. Awareness of Prior Records of Assessment and Treatment

16. Explicitly Indicate All Reservations Concerning Reliability and Validity

17. Staying Current

The American Psychological Association has Specialty Guidelines for the Delivery of Services by Clinical Psychologists (APA, 1981b), Specialty Guidelines for the Delivery of Services by Industrial/Organizational Psychologists (APA, 1981c), and Guidelines for Computer-Based Test and Interpretations (APA, 1986).

Standards for Educational and Psychological Testing have been adopted by the American Educational Research Association, the American Psychological Association, and the National Council on Measurement in Education (1985). In 1988, these three groups were joined by the American Association for Counseling and Development, the Association for Measurement and Evaluation in Counseling and Development, and the American Speech-Language Hearing Association in developing a Code of Fair Testing Practices in Education. This code sets forth obligations for test developers and test users in developing and selecting appropriate tests, interpreting scores, striving for fairness, and informing test takers.

Professionals involved with assessments must keep up with current issues in the field. Recently, integrity tests in pre-employment screenings have come under criticism (Bales, 1988). Failure to take account of changes in personality concepts (Kagan, 1988) and failure to pay attention to construct validity in personality tests (Hogan and Nicholson, 1988) have been challenged.

In addition to keeping up with new developments in the field of clergy assessment, such as those described in other chapters of this book, it can be useful to be aware of problems described for other professions being assessed. Extensive evaluations are done in the police and law enforcement fields. Professionals have written of the legal and ethical problems there (Ostrov, 1986; Flanagan, 1986; Coleman, 1987; and Moore and Unsinger, 1987). Often issues—such as professional responsibilities to the person ordering the assessment and the person being assessed or confidentiality of potentially damaging information—parallel the problems in the field of clergy assessment.

Practical Suggestions for Legal and Ethical Practices

If the professional involved in clergy assessments tries to maintain a legal and ethical practice in harmony with the various codes, standards, and guidelines, is there anything else the professional can do? The answer is yes. Some problems can be prevented with forethought. Other challenges can be met more easily if resources and procedures are in place to deal with them.

Situations that arise in practice are often not packaged in the neat forms that may be presented in legal precedents and ethical codes. Network connections with other professionals in the field will allow for discussion of cases that fit in a "gray zone," neither clearly right nor clearly wrong. Moreover, if a matter is litigated, consultation with others enhances the image of responsibility.

Selection of a lawyer who is knowledgeable about psychological and religious issues and with whom the professional plans an ongoing relationship is useful. When a subpoena is served on a professional, the anxiety level is likely to be high. If the professional has already established contact with a lawyer who can give specific advice, he or she will not be faced with the additional task of selecting a counselor who works with the issues of the litigation. With prior contact, the lawyer will have some idea of the professional work involved in potential disputes. The lawyer can be of help in suggesting forms, contracts, and standards to be used in the practice. Too often, professionals do not seek legal advice before they act in situations with potential liability to them. Sometimes they rely on lawyers who represent other clients, employers, or insurers when they need an attorney who is retained to protect them.

Often professionals do not give sufficient thought to the training of persons who work with them and for whom they bear a legal responsibility. Professionals within the same organization, students, secretaries, record keepers, receptionists—all these persons are in a position to engage in illegal and unethical practices that can harm. Any one of these colleagues or employees could leak confidential information that could cause great harm to a person being assessed.

In organizations consisting of more than one person, written rules and procedures can be very useful. Training sessions on legal and ethical issues that involve both the professional and the nonprofessional staffs can be productive in providing important information and establishing a setting in which the clients and their records are treated with respect. These sessions need to be repeated at least annually, especially in units where there is a turnover in personnel. If the sessions are carried on in a routine manner when there is no crisis confronting people, situations and standards can be discussed without the defensiveness that may be present when litigation is pending. New employees, students, and consultants need to be informed of legal and ethical safeguards that are in place in the setting in which they are coming to work. This training does not just happen. It needs to be planned.

The responsibilities of professionals do not end with the front door of their offices. The results of assessments are often given to persons other than the ones being assessed. The potential damage to careers and lives if the assessments are misused is great. Professionals need to help persons who have access to assessments to use them in a legal and ethical manner. Contract provisions to protect the professional from unauthorized use by others may be necessary.

Not only do issues in the treatment of persons need to be considered, but also the risks and the advantages of the paper trail left behind the assessment process need to be analyzed. What is put on paper can sometimes help and sometimes hurt the professional doing assessments when that paper is put into evidence in litigation. Issues like who gets what records and who keeps possession of the records in case of termination of employment by the professional can be thought through before the question is presented. Policies regarding how long records are retained and the safety and privacy of information need to be set.

Professionals must give attention to the business and professional relationships and to the organization of their practice in order to see that their work is in harmony with legal and ethical principles. Planning before a crisis is desirable. The "ounce of prevention" that comes from a careful analysis of what needs to be included in assessments tailored to the specific purpose of the evaluation, the attention to the legal and ethical standards when assessments are done, and the action required to be prepared for problems that may arise can provide professionals with a solid foundation for a more trouble-free practice of assessing clergy.

Gender and Cultural Issues
in Assessment

24

Culture Fair and Gender Fair Assessment

HARVEY HUNTLEY, JR.

Between 1983 and 1987, I was involved in spearheading a review of candidate psychological assessment for the Lutheran Church in America (LCA) concerning cultural and gender bias. This chapter describes procedures used in exploring issues related to culture fair and gender fair assessment, findings and recommendations that emerged from a series of consultations with respected practitioners, and some of the implications of the findings for future candidate assessment. Although this work was within a single national church body, the consultation and data collection encompassed a diverse group of experts. The results, therefore, represent a fairly broad consensus among clinicians of divergent backgrounds and should be applicable to most denominational contexts.

Background

At the time of the review, the LCA was operating its candidacy process through a system of synodical preparation committees composed of clergy and laity. The national church strongly recommended candidate assessment by an approved clinical psychologist or a church career center during the early phase of the seminary endorsement process (normally by the end of the first year in seminary).

Minimal guidelines were available from the national church pertaining to criteria for candidate assessment, the form and manner of reporting by clinicians to synodical committees, recommended instrumentation, and expectations of the church for clinical assessment (Preparation Committee, 1981). Synodical preparation committees typically utilized three key evaluative tools for granting endorsement to candidates: a report from a clinician, a structured interview by a trained interviewer from the synod (often a committee member), and personal references submitted by the candidate as part of the registration process. The clinician's report had primary impact during the early phase of candidacy,

unless the candidate did not develop a relationship with a synodical committee until late in the process—that is, near the end of seminary studies or as a transfer from another denomination. The influence of the psychological assessment diminished dramatically once the committee endorsed a candidate and became familiar with the candidate on its own. When major developmental issues were identified by a clinician, committees generally attempted over a period of time to monitor a candidate's growth and progress in that area. In a few instances the clinician's report may have been allotted inordinate influence in committee proceedings, but such tendencies were clearly the exception, not the rule.

In the early 1980s, concerns about cultural and gender bias in psychological assessments came to the attention of the Division for Professional Leadership (DPL) of the LCA. Some critics claimed that women and ethnic minorities were unfairly evaluated by clinicians and testing instruments that were insensitive to cultural and gender realities. White male candidates, it was claimed, enjoyed an unfair advantage over women and ethnic minorities in clinical assessments.

In response, I conducted a preliminary survey of knowledgeable clinicians by mail and telephone to determine whether such allegations were well founded. The information I gathered convinced me that there was reason for concern among women and ethnic minorities about clinical assessments. In a report I prepared in 1983 for the DPL Management Committee, I recommended that the division convene a consultation of clinicians representative of women and ethnic minorities to review the issue of culture and gender fairness and make recommendations for remedial action (DPL Management Committee, 1983). Due to a lack of funding at the time, the DPL Management Committee received the report as information, but took no further action. Three years later, I succeeded in procuring external funding for a serious effort to address the issue.

Project Methodology

As a result of the preliminary survey of clinicians, in late 1986 I invited a small group of carefully selected practitioners to Philadelphia for a two-day consultation on the issue of culture and gender fair assessment. Although attendance of women and ethnic persons was less than what we wanted, this first consultation prepared a preliminary report for wider dissemination among the appropriate church leaders. (The contents of the preliminary report of the December 1986 consultation are included in the findings discussed in this chapter, since the tentative conclusions of the first consultation needed to be corroborated by ethnic minority representatives at the second consultation.)

After gaining approval from a joint work group of the merging Lutheran churches to proceed with a second consultation, a more inclusive group of consultants was invited to a second meeting in April, 1987.* The objectives for the second consultation were as follows:

1. To review key factors contributing to cultural and gender bias in psychological testing and develop strategies for reducing cultural and gender bias in candidate psychological evaluations.
2. To examine the relationship between Christian theology and psychology in church candidacy processes.
3. To make tentative recommendations for candidate psychological evaluations in the Evangelical Lutheran Church in America (ELCA).

After reviewing the purpose and objectives for the meeting, updates and background information on the candidacy process being developed for the new ELCA, and recommendations formulated by the first consultation (see above), the consultation identified further issues to address. Once agreement had been reached on the issues and topics to be explored, the consultation formed into work groups on specific topics. Each work group prepared written statements on the issues assigned as well as specific recommendations to forward to the participating churches. In a closing plenary session on the second day, each small group presented its conclusions and recommendations, which the total consultation then discussed and refined.

As convener, I compiled the group statements into a final report with recommendations. A supplementary group of additional consultants who were unable to attend the April 1987 consultation reviewed the work of the larger consultation and conferred with them via a conference telephone call. All consultants then approved a final draft of the report, which was then submitted to the joint work group.

Major Findings

The consultation reached consensus on a broad range of concerns clustered into two categories: (1) perspectives on candidate assessment and (2) recommendations to the church for future praxis (Transition Work Group on Ministry, 1987).

1. Perspectives on Candidate Assessment

In response to allegations of cultural and gender bias in psychological assessment, the consultation noted claims that ethnic minority candidates in the LCA were receiving psychological assessment earlier in the candidacy process than were other candidates and were being denied ecclesiastical endorsement on the basis of such assessment. Also, according to critics, many ethnic minority candidates had dropped out because of seminary stress and other unidentified factors. Recognizing the lack of empirical verification and documentation for such claims, the consultation nevertheless basically confirmed the validity of the foregoing assertions.

The consultation further pointed out that among ethnic minority candidates, psychological assessment induces anxiety, which has an impact on their interaction during an interview. Power or authority figures often spark internal conflicts within ethnic minority persons because of their familiarity with being powerless. All such contextual factors can alter the way a candidate functions during an interview.

A critical variable in the assessment of both women and ethnic minorities, the consultation stressed, is the "quality and sensitivity of the clinicians who administer the instruments, interpret scores to candidates, interview candidates, and prepare reports" (Transition Work Group on Ministry, 1987). The relationship between the clinician and the instrument is just as significant for reliability as is the quality of the instrument itself. Accordingly, a significant corrective

*The merging churches were the Lutheran Church in America (LCA), the American Lutheran Church (ALC), and the Association of Evangelical Lutheran Churches (AELC). The joint work group was officially called the Transition Work Group on Ministry. It consisted of staff and board representatives from the LCA's Division for Professional Leadership, the Office of Support for Ministry (ALC), the Division for Theological Education and Ministry (ALC), and the AELC. Participants in the April 1987 ALC/LCA Consultation on Candidate Psychological Assessment were: Nancy Y. Arndt; Anderson J. Franklin; Joaquin Garcia; Gary Harbaugh; John Hinkle; Harvey L. Huntley, Jr.; Craig J. Lewis; Shirley Lucore; Albert Pero, Jr.; Patrick Persaud; George P. Polk, Jr.; Arthur Pressley; Thomas Pugh; Nicole Sperekas; Murphy Thomas; and Walter R. Wietzke.

for culture and gender bias in psychological instruments is the participation of a clinician of the same cultural background and/or gender as the candidate. In some instances, clinicians can bias the assessment in the opposite direction by becoming advocates for specific candidates, and such "alliance factors" need to be carefully avoided.

A further corrective to cultural and gender bias is the establishment of an approved core of instruments to be used as part of a churchwide standardized approach that provides both consistency and flexibility in providing clinicians freedom to select additional instrumentation beyond the minimal expectations of the standard core.

Due to the likelihood of both cultural and gender bias in candidate psychological assessment, the consultation took the further step of advocating regular monitoring of the *entire* candidacy process, as well as psychological assessment per se. The intent behind such oversight is to enable the church to be "proactive" in the domain of gender and cultural equity.

Finally, the consultation cited the necessity for consistent and clear criteria for candidate selection in order for clinicians to know what types of information the church is seeking. Based on the extensive experience of the participants, the consultation suggested seventeen areas of criteria as suitable for assessment (Transition Work Group on Ministry, 1987): Self-image or self-concept of the candidate vis-à-vis the role of pastor or other church occupations, interpersonal skills, personal identity, potential for professional identity, flexibility or malleability, vocational interests, motivation, coping ability and durability, maturity, self-nurture, tolerance, sense of vision, intellectual functioning and honesty, empathy and affective expression, imaginative ability, leadership style, and family relationships.

2. Recommendations

In consultation with two other churchwide agencies with specific advocacy responsibilities, the following recommendations were made. First, it was recommended that the Division for Ministry of the ELCA should create and oversee a churchwide psychological standards panel of four to eight members representative of appropriate groupings within the church and familiar with psychological issues. This panel would approve all clinicians, review and assess their written reports, and have general oversight and monitoring of candidate assessment.

In each location where psychological assessment is done, both female and ethnic minority clinicians should be available. Candidates would be free to select a psychologist from those who had been approved by the panel. In instances where allegations of gender or cultural bias arise, the churchwide panel could provide a "technical review" of the challenged assessment through the services of carefully chosen professional consultants of appropriate gender and/or cultural background. The churchwide panel would be involved as a consulting body to advise the Division for Ministry on any cases where bias has been claimed (Transition Work Group on Ministry, 1987).

Second, it was recommended that candidates would assume the initiative for scheduling their psychological assessments within the time frames established for the ELCA candidacy process. By giving candidates more control over the assessment process, the consultation was hopeful that anxiety about the timing of the process could be reduced.

Third, it was noted that clear ecclesiastical guidelines that reflect a strong sensitivity to gender and cultural concerns are needed for candidate assessment. These guidelines should address the choice, use, and interpretation of psychological instruments, interview processes, interviewers, and the structure and content of interviews. There also needs to be provision for a "second opinion" from a clinician approved by the churchwide panel at the candidate's expense. The second opinion will minimally include the core of instruments required by the churchwide panel. Normally, both reports—the original and the second opinion—will be available to the candidacy committee, but at least one such report is required for the candidate to continue in the process.

Fourth, a "core battery of assessment instruments" that are culture and gender fair and consistent with variables commonly utilized by clinicians for personnel selection should be identified by the Division for Ministry. Such instruments should be capable of measuring the following: intrapsychic structure/function, interpersonal styles and skills, self-image, intellectual functioning, coping ability and durability, psychological sources of motivation for ministry, creativity, conventionality, and vocational interests.

The recommendation further stipulated specific instruments for each of five variables: personality (the MMPI), vocational interests (SCII), intelligence quotient (Shipley-Hartford Institute of Living Scale), self-image (Tennessee Self-Concept Scale, or the Adjective Checklist), and values (Allport's Study of Values, or the Hall-Tonna Inventory of Values). As knowledge of culture and gender fair instrumentation expands or changes, the core battery could be appropriately modified. Other instruments recommended for optional use were Sixteen Personality

Factor (16PF), California Psychological Inventory (CPI), Edwards Personnel Preference Schedule (EPPS), Myers-Briggs Temperament Inventory (MBTI), Inventory of Religious Activities and Interests (IRAI), Theological School Inventory, and Profiles of Ministry.

Fifth it was noted that an "informed consent procedure" needs to be available to all candidates, detailing a theological rationale for candidate assessment, the purpose of assessment, procedures and criteria to be employed, the place of confidentiality in the process, and an explanation of how information gained through assessment will be used in the candidacy process.

Additional recommendations included the need for orientation and continuing education of clinicians with focus on cultural and gender fairness, as well as the instruments and procedures of assessment, along with continuing research. In the words of the report, "the development of reliable research data is essential for maintaining the integrity of psychological assessment that is sensitive to gender and cultural factors" (Transition Work Group on Ministry, 1987).

Some Reflections

Candidate psychological assessment is a natural target for accusations of cultural and gender bias, partly because it is a readily identifiable and highly visible part of the candidacy process in mainline denominations. Although some psychological assessment has had a white male bias, so have academic traditions and methods used in seminary education, field work supervision, written evaluations used by church bodies at the conclusion of a candidacy process, and standard interview procedures. The whole system that the churches use for candidates is suspect from the perspectives of women and ethnic minorities; therefore, the whole system needs to be analyzed, scrutinized, evaluated, and modified in the light of criteria for culture and gender fairness.

The consultation described here recognized the systemic nature of the need for culture and gender fairness. In the concluding section of its report, the consultation issued a stern warning to the church:

Of critical concern is a pervasive awareness on the part of the consultation that gender and cultural bias is *not* limited to psychological assessment. It is a factor both in the total church candidacy process and in theological education. To address such bias in only one segment of the total system in which candidates are involved is to invite dysfunction and disillusionment once candidates enter the larger system. Unless and until the church chooses to recognize and address its systemic and endemic gender and cultural biases, the implementation of the recommendations contained in this report will at best be little more than window dressing and at worst a travesty of tragic proportions. (Transition Work Group on Ministry, 1987)

To implement the foregoing concerns, it is indispensable for churches to involve women and ethnic minorities at key points in candidacy procedures, including, but certainly not limited to, psychological assessment.

Implementing the recommendations from the consultation means coping with constraints that are likely to affect the integrity and viability of the consultation's approach. A major obstacle is cost. None of the predecessor churches has made a budgetary commitment sufficient to underwrite the sophisticated and ongoing structure envisioned for establishing and monitoring culture and gender fairness. In fact, the consultation submitted no estimates of the costs that would be involved in implementing the recommendations.

Another hurdle is the logistics on a national or churchwide basis required to give candidates access to female and ethnic minority practitioners or clinicians. In the predecessor church bodies, candidates saw clinicians near their home base. The consultation recommended centering assessments in locations accessible to each of the ELCA seminaries. Significant effort could be required to locate qualified persons with the necessary gender and cultural backgrounds in each of the proposed eight locations. While not an insurmountable problem, the logistical considerations may not be nearly so facile as they might at first sound.

Consistent enforcement of standards for culture and gender fairness will also be essential for any approach to be viable. Effective monitoring of assessment procedures of the sort envisioned by the consultation will entail significant time commitments by the churchwide panel. The key to the effectiveness of any plan for culture and gender fair assessment is the commitment of the institution, in this case the church, to the goal and the willingness of the institution to allocate funds, time, and staff for implementation on an ongoing basis. Culture and gender fair assessment is an attainable goal, if the church is willing to pay the price and make the necessary effort.

In this chapter, I have identified some major findings and recommendations for culture and gender fairness in candidate assessment from the perspective of one large Protestant denomination. The findings and their implications, however, are not denominationally specific. They are applicable to any ecclesiastical system that is concerned about the issues addressed. My hope in sharing the results of the consultation is that these recommendations will receive a wider reading across denominational lines and prove to be useful in a variety of church candidacy systems.

25

Issues in the Assessment of Women

JOAN SCANLON

The psychological assessment of women as potential candidates for ministerial roles in the church of the late twentieth century is a topic that demands a sensitive exploration and critique of the questions of gender, female psychology, and the feminist critique of theology and spirituality, and a critical understanding of the sociological structures of the institution known as the church. The purpose of this chapter is to explore some of the gender related differences that must be taken into account as we go about the task and ministry of assessment of women for ministerial roles in the church.

If we are to define assessment of candidates for ministry as the ongoing discernment of vocation throughout the life cycle, then the assessment process is an introduction to a life-style of sensitively discerning God's compassionate care as it is revealed in individual lives. The call to this form of asceticism and reflection is a lifelong call that is tempered and flavored by the particular demands of the life cycle and the needs of the contemporary church. The professional involved in the assessment of candidates faces the dilemma so clearly outlined by Browning (1987, p. 2): "Will our culture be overruled and directed by our inherited religious traditions or will it increasingly gain its orientation, especially with regard to the inner life, from the modern psychologies? Or is there a way to state the appropriate relationship between these two perspectives thereby giving each its proper space?" Those who question whether women should be ordained may profit from Jewett's carefully documented study (Jewett, 1980).

The psychological assessor of ministerial candidates faces this issue in a very specific and focused form. How do we understand the limits and boundaries of the modern psychologies, and in what ways do they apply to the assessment process? A parallel issue is the adequacy of the modern psychologies and theologies to contribute to the assessment of women ministerial candidates.

The assessment of female candidates for membership in religious orders in the Roman Catholic Church presents even more challenging parameters for inquiry. Because the Roman Catholic Church has taken such a rigid and focused approach to the role of women in the church, religious communities have become subcultures that express a wide range of response, reaction, and integration of the role of women in the institutional church. The assessor must then also function as an anthropologist, assessing the cultural identity of the community and its perceived response to the role of women in the institutional church.

This response is typically formulated in constitutions and mission statements, which may range from those committing themselves to expressed loyalty to the tradition of the church to those communities whose mission statement commits the membership to challenging oppressive structures and systems as works of justice. The assessor is challenged to have some rudimentary understanding of both a psychological and a theological profile of the community that is requesting the assessment. This awareness is also necessary for assessing candidates for membership in religious orders of men, but the role of men in the Roman Catholic Church is not in question precisely because of gender.

The assessment of female candidates for ministry must take seriously the issue of gender differences because the candidate herself will be constantly confronted with the issue as she works out her commitment to a ministry and a life-style in the church. The recognition of the feminine voice in denominations that have admitted women to ordination and full participation in the administration of the church may still continue to be a critical issue, but one that is more subtly expressed. Dioceses, judicatories, and districts may all be considered subcultures that express a range of response to the acceptance and inclusion of women in the ministry. As the family therapist carefully analyzes the genogram, or family map, the psychological assessor needs to carefully analyze the emotional and sociological terrain of the receiving culture.

The psychological assessment of female ministerial

candidates must be understood as part of a more comprehensive process traditionally understood as discernment. The classic definition of discernment in the spiritual tradition is the process of determining whether one's feelings and interior dispositions are indicative of God's spirit moving in one's life. The process of discernment presupposes a commitment to the discipline of prayer, reflection, and companioning by a spiritual advisor or mentor.

The process of assessment, or evaluation, is an integral part of the life and growth of the candidate as she continues to discern her call to ministry throughout the life cycle in the context of communities of faith. This process will include different mentors, guides, and evaluators, and it will be situated in differing communities of faith as the process develops and unfolds. These turning points or marker events differ according to the system, structures, and requirements of each denomination.

The psychological assessment of female ministerial candidates can be understood as an introduction to a lifelong process of critical discernment and evaluation. The primary tools of this process include assessment through life history methodologies and the use of psychometrics. The generic goal of the psychological assessment process is to evaluate the candidate's fitness and aptitude to pursue further training, formation, and preparation for full acceptance into the ministry. Within this framework, the process must become fine tuned to relate to the particular needs of the candidate and the receiving community, district, or diocese. The tools of assessment must also be fine tuned to capture adequately and relate to the feminine experience. The exploration of gender bias in psychological instruments must be a part of the assessor's awareness as he or she uses psychometrics in the assessment process.

The use of the life history as an evaluative tool raises the issue of developmental theory and gender differences. Developmental theory provides conceptually for the inclusion of gender differences, but in practice these theories predominantly describe the male experience. The questions of gender differences and the bias of life cycle theorists have been raised by Carol Gilligan (1982), who challenges the gender biases of major developmental theorists who have constructed a masculine image that has then become normative for female development.

Freud, for example, based his theory of psychosexual development on the experiences of the male with particular emphasis on the Oedipal conflict. When the young female did not fit into the masculine patterns, he theorized that she envied that which she lacked anatomically (Gilligan, 1982, p. 6). The treatment of

moral development by Piaget concluded that little girls lack the legal sense of little boys and thus could not develop the moral judgment of the male. Kohlberg's six stages of moral development were derived empirically from a study of eighty-four boys. In this schema, women are considered to be deficient in moral judgment, generally progressing only to the third stage in a six stage sequence (Gilligan, 1982, p. 18).

Erikson's eight stages of psychosocial development have as their focal point the fifth stage of identity vs. identity diffusion. At this juncture in development, the female adolescent does not fit into the schema. Erikson claims that the sequence is different for females, but the theory of development remains unchanged to accommodate the masculine perspective. Erikson developed a theory in which the experiences of women can only be contrasted with that of men and not accommodated by the theory (Doherty, 1978, p. 9).

Gilligan concludes that the construction of masculine theories of personality development has failed to take into account the construction of reality from the feminine perspective. Further she suggests that the genesis of the feminine perspective begins in infancy and early childhood, basing her argument on the works of sociologist Nancy Chodorow.

Chodorow attributes the continuing differences between the sexes, not to anatomy, but rather to the fact that women are largely responsible for early child care and later female socialization. The context of this early socialization differs for males and females and makes a major contribution to gender difference in personality development. Because of the early mother-child relationship, girls tend to experience themselves as more continuous with and related to the external object world and differently related to the inner object world (Chodorow, 1978, p. 167). By contrast, since sons are experienced as being opposite by mothers, they are encouraged to break out of the mother-child dyad. Male development thus becomes equated with separation and individuation, while empathy and attachment are central to the female self-definition.

Gilligan (1982, p. 89) theorizes that the issues of identity and intimacy are extensions of the core issues of attachment and separation and are defining constructs for the psychology of human development. The issues of attachment and separation are the key issues in infancy. They reemerge as identity and intimacy in adolescence and are redefined as love and work in adulthood.

Although the achievement of intimacy and generativity are regarded by Erikson as the hallmark of adulthood, the studies of adult male development (Vaillant, 1977; Levinson et al., 1978) are postulated primarily in terms of achievement and individuation. The models of healthy American male achievement in both the Vaillant and the Levinson studies are characterized by interpersonal distance and lack of friendship. Relationality does not assume the importance and saliency in men's lives that it does in women's lives.

The female experience does not fit the linear, hierarchical sequence of the male model, which is organized around achievement. Theorists in female psychology argue that identity, intimacy, and generativity occur simultaneously throughout the course of life and that these developmental roots can be traced back to the socialization patterns of early childhood. In other words, who a woman is (identity) is woven together with to whom she is relating (intimacy) and for whom she is caring (generativity) (Scanlon and Zullo, 1987).

According to psychologist Ruthellen Josselson (1987, p. 26), psychology at present does not have a comprehensive theory of normal female development that would adequately encompass both the centrality of attachment and relatedness in women's lives and the multiplicity of roles and circumstances in women's worlds.

The feminist critique of developmental psychology would suggest that current models of development are inadequate for evaluating and assessing the female life history. This is not to say that existing models of assessment employing a life cycle perspective are not useful. It is to say that they must be nuanced and reinterpreted in the light of a feminist critique of developmental theory.

Just as the assessment of women ministerial candidates must take into consideration the feminist critique of psychology, it must also remain open to the contributions of feminist theology and spirituality. The major shifts expressed in the radical or secular theology of the twentieth century have been the use of psychology, evolutionary theory, and economics as resources.

This dialogue between theology and the social sciences has permitted the asking of new questions in new contexts. The timeless, traditional questions of who God is, who the Christ is, and how we should live in right relationships with God, ourselves, and others are now being asked by new sectors within the human community who are viewing the world from their own unique perspective. Theological schools, seminaries, and pulpits were formerly the domain of white males who were the exclusive "doers" of theology. As new tools were used in the study of theology (hermeneutics, anthropology, sociology, psychology), new groups of people began to raise theological questions, and new theologies emerged that took seriously the context out of which the questions arose.

Feminist theology, therefore, takes seriously the scholarship and tradition of the past, including the unspoken and unheard experience of women of the past. At the same time, it reflects, critiques, and interprets the contemporary experience of women in differing cultural contexts. Building on a feminist theology, a feminist spirituality would be the mode of relating deeply to a personal God out of the convictions that arise from a feminist consciousness. It is a spirituality that envisions a world characterized by mutuality, reciprocity, and equality (Carr, 1986, p. 54).

Feminist spirituality is distinct from feminine spirituality, which can be correlated with the distinctive female developmental agenda. Female spirituality may be described as "more related to nature and natural process than to culture; more personal and relational than objective and structural; more diffuse, concrete, and general than focused, universal, abstract; more emotional than intellectual" (Carr, 1986, p. 53).

Female psychologies, theologies, and spiritualities become feminist when they not only affirm the validity and authenticity of the feminine experience but stand over against the dominant culture that promotes the subordination of women and enhances the dominance of the male culture. They become feminist when they envision a world community of mutuality, reciprocity, and interdependence.

Female candidates for the ministry will present themselves for psychological assessments carrying both conscious and unconscious histories and awareness of their own internalization of female and feminist psychology, theology, and spirituality. Their motivations, self-awareness, consciousness, and sensitivity to the emerging cultural and intellectual understanding of the role of women in the church and the world will vary widely, dramatically, and uniquely within the context of their own life themes.

The challenge and task of the psychological assessor engaged in a process of discernment with a female candidate for ministry is to be prepared to view the candidate through the lens of female developmental theory and feminist theology and spirituality, and to situate this understanding in the context of the denominational or congregational receiving culture. Using the life history narrative as an assessment tool, the assessor must be able to receive and interpret the life themes as valid representatives of the female life cycle and not subject to evaluation using male models.

It could be hypothesized that the female life theme is oriented to attachment and that the personal narrative is given meaning over the life course through attachment experiences (Scanlon, 1985). The path to self-actualization in the female narrative begins in the early attachment experiences, is fostered and nurtured by a widening range of attachment objects and experiences, is frequently plagued by ambivalence and anger in the face of the culture of autonomy with its emphasis on competition and achievement, and comes to resolution in the internalization and integration of both secure attachment and firm self-reliance.

Assessment, understood as the ongoing discernment of vocation throughout the life cycle, must include the insight of the modern psychologies as well as the wisdom of the religious tradition. As the criteria for ministerial preparation shift and change to accommodate diversity in both gender and life-style, the models of assessment must also change. We could envision assessment in the future changing in four major areas. These changes could best be understood as movements along a continuum from less to more: (1) from less time limited to more ongoing; (2) from less detached to more mutual; (3) from less unilateral to more mutual; and (4) from less individually focused to more group focused (Scanlon and Zullo, 1987).

Currently assessment takes place as part of an entrance requirement for seminaries and novitiates. It becomes intensified during the period prior to ordination or profession of vows, and after ordination or final profession it is no longer used as a tool for growth and development. Evaluation that takes life cycle theory seriously would not be limited to the initial assessment of candidates but would be a process that is used to foster and enhance growth and development throughout the life cycle.

The style of evaluation in a more pyramidal or hierarchical structure has been characterized by detachment. The evaluator assumes a detached stance from the candidate and assesses her fitness for the next step in religious formation. Developing new models of evaluation would include the movement from detachment to engagement. Engagement with the candidate in the evaluation process focuses on the value of support, affirmation, and growth of the candidate throughout the process. An engaged style of evaluation enables the candidate to assess his or her own progress and to use the relationship with the evaluator as an opportunity and an environment for insight, challenge, and deeper self-knowledge. A more engaged model of assessment is also more congruent with the notion of attachment as a defining construct in female developmental psychology.

As the process of evaluation unfolds, it has the possibility of movement from a unilateral to a mutual discernment experience. The candidate receives feedback and at the same time is invited to share her experiences of ministry; the spirit; and the spirituality of the diocese, district, or congregation and its relationship to the church. In this mutual process, the feminine voice is used to bring new life and growth to the diocese, district, or congregation. This approach to evaluation takes into consideration the ongoing tension between appropriation and criticism. The candidate or new minister is in the unique position of both appropriating the spirit, style, and structure of the institution as well as bringing fresh insights and awareness to critique the existing structures. An evaluation process that is attempting to move from a very unilateral to a more mutually interdependent model must take into account the tension that always exists between appropriation and critique.

Finally, if the female and feminist critique of psychology and theology is taken seriously, the process of evaluation as it evolves over the life cycle would include evaluation in the Christian context of communities of faith. Christianity has always been understood as a communal venture rather than an individual enterprise. Within this tradition, communities of faith could be understood as being both psychological experiences and sociological structures. As a psychological experience, community could be defined as a sense of belonging, an awareness of support, a recognition of shared belief. As a sociological structure, it would include a group's formal structure, which could range from a religious community that actually shares life together, to a support group that meets on a regular basis, to a parish staff that forms a community as part of the ministerial task (Whitehead and Whitehead, 1982, p. 24).

In the context of community, individual growth is intimately connected to the growth of the community as a whole. In communities of faith, the members confront the meaning of their lives together, assess their strengths and weaknesses, and plan for their future. Evaluation of candidates in isolation from the community often becomes an opportunity for scapegoating and siphoning off anger and resentment that more appropriately belongs to the group itself.

Each of these movements in some way represents the inclusion of the feminine voice and world view that could contribute significantly to the development of new models and styles of assessment. It will be the task of individual dioceses, judicatories, and congregations to enflesh the particulars of these movements in their assessment programs, while at the same time retaining the integrity of the process.

Summary

This chapter has attempted to overview the challenges and demands of the issue of psychological assessment of female ministerial candidates for the churches of the late twentieth century. Holding the insight of the modern psychologies and the wisdom of the religious traditions in tension, the psychological assessor is challenged to take seriously the contributions of female psychology as well as the feminist critique of theology and spirituality.

It is hypothesized that the female sense of identity is forged from a history of attachment and that relatedness, care, and responsibility further shape and nuance the call to ministry in the church. Each female candidate for the ministry will present a unique history of attachment and will also present both conscious and unconscious awarenesses of the impact of female and feminist psychology, theology, and spirituality. It is suggested that the task of the psychological assessor is to become cognizant of these dynamics and to assess the goodness of fit between the female candidate and the receiving congregation, diocese, or district.

Finally, as we look to the future, some recommendations are made that can shape the models of evaluation to include the growing feminine consciousness in our culture.

26

Black Populations

EDWARD WIMBERLY

The literature written on psychological and personality assessment of black people has been reviewed from a black perspective (Jones, 1980). There have been several conclusions: (1) assessment instruments are not culturally free; (2) many test interpretations employ a culturally deviant model in which comparisons are made with dominant culture; (3) many of the norming populations are white and middle class; (4) the instruments do not take full cognizance of the cultural context of ethnic groups; (5) the test taking environment has a critical impact on the test results; and (6) psychological assessment instruments could be culturally relevant to ethnic groups if certain conditions are met.

Black clergy in predominantly white denominations that require psychological assessment as part of the evaluation process of ordination are aware of the limitations of the assessment instruments enumerated in the above paragraph. They have questioned the usefulness of objective psychological instruments for evaluation of black candidates for ordination, given some of the cultural limitations of the instruments. Yet, some black pastors who have witnessed the viability and accuracy of descriptions of certain black candidates for ordination and ministry by experienced test interpreters familiar with the black culture have become lukewarm advocates of the pastoral assessment process.

On the whole, many black pastors remain skeptical about the fairness of those tests to accurately describe a person and to predict effectiveness in ministry. Some black pastors would like to do away with psychological assessment altogether, while others feel that testing is important, particularly if there is a way to make the testing instrumentation less culturally biased.

This chapter seeks to address the issue of making existing assessment instruments more culturally relevant to the assessment of black candidates for ministry and ordination. The basic assumption undergirding this chapter is that psychological assessment can be a valuable tool for assessment of black clergy candidates for ministry and for ordination.

Cultural theory forms the background of the analysis employed in this effort. The questions raised about the efficacy of psychological assessment with black people have come as a result of the theory of cultural deviancy. This theory states that wider culture should be the universal yardstick for assessing all human behavior, and any deviations from the norm are deemed abnormal and pathological. In response to this model, the cultural variance model states that differences between minority cultures and the dominant culture can be accounted for by cultural patterns within the minority group that are not pathological or deviant. Rather, these cultural differences are patterns of response that make for the expression of cultural uniqueness as well as for healthy adjustment to difficult social conditions.

Cultural variance theory informs the use of psychological assessment for black ministerial candidates. It sets the stage for comparing black clergy candidates with other black clergy candidates. It creates a context for developing norms for black clergy candidates based on black clergy populations. It also establishes a conceptual model for employing cultural context factors in interpreting test results.

This chapter will present an approach to the assessment of black clergy candidates for ministry and ordination that is culturally relevant. Its focus is on the development of test norms and interpretation of psychological tests that are from within the cultural context of black clergy candidates for ministry. It will deemphasize the comparison of black candidates for ministry and ordination with other groups, especially white candidates for ministry and ordination. It will primarily emphasize comparison of black ministerial candidates with other black ministerial candidates.

Cultural Variance

The cultural variant model attempts to address the cultural uniqueness of minority groups (Wimberly,

1985). This approach recognizes that differences exist between the black ethnic culture and the wider culture, and it determines how these differences and cultural divergences influence the behavior of ethnic minority people. This model also focuses on the normal majority within a well defined ethnic minority group and their strengths and attributes.

At the same time, the cultural variant model is very critical of the researchers and theorists who focus on the convenient problem populations in describing ethnic minority people. These convenient problem populations include mental health patients, prisoners, and welfare clients. In contrast to the convenient problem populations orientation, the culture variant model seeks to describe what is normal, standard, and general as well as the strengths of ethnic minority people.

A culturally variant model would attempt to describe the cultural inheritance of a particular group and how it contributes to a world view that orients the group to reality. It attempts to describe kinship ties, economic organization, and values concerning time, work, and the nature of human beings. It focuses on how the language of specific groups influences how people may interact within the majority culture. In short, the cultural variant model seeks to present a picture of ethnic and cultural inheritance of a specific group.

The cultural variant model has specific implications for psychological assessment and pastoral evaluation. These implications are concerned with developing culturally fair assessment instruments and culturally specific instruments (Abel, 1973; Samuda, 1975). Culturally fair relates to assessment instruments that present problems, tasks, ideas, and concepts that are familiar to those who are being assessed. Culturally specific refers to comparing individuals with members of their own ethnic minority groups, which have the same linguistic and cultural background.

Culturally fair and specific instruments involve the questions of standardization or developing assessment norms based on particular populations. This involves considerable expense and time. Moreover, it involves delimiting the boundaries of a particular ethnic minority group.

In general, the cultural variant model as applied to psychological assessment and evaluation seeks to be culturally fair and specific. It recognizes the cultural limitations of existing instrumentation; and therefore, it recommends certain ideas to make psychological instrumentation accessible to ethnic minority groups.

The emphasis is on a cultural variant model that makes existing psychological instrumentation more available to be used in the assessment of black ministerial candidates for ordained ministry. The emphasis will be on culturally fair and culturally specific instrumentation rather than abolishing the assessment process altogether.

The Division of Ordained Ministry, United Methodist Church

In 1978 the National Task Force on Psychological Testing and Pastoral Evaluation, Division of Ordained Ministry of the Board of Higher Education and Ministry of The United Methodist Church, decided that the issue of developing norms for black clergy was an important research step to take. This research step was based on the Task Force's awareness of some sensitive cultural and racial issues involving psychological assessment and pastoral evaluation within The United Methodist Church.

When The United Methodist Church was formed in 1968, racial segregation was eliminated from its structures. This meant that integrated committees of the Boards of the Ordained Ministry on the conference level would be assessing all candidates for ministry, including black candidates. In this context, black ministers were very suspicious of the use of psychological assessment instruments and the possibility of their discriminatory use. The major concerns of black clergy were (1) the subjective nature of assessment, (2) the use of white test interpreters, (3) and the lack of culturally sensitive interpreters of tests (Jones, 1985).

Because of the nature of the racial tension, lack of trust, and the Task Force's awareness of the cultural bias of assessment, the Task Force set out to develop norms on the Minnesota Multiphasic Personality Inventory (MMPI) so that black ministerial candidates could be compared with their own black peers rather than solely with their white counterparts. The concern of the Task Force was to develop a culture fair and culture specific use of the MMPI instrument. The MMPI was chosen by the Task Force because of its research possibilities with regard to developing norms and because this test raised considerable conflict for many black candidates for the ministry.

The Task Force discovered that several seminaries in the United States used psychological assessment and evaluation of seminary students. Two institutions with long histories of testing black students were Interdenominational Theological Center (ITC) in Atlanta, Georgia, and Garrett-Evangelical Theological Seminary (G-ETS) in Evanston, Illinois. A brief review of these two institution's testing problem is important.

Psychological testing began at ITC in the 1960s under the direction of Thomas J. Pugh, professor of psychology of religion and pastoral care. He administered a battery of tests to every incoming seminary class during orientation, and this testing continues today. Over the years, the battery included the Edwards Personal Preference Schedule, the MMPI, the Gilmore Health Inventory, the Sequential Tests of Educational Progress, and the Wechsler Adult Intelligence Scale. Later the Theological School Inventory and the Study of Values were added to the battery.

Over a fifteen- to eighteen-year period, over four hundred black seminary students took these tests for evaluation purposes. Of significance is the fact that Pugh, black students, faculty, and administration valued the testing and saw its significance in nurturing students in their seminary career. In the early years, Pugh would interpret the battery to all the students in individual interviews; however, when the student body grew, he interpreted the tests only to those whose profiles showed certain patterns that needed addressing. He also encouraged students to take the initiative to contact him for test interpretation.

It was found that ITC had appropriate answer sheets with raw data that could be used for research purposes. These data were included as part of the norming process.

Several members of the G-ETS's faculty were on the Task Force, and they informed Task Force members of the assessment of black students that occurred there. G-ETS had been testing students since the 1950s (Hinkle and Haight, 1988), and black students began to be tested in the 1970s, when they applied for participation in Clinical Pastoral Education. There were twenty-four black seminary students whose answer sheets could be used in the research of black norms (Pressley et al., 1981).

At least four black Ph.D. candidates participated in the administration and interpretation of psychological tests for black seminary students at G-ETS. These students formed a significant pool of knowledge regarding administering and interpreting psychological tests for black seminary students. Because of G-ETS's history of psychological assessment, the participation of black Ph.D. candidates in their testing program, and the facilities to carry out research, the Task Force pursued the possibility of developing the black norms on the MMPI at G-ETS. Two of the black Ph.D. candidates were selected to carry out the research under the supervision of their doctoral advisor, John Hinkle.

The MMPI and Black Ministerial Students

The researchers received 174 usable answer sheets from ITC and 24 from G-ETS (Pressley et al., 1981). One hundred ninety-eight answer sheets were used in

building norms. These research subjects had attended ITC and G-ETS between the years 1972 and 1977. Each student had taken the 556 item MMPI, and the Kleemult scoring was used to generate 127 scales. The research is contained in an article entitled "The MMPI and Black Ministerial Students" by Haight and McNair (1981), which is available through the Division of Ordained Ministry of The United Methodist Church.

A third group was added for research purposes. This was a group of 74 white students who would serve as a comparison group for discerning cultural differences. Moreover, the Midwestern black ministerial students were compared with Southern black ministerial students to discern any regional differences. A summary of the findings is contained below:

1. Previous research on black people and the MMPI scores used only the validity and the 10 clinical scales, whereas this study used 127 scales.

2. When Midwestern black seminary students were compared to Southern black seminary students, the profiles were essentially the same.

3. Black seminary students are distinctive from the general population (mean scores above 60) in their tendency to challenge societal tradition or institutional structures to achieve desired goals (PD, PD-S). They acknowledge more unusual thoughts or experience (SC) and evidence a high degree of physical, mental, and emotional drive and energy, probably motivated by a strong sense of special calling or high personal expectations (MA, MA-S, PMA). Black male students indicate having traditional feminine interests similar to most male graduate students (FM, FEM). The Black students' scores also suggest a tendency toward religious fundamentalism (REL) and responses similar to persons who choose the nursing profession (NURC) (Pressley et al., 1981).

4. White seminary students were distinctive in that they tended to see themselves in the most positive light, perceived themselves to be deserving of special privilege or status, experienced major depression in the face of loss or setbacks, showed a high need for approval and emotional support, showed emotional strength in coping with life, were generous and self-giving, worked to fulfill role expectations, and suppressed the emotional expression of themselves (Pressley et al., 1981).

5. Midwestern blacks attending the predominantly white seminary tended to present themselves in

a more socially desirable light, as did the white students.

6. White students as a whole tend to present themselves in a more socially acceptable manner than black students and to portray themselves as emotionally strong and capable of handling stress.

These data suggest that the primary area of distinction between black and white ministerial students is in self-presentation. The difference is in the area of test taking attitudes rather than in pathology, according to the researchers. They have pointed out that self-presentation is a cultural issue that has economic and socio-cultural bases. They have reported that the higher socioeconomic status groups present themselves as self-sufficient and unwilling to admit problems, while lower socioeconomic groups present themselves as having more concerns and cautions, as conforming to authority figures, and as self-critical. Another distinguishing dimension has been the feeling by black test takers that their traditional defenses would not serve them well in the test taking circumstance, and they have felt as if they have lost control of their destiny in test taking circumstances.

These researchers have drawn several implications from the study of black norms. The first is that it is important to begin the testing with a contracting process to help the testee to have a sense of ownership and control in the process and its outcome. Second, test taking attitude affects the scores on the MMPI. Therefore, they have recommended that pastoral evaluation specialists need to be cautious in interpreting profile evaluations. This is especially true if only the clinical scales are used. Third, computer scoring enables cross-checking sources of the main scales that provide differentiation between subtle and obvious item responses. This will help to go beyond the clinical scales to envisage a more complete profile.

Issues and Recommendations

It is very clear that cultural factors enter into the development of assessment instruments, in their employment in psychological evaluation, and in the test taking process. Therefore, certain issues and recommendations are essential for pastoral evaluation specialists to recognize.

The first issue concerns the relationship between the MMPI norms and other assessment instruments in a test battery. It is important to realize that building special ethnic norms on every assessment instrument is important, but not necessary. The cost would be expensive and time consuming. As an alternative, it is recommended that the MMPI norms be used as a basis of comparison to ascertain how cultural factors affect the other instruments. For example, other instruments could be checked to see if the cultural factors revealed by the MMPI turn up in their results. Moreover, other instruments could be used to complete the profile of the individual, and the cultural factors to be included in the interpretation of the profile could be verified.

Second, pluralistic evaluation is essential. Pluralistic evaluation is comparing ethnic clergy with persons in similar geographical locations and with similar training and preparation.

Third, the test taking environment influences the outcome of testing. Therefore, using experienced testers and interpreters from the same ethnic and cultural background of the testee is recommended. When this is not possible, testers and interpreters who are culturally sensitive and experienced are a must.

Fourth, there is need to balance objective results on assessment with clinical interviews and the use of projective instruments. The clinical interview and the use of projective instruments allow for personal factors to emerge that give a more complete picture of the individual. They also allow further exploration of factors that may account for scores that have been influenced by cultural factors.

Fifth, developing culturally specific content in assessment instruments is a task that remains to be done. This is, indeed, possible. However, in the meantime, this chapter has presented a model that makes use of the existing testing instruments. The emphasis in this model is on the culturally sensitive pastoral evaluation specialist or the ethnic pastoral evaluation specialist.

The sixth and final issue concerns the next immediate research task. This involves developing longitudinal research studies that are predictive of ministerial success with regard to ethnic ministerial students. This means building criteria for the differences between successful and unsuccessful pastors in culture specific situations and tracing ethnic minority pastors' activities within and outside of ministry over a period of years.

This chapter has described the cultural factors that enter into the assessment process from the beginning to the end. A culturally variant model of pastoral assessment has been introduced that makes the use of existing instruments more effective in the hands of a culturally sensitive pastoral evaluation specialist. This model also compares black ministerial candidates with other black ministerial candidates. The model draws on what is normal and standard for a specific group of black seminary students without making the white seminary student populations a normative yardstick.

Black Populations

The value of a culturally variant model for psychological assessment and pastoral evaluation in predominantly white denominations is that it recognizes the cultural richness that makes up God's creation of the human family. Excluding individuals from the ordained ministry solely because of cultural differences that are deemed pathological diminishes the church and its ability to accomplish its mission in the world. It makes the church a social and class enclave, isolated from many of the people of the world who need to hear the message of the church. Having culturally inclusive leadership within the church helps the church to carry out its ministry to the world.

153

27

Hispanic Populations

PABLO POLISCHUK

The Hispanic presence is felt in most urban centers throughout the United States. According to the 1980 United States census, the number of Hispanics in this country was 14.6 million, at least 6.4 percent of the general population. The numbers have increased 30 percent since 1980 to 19 million. Most trace their roots to Mexico (63 percent), Puerto Rico (12 percent), and Cuba (5 percent); the rest trace their roots to the nations of Central and South America and the Caribbean. The Census Bureau has projected such minorities to reach 22 million in 1990, and between 23.07 to 31.21 million by the year 2000, and it is estimated that they will eventually comprise 15 percent of the whole population.

A wide variety of cultural idiosyncrasies exists among Hispanics, with distinct manifestations of life-styles and customs and varying degrees of acculturation.

The Religious Dimension

Most Hispanics in United States are of Catholic persuasion. Until recently, the ecclesiastical hierarchy of the Roman Catholic Church was non-Hispanic, but in recent years, a number of Hispanics have begun to occupy positions of authority in the Church. In 1969, the National Conference of Catholic Bishops established a Division for the Spanish Speaking. Rodriguez (1986) and Gonzalez (1988) presented some data on Catholic constituency, with two archbishops (San Antonio and Santa Fe), six diocesan bishops, eleven auxiliary bishops, and a total of 1,954 priests of Hispanic descent representing the Hispanic presence.

Protestantism among Hispanics has been gaining a steady increase in the United States. Estimates place the numbers of churches across this country at 5,000 (Miranda, 1988). Between 700 and 1,000 Hispanic Protestant churches saturate the Los Angeles area alone. More than 1,000 Hispanic churches have made New York their basis of operations, with Pentecostal, Fundamentalist, and Baptist persuasions in the lead,

followed by mainline denominations (Gonzalez, 1988). The Assemblies of God alone reported 1,217 Hispanic churches and 2,717 ministers affiliated with the denomination in six districts throughout the country.

The Hispanic Clergy

Since 1972 the Association of Theological Schools (ATS) has kept statistics on Hispanics enrolled in accredited seminaries and schools. Under the category of professional degrees (3- or 4-year programs), 7 women and 202 men enrolled in 1972; the number grew to 100 women and 609 men in 1986. Taking into account all degree programs, the number rose from 264 to 1,297 in 14 years. Still, it represents only 2.3 percent of all seminarians in the ATS programs.

Besides the formal or traditional ways of training ministers in accredited schools, Hispanics have opted for Bible institutes, local night schools and even correspondence courses for those who already have worked as laypersons and have proven their ministries in a more existential, ongoing fashion. As an example, the Latin American Bible Institute of La Puente, California, reported having 100 daytime and 600 evening students in 1987. The number of Hispanics enrolled in graduate institutions of higher learning in the New York area was 100 pursuing M.Div. or doctoral degrees. On the other hand, more than 40 Bible institutes in the New York area report an estimated enrollment of 6,000 (Gonzalez, 1988). In most cases, the leadership and institutions involved in the recruitment and training of candidates have not taken into account the issue of psychological-mindedness or assessment of clergy as part of their policies.

Assessment of Hispanics: Review of Literature

Psychological assessment of Hispanics has been surrounded by much controversy since its inception in the research arena. The questionable practice of assessing ethnic, socioeconomic, or linguistic minorities with instruments that have been designed, standardized, and validated from middle-class, English-speaking perspectives has been adequately stressed (Padilla, 1979; Olmedo, 1981). Differences along value orientations between Anglo and Hispanic cultures have been pointed out (Levine and Padilla, 1980).

Projective Measures

Instruments such as the Rorschach, the Thematic Apperception Test, and the Holtzman Inkblot Test have been employed for over thirty years, but no studies involving Hispanic religious professionals have been reported. Open-ended techniques have often characterized Hispanics as less verbally fluent compared to Anglos and as being more reserved or apprehensive about openness or vulnerability in testing situations involving self-disclosure. Levine and Padilla (1980) listed a number of personality traits in which Hispanics' performance differed from that of other ethnic groups, concluding that projective tests tap into personality factors as they vary with cultural and social context.

Objective Measures

The question of "objectivity" needs to be ascertained, as most paper-and-pencil tests have borrowed, translated, adapted, and tried to validate instruments devised and standardized in a dominant culture that implicitly has reserved its own "right" to establish norms for comparison.

Correlations between English-Spanish parallel forms of these instruments have been found acceptable; yet, criterion-related validities for Hispanics have not been established, and the internal factor structure has not been proven invariant between forms. The 16PF test developed by Cattell (1949) has been translated in Spain; another version circulates in Latin America and a third in Mexico, the *Cuestionario de 16 Factores de la Personalidad* (translated by del Castillo et al., 1980). Absence of data on its validity and reliability does not appear to act in any deterrent fashion as to its utilization.

The most comprehensive self-report inventory widely used for personality assessment has been the Minnesota Multiphasic Personality Inventory (MMPI). Earlier versions of the Spanish MMPI appeared in Cuba (Paz, 1952) and Puerto Rico (Bernal, 1959). Nuñez utilized items of Bernal's translation in adapting the MMPI for Mexican populations (Nuñez, 1967; 1968). Other Spanish versions have appeared in Chile (Risetti, 1981) reported by Butcher and Pancheri (1976) and Butcher and Clark (1979), and in Spain (Echevarría et al., 1969). The Puerto Rican translation has been investigated by Glatt (1969), and the assertions were made as to its adequacy and clinical utility. Yet, no standardization data or norms are available (Butcher and Pancheri, 1976). More recently, yet another version appeared in Puerto Rico (Dìaz, Nogueras, and Draguns, 1984).

The MMPI has been utilized with adolescents, college students, offenders, prisoners, and psychiatric patients, as exemplified by an emerging body of research (Reilly and Knight, 1970; Navarro, 1971; Quiroga, 1972; McCreary and Padilla, 1977; Hibbs, Kobos and Gonzalez, 1979; Holland, 1979; Padilla, Olmedo and Loya, 1982). General reviews were provided by Greene (1987), in which MMPI performance as a function of ethnicity indicated that moderator variables—such as social class, education, and type of setting—seem to play an important role in determining the specific patterns of scores that are found in different research publications.

Personality Measures

Clergy have been under-represented in research with Hispanics utilizing psychological measures. Cattell's Spanish version of the 16PF has been utilized to assess priests in Peru (del Castillo et al., 1980). Among MMPI studies, only Velazquez (1970, cited in Butcher and Pancheri, 1976), comparing Mexican priests with North American counterparts, and Polischuk (1980), assessing Hispanic Protestant religious professionals, have targeted on such populations.

The subjects in Velazquez's study were sixty Mexican priests (twenty-five to fifty years of age) from several cities of Mexico, and forty-one North American priests (twenty-five to fifty years of age) who lived in bordering cities in the United States. The Mexican subjects were predominantly from low income backgrounds, while the majority of Anglos came from middle income families. The greatest differences between the matched samples appeared on scales D and Sc, consistent with findings of most reported data using North American plotting norms. A greater number of items on the L scale were endorsed by Mexican priests, who also as a group were represented by a two-eight profile type, with Hs, Hy, Pa, Pt, and Si bordering 1 SD above the norms.

The Protestant sample studied by Polischuk (1980) was drawn from a pool of Hispanic churches of the Los Angeles area, from which 87 ministers agreed to participate. The average age was 44.64 (SD = 11.03); the educational level was 16.7 years (SD = 2.15). Subjects from Mexican-American, Central and South American, as well as from Puerto Rico and the Caribbean areas were included in the term *Hispanic*. Pentecostal, Assemblies of God, Baptist type organizations, United Methodists, Presbyterians, Nazarenes, and independent associations participated in the study.

The Spanish version of the MMPI by Nuñez (1967) was employed and was judged to be the instrument that would approximate the cultural expressions and customs prevalent in the Southwest, with a large Mexican influx. Besides the MMPI, a demographic questionnaire was administered via bilingual research assistants, in which acculturation levels could be inferred from data pertaining to setting, language utilization in conversation, preaching and teaching, family composition, educational level, earning power, and years in ministry.

Cross comparisons were made, employing Anglo samples (Davis, 1963; Cardwell, 1967; Munger, 1974). Hispanics scored consistently higher on scale L, as compared to Anglos, and differences were noted along scales Hs, D, Hy, Sc, and Si, with higher elevations for Hispanics. Lower scores were found on scales F and Mf for Hispanics.

The differences were taken to represent cultural differences in approaching psychological measures, compounded by issues of language, meaning, and idiosyncratic elements. Hispanic Protestant ministers in the Southwest share with their Roman Catholic counterparts some characteristics, if the samples of Velazquez and Polischuk are perceived as somewhat representative. Both groups scored higher on L, Hs, D, Sc, and Si scales as compared to their Anglo counterparts.

The Inventory of Religious Activities and Interests (IRAI) developed by Webb (1968; 1970) was translated and adapted into Spanish by Polischuk (1980). Functional equivalents of words, thoughts, concepts, and idiomatic expressions were sought, using back-translations by competent bilinguals. Professionals with degrees in theology and education were employed for that purpose. This version was administered to a group of twenty bilingual subjects, with parallel forms given a week apart. Correlation coefficients were calculated for each scale, ranging from .73 to .96. The instrument was regarded as adequate for research purposes and viable for cross-cultural comparisons. Of the sample who initially agreed to participate and provide data on the MMPI, eighty-four also returned the IRAI. As judged by existing Anglo norms (Webb, 1968) a general elevation of the Hispanic profile was obtained. The highest ranked role preference was the spiritual guide, followed by the evangelist and the priest roles. At the lower end, the musician, reformer, and scholar roles were encountered. In between fell the roles of counselor, preacher, teacher, and administrator.

Although elevated above the Anglo norms, the profile in general (except for the reformer role) followed a remarkable parallel trend. Stereotyping in ministry, acculturation to what "successful" clergymen are supposed to prefer in vocational terms, were given as explanations.

The Check scale reflected a tendency among Hispanics to comply or acquiesce with what they might have perceived as representative of expected answers along roles in ministry. Correlations were performed between MMPI and IRAI responses among Hispanic clergy, failing to reach levels of statistical significance, indicating that there are no discrete types or given personality characteristics associated with role preferences.

Discussion

The assessment of Hispanics in general, and clergy in particular, reflects differences with Anglo norms along psychological measures of personality and vocational preferences. What do these differences mean? Explanations of such findings may represent: (1) lack of linguistic equivalence, rendering the measures less than comparable; (2) responses to reality as presented in the testing situation, by the utilization of developmental filters based on cognitive-behavioral-affective structures and processes (cognition, perception, learning, attribution of meaning, and judgment); (3) degrees of acculturation or the complex multidimensional factor involving education, socioeconomic status, dominant language, years in this country, generation, and family structure and size; and (4) degree of being prone to acquiescence among Hispanics.

Several versions of tests like the MMPI and the 16PF have made their appearance. Such phenomena tend to confuse issues, pose questions as to the parallelism of forms, linguistic or functional equivalences, and difficulties in ascertaining cross-cultural comparability. Revalidation, standardization, and normalization are necessary, even if "better" versions are established among such measures.

Acculturation has proven to be a complex, multidimensional variable. Empirical scales have been developed for Hispanics of Mexican descent (Olmedo, Martinez, and Martinez, 1978; Cuellar, Harris, and Jasso, 1980), for Hispanics of Cuban ancestry (Szapocznik, Scopetta, Kurtines and Arnalde, 1978; Szapocznik and Kurtines, 1980), and Puerto Ricans (Inclan, 1979).

Differences in language utilization, generation, and citizenship of the heads of households appear to be related to differences in MMPI scales L, Hs, and Mf. Differences in socioeconomic status appear to be related to impinge upon scales L, K, and Pd. Thus acculturation seems to impinge upon responses on personality measures, affecting them in both directions, depending on which component factor we focus. Different dimensions of acculturation may serve as independent variables, acting as predictors of variance in responses to measures of constructs labeled as personality.

Although employed in a number of empirical investigations with a variety of Hispanic populations, few validity studies were conducted with the MMPI. Fuller and Malony (1984) presented some data that revealed doubts as to the appropriateness or interchangeability of the measures. Prewitt Diaz (1984) on the other hand, gathered some initial data on reliability and validity on the Puerto Rican MMPI.

Beyond the impressionistic data from the past, more empirical findings have demonstrated the tendency of Hispanics to agree to items that would place them in idealistic, expected, or agreeable light. Not only on personality measures, but in vocational preferences as well, clergy gave answers that allowed for elevations toward the "true" or "yes-saying" set in responding.

Several decisions must be made in utilizing translated measures. The assessor may accept the instrument "as if" it is adequate and interpret the results "as if" they correspond to the original. Most evaluators, nevertheless, suspect the results and are tentative in their conclusions, being conservative in their claims due to possible contamination. The establishment of linguistic accuracy, functional equivalence, validity, and reliability at times present such difficulties that some researchers would prefer to regard the measure as a "new test" and investigate empirically the correlates in the Hispanic culture, gathering empirical validity. In doing so, the measures depart from one another and cannot be considered equivalent entities. Yet, most evaluators do not take the time to ascertain whether or not all the variables are taken into consideration.

Item-endorsement analysis among different Hispanic groups is necessary to gather information with regard to resemblance or differences in approaches to the same measures. Some data have emerged among Mexicans and Chileans, reported by Butcher and Pancheri (1976), but such efforts need to be directed to the diverse populations of Hispanics in the United States.

It is quite regretful that Hispanic clergy have not been the object of study more often, as they represent such a key leadership role in terms of their relatedness to the masses, with personalistic styles and influencing power and guidance. These individuals must be regarded as being endowed with personal characteristics that make them able to be good leaders. Transcending many limitations in solidarity with the poor, the dispossessed, and struggling minorities, such individuals may offer valuable information as to what constitutes a minister to the Hispanics, considered an exemplary person in the community. By necessity, such persons must be "out of the ordinary" and "different."

Such persons must have a minimum of mental health (however we define the construct), humanistic skills, abilities to lead, sensitivity to the needs of the parishioners, and some degree of maturity and emotional adjustment beyond the basic response to the call from God. We may add that stamina, fortitude, and assertiveness to challenge the status quo may prove to be necessary traits. Further research into such constructs, attitudes, values, and coping strategies is crucial.

Given the existing negative attitudes of Hispanics toward mental health issues in general, and toward assessment in particular, the need is justified for approaches focusing on cultural sensitivity. Education as to what psychological assessment may offer is needed to elucidate the proper place, not so much in selection, but rather in guidance and counseling situations along training endeavors.

Instruments emerging from the cultures in question are needed, with original, autochthonous, relevant, and appropriate measures of personality structure and functioning and ministerial vocations, roles, and gifts. Such efforts may prove costly, but perhaps the time has come for Hispanics to count themselves as worthy of the endeavor. Further normative data on existing instruments is needed before an indiscriminate procrustean approach is employed, if cross-cultural comparisons are still functional and in vogue.

28

Asian Populations

CHAN-HIE KIM

The term *Asian American* designates a very broad range of people living in America. Because of the vast geographical area and cultural diversity represented by this group of people, it is not easy to identify them in a simple term. We have Southeast Asians (Vietnamese, Laotians, Indonesians, Filipinos), Southern Asians (Indians, Sri Lankans), and East Asians (Chinese, Japanese, Koreans). These Asian Americans are from lands that historically have been dominated by the two great, yet different, cultural traditions, those of China and India. These people also have different political and economic histories and experiences in America as well as in their respective ancestral lands. Thus the effort to identify the Asian Americans is not easy, if not impossible.

However, the situation is not that impossible or hopeless. Since the four major groups among the Asian Americans—Chinese, Filipino, Japanese, and Korean—make up more than 80 percent of the total Asian population in America, it is a general practice in academic circles to confine the term to these four groups of Asians, unless specified otherwise. This chapter will focus primarily on these four groups, since they represent more than 95 percent of the total Asian churches within the United Methodist family and share so many things in common with other subgroups (Directory, 1987).

Immigration

The first Asian group that began to come to the American continent was the Chinese. The gold rush in the West in the mid-nineteenth century brought the Chinese adventurers to this side of the Pacific Ocean. Most of these people, male singles, had never intended to stay in the new land; they simply wanted to make fortunes and return home. But the dream was not easy to accomplish. Because of the racism and various kinds of discriminatory immigration acts and other federal and state laws and codes, their dream was totally shattered. They were no longer able to go home but only to sell themselves to the cheap labor market. Thus the first wave of Chinese migration took place between the 1850s and 1882 (Kim, 1978, p. 2). Many of the third and fourth generation (even fifth generation) Chinese Americans are descendants of these first immigrants. Since 1882, however, the Chinese have migrated to this country steadily in small numbers during those periods of political turmoil.

The Japanese migration took place during the period of 1890 to 1908 (Kim, 1978, p. 2). They first came to Hawaii to be hired by the sugar plantations as cheap laborers. Owners of the plantations brought them here to replace existing laborers from Portugal and China, who were demanding higher wages. But the Japanese, too, were later replaced by Korean and Filipino immigrants. Some of the first immigrants further moved to the mainland and settled down in California and other West coast states. The events of World War II have left permanent scars in the minds of many Japanese Americans who are now in their fifties and older. The recent act of reparation by Congress can only console their pain, but will never help them to recover from their psychological wounds. The postwar economic boom in Japan halted further immigration to this shore of the Pacific Ocean, except for a few cases in which Asian women married American service men.

Most of the first Filipino immigrations took place during the period of 1900 to 1930, when the Philippines was still under the control of the United States (Kim, 1978, p. 2). Their immigration in this period was not as massive as we see it today. It was more or less a gradual process in small numbers. Like other earlier Asian immigrants, they, too, came first to Hawaii as cheap laborers. But most of the recent immigrants are highly educated professionals, as are other new Asian immigrants.

The first official Korean immigrants came to Hawaiian plantations just like other previous Asian immigrants. A total of around 8,000 people finally settled in all parts of the Hawaiian islands until 1905, when Korea lost its diplomatic independence to Japan. A few thousand more immigrants moved to the mainland until the Korean War, but there was no massive migration until 1965.

The turning point in Asian immigration history was the new Immigration Act passed by Congress in 1965 (Public Law 89-236), abolishing all the previous discriminatory acts in immigration. The law was fully implemented in 1968, and since then there has been a massive flow of Asian immigrants (other than Japanese) moving to America. The Asian groups are, therefore, the fastest growing community in the United States today.

It is estimated that Asian Americans comprise less than 2 percent of the total population of the United States. Compared with the earlier immigration pattern, it is striking to note that the new immigrants are not blue collar workers or uneducated laborers or farmers. A recent study conducted at the Center for Asian American Ministry found that most of these new immigrants are highly educated professionals, such as nurses, doctors, engineers, and businesspersons. Consequently, their income is either on a par with or higher than that of the white majority in the United States. Of course, this does not mean that the quality of life they enjoy is completely satisfactory. Racial discrimination, which must be eradicated, still exists against Asian Americans. Adjustment to the newly adopted country is not easy for the newcomers. There are many cultural and psychological obstacles they must overcome to fully assimilate into mainstream American life.

Demographic Characteristics

The majority of Asian Americans are first generation new settlers who have immigrated since 1965. We do not have statistics on the percentage of new arrivals against the number of those born United States citizens, but it is roughly estimated that about 80 percent of the Chinese, 40 percent of the Japanese, and over 90 percent of both Filipinos and Koreans are newcomers. The majority of Asians are persons who need special care and attention when we evaluate them for any kind of purpose because they are new to American culture. These are the persons who still live in America with Asian values and viewpoints. They still use their native languages at home and in their respective communities. Even though their life-styles might have undergone some changes, their basic pattern of thinking and living is still Asian. The Chinese, Japanese, and Korean Asian groups are under the influence of Chinese culture, whose predominant value system is the Confucian ethics.

Most Asian Americans are concentrated on the West coast. For instance, the 1980 United States Census shows that 40 percent of the total Chinese in the United States, 46.1 percent of the Filipinos, 37.4 percent of the Japanese, and 29.3 percent of the Koreans were living in California (Yu, 1982, p. 29). Asians outside the West coast are found mostly in large metropolitan areas like New York City, Chicago, Washington, D.C., and Dallas.

One of the most noticeable demographic characteristics among the Asians is their comparatively young age. Around 65 percent of the breadwinners of the Asian families are in their thirties and forties with younger children and often with the parents of one of the spouses.

Another distinctive characteristic of the Asians in America is their exceptionally high level of education. The 1980 Census indicates that the number of adults with four years of college include 33 percent of Asians, 17 percent of whites, and 8 percent of blacks (*U. S. News and World Report*, October 18, 1982). According to a survey conducted by this writer, 70.7 percent of Korean American adults have at least four years or more of college education (49.1 percent in Korea and 21.6 percent in America) (Kim, 1981, p. 8). The high percentage of people with college educations can easily be seen among Asian blue-collar workers and small store owners.

The downward professional mobility is also evident among the Asian immigrants. This is primarily because of language barriers and racism. Therefore, one of the most important ministries in the Asian churches is to help these people gain self-confidence and lost dignity. Consequently, the type of leadership the Asian churches are looking for is the one that is quite well acquainted with the two worlds—that is, bilingual and bicultural persons who can also give the first generation Asian immigrants hope for a bright future despite their difficulties in adjusting themselves to American life and value systems.

Cross-cultural Observations

Understanding Asian Americans requires a good knowledge of their cultural roots in comparison to American views and perspectives, which are predominantly European. Here cultural anthropology can help us to understand other cultures and value systems that are foreign to us.

Recently some biblical scholars have begun to take cultural dimensions in biblical studies quite seriously, and they have recognized the usefulness of the sociology of religion and cross-cultural anthropology for the understanding of the biblical world. The Mediterranean world that gave birth to the Bible is too far removed from our own in terms of time and culture. Unless we overcome these wide gaps, the biblical messages can hardly be heard again. Some of these studies are quite relevant in our understanding of Asian cultures because the Asians share so much in common with the ancient Mediterranean views.

I have adopted as our guide through the American and Asian worlds for observation of their cultural differences most of the list "Comparing U. S. Values with the Mediterranean View" (Malina and Neyrey, 1988, pp. 145-51), which they composed from data provided by Jeremy Boissevain (1982), Geert Hofstede (1984), and Bruce J. Malina (1981) . Both the "U.S. View" and the "Asian View" below are exact quotations from the list; only the title has been changed from the "Mediterranean View" to the "Asian View," because what they describe as "the Mediterranean View" can also be seen as the "Asian View." But the sections under the heading "A-A (Asian American) View" are my own. Since the sections headed by "U.S. View" and "Asian View" are quotations from Malina and Neyrey (1988, Table 1 in their Appendix), I have not put them in quotation marks.

There are major differences among Asian Americans as to the measure of their acculturation. Most of the American born Asians are much more like the general American population in terms of their perceptions of life and life-styles. Of course, those second generation Asians who are directly influenced by their first generation parents and share much of their world views are more like bicultural persons, but the third and following generations are somewhat different; these people are culturally very well assimilated into the mainstream of American life. Since, however, the majority of Asian Americans are first generation Asians, it is appropriate to concentrate our effort in examining the culture of these not so well-known immigrants. Therefore, the "A-A View" below is focused generally on the first generation Asian Americans.

Self-perspectives 1

U.S. View: Emphasis on autonomy and individualism, with adults presumed to be equal with regard to law and customs; adult children dissociated from parents, husband, and wife in egalitarian relationship; siblings treated equally.

Asian View: Emphasis on sociality and group orientation, with adults in patron-client relation, sons and fathers interacting over a lifetime, wives subject to husbands, younger brothers subject to the elder.

A-A View: Nothing much has been changed in the Asian American families. The feminist movement in America has had almost no impact on the Asian communities. Because of the minority status, solidarity and group orientation are much more strongly emphasized. Children are still very much obedient to their parents. Parents mostly dictate the future of their children's professional careers.

Self-perspectives 2

U.S. View: Friends are expected to provide emotional support and companionship; chosen from both sexes and a range of social groups.

Asian View: Friends are expected to readily provide material and emotional support; chosen from males only within a limited group, e.g., village, neighborhood.

A-A View: Once persons become friends, the relationship is regarded to be like that of brothers and sisters. Sometimes the friendship is much more valued than the relationship between siblings. Particularly in the immigration context, material support to friends is strongly urged.

Emotional support in the foreign environment is generally carried by church and other community activities. Fraternal organizations, hometown reunion meetings, alumni associations, and similar organizations like this are doing indispensable service to the Asian community in terms of moral as well as emotional support.

Self-perspectives 3

U.S. View: Emphasis on rights and the right to experiment and change individually and socially.

Asian View: Emphasis on duty and loyalty with the obligation to remain in one's group(s) and abide by its decisions.

A-A View: Among social groups, the family is the most important one. Individuals in a family seldom do something against the will and hope of the family. The highest virtue is to obey the decision of the family. In assessment interviews, Asian candidates quite often express that their decisions are approved by the family members and/or its elders, in most cases, by their fathers. They also indicate that even though they may not like to become ministers or have some reservation about the profession, they simply follow the wishes of their parents. By doing this they are trying to prove what good children they are; this does not mean that they are not in control of their lives.

Self-perspectives 4

U.S. View: Preference for majoritarian decision making, with the willingness to abide by the will of the majority.

Asian View: Preference for consensual decision making, with dissatisfaction should one be omitted from the consensual process of one's peers.

A-A View: This is an indication that Asians are not yet accustomed to democratic processes and principles. The representative principle and delegation of powers are sometimes not clearly understood. Thus omission from the representative decision making body is often regarded as being isolated from the group. Therefore, it takes another kind of leadership skill to enable people to abide by the majority decision.

Self-perspectives 5

U.S. View: Respect for efficiency, ability, success.

Asian View: Respect for hierarchy, seniority, family.

A-A View: Not because of ability or efficiency, but because of seniority and family ties, are people put in the leadership position. The practice is now somewhat modified in order to survive in the competitive industrial world.

Self-perspectives 6

U.S. View: Quality of life assessed in terms of individual success, achievement, self-actualization, self-respect.

Asian View: Quality of life assessed in terms of family/group success, achievement, respect of others for the group.

A-A View: Not how I am doing, but who in my family—including myself—has accomplished something others might admire is more important. Individuals must sacrifice themselves for the sake of the honor of one's family.

Respect of others is directly related to the "shame culture." Saving face is highly valued. Pushing children for the Ivy League schools, irrespective of their children's abilities, is an example. Self-realization through an appropriate school is ignored at the expense of family showcasing.

Self-perspectives 7

U.S. View: Quality of work life judged by a task's challenge to the individual and the intrinsic needs of the individual that it meets.

Asian View: Quality of work life judged by degree to which a job allows the individual to fulfill obligations to the family/groups.

A-A View: In this thoroughly individualistic society Asian Americans are suffering from these two value systems. What would be the best way to satisfy both my own intrinsic needs and at the same time my obligation to the family? Many individuals opt for fulfilling their obligations to the family rather than one's own individual needs. Most Asian Americans are engaged in a business they are not trained for nor would give them satisfaction. Survival of the family is the most urgent priority concern for them.

Self-perspectives 8

U.S. View: Satisfaction comes from a job well done.

Asian View: Satisfaction comes from a job well recognized.

A-A View: Desire for recognition is a universal instinct of all human beings regardless of one's own cultural orientation. But the desire for recognition in the Asian context is directly linked to "face saving."

Asians are more concerned about how others—neighbors, friends, peers, seniors, teachers—would think of the job they have done.

Self-perspectives 9

U.S. View: Students are motivated by a need to master the subject and the desire to get good grades for some future occupation.

Asian View: Disciples are motivated by a need to acquire the status that a discipleship can provide.

A-A View: Asian American students are highly motived to get good grades as well; in fact they are strongly pushed by their parents for this. But much more important than this is admission into a prestigious educational institution and becoming a student of renowned professors. Being a student of famous professors itself carries much more weight than mastery of the subject.

Self-perspectives 10

U.S. View: Avoiding guilt, either internalized or applied by another for some infraction, is a fundamental concern.

Asian View: Avoiding being shamed by others, and thus maintaining one's family's/group's honor, is a fundamental concern.

A-A View: Asian Americans are not so much different from Asians in this regard. "Shame" rather than "guilt" is the primary concern of the people. It is to be noted that this is one of the basic, important cultural differences between the U.S. and Asian value systems.

Self-perspectives 11

U.S. View: Preserving self-respect is basic.

Asian View: Preserving face—that is, respect from one's reference groups, is basic.

A-A View: "Self-respect" is also highly valued because it is a means of preserving one's face.

Self-perspectives 12

U.S. View: Children learn to think of themselves as "I."

Asian View: Children learn to think of themselves as "we."

A-A View: Children learn to think of themselves as both "I" and "we," depending on the degree of acculturation.

Self-perspectives 13

U.S. View: Just as children are socialized to think of themselves as individualists, so also they are taught to relate to others as individuals.

Asian View: Just as children are socialized to think of themselves as dyadic group members, so also they are taught to relate to others in terms of the stereotypes characteristic of the groups to which others might belong.

A-A View: Here again, Asian American children are not much different from Asian children. Too much self-assertion can easily lead one to isolation and excommunication. This is also true for adults.

Concluding Remarks

It must be emphasized again that, depending on the measure of cultural assimilation, there are wide gaps and diversities among Asian Americans in their perception about self, relation with others, and everyday affairs. The degree of assimilation generally depends much on the length of their stay in America. Thus the longer they have lived here the more they tend to think and behave like an average American. But we should not forget that their basic mind-set is already formed in their native country; they can never be completely assimilated here.

Another group of Asian Americans we should not ignore is the Asian populace who were born here. As I mentioned earlier, we have not specifically dealt with these people in this paper because they are already assimilated to a certain degree into the mainstream of American life. However, it should not be misunderstood that they are completely immersed in the pool of Western thinking and perception. They, too, are Asians. We cannot deny the fact that they have inherited some of the Asian views as noted above. Their views of life and behavioral patterns are sometimes very much Asian. This reality must be kept in mind in our assessment of candidates.

29

Native American Populations

J. David Pierce

Who Are the Native Americans?

A little over ten years ago the United States Congress concluded its most detailed and intensive investigative work encompassing the entire field of Federal-Indian relations. The American Indian Policy Review Commission began by asking questions such as "Who is an Indian?" and "What are the conditions under which they live?" Such questions are also relevant for our study of assessment issues and the Native American cultures. When we are concerned with assessing someone for the role of ministry, it seems only reasonable that we allow our assessments to be informed by the culture and society from which the candidate came and to which he or she may return.

First of all, the term *Native Americans* is used to refer to all indigenous tribal groups in the United States of America and includes the American Indians, Aleuts, and Eskimos. A second point of clarification is that historically—and to a degree to the present—there is no such thing as "the Native American culture," or the "Indian view," or "the Indian religion" (Beaver, no date). The hundreds of tribes in North America can be traced to many different cultures, religions, languages, and views. But today we see a certain amount of intermingling of tribes; there is some commonality among Native American peoples in terms of political, economic, social, and ecological realities and pressures. Thus although the Native American groups retain their important distinctiveness from one another, we can identify Native American cultures (plural) as a collectivity distinguished in many ways from Euro-Americans and other ethnic American groups.

Who qualifies to be considered a Native American at the individual level, however, is a matter of whom you consult. For instance, the various federal government agencies, the different state governments, and the Census Bureau all have different criteria for their definitions used for statistics and eligibility for programs and laws affecting Native Americans (examples include various amounts of Indian blood, enrollment records from a federally recognized tribe, anyone of Indian descent, an individual's own determination, whether or not one is recognized in the community as being Native American, and/or having residence on a reservation).

However one defines who the Native Americans are, the pattern is essentially the same. Incomes are lower than that of the population at large, with more Native Americans below the poverty level (U.S. Dept. of HEW, 1984). According to the Standard Metropolitan Statistical Areas, Native Americans generally have triple the national average of deaths from each of the following categories: accidents, cirrhosis of the liver, tuberculosis, and gastritis (U.S. Government Printing Office, 1977).

The American Indian Policy Review Commission found that both Native American women and men suffer from inadequate and inappropriate education as well as from unemployment and low income. In fact, the conditions of poverty among Native Americans who live in rural areas are worse than the conditions of those residing in cities. A large percentage of Native Americans were found to be in the ranks of the unemployed or working poor. Further, the statistics fail to reveal the extent of unemployment since they are determined by registering those seeking work; with few, if any, jobs available on reservations, many do not register and are not included in the statistics (U.S. Government Printing Office, 1977, p. 92). Although the commission's study is now slightly over a decade old, there is little evidence that the trend has changed significantly.

Crisis in Native American Church Leadership

Certainly not all individual Native Americans can be understood by census statistics; yet, it appears clear that many of the Native American communities have been experiencing a great need for the liberating and witnessing presence of the church. Unfortunately, there has also been a crisis of Native American leadership in the church. In 1974, the Indian Church Career Research and Planning Project was launched with initial funding from the Vocation Agency of the United Presbyterian Church. Seven denominations (United Presbyterian, Reformed Church in America, American Baptist, United Church of Christ, United Methodist, Episcopal, and Christian Reformed) cooperated in a massive research into the extent, nature, cause, and possible solutions to the leadership crisis.

The results of the Career Project can be found in the document titled "Mending the Hoop: A Comprehensive Report" (Corbett and Kush, 1974). At the time of the report, there were 65 fully credentialed pastors for 452 churches affiliated with the seven denominations, and only four Native American students were in seminary. Other data concerning language and education are important for our study of candidate assessment—namely, 56 percent of the Native American pastors stated that they used both English and a tribal language in their ministry. Further, on the average, Native American clergy have been less schooled than non-Native pastors serving Native American congregations. The Native American Episcopal priests tended to have completed the highest level of school with the least schooled being United Methodist pastors. The average educational level was 15 years of schooling for the Native American clergy, but that compares to 9.8 years for the general Native American population (Corbett and Kush, 1974).

Perhaps the most significant finding relevant to assessments of clergy candidates emerged from the Career Project's investigation of the explanations for the leadership crisis. Ordained Native American clergy serving Native American churches ranked the leading causes to be "a lack of support from denominational executives" and "educational requirements being too high." When surveyed, a large majority of Native American church workers felt that the basis for ordination should be demonstrated competency in the parish rather than school records. This opinion was statistically unrelated to the respondents' own level of education (Corbett and Kush, 1974).

During the fourteen years since the "Mending the Hoop" document, there has been a noticeable increase in Native American clergy candidates, especially in schools like the University of Dubuque Theological Seminary, which has an established Native American program and director. The Native American Theological Education Consortium (NATEC) was formed in response to the leadership crisis and set as its goal the equipping of Native American church leaders and pastors through theological education by extension. Nonetheless, the Native American churches still need a great many more pastors and leaders who are theologically, personally, and culturally competent. The ordination examinations and certain psychological assessment procedures, however, can at times be cultural stumbling blocks that the Native American churches cannot afford.

Preparation for Native American Ministry

According to the churchwide policy statement of the United Presbyterian Church (1979) several areas of training and sensitivity are important for Native American ministerial candidates and non-Native American pastors engaged in ministry with Native Americans. Perhaps the most critically needed areas of training include an awareness of Native American cultures, heritage, history, and religious thought.

It has become evident to many theological educators who are involved with the training of Native American seminary students that the general historical understandings of culture, history, and religious thought are not enough. Since there is not "one" Native American culture, further training is needed to take seriously such concerns as community values and local patterns of leadership. As of this time, however, ordination examinations that are used to assess a Native American candidate's readiness for ministry have generally ignored any reference to these critical areas of training.

Native American Readiness for Ministry

It is the general practice of the various denominations to be committed to their prescribed standards for the training, ordination, and installation of clergy. A modification of those standards to take into account Native American issues does not necessitate a substandard process; in fact, the opposite may be the case. The available literature at this time does not offer us empirical data concerning the predictive validity of the various ordination standards for Native American pastors in Native American settings. Nonetheless, it is plausible to assume from observation that formal accreditation as a minister is not necessarily the only, or even the most heavily weighted, predictive factor of pastoral effectiveness in a Native American congregation. Perhaps this is due to the fact that the training and the assessment of clergy candidates as related to the ordination standards have arisen out of the experiences of the church in settings other than Native American.

When assessing an individual from a group that is culturally different from the normative population, the validity of any assessment instrument or evaluative procedure is fundamentally dependent on the certainty that (a) the constructs being measured are the important and relevant variables in that minority culture; (b) the symbols (language and content) of the instrument are meaningfully associated with the constructs in the same way as they are in the normative population; and (c) the procedures used in the assessment are congruent with the communication patterns within the culture of the individual. In essence, this means that the judicatories overseeing the assessments for ordination standards may need to review and modify their procedures for Native American candidates. In order for our assessments to have predictive, construct, content, concurrent, or even face validity, we must take into account Native American life-styles, experiences, values, and the way the individual processes information (the meaning-making system of the individual).

Three important constructs, for example, that are sometimes assessed as elements of pastoral identity and ministry are the ability to translate experience into insight, the ability to form empathic relationships, and an understanding of the self in relation to the role of ministry. Each of these qualities must be evaluated in specific ways, informed by existing Native American cultural and social conditions. Only in this way will they be relevant to the setting in which they will be used in ministry.

The "insight ability" can be assessed at least partially by a measure of a clergy candidate's comprehension of the dominant culture, his or her own native view, and the ability to use this insight effectively. The "empathic ability" might include an assessment of one's facility in the use of a particular native language and its use in storytelling. Further, the acceptance by one's racial peers and native community may well be an essential part of the candidate's ability to understand and to fill effectively the role of pastor. As an illustration, according to a report from the Native American Theological Association (NATA), it was not until he had killed his first whale that one of the first Eskimo pastors to graduate from a seminary was accorded respect by his community. The report concludes that "the community did not care as much about his degrees as they did about whether or not he was a 'good Eskimo' " (NATA, 1980, p. 10).

Culture Fair and Relevant Ordination Examinations

NATA affirmed the need for denominational ordination examinations, but it also reported several representative problems in the content, testing methodology, and grading procedures. After reviewing some of the example biases found in ordination examinations, we will explore some suggestions concerning how to make the examinations more culturally fair and relevant to a Native American clergy candidate.

With reference to content, for example, a Native American was examined on worship with a question involving a choir director, a treasurer, and her assistant. The examination over polity contained questions involving a board of trustees and a Sunday school superintendent. The typical Native American congregation is small and not likely to have the formal designation of staff titles or even trustees, for that matter! Indeed, these churches often survive because of the commitment and the training of the laity (NATA, 1980). Further, if the purpose of an ordination examination includes the opportunity for the clergy candidate to apply what has been learned, how can we expect the Native American to apply insight and pastoral wisdom to his or her world when that world has received little or no focus of study in the seminary?

Perhaps even more problematic than the content of the questions, however, is the fact that three potential types of biases against Native American cultures can be found in the testing method and evaluation criteria often used in ordination examinations. Some of these biases are also present in a few of the psychological instruments used to assess clergy candidates. Without an understanding of the Native American cultures, such biases may seem insignificant or even remain unnoticed. These constraints include (a) the use of controlled time limits for responses, (b) the requirement of written as opposed to oral communication, and (c) the positive evaluation of the responses being dependent on a logical and linear progression of ideas.

Many Native American cultures do not value speed or even punctuality as a sign of intelligence or competence. An individual Native American may require longer response times compared to other groups due to a variety of interacting factors. Along with a cultural expression of "unhurried" time, some Native American clergy candidates may have less experience than other groups in writing skills and linear problem solving strategies. Also, while some non-Indians may regard a quick answer to a question to be polite, some Native American cultures emphasize the impoliteness of answering too quickly because it shows disrespect for the question. "Slowness," then, may be a result of politeness and/or difficulty in expression rather than an indication of a lack of knowledge or ability.

Many ordination examinations and assessment tools focus on impersonal tasks, such as writing skills and paper/pencil questionnaires, more than on relational skills and oral communication. Given the fact that many

Native Americans have been reared in a traditional culture in which people look for and find meaning primarily in relational terms, it seems a bit strange to expect them to clarify their understanding of themselves and of ultimate meaning apart from their concrete experience of their story—a story or faith history in which "all are relatives"; it is usually a story centered in a "circle of meaning," devaluing dichotomies and impersonal forced choices between two or more alternatives.

According to a NATA (1980) report on culture fair testing, Native American pastors must be good speakers if they are to be considered competent. The report also cites the conclusions of Robert Havighurst, who has done several major studies of Indian education and who has supported the thesis that verbal intelligence tests are an unfair measure of Native American intelligence. While the NATA report avoids the suggestion that individual Native American clergy candidates cannot write well or that all the examinations should be oral, their study does raise questions about testing options for Native American cultures that have an oral tradition and a storytelling method of communication.

At least somewhat connected to the oral and story culture is the problem of grading or evaluating some Native American answers on the ordination examinations. Non-Native evaluators usually expect the written (or even spoken) answers to demonstrate a logical progression of ideas in order to "make sense." But who (or which culture) is to decide what a logical progression is? There is much evidence that there are cultural aspects of logic.

Ashbrook (1984; 1988) describes patterns of belief in terms of the processing patterns of the working brain. In his research, he suggests that certain cultures can begin to depend on and thus value a preference for left or right mind patterns of meaning-making. His description of the Byzantine mind-set (predominantly right brain patterns) seems to match rather closely the attributes that many Native Americans claim for themselves. In summary this would mean that many Native Americans engage life by being immersed in a contextual universe around them and thus relationally hold to a logic of "manifestation," in which everything is affirmed and everything is related as an inseparable, unanalyzable whole. This is quite different from a logic of "proclamation," in which immediate values can be rejected in the service of a distanced rationality and an objective naming process (including analysis).

Ashbrook's (1988) work helps to clarify the Native Americans' difficulty when they are expected to give answers that demonstrate step-by-step deliberate responses—responses that are specific, logical, and based

on a rational analytic strategy. Such a conceptual rationality is countercultural to most Native Americans who come from a community setting in which meaning is constructed and conveyed by leaps of inference; the Native Americans will most likely be misunderstood in such cases when they use personally symbolic and relational strategies to answer theological questions.

Recommendations

The Native American Theological Association (NATA, 1980) has made several basic recommendations concerning examinations as they relate to assessing its clergy candidates. In the light of the issues discussed in this chapter, these are worth noting:

1. We recommend that the "large church" biases in questions be removed.

2. We recommend that questions which allow Native Americans to respond in the context of their ministry be added. Questions in this area should be based upon studies of desired competencies.

3. We recommend that it be an option for some people that the examinations be translated into tribal languages and graded by someone who can read those languages and understand the culture.

4. We recommend for those for whom oral examinations would be more fair that the essay questions be administered orally as an option and graded by persons familiar with that Native American language and culture. When this is done the predictive validity of these scores should be examined.

5. We recommend that Native American candidates who are studying for ordination by alternative routes, such as Theological Education by Extension, be allowed to take ordination examinations.

The above recommendations take seriously the need for cooperation among seminaries, evaluating judicatories, and the Native American communities of faith in the preparation, interpretation, and grading of examinations. What they fail to address adequately is the possibility of redefining evaluation in terms of competency-based field work. If the Native American cultures generally tend to be more experientially and relationally focused than they are oriented toward abstract conceptualization, then it would seem important to assess their ability to "do theology" under the supervision of an experienced Native American leader.

These recommendations relate in general ways to the use of psychological tests. On the one hand, the issues of time constraints, the content relevancy of questions, the use of impersonal tasks to assess people who assign and find meaning primarily through relationships, and the possibility of right brain information processing patterns may have the effect of skewing the data.

On the other hand, there is little research or empirical evidence upon which to make specific recommendations concerning the construct or predictive validity of many of the psychological instruments most often used in assessment of Native Americans. For example, the Minnesota Multiphasic Personality Inventory (MMPI) is criterion-keyed, and its interpretation demands normative data on population groups. Given the cultural and social distinctiveness of the Native American groups, it would be difficult, if not unfortunate, to interpret a candidate's MMPI profile by referencing it to "the usual seminary student patterns."

If psychological testing is to be used to make decisions about the career or the mental health of Native Americans, the task before us is clear: Research and norm building are critically needed.

Applications Among Church Structures

30

Seminary Applications

SUE WEBB CARDWELL

The general purpose of seminary education is professional formation for ministry. This is more complex than many other kinds of professional education, since it involves academic, professional, personal, and spiritual aspects. Assessment needs for each of these aspects will vary accordingly.

The *Readiness for Ministry* project (see chap. 16 of this volume) found seven most highly rated ministry themes. "The most highly rated themes portray a merger of certain qualities of personhood and character with a certain competence in ministry skills. The themes evaluated as most detrimental reflect a similar merger of personal qualities . . . that reflect incompetence in real practice. The personal self is not separated from the professional self at either the positive or negative ends. The patterns in the data imply an integrated perception of ministry not unlike the Christian concept of incarnation" (Schuller et al., 1980, p. 51).

The theme rated as most important, with the most unanimous agreement, was that called "open, affirming style" that is "highly sensitive to the character and spirit of the person who carries out these functions" (Schuller, 1980, p. 30). The characteristics—positive approach, responsible functioning, flexibility of spirit, personal integrity, and acceptance of clergy role—are seen to be very similar to those listed in I Timothy—above reproach, sensible, dignified, temperate, hospitable, gentle, not quarrelsome, not a lover of money, and well thought of by others.

The importance of these characteristics was further emphasized by the almost unanimous agreement on the factor "Disqualifying Personal and Behavioral Characteristics." These were the opposites of those listed above, emphasizing intra- and interpersonal relationship qualities. Some persons question whether the seminary can teach these desired characteristics, or only help develop them in persons who come with a certain degree of them already (Holmes, 1978, p. 183). However, their primary importance indicates that assessment of these would be a very important part of any program in a seminary, and especially so for any selection process.

In clergy and candidate assessment the first question is "What do you want/need to know?" The second is "What assessment tool will give that information?" Academically, for example, learning in a certain course is usually measured by teacher-made tests. However, at times, there is a need to know what factors are involved in the poor performance of certain students, whether lack of ability, lack of interest, poor study habits, or interference by emotional difficulties. The choice of appropriate measures is crucial for each of the aspects, and these concerns are discussed in other chapters of this book.

In this chapter, a discussion of seminary applications will be based largely on the report of a survey of the assessment process in most of the seminaries belonging to the Association of Theological Schools.

Survey of Seminary Assessment Programs

An information form was sent to all 202 seminaries listed in the current directory of the Association of Theological Schools (ATS), asking about their use of assessment inventories—which ones were used; how, when, and by whom they were administered; the purposes; access to results; interpretation and by whom; response of students; opportunity for counseling; changes in the battery of inventories and they were how scored; and an opportunity for comments.

Returns were received from 157 of the 202 seminaries (16 Canadian, 141 in the United States), a very acceptable 77 percent return rate. The results can be compared with a previous survey done in 1961 (Ashbrook, 1970, p. 93), in which 108 schools answered the questionnaire. In 1961, 89 (82 percent) of those reporting were using inventories, compared to 93 (59 percent) for 1988, though we do not know the return rate represented in 1961. We do know that of the 157 in

1988, 50 have never used assessment inventories, and 14 seminaries who formerly used them have discontinued their use for various reasons, most frequently because the faculty person qualified to do it left or because of the student unrest and opposition in the late 1960s and early 1970s or because of limitations of time and money, or, for several, judicatories were doing the testing now.

Inventories Used

It seems that there has been a great deal of change since 1961 in the number of inventories and which ones are used. In 1961, 72 different instruments were reported—30 of them personality, 25 achievement, and 17 vocational/interest tests. The eight most frequently used by seminaries included the Minnesota Multiphasic Personality Inventory (MMPI), the Strong Vocational Interest Blank (SVIB), the S-O Rorschach, the Miller Analogies Test, the Graduate Record Examination (GRE), the Ohio State Psychological, the Guilford-Zimmerman, and the California Test of Mental Maturity (CTMM), in descending order (see Table 1). Currently the most used—with the number of seminaries using them in parentheses—are the Myers-Briggs Temperament Inventory (63), the MMPI (42), the *Profiles of Ministry* (39), the Theological School Inventory (28), the Taylor-Johnson Temperament Analysis (24), the Sixteen Personality Factor (16PF; 17), the California Psychological Inventory (CPI; 14), and the Strong-Campbell Interest Inventory (SCII; 11).

It is interesting that only two inventories overlap in these two lists. It is also notable that two on the 1988 list were not available in 1961, the TSI and the *Profiles of Ministry*, both specially developed for use in seminary.

Table 1.

Most Frequently Used Instruments—1961 and 1988

Instruments	1961 N = 89			1988 N = 93		
	Seminaries	%	Order	Seminaries	%	Order
MMPI	52	58	1	42	45	2
SVIB (SCII)	28	31	2	11	12	8
S-O Rorschach	17	19	3			
Miller Analogies	15	17	4	7	8	
GRE	14	17	5	3	3	
Ohio State Psych.	13	15	6			
Guilford-Zimmerman	9	10	7			
CTMM	7	8	8			
MBTI				63	68	1
Readiness/Profiles	Not Available			39	42	3
TSI	Not Available			28	30	4
TJTA		24	26	5		
16PF				17	18	6
CPI				14	15	7

Administration of Instruments

In response to whether inventories were administered to all entering students, 63 (67 percent) schools do, 23 do not, and 6 did not respond. Twenty-seven administered them before entrance, 64 after; 18 administered them to some groups; and 23 administered some inventories to seniors before graduation. Eighteen seminaries reported administration to certain selected groups—to M. Div. only, to those preparing for Field Education or CPE, or in conjunction with a specific course or for special purposes. The instruments were usually administered by someone inside the seminary, with only 12 using outside agencies/persons. In 32 instances, it was the staff in pastoral care/counseling, while another 36 named faculty or staff, with no specification. The high cost of paying an outside agency seems to be one reason for keeping it inside, though other reasons might well be the greater possibility for further input, more use of the results with the student, or for other purposes relative to the needs of the seminary. As part of this, the use of seminary norms for the various inventories is essential to avoid misinterpretation.

Purposes of Assessment

Since the purpose of seminary education is professional formation for ministry, the two main purposes of assessment are selection/screening and the growth/development of the seminarians. These can be subdivided into five purposes as shown in Table 2.

Table 2.

Purposes of Assessment

	Seminaries	%
Screening	27	29.7
Self-understanding	82	90.1
Counseling/guidance	49	53.8
Seminary understanding	49	53.8
Research	13	14.3

Screening

Twenty-nine (31 percent) of the seminaries gave screening as a purpose for the assessment. This raises an important issue: Who is the client?

In the first case, that of screening, the primary client is the seminary or judicatory, and the secondary client is the student. The seminary stands between the student and the denomination, always with a sense of tension between the needs/welfare of the student and the welfare of the church/denomination. The seminary sometimes says, "We educate, it is the judicatory/church who ordains and hires; therefore, they are the ones to make the decisions about ordination, do the screening." On the other hand the judicatory says, "You have students for about four years. You know how they are doing. You have the personal contact with them; therefore, you should weed out the unfit (or marginal) ones."

It is never easy to tell a student who "feels a call" that you do not consider him or her a suitable candidate for ordination. So it is easier to put off the uncomfortable task on someone else. However, even though there seems to be a natural division of labor between seminary and judicatory, still the question of how the two might cooperate in the assessment task does not always have a simple answer.

Self-Understanding of the Student

Ninety percent of the seminaries using assessment indicated that one purpose was the self-understanding of the student. We know that students are self-selected, having made a response to a "call" and having made a vocational decision. Except for a few situations, these students will be making career decisions all along the way, and who they are, and their intra- and interpersonal dynamics and relationships will crucially affect their effectiveness and their fulfilment. Therefore, the most important factor involved in their ministry is themselves, and anything that can contribute to their self-understanding and help them make more informed choices—even, perhaps, a choice not to pursue ministry—is of urgent importance. These would include understanding of and consideration of motivations for ministry, background influences, academic ability, personality, vocational interests, temperament, and strengths and weaknesses—or as I prefer to call them, growing edges. The whole thrust in this case is *growth* and development. In some cases, remediation may be called for, which may lead to special experiences and/or counseling.

Counseling and Guidance

The ATS Procedures, Standards and Criteria for Membership (1986, p. 31) requires that "Programs include adequate counseling, personal and spiritual, as well as academic" with "particular attention to the personal and spiritual qualifications."

A National Institute of Mental Health (NIMH) study has shown that 19 percent of the general population suffers from a mental disorder, but only one-fifth of these get help for it. Thus between 10 and 20 percent of seminary students can be expected to have some need for counseling at some point in their seminary experience. This can involve vocational decision, faith questions, marital and family problems, as well as depression and more clinical conditions. The assessment process can indicate such a need, and its process of interpretation to students gives the student an unequalled opportunity to acknowledge such a need and to receive help, whether from someone inside or outside the seminary.

In seminaries where there is also a counseling center and/or training program in counseling, this can be an invaluable asset for the personal/professional development of the students. For example, at Christian Theological Seminary—which has a training center accredited by the American Association of Pastoral Counselors (AAPC) in connection with master's and D. Min. degrees in pastoral counseling—students are counseled principally by three part-time staff persons and by advanced trainees. In the last two years, 63 (including family members) out of a student body of about 325 were counseled in 1986–87, and 71 in 1987–88. Students as counselees are never discussed in case conferences, only in individual supervision in the case of the advanced trainees.

Eighty-one (87 percent) seminaries responded that opportunity for counseling is provided. Of the 71 seminaries that responded to the question as to who does the counseling, 45 (63 percent) said that it was the seminary staff or faculty. Eight said "counseling center or referral," and five said "university service." Other responses included campus pastor, outside therapist, local mental health agencies or outpatient clinic, or licensed psychologist or other local professional.

As to the number of sessions, 28 indicated these were unlimited, 30 indicated "limited," while 33 did not respond. Frequently, cost or the time limitations of the seminary staff lead to the limitation of the number of sessions. It is a great advantage to have access to a service on a sliding scale that is affordable for the student.

How the Results Were Interpreted to Students

Interpretation to students is integral to self-understanding and counseling/guidance. Ninety (97 percent) of the seminaries responded that the results were interpreted to students. This interpretation was done by persons outside the seminary in fourteen cases, usually by the same service that administered them.

Students' Response

Seventy-one seminaries (80 percent) rated the response of students to the interpretation process as Very Favorable (24) or Favorable (47). Sixteen rated it "Mixed," with eight of these using the assessment for selection/screening, which provokes considerable anxiety in the students. It seems that students appreciate the assessment and interpretation process and its contribution to their self-understanding and/or counseling, especially when its main purpose is their growth and development. The expertise and attitude of the person doing the interpretation are also critical here. This kind of response should encourage seminaries who do not currently have such a program to initiate one.

Basis of Interpretation

Should interpretation be voluntary or compulsory? Group or individual? Forty-nine seminaries (52 percent) believe that it should be compulsory; thirty-two (35 percent) think it should be voluntary; and twelve (13 percent) "if need is seen." This raises the questions of who sees the need, and how it is communicated to the student, and what the student's response and feelings about this are.

The split between group and individual interpretations is 61 percent individual and 38 percent group. Those who use assessment instruments for specific class purposes would ordinarily use group interpretation. This is very helpful, but to use only group interpretations loses the opportunity to go more deeply into a student's concerns and provide the occasion needed for growth in personality and coping and interpersonal skills that are so essential for effective ministry.

The advantage of making the interpretation voluntary is in the attitude of the student as he or she comes to the interpretation. Some students may still be hesitant about whatever is required or compulsory, and that resistance can be the first thing that needs to be dealt with and overcome in doing the interpretation with the student.

On the other hand, if one comes voluntarily, the beginning attitude is better, and if the general feedback among the students is favorable to the process due to positive experiences with it, the person comes with positive expectations. The drawback is that some of the students who most need the interpretation may not seek it voluntarily. Where the experience is positive, 75 to 85 percent of the students do come voluntarily. Just as in counseling, it is best for the student to make the appointment and to take that initiative.

Who Has Access to Results?

The issue of confidentiality and access to assessment results is a sticky one. It raises the question of who the client is. Hinkle, in describing the philosophy of Clinical Pastoral Psychological Assessment at Garrett-Evangelical Theological Seminary, says, "Assessment within a seminary setting is understood as a three-person two-party contract. The seminary provides the service as a part of its educational resources, and so has an investment in what will augment its ability to prepare students for ministry. However strong this investment may be, the right of privacy and confidentiality for students is a primary and legal concern for the assessment staff. This tension is always a relevant feature of the milieu in which pastoral assessment is done" (Hinkle, 1988, pp. 238-39).

In the case of screening, the primary client is the judicatory or seminary, and the secondary one is the person being tested—though the respective needs, rights, and feelings of each need to be kept in delicate balance. The limits of confidentiality need to be spelled out carefully and specifically before the assessment process is undertaken. Under the Family Education Rights and Privacy Statement, students have the right to see what is in their files, unless they have specifically signed a waiver. In doing the test interpretation individually or in a group, students usually do see their test scores. The atmosphere should be one of openness, not secrecy. Eighty-nine of the ninety-three seminaries indicated that the results were accessible to students.

If the seminary makes the test results available to judicatories, it must be only on the informed, written consent of the student, unless that is specifically spelled out at the time of testing. Just exactly who will have access must be clearly understood and adhered to. This can make for a dilemma for the person doing the testing and interpretation to students, in cases where some important information bearing on the student's possible effectiveness in ministry is uncovered. Should the interpreter only discuss this openly and frankly with the student, hoping whatever action needs to be taken will be taken by the student? What if the student is unwilling to take action? Tarasoff et al. define the limits of confidentiality as being a time when there is danger to another person. As examined in chapter 23 of this book, which deals with legal and ethical issues, this is a thorny question! What is the seminary's responsibility here? What is the judicatory's, when reports are requested? How much does the interpreter reveal that may have been outside the test results themselves? Where the contract is clear, it is easier. It is harder in cases when the first contract is self-understanding/counseling, and later permission is given to release results to judicatories.

As the seminaries responded, there was a wide range of persons other than the student who may have access to results. This may represent the wide range of purposes and situations in which assessment was done. The largest number, 70, listed faculty/staff in the blank provided. Some listed more than one of the following: faculty advisor, 10; Dean, 12; faculty of specific classes or program, 16; with student permission, 2; faculty psychologist, 5; field director, 5; 1 each for Dean of Student Life, test administrator, academic staff, president, specific department faculty, assistant dean, staff, appropriate faculty, and assessment team. Additionally, 7 listed counseling staff, and 16 did not specify.

Seminary Understanding of Students

Just over half of the seminaries using assessment list as one purpose the seminary's understanding of its students, meaning through group profiles. As in all assessment with clergy, group norms are essential to avoid misinterpretation and to make adequate comparisons. In most of the personality inventories, clergy/seminary students score differently from the general population in several significant ways. In addition to expertise with the instrument in general, a good knowledge of the group norms is necessary (Cardwell, 1967).

Changes in motivation through the years in entering classes can sometimes be very significant, as, for example, during the 1968–71 years compared with the years preceding and following. Since the measures represent what the students bring with them through social influences and self-selection, understanding these can be useful in understanding and in avoiding frustration and surprise in teaching these students (Hunt, Cardwell, and Dittes, 1976).

Ministry Inventories, as part of its scoring service, includes a summary of the demographic data in Part I of the TSI, giving very helpful information about the group. This is especially useful now with more women and older and second-career students entering seminary.

Research

Closely related to the above is the whole matter of research. Where assessment has been done and results are available, important research on seminary students and their subsequent ministry is possible. A recent example of this is the Spring 1988 issue of *Theological Education,* in which Larsen and Shopshire were able to use data from the TSI from 1962 and 1975 and other specially gathered data to produce "A Profile of Contemporary Seminarians." Other research studies are listed in bibliographies of sources cited in the reference section of this book. The importance of research possibilities cannot be overstated. Only 15 percent of seminaries using assessment reported using the results for research purposes. It is hoped that in the future many more will do so.

31

Ecumenical Career Development Centers

THOMAS E. BROWN

Assessment, as part of career development planning and counseling, was "institutionalized" with the opening of the first church church sponsored career counseling center in late 1965. No doubt clergy had sought consultation from psychologists and other counselors before then and had been subjected to assessment as part of the process, but the opening of the Northeast Career Center in Princeton, New Jersey, placed it in a new context. In a pilot program, a model for provision of assessment and planning services to clergy was tested, revised, and implemented, then replicated in regional, ecumenically sponsored centers across the United States.

Today there are twelve centers and a group in Canada related to the Church Career Development Council (CCDC). These centers are located in Arlington, Texas; Atlanta, Georgia; Boston, Massachusetts; Chicago, Illinois; Columbus, Ohio; Lancaster, Pennsylvania; Laurinburg, North Carolina; Los Angeles and Oakland, California; Princeton, New Jersey; St. Paul, Minnesota; St. Petersburg, Florida; and Toronto, Ontario. The CCDC, located in Room 774, 475 Riverside Drive, New York, NY 10015, is sponsored and managed by twelve major church denominations as a coordinating and standard-setting organization. In addition to the CCDC related centers, there are two others that grew out of the Princeton experiment: The Center for Professional Development in Ministry, owned by Lancaster Theological Seminary in Pennsylvania, and Career Planning Centers of America, Inc., in St. Louis, MO, which is independently owned.

The context in which this work is done today is significantly different from what it was in 1965. Then, even the phrase "career counseling" was not at all common, and the availability of such services for adults was scarce. Literature about adult career development was in its infancy. The church was for once, it seems, ahead of the culture. Now, career assessment and counseling are available to adults on a widespread basis: colleges, universities, community agencies, and corporations offer many opportunities to evaluate and plan, and career counseling is a common phrase.

However, the holistically comprehensive approach originally tested in Princeton, and still followed for the most part (in principle if not in exactness) by the centers that grew out of Princeton, is difficult to find elsewhere. Economic considerations, as well as a lack of awareness of and concern for some of the things that are givens in the church-related centers, account for this. In the ministry, it is recognized that career represents more than simply a job or an income, and thus the centers serving clergy must help them assess a lot more than career if the work is to be relevant and effective. In fact, while some of the secular centers have focused too little on issues of meaning and value, probed at some depth, the church centers have failed at times to focus sufficiently on the practical sociological aspects of career development. There seems today to be more balance than there was in the beginning.

A holistic approach to assessment involves the individual in a process that combines self-assessment with objective, external input. It considers occupational facts as well as personal feelings and is open to exploration of options outside ministry as well as within. It confronts the individual with potential failure as well as success. A holistic approach to assessment respects the theological system operative for the individual, but seeks to avoid distortion of reality in the name of theology. It views the individual from a variety of perspectives—values, personality, needs, interests, abilities—and fosters self-actualization rather than dependency. It takes seriously the whole person—physical, emotional, and spiritual—and the occupational and family contexts in which the individual is functioning. This form of assessment is developmental in approach; it is seen as a process, not an event. (An early statement of "guiding principles" is available in my article, "Career Counseling for Ministers," *The Journal of Pastoral Care* [March 1971]: 33-40.)

Maintaining a balance in the programs offered has been a problem from the very beginning of the centers. Because of a heavy concern for emotional health, the CCDC standards have required that each client be seen by a clinical psychologist as well as by a career counselor (almost always an ordained person with special training). It has taken a special effort to keep this from tilting the services too much in the direction of clinical analysis of personality, referral to therapy, and such at the expense of the practical aspects of occupational functioning. A focus on the individual has inhibited the utilization of group resources. A review of literature from the centers shows that today there is much more balance than in the early days. Every center offers specific help with career direction and job seeking, and all offer opportunities for group experiences.

What actually happens when a person goes to a center will vary a bit, depending on the particular center and on the individual counselor that one has within a center, but there is a pattern that is fairly common. The person will be at the center for two to three days. The spouse is encouraged to participate. Prior to arrival, preparation has included the completion of objective tests, biographical surveys (life history and achievement), and a physical examination. During the time at the center, six to eight hours are spent in consultation with a counselor and an hour or more with the clinical psychologist. The sessions begin with exploration and review, move through feedback, and conclude with planning. Provision is made for follow up visits, or if the individual lives near enough the whole process might be done on a weekly basis for a number of months.

The instruments used vary according to preferences of the staff, but all centers evaluate basic emotional and mental health, intellectual abilities, orientation to ministry, vocational interests, marital health, and functional abilities.

While at first glance it may seem that these centers simply "test and report," the services and emphases are actually much broader. As the brochure for the Center for the Ministry, in Oakland, California, states:

In response to the life-planning needs of a decade of clients, we have evolved programs to help with self-understanding, using talents and skills effectively, clarifying personal and work values, advantageous use of personal style, time management, making the most of one's present job, conflict management, effectiveness as an administrator, planning a meaningful "sabbatical" or continuing education program, becoming bi-vocational, synchronizing dual careers, reentering the job market, retooling for a different career, mobility, writing an effective resume, particular career crises, retirement planning, and team building.

Programs to meet these needs have more variety than ever. For example, Northeast (Princeton) now offers a four-month process for individuals or dual career couples, involving from ten to eighteen hours of consultation time spread over six visits to the center. Midwest offers a four day out placement counseling program for persons leaving ministry as an occupation. North Central (St. Paul) provides staff for marriage counseling on a continuing basis. Southwest (Arlington) has a special program for persons considering work together on a staff. Several of the centers offer retreats and workshops on a wide variety of topics. Northeast offers the following programs that deal with adjustments related to early career, mid-career or pre-retirement, team building for multiple staff situations, career review and planning, dual career couples retreats, clergy couples workshops, stress reduction, couple enrichment, special concerns of the clergy family, and successful interviewing.

Midwest offers the above programs and others, such as conflict management, spirituality and the minister, leadership styles in ministry, mid-life malaise in ministry, pre-retirement planning, women in ministry, and time management.

A special emphasis in several centers is on the evaluation and counseling of candidates for the ministry. Lancaster reports that 60 percent of its caseload is now with candidates, 50 percent of whom are women. At Lancaster this is a two-step process: a first evaluation at the beginning of seminary, and a mid-seminary consultation, with an emphasis on discernment of vocational aptitudes for ministry and training of those aptitudes. North Central offers a program for "Seminarian Developmental Counseling" in which seminarians are tested and counseled each year they are in seminary. Princeton offers a one and one-half day Vocational Inventory Program for persons at the beginning of their careers. Midwest offers a pre-candidacy group program, a two-day candidate evaluation program, and a two and one-half day "vocational and psychological assessment program."

Several centers (Midwest and North Central emphasize it in their published materials) offer evaluation services for persons being considered for missionary assignment or for special positions of leadership in the church.

While confidentiality is respected by all of the centers, and no information is released without written consent of the individual client, the evaluation programs—whether for seminary candidates or for missionaries or leaders—all depend for effectiveness, as far as the sponsoring organizations are concerned, on release of a report from the center. Some special considerations must be kept in mind when a center staff moves from evaluation and counseling with a person to evaluation of a person and the sharing of that evaluation with a credentialing or certifying or hiring organization. Issues raised include the following:

- What is the objective basis for any predictions of "fit" made?

- How free is the candidate to be forthright and honest?

- If the consultation is not based on strictly objective data (job specific criterion-based tests), how is philosophical and emotional bias by the counselor or psychologist protected against?

- How are distortions of the data by committees and others interpreting it without the presence of a professional person avoided?

- Is there any difference in the success or failure rates of those who have been so evaluated and those who have not?

- How is balance between developmental counseling and candidate evaluation to be maintained?

- How does a center focusing on evaluation as a major effort prevent itself from being seen by its constituent clergy population as first and foremost a place of evaluation rather than of consultation?

- How does the center avoid the tendency of a committee or employer to use the center report as a way to shift its own responsibility for decision making, or for guidance, to the center staff?

These are not new questions, nor are they avoided or ignored by the staffs of the centers. Industry has dealt with this problem by keeping assessment centers and career counseling separate. The temptation in the churches from the very beginning of the career center concept has been to tie them together. It is logical to do so when approaching the task from the perspective that the individual is a professional, not an employee, seeking assistance and choosing freely with whom data will be shared. It is potentially more of a problem when the churches are sponsoring an organization that is expected with some persons to be evaluative and with others to be consultative. The centers walk a tight rope in this regard.

Trends for the Future

With career counseling now a common term, and with services widely available throughout the United States, a question must be raised about the efficacy of providing centers on a regional basis, aimed specifically at a special group of persons. A question also to be considered has to do with the potential bias in a staff that is working almost, if not entirely, exclusively with persons in, or wanting to be in, ministry. To what extent are the advantages of focus outweighed by the disadvantages of cultural isolation? This problem has always been corrected for somewhat by employing psychologists as consultants rather than as staff so that they bring in a perspective from the other persons and worlds to which and in which they relate. But is that adequate?

A trend that may help with these issues is seen in the emphasis in the Northeast brochure on services to persons in government, education, social services, and industry as well as in religion. Midwest reports that 15 percent of its client load is laypersons. The centers in Florida, Georgia, and North Carolina are all part of more broadly based services offered to youth and adults considering any occupation, a program offered by the Presbyterian Church in the south for more than forty years. The privately owned center in St. Louis serves a clientele that is 80 percent "secular" and 20 percent clergy, and accepts no contracts with church organizations on an ongoing basis, though it will accept payment by the organization for services to an individual.

Northeast mentions among its services the availability of supervision for persons training in counseling or psychology. In the interest of spreading availability of services to more locations, the centers might consider establishing a training program in career counseling with a focus on ministry for persons who are professionally trained in career counseling, but who are not familiar with the nuances of "clergy life." There are among the counselors certified by the National Board for Counselor Certification many persons who are active in the church, theologically sensitive, and professionally competent. A program to certify them for counseling with clergy would be welcomed by many of them.

This would have the advantage of exposing center staff to persons who are doing career counseling regularly with a broad cross-section of persons, and, when combined with other efforts, would heighten the staff's awareness of possibilities for work beyond the professional ministry. When one counsels with an executive one day (or hour), a teacher the next, an unemployed banker on the third day, and a minister on the fourth, one's perceptions of all of them are affected. There is a tendency in most career counselors to counsel toward the occupations with which one is most familiar. The broader the familiarity the less likely there is to be a bias in one direction or another. Some of this tendency is corrected by extensive study in the sociology of occupations, but there is probably nothing that affects one the way personal experience does. For example, it is a lot easier to counsel a minister toward being a banker if you've never counseled with a banker who found banking to be the pits, or to counsel a minister toward ministry as the strongest source of meaning if you've never listened to an engineer wax philosophically about the meaning in his or her work. These are over simplified examples, but they are not unrealistic ones.

As stated at the outset of this chapter, it is difficult to match the holistic comprehensiveness of the CCDC centers in the world of commercial or private services. Yet, thousands of laypersons who are related to the churches that sponsor the CCDC centers are trying to live out a life of faith in the midst of the secular community. They hunger for the kind of assessment and counsel that the CCDC centers offer, but very little attention is paid to that hunger. It is obvious why this is so, considering the economies of time and money, but could not CCDC personnel be more active in the American Association for Counseling and Development, or the state chapters related to it, or the National Career Development Association and the Association for Religious Values in Counseling, both affiliates of AACD? Through such affiliations, an influence could be exercised to broaden the view of counseling held by the professional persons who do belong and participate in those organizations. For a few years, CCDC held its annual meeting in conjunction with the AACD annual meeting, but that is no longer the case.

A trend that is somewhat evident, but not very strong, then, is toward a broader view of ministry by the ecumenical centers. In the light of an increase in tent-making ministries, more mid-life changes into ministry as well as out of ministry, and the ongoing search for meaning by persons in all walks of life, this trend needs encouragement. Evaluation (assessment) at its best has to do with testing of values, and many would respond to the opportunity for that when done in a non-threatening, supportive, professional climate.

Another trend, stronger in some centers than in others, is toward more group work. The Center for Professional Development in Ministry at Lancaster, Pennsylvania, was organized around a concept of group-based assessment and planning for continuing development in ministry. Using the Survey of Resources for Development in Ministry handbook, published by the center, thousands of ministers, priests, brothers, and nuns have assessed their ministry and planned for developmental growth. The handbook is based on the same assessment approaches that guided the development of the first career centers but replaces psychologists and counselors with peers in the group, guided by a trained consultant. This approach is not only economic and inclusive, but it also promotes cooperation in ministry. It teaches a way to use assessment as a community building experience. Such group approaches are a trend of the future. They lack the clinical depth found in the individual programs, but have a power to influence that is based on equality rather than authority, interdependence rather than dependency, colleague dialogue rather than consultant approval.

32

Alban Institute Approaches to Assessment

ROY OSWALD

Problems, Pitfalls, and Paradoxes

For the past ten years the Alban Institute has been consulting with clergy and congregations on the subject of clergy assessment. We have conducted workshops for clergy and lay leaders, and we have provided consultations for congregations as they have constructed assessment processes for themselves.

Ten years ago I set out to write a book on this subject. Fortunately, I did not complete that book. I have become more cautious about clergy assessment as I have seen how many clergy have been hurt by ill-conceived evaluation attempts. A religious voluntary system provides ample room for scapegoats.

Clergy assessment is one area where we at the Alban Institute believe secular technologies do not belong. Congregational members with confidence in their evaluative skills may volunteer to set up processes for the assessment of their pastors. They may then proceed to objectify the roles and functions of clergy on the assumption that these factors are quantifiable. But how do you measure the quality of an interaction between a pastor and a parishioner?

Many such assessments oversimplify the pastoral role. I do not believe that a quantifiable assessment can ever get at the essence of that role. In my basement, I have a foot-high pile of articles and instruments produced by consultants using this orientation. Few are worth the paper they are written on, as far as clergy are concerned.

Any system that purports to evaluate clergy without regard to context is a career assessment, not a performance review. When persons rate clergy on separate scales, such as "Preaching, Grade from 1 to 6" and "Church Administration Grade from 1 to 6," the raters are placing clergy on a universal scale and are failing to measure these qualities in the context of specific settings.

The Alban Institute constantly receives calls and letters requesting forms and procedures for clergy assessment. To date we have resisted putting into print one recommended process. My own response to such requests continues to be that it is best to hire someone to work with the pastor and congregation to tailor a process for that particular context.

There are two reasons for holding this position. First, the pastor needs someone in his or her corner to assist in dealing with unexpected and difficult information. Clergy are too vulnerable in the assessment process without outside advocates. Second, the congregation needs to know that an authority figure of some kind is available to manage the process in the eventuality that the religious authority for their parish comes under attack. (Laypeople do not like to confront the clay feet of their pastors.)

In addition to these concerns, other complexities in the clergy assessment process continue to trouble us. Those clergy who need an assessment are often least able to handle candid feedback. Those who eagerly engage in such a review are usually not the ones who will benefit most; they are, in fact, the types who will constantly ask their parishioners for feedback.

A second problem has to do with timing. When congregational life is going well, no one seems to want to evaluate. When things are going poorly, they do. Yet, when trouble exists between pastor and people, it is the worst possible time to engage in assessment activity. No matter how well grounded the process, it will be used by laypeople primarily as an expression of their discontent over what is or is not happening. Generally clergy are damaged in such situations, and nothing really changes. The best time to evaluate is when clergy and congregation are feeling good about one another.

Another troubling problem we often encounter is the notion that in an evaluation we should focus on what is not being done well. The inference is that if we tell people how they fail, they will be able to change and improve. In fact, the very opposite usually takes place. When people receive negative feedback, they become discouraged and disheartened. Rather than focussing on change and improvement, they begin to consider leaving or moving into some other kind of employment.

In a study conducted for General Electric by Meyer, Kay, and French (1965, p. 123), such an unintended consequence of performance review became clear. General Electric management had assumed that a clear comparison system would have a positive, or at least a neutral, effect on performance. The assumption was that such results would inspire good people to work harder and would alert the poor performers to the need for focused improvement. Here is what the study discovered:

1. criticism had a negative effect upon achievement and goal-setting;
2. praise had little effect one way or another;
3. the average person reacted defensively to criticism during the appraisal interview;
4. defensiveness then produced inferior performance;
5. the disruptive effects of repeated criticism on subsequent performance were greater among those individuals who were already low in self-esteem.

W. Edwards Deming believes that performance appraisal is a substitute for a primary function of organizational leadership, helping people function at their best. He calls the annual appraisal "the destroyer of people" and "the most powerful inhibitor to quality and productivity in the Western world" (Deming, 1986).

Critics like Deming see this process not only inflicting personal damage but also ascribing to individuals in a group differences that may be caused totally by the system in which they work. For clergy that means they are being reviewed according to people's frustrations with a church system in which they are joint participants and for which more than one person must bear responsibility.

We have often observed that before a formal assessment is initiated, clergy and congregation may have functioned reasonably well. Following the assessment, clergy may become depressed and unmotivated and laypeople may become bogged down by anger that has surfaced through the process. It is all too easy for even the most objective participants to become discouraged by the way their minister may not be measuring up to the criteria that have been set.

Lyle Schaller has often said that 90 percent of what clergy do is invisible to 90 percent of the laity 90 percent of the time. When simplistic images of the clergy role are brought to an evaluation session, an enormous

collection of individual expectations can easily be laid on clergy. When good-hearted clergy try to live up to all those expectations, role overload can quickly occur. (See chapter 5 of this volume for some of these negative results.)

Anderson and Hahn (1979) make a strong case in an article they wrote about the call of clergy. They argue that the call is more to a role than to a series of functions or a performance of a set of discrete tasks.

Functional performance is much more easily evaluated than the full dimensions of a role. Think of how we would expect parents to be evaluated. We would not be satisfied with an appraisal that focussed only on clean clothes and nutritious meals. We would want to take a look at the quality of presence a parent had with a child, the self-discipline and modeling offered, the congruence between actual behavior and espoused values, and spiritual depth and how it is communicated.

These issues of role in parenting are much harder to evaluate. They do not lend themselves to a simple check for food on the table or the absence of dust on a counter. Much clergy evaluation is like checking for dust. It involves the teaching, preaching, administering, and visiting functions, but there is more to the clergy role than the performance of those specific functions.

All these concerns about the problems, pitfalls, and paradoxes of clergy assessment have caused us to broaden our view. Our focus is now on evaluative processes that clergy themselves initiate in order to get a better fix on their professional development needs. The prelude to personal growth is an openness and vulnerability that allows clergy to confront areas where they feel uncertain, fearful, or inadequate. I believe that clergy will not open themselves to these unknowns without the confidence that they maintain some control over the process.

Ministry Evaluation: A Broader View

Alban Institute considers it essential that clergy have primary input into the assessment process. But if a church is going for a thorough "top-down" evaluation, it is vital that the process not work to isolate the individual. A broader approach, which we call "ministry evaluation," involves the entire parish, not just its full-time professionals. Clergy and lay leaders can reflect together on the quality of their shared efforts. The operative question is "How are we doing?"

We assist congregations in asking that question by turning to the words developed by the early church leaders to describe the marks of the true church of Jesus Christ. They said that the church of Jesus Christ was present if there were three elements:

kerygma—the proclamation of the good news; *koinonia*—a Christ-centered fellowship; and *diakonia*—a ministry to those in pain, need, or difficulty.

Some would add a fourth dimension, *didache* (teachings about Jesus), but we place that in a sub-category under kerygma. I have used these categories in a half-dozen parish evaluations and have found them quite workable.

Under the heading of *kerygma*, we ask about the quality of proclamation in the parish. To what extent is this a "good news" place? When people come to the parish are they consistently offered a message of faith, hope, and love? To be sure, much of this depends on the quality of sermons that are preached on a regular basis, but if that is the only place good news is shared, the congregation is in trouble. Members need to be sharing good news with one another. Are people helped to share openly the deeper dimensions of their lives? Are people encouraged to try to articulate what their faith means to them? Does the parish have a vision for itself that is shared by the membership? Are children being taught well the basics of the faith? Are there adult opportunities for learning? These are all kerygma issues.

When it comes to *koinonia*, we look at the quality of the fellowship in the parish. Are people feeling accepted? Are some valued more than others? Do newcomers experience warm caring immediately when they step inside the door? Is the parish leadership consciously teaching members how to be more compassionate and openly affectionate with one another? Are conflicts resolved with candor, yet in ways that allow persons to maintain integrity and self-respect? Does the parish have frequent opportunities to experience their oneness in Christ?

The *diakonia* aspects of parish life have to do with caring for others—being a servant community. To what extent are people satisfied with the way the parish initiates community involvement on behalf of its members? Is the congregation involved in peacemaking, in being a reconciler in the community and the world? Does the parish support its members in their daily ministry at home and place of work? Christians are busy at the work of transforming a broken world to wholeness. To what extent are members satisfied with their roles in this regard?

In the churches where I have used this model, I have been the outside person who came in to facilitate the process. If congregations want to do a quality parish review (a process that need not occur any more often than every three to five years), we feel it is wise to hire an outside consultant.

In this instance, the board makes that decision, and the consultant is accountable to the board. The board's decision communicates to church members that their input is taken seriously and that there is a planned outcome to the process. It ensures that corners aren't cut. Most important, the presence of the consultant gives everyone—clergy and laity—a sense that there is someone monitoring the process and, as noted earlier in this article, someone to fill a void if the religious authority for the parish is under attack.

Growth-oriented Performance Appraisal

There is another model that we endorse, which is designed specifically as a growth-oriented experience for the individual. This is the option to take when the individual is genuinely curious about how he or she is doing and wants to know how to improve performance.

It is important that this kind of evaluation not be confused with what I refer to as "administrative review." That process is often used by CEOs, supervisors, or vestries to ascertain salary issues, promotion policies, job descriptions, and the utilization of employee resources. It is a "top-down" process. Most people grit their teeth and put up with the routine even though they may be unhappy about what is happening to them. When this kind of review occurs in a church environment, it may remind laypeople of what they have experienced at work. They may want to avoid involvement in the process. Others, as noted earlier, may mistakenly assume that their own workplace evaluative skills can be applied to a church system.

Most research on assessment indicates that a beneficial performance appraisal cannot be routinely meshed with a standard administrative review without potentially harmful results. The performance appraisal offers a situation in which clergy are willing to explore their more vulnerable sides, those places where they feel afraid and insecure and those places where their work may be pinching them.

We suggest that the individual carefully test the appraisal ground rules in advance by asking these questions:

1. Is someone else imposing an appraisal process on me for decisions to be made for the church, or am I imposing the process on myself to enhance my own ministry?
2. Who owns the findings once they are received?
3. Who is in charge of the process?

If the person is able to decide what to do with the findings (even if shared with others) and is in charge throughout the process, then he or she is engaged in a performance appraisal process with potential for growth and development. If the data are owned by someone else, and the process is controlled by others who decide what will be evaluated and how findings will be used, then what is proposed is an administrative review.

I am not trying to suggest that one process is right and the other is wrong. Administrative review is a necessary ingredient in the personnel system of any organization concerned about appropriate allocation of its human resources. But it is a restricted focus and does not provide the kind of ownership that impels the clergy to open up to further personal growth.

Now that the ground rules have been established, additional safeguards can be taken. When choosing the areas of ministry to be evaluated—such as preaching, pastoral care, or administration—it is best not to choose more than two or three. Although it is tempting to go for a shotgun approach: the more specific one can be, the more helpful the experience.

Once areas of ministry to be evaluated have been selected, a list should be made of the questions to be addressed about performance within these areas. We next advise the person to identify the congregational members who will participate in gathering information. This means consideration of those who can act as a support group throughout the process. The selection should include persons with whom one is willing to share the painful and vulnerable aspects of life and ministry—persons who are or have been at the core of the congregation and understand its dynamics—and persons who are not currently in decision making positions (church leadership must be protected from a conflict of interest situation).

The laypersons selected need to feel totally invested in the experience. The pastor can help ease their anxieties by sharing with them the following:

1. His or her own assessment of performance in very specific terms;
2. Why feedback would be especially helpful in the areas chosen; and
3. Their specific role in making that feedback meaningful.

There is value in informing the church board of the appraisal process put into place. Board members should expect to hear only that care has been taken to safeguard that process and the ongoing needs of the congregation. Learnings may be shared with the board by clergy at the end of the process, but the specific feedback is confidential. Here again is another situation

in which the involvement of a consultant provides space for all parties. The consultant can assist right from the start as the support group is formed, the areas of inquiry are identified, and the system of feedback is designed.

In this design, the consultant is hired by and is accountable to the pastor. Often a board may be willing to cover the costs as a way of supporting its minister's developmental goals.

In designing the feedback process, those in the congregation from whom information will be sought must be targeted. At Alban Institute, we feel that it is best to engage a representative sample of the congregation in the evaluation process (⅓ active leadership, ⅓ active attenders, ⅓ fringe members). This follows the established practice of pollsters like Gallup and Harris. A group of as few as twelve or no more than twenty-four will work well. A larger group will make the collation of data difficult and may seem like a major intervention into the life of the congregation.

The method used to gather data should fit both the size of the sample and the number of issues to be explored. Those issues should help frame the task. For example, when seeking a better fix on leadership style, engage those who see clergy most often in a leadership capacity. When looking for insights on effectiveness as a pastoral counselor, people who have been counseled should be among those contacted.

In the actual execution of the evaluation process, it is difficult for clergy to serve as both leaders and active listeners. Either those in the support group or the consultant should fill the leadership function. For a focussed group discussion, the consultant can chair the meeting. This allows clergy the freedom to listen, to take notes, and possibly to share reactions to the feedback. The consultant is also a good resource for collating and interpreting data, or the support group may be involved in that task.

The process may not be completed on the first round. There may be a need to review ambiguous returns and sharpen questions for another round. If the feedback is particularly stimulating, the inquiry can be broadened.

Alban's recommendation at this juncture is for a pre-negotiated incubation period. Instantaneous reaction is a mistake. There is more meaning in this information than will be grasped at its first reporting. We counsel some space and time.

The last step is essential: development of a plan of action. The process needs a conclusion. The pastor needs some concrete form for long-term growth and development. This plan should include two key elements: first, provision for behavioral changes to make within the parish; and second, long-term personal/professional development plans for the next three to five years. In short, the plan must respond to questions of what is to be done differently as a result of the process, both in terms of day-to-day parish life and continuing education over the months and years ahead.

This plan of action should be tested with the consultant and the support group. They should be able to give an objective judgment as to whether or not the plan responds adequately to the feedback received. They also should be able to sense whether the plan is a realistic fit with career-path and personal qualities.

Putting oneself in charge of a process like this one is a remarkable learning experience. In fact, a well-constructed performance appraisal with built-in supports is like turning a page to a new chapter in our lives. Yet, at Alban Institute we refer to clergy performance appraisal as a mine field, often haphazard in its construction and sadly lacking in humanity on so many occasions.

In its simplest construction, performance appraisal should come down to the pastor and the people being clear and candid about the things that matter most in their corporate life together. This type of experience must be approached with extreme caution. That is why we have proposed both a broad view of ministry evaluation and a practical series of steps to be followed to protect the interests of all involved.

At the outset, we have urged clarity of purpose and ownership. The clergy must take the lead to define the process and the outcome. A group of laypersons must be assembled to mentor and support. They will need encouragement and training. Those who will provide information must also feel invested. Church leaders will benefit from an understanding of the procedures to be followed. The religious authority of the congregation must be safeguarded.

To nurture this special environment within the larger environment of a functioning church, a consultant can provide objectivity and reassurance. There will be more confidence that the process will not spin out of control or neutralize itself before a productive payoff.

While we have called for precision and objectivity in the formulation of ground rules and guidelines, we support the broadest possible interpretation of clergy performance. This mystical, mysterious role of "resident holy person" challenges us to reach beyond the limits of a 1 to 10 numerical scale.

33

A Protestant Denominational Application

ROBERT F. KOHLER

There has been a steady increase in the use of psychological assessment as a means by which candidates for ordained ministry, diaconal ministry, and mission service are evaluated in The United Methodist Church. Although the history of such evaluation is relatively short, the development of psychological assessment processes has been rather dramatic in recent years. While the General Board of Global Ministries of The United Methodist Church has used psychological assessment of candidates for mission service for over thirty years, its use in the selection of candidates for ordination has a more recent history.

During the decade of the 1960s, psychological assessment became a regular part of the student assessment program of many Methodist seminaries. Although not used as an entrance requirement, psychological assessment became a significant part of the guidance and evaluation of seminary students. Once introduced into this context, Annual Conference boards of ordained ministry discovered the value of such assessment in the selection and training of candidates. As a consequence, many boards of ordained ministry contracted with the seminaries for a report on psychological assessment that would be used in the selection process outside of the seminary setting. The progressive use of psychological assessment in The United Methodist Church, therefore, moved from the assessment of mission personnel to seminary students and then from seminary students to candidates for ordination in the Annual Conferences.

The shift of psychological assessment from the seminary to the Annual Conference was accompanied by a reduction in the number of seminaries using psychological assessment as a tool in the guidance of students. Although it is difficult to say whether it was the seminaries' initial commitment to psychological assessment or their decision to discontinue such assessment that served as the catalyst for Annual Conferences to contract independently for psychological assessment of candidates, what is clear is

the fact that in the mid 1960s, Annual Conferences began to turn to psychologists for the assessment services they wanted and needed.

By 1972, the use of psychological assessment by boards of ordained ministry in the North Central Jurisdiction led a subcommittee of the Committee on Ministry to carry out a series of workshops for boards of ordained ministry and persons doing psychological assessment of candidates. These workshops led directly to the construction of a set of guidelines for psychological assessment, which, after undergoing several revisions, still articulate the basic principles and procedures for assessment through the Annual Conferences of The United Methodist Church.

About the same time a national consultation on psychological assessment, sponsored by the Division of Ordained Ministry, in 1978 served to extend the dialogue about candidate assessment to the national level. Through this consultation, a committee was established to advise the Annual Conferences, pastoral evaluation specialists, and the Division of Ordained Ministry on the issues related to psychological assessment of candidates for ordained ministry. It is the work of this committee, now known as the Advisory Committee on Psychological Assessment, that has guided the application of psychological assessment to the selection of candidates for ordained and diaconal ministry in The United Methodist Church (see chap. 9, pp. 62-63). The importance of the work of this committee in the development of psychological assessment processes cannot be overstated.

In response to the 1978 national consultation, the advisory committee surveyed all conference boards of ordained ministry to document how psychological assessment was being applied to the assessment of candidates for ordained ministry. This survey was conducted by Harry DeWire. His survey (1979) wanted to know (1) how many conferences were using psychological assessment; (2) how assessment reports were being used; (3) who was administering and

Applications of Psychological Assessment by Annual Conference Boards of Ordained Ministry in The United Methodist Church

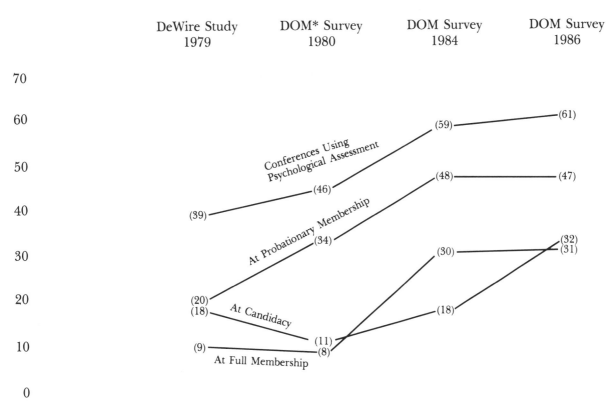

* Division of Ordained Ministry, The United Methodist Church

interpreting the assessment data; (4) what degree of satisfaction with and confidence in the assessment process was in evidence; (5) who received and reviewed the reports and how they were handled and kept; and (6) the kind of assistance and research that would make programs of psychological assessment more effective.

DeWire found that about half of the Annual Conferences (39 out of 73) were using psychological assessment procedures in 1978, and that assessment was being done for both selection and guidance purposes. He concluded that interest in the area of psychological assessment was intense and that further work was needed to assist boards of ordained ministry in these matters. DeWire also discovered that 30 of the 39 conferences doing psychological assessment were using the Minnesota Multiphasic Personality Inventory (MMPI), 19 were using the Strong-Campbell Interest Inventory (SCII), 15 were using the Edwards Personal Preference Test, and 10 were employing a version of the Incomplete Sentences Blank. DeWire's research provided an empirical basis for structuring the work of the advisory committee and the Division of Ordained Ministry in the application of psychological assessment to the selection process of candidates for ordained ministry.

Among other things, the DeWire study revealed that most Annual Conferences were using psychological assessment as part of the selection process for probationary membership and deacon's orders. This meant that most candidates were being evaluated during their first year of seminary; a psychological report was included among the material reviewed by their boards of ordained ministry at this decision point. A few conferences (9) also required a psychological report for full conference membership and elder's orders after graduation from seminary. Others were willing to offer or require assessment services for candidates when questions of psychological fitness surfaced at a variety of points in the selection process.

When the Division of Ordained Ministry surveyed the work of boards of ordained ministry in 1980, the same pattern of psychological assessment emerged with one exception; the number of conferences using psychological assessment in the selection and guidance of candidates for ordained ministry increased from 39 to 46. While 34 of the Annual Conferences were doing psychological assessment of applicants for probationary membership, only 11 were offering assessment to persons seeking certification as candidates for ordained ministry, the first required step a person takes on the road to ordination in The United Methodist Church, a step that precedes probationary membership and ordination as a deacon by at least a year. This pattern, which stressed psychological assessment at probationary membership, was further reinforced by the fact that in 1980 only 8 conferences were doing psychological assessment of post-seminary probationers preparing for full conference membership, and only 5 conferences were assessing persons licensed as local (lay) pastors.

In retrospect, it seems apparent that the increase in the number of conferences doing psychological assessment was directly attributable to the work of the advisory committee that provided guidelines, resources, research, consultative services, and a network of communication among those doing assessment of candidates for ordained ministry. Such a conclusion is justifiable in the light of the significant increase in the number of conferences doing psychological assessment between 1980 and 1984. (See p. 185.)

When the Division of Ordained Ministry surveyed the work of the 73 boards of ordained ministry in 1984, it discovered that the total number of conferences using psychological assessment for the guidance and selection of candidates for ordained ministry had increased to 59. Although the predominant application of assessment continued to be at the probationary membership decision point in the Annual Conference (48 of the 59 conferences), there was a significant increase in the number of conferences doing psychological assessment of applicants for candidacy certification and of applicants for full conference membership. While in 1980 only 8 conferences indicated that they were doing assessment at the full membership decision point, 30 conferences so indicated in 1984. While only 11 conferences were doing psychological assessment of candidates applying for candidacy certification in 1980, 18 conferences were doing so in 1984, and 32 in 1986. By 1986, therefore, it was apparent that a change in the pattern of applications of psychological assessment had occurred in The United Methodist Church.

Although there was a slight decrease in the number of conferences requiring psychological assessment as a prerequisite for probationary membership (from 48 to 47), there was a large increase in the number of Annual Conferences including psychological assessment at the candidacy level (from 18 to 32 conferences). Since it was the advisory committee and the staff of the Division of Ordained Ministry that, in the 1984 training of new board of ordained ministry leadership, presented the rationale for shifting psychological assessment to candidacy certification where the primary issues of "fitness" for ordained ministry are examined, it is logical to conclude that the boards, recognizing the logic of such a shift, moved rapidly in that direction.

One of the other factors in the development and application of a system of psychological assessment of candidates for ordained ministry in The United Methodist Church was the selection of a standard set of assessment instruments by the advisory committee and the Division of Ordained Ministry. With the knowledge gained from the DeWire study that the most commonly used instruments for psychological assessment were the MMPI, the SCII, and a sentence completion form, the advisory committee recommended the use of these or comparable instruments along with a standard intelligence test, a personal data inventory, a set of references, and a clinical interview with a qualified pastoral evaluation specialist. The advisory committee later added the Adjective Check List to the core group of standard instruments. The establishment of this core battery of instruments, combined with an assessment interview by a qualified pastoral evaluation specialist, not only served to focus attention on a variety of instruments examining issues related to personality, intelligence, and interests, but it also had the advantage of providing the committee with an agenda for research into the validity and normative bases of the instruments and the usefulness of the psychological assessment in the selection and guidance of candidates for ordained ministry.

The rationale for establishing the core battery of inventories, as presented by John Hinkle in *A Guidebook on Psychological Assessment in a Pastoral Evaluation Process*, published by the Division of Ordained Ministry in 1988, included concerns to standardize procedures in the interest of (1) greater consistency and quality in reports, (2) establishing appropriate norms for scoring and interpretation of candidate test materials, (3) reducing duplication of efforts on the part of candidates for multiple contexts of assessment, and (4) consistency of data collection necessary to ongoing research essential to the further improvement of the consistency and quality of psychological evaluation processes of current and future clergy candidates. It was believed that the standard core battery would reduce duplication of effort by the candidate, facilitate the development of norms for sub-populations, standardize data collection and reporting, allow for a greater degree of quality control, enhance the possibility for ongoing long-term research, and provide an empirical basis for refinement of theory and practice in the assessment of candidates for ordained ministry in The United Methodist Church.

Once the advisory committee committed itself to a set of standard instruments for psychological assessment, it then turned its attention to a series of research projects related to the use of those instruments in order to enhance the quality of psychological assessment in the denomination.

1. In 1980, the Division of Ordained Ministry published *The Guidebook for Pastoral Evaluation Specialists,* edited by Doris M. Jones, which contains Jeffrey Means' paper on "Key Concepts in the Selection and Application of Criteria in the Nurture, Preparation, and Selection of Persons for the Ordained Ministry." This paper identifies several key concepts within the process of selection and nurture of candidates that affect the manner in which criteria are chosen and applied in the assessment process.

2. *The Guidebook for Pastoral Evaluation Specialists* also contains an abstract of Emily Demme Haight's 1980 dissertation on the "Psychological Criteria for the Selection of Ministerial Candidates," which outlines the relationship between the recommendations of pastoral evaluation specialists and the decisions of boards of ordained ministry regarding candidates for ordained ministry.

3. In 1983, Michael P. Comer (see chap. 11 of this book) conducted an empirical study of the United Methodist psychological assessment program. The data involved prediction based on the pastoral evaluation specialist's use of the MMPI, Adjective Check List, Strong-Campbell Interest Inventory, Shipley Intelligence Test, and letters of recommendation. Multiple regression based on data from the test scores and the pastoral evaluation specialist's judgment ratings was used to predict the recommendation to the boards of ordained ministry. Comer's finding was that the psychologist's rating could be predicted from the data. He further concluded that the Shipley Intelligence Test does not add enough additional information to justify its inclusion in the core battery.

4. In 1985, Pamela Holliman completed "A Study of Psychological Assessment Procedures as Adjunctive to Personnel Selection Processes in a Religious Organization" (see chap. 12 of this book). Her theological framework served as a context for determining the link between the goals and programs of psychological assessment in seven Annual Conferences of The United Methodist Church. Her study provided empirical documentation in support of the general notion of a widespread consensus among boards of ordained ministry and candidates about the prioritizing of candidate application materials for use in selection decision making. The study also found a high degree of satisfaction among boards in terms of the usefulness of psychological assessment reports in the selection process. These and other similar research projects, sponsored in part by the Advisory Committee on Psychological Assessment and supported through the development of an archive of assessment data, have strengthened the applications of psychological assessment in the guidance and selection of candidates for ordained ministry.

One of the most significant shifts in the application of psychological assessment occurred in 1984, when the advisory committee suggested that the boards of ordained ministry make it a part of the required studies in the Candidacy studies. As noted above, the number of conferences choosing to do assessment at this decision point nearly doubled within the next two years, moving from 18 to 32 Annual Conferences. This meant that by 1986, approximately half of all conferences engaged in psychological assessment of candidates for ordained ministry were doing so as a part of the candidacy process.

Although most of these conferences were also continuing to use assessment at the decision point for probationary membership, it became increasingly clear that a significant change in the pattern of psychological assessment was under way. To encourage this shift to what was seen as a more appropriate place for psychological assessment, the advisory committee recommended that part of the fees for enrollment in candidacy for ordained ministry be used for the establishment of a Candidacy Assessment Office in the Division of Ordained Ministry, the purpose of which was to create a central scoring service for the core battery used in the assessment process. As a result of this suggestion and the creative work of the advisory committee, a procedure was developed in which supervising pastors working with candidates in the vocational exploration process were trained to administer the core battery of assessment instruments upon application to the Division of Ordained Ministry. Assessment materials and score sheets then were sent to the Candidacy Assessment Office at the division for central scoring. Assessment profiles, references, and the Personal Data Inventory were sent to a qualified pastoral evaluation specialist (PES) for use in a clinical interview. From these materials and the interview with the candidate, the PES developed a psychological report that was shared first with the candidate for the purpose of self-understanding and growth, then, in most cases, with the district committee or board of ordained ministry, to be used in a decision for certification of candidacy.

As a result of the development of the Candidacy Assessment Office, the number of conferences doing assessment at the candidacy level has continued to increase. As of this writing, 30 Annual Conferences use the services of the Candidacy Assessment Office, while a number of other conferences have developed their own systems of psychological assessment for use as part of the candidacy program.

The most recent application for psychological assessment in The United Methodist Church has been the assessment of candidates for diaconal ministry. Diaconal ministers are laypersons with a master's level education in such areas of service as church music, Christian education, and church administration. As of January 1, 1989, denominational rules have required that every candidate for consecration as a diaconal minister participate in a program of psychological assessment. Since most Annual Conferences already had a system of assessment for ordained ministry in place, many responded to this legislative requirement by using the same system for diaconal ministry. Since it cannot be assumed that the standards for ministry and criteria for psychological assessment of candidates for diaconal ministry are identical to those of ordained ministry, the Advisory Committee on Psychological Assessment has expanded its membership and its vision of assessment to include diaconal ministers. It is anticipated that specific adaptations of the assessment program will emerge as the work of the advisory committee continues to address this area of responsibility.

As seen through this review of the applications of psychological assessment in The United Methodist Church, the key to understanding the development of the system of assessment of candidates for ordained and diaconal ministry is the work of the Advisory Committee on Psychological Assessment. For more than a decade, this committee has probed the assessment procedures of Annual Conferences and pastoral evaluation specialists. In the process, it has provoked discussion and consideration of the issues related to psychological assessment. It has recommended a core battery of assessment instruments to be used in the evaluation of a candidate's fitness for ordained or diaconal ministry in The United Methodist Church, and it has developed a centralized scoring procedure that not only standardizes the assessment process, but also provides a data base for research into the norms and values of the assessment instruments themselves. With the support of the Division of Ordained Ministry, the advisory committee has engaged in an ongoing series of research projects that have created a significant body of literature on clergy assessment—literature that has become the basis of consultation and training of both boards of ordained ministry and pastoral evaluation specialists.

The committee has also provided consultative services for Annual Conferences as they developed application for psychological assessment, and it published a directory of pastoral evaluation specialists, which is used by Annual Conference boards of ordained and diaconal ministry. A newsletter of the Network of Pastoral Evaluators, published by the advisory committee, seeks to provide regular communication with those directly involved in assessment. Without the vision, the dedicated commitment, and the hard work of this committee, one can assume that the applications of psychological assessment in The United Methodist Church would be inconsistent and less effective. With its commitment to a high quality program of assessment, a system has emerged for the development and support of psychological assessment in The United Methodist Church.

34

Clergy Assessment in Roman Catholic Applications

BRIAN P. HALL

A major expectation held by Roman Catholics about beginning priests is that they manifest an openness in their ministerial style while remaining sensitive to the history and tradition of the church. A stereotype that focuses heavily on the sacramental and liturgical roles of the priests is destroyed, for a greater concern emerges that young priests relate the faith to daily life, preach well, and encourage the building up of the Body of Christ within their congregations. (Schuller, Stommen, and Brekke, 1980, p. 467)

This chapter will address issues about assessment of candidates for the priesthood in the Roman Catholic Church, while highlighting areas that are unique to this denominational perspective.

Clearly, anyone dealing with clergy assessment is not going to see the Roman Catholic situation as one among many other denominations. The world population of the Catholic Church is approximately 700,000,000 and, therefore, must be seen as a central influence on the whole Christian paradigm as it is experienced in the world today.

The admission of persons into the rite of ordination, their worthiness of such a vocation, and the difficulty of assessing that worthiness must be seen within the historical context in which we find ourselves. As such, we will begin with a brief historical review, particularly in North America, and how that affects the candidacy for the priesthood. Second, we will look at the norms for admission to candidacy to the priesthood as they arise out of Canon Law. Finally, we will look at some of the new developments in assessment instrumentation and approaches, which might add a dimension that is perhaps a unique contribution from Roman Catholicism.

The Historical Perspective

As with all churches, the presence of Roman Catholicism on the North American continent grew considerably with the great emigrant missionary efforts from Europe into the New World in the nineteenth and the first half of the twentieth centuries. Roman Catholicism was identified very much with the needs of specific ethnic populations that were settling in various parts of the country, German, Polish, Irish, and so on. It was this union between cultural survival and religious fervor, related to mission in the New World, that did so much to establish Roman Catholicism's stronghold in North America.

One indication of the strength of the relationship between the culture and religion of Catholicism was the manner in which the church and the laity joined in a strong physical liaison to perpetuate their mutual development. For example, Catholic parents were encouraged to have large families. These families would receive pastoral care from the church, which provided education and health care staffed by priests and nuns. In return, families were expected to dedicate their youngest children to the priesthood and sisterhood.

Catholic education was very much a nurturing environment for new vocations. As such, in the 1950s there was a plethora of minor seminaries that would take care of a young man's high school education and at the same time prepare him for seminary.

The role of women in the church in the nineteenth century was a very important factor in the formation of modern social and welfare institutions. The wives of wealthy Protestant and Roman Catholic industrialists, on the one hand, and a growing number of women's religious congregations in the Roman Catholic Church brought with them a strong caring element that gave rise to many of the social institutions so important to the development of the new society. Within the Roman Catholic Church, health care and education were of particular significance.

Another important aspect of Roman Catholicism is understanding its uniform system of authority. Unlike the majority of other churches, the central focus is not so much in the congregation but in the diocese, the geographic area presided over by the bishop. Each bishop is connected to the other bishops and to the primary bishop in Rome, the pope, through a hierarchical system of management that has not been equaled in the modern world. As the new world of the industrial revolution centralized administrative management and employee populations in the cities, so the Roman Catholic Church did this par excellence in the early 1900s through the new Canon Law in its development of worldwide administration of bishops and priests working in coordination through a singular hierarchy whose headquarters were at the Vatican in Rome.

Uniformity through Canon Law, carried over into education, dress, and moral dictates, was felt throughout the church as a whole, giving its membership a sense of belonging and nurturance that was effective in the way it developed its mission and services through hospitals and schools. It was a church that was dominantly male in its orientation and required radical commitment from its priests, brothers, and sisters in the form of celibacy.

Vatican II

The second Vatican Council in the mid 1960s, led by Pope John XXIII, signaled a change in the Roman Catholic Church and consequently in Christendom itself, which was at the same time adjusting and reacting to the huge shifts going on in Western society (Arbuckle, 1987). Those shifts that have radically affected the nature of the Roman Catholic Church and society are in part as follows:

1. Central services, such as education, health care and welfare, previously managed to a significant degree by the church are being taken over by society. This process has not ended but continues today, especially in North America, Europe, and Canada.

2. Many of the differences that kept major denominations apart were dissolved by new knowledge from an information explosion at every level of scholarship. As such, theological differences regarding interpretation of the Bible, common understanding of history and its development in the church, and awareness of global suffering and the need for ecumenical collaboration have eroded many differences between the churches and brought about new levels of collaboration.

3. New understanding of the human being through the social sciences (Tonna, 1982) has broadened the base of spirituality and its meaning and increased our sensitivity to the unique contribution women make to

society, undermining earlier sexual stereotypes and raising questions across all denominations about the nature of ministry.

Prior to the second Vatican Council, the Roman Catholic Church placed enormous importance on the central focus of the control of ministry through the male cleric. Within this framework, the role of "non-clerics," including religious, was to assist the cleric in fulfilling the responsibility of ministry (see Coriden, Green, and Heintschel, 1985, p. 713).

This premise, which was a part of the 1917 code of Canon Law, reflected the unchallenged ecclesiology of the time. An Apostolic Letter in 1972 from Pope Paul VI changed all that by restoring the permanent diaconate. This was followed by renewed affirmation of the importance of lay ministry as flowing from the sacrament of baptism. The critical issue here is that these official changes reflected a shift in consciousness in the church itself, that ministry as based in the sacrament of baptism must be reflected in ecclesial polity.

The issues that have been summarized above serve to put in focus the difficulty that any person has in a seminary or working in a vocation office for a bishop with the process of assessment of a candidate's worthiness for priesthood. Assessment in the Roman Catholic Church is made difficult at this time within a church that is in radical transition.

The Present Reality

The historical changes outlined above have brought about a reality whereby vocations for the priesthood within the Roman Catholic Church have declined radically since the late 1960s (Arbuckle, 1986). When viewing this system as a whole, it is necessary to consider that the Roman Catholic Church, although exhibiting an outward sign of unity, consists of two systems of authority within.

The first system of authority is centralized authority through the diocesan structure. That is, the total geographic area of the United States and Canada is divided into dioceses, each governed by a bishop. Within each diocese there is a series of parishes, each ideally governed by a priest. The role of the bishop is to nurture and administrate, for the purpose of unity, his priests, who in turn have oversight over each of their parishioners. At the same time, the bishop is responsible to the other bishops and to the primary bishop in Rome, the pope.

The second and parallel system of authority is the

complex of international, independent religious orders and congregations. This constitutes a system of dispersed authority, which, although theoretically under the authority of the pope, operates independently and cooperatively with local bishops in their dioceses.

There are religious congregations that are under the authority of the local bishop, but for the purpose here I am referring to those congregations that are independent of the local diocese. In most cases, a religious congregation will be invited to a diocese to assist in giving educational or health services or running a parish that has no priest. However, the local bishop has no authority over the internal workings of a given congregation, whether or not it is working in his diocese.

At present there are about 300 men's congregations worldwide and 2,500 women's congregations. The members of such a congregation commit themselves to lives of service through the vows of obedience, poverty, and chastity. They also commit themselves to an expression of gospel living as interpreted through the particular charism, or values, of the religious congregation to which they belong.

In the Roman Catholic system, candidates for priesthood are limited to males who are baptized Christians and who have been confirmed in the Roman Catholic Church. Candidates for the priesthood are, therefore, those who are going to be diocesan priests or priests within the membership of a religious congregation. The person who is ultimately responsible for the worthiness of the priest is the ordaining bishop. Assessment concerns come, therefore, from up to three parties: (1) the bishops who are ordaining candidates, (2) superiors of religious congregations, and (3) seminaries who are training candidates for the priesthood in both categories.

Another important factor is the fact that since the decline in vocations for the priesthood is so great and the emphasis is on ministry shared by laity, the assessment of lay ministers is an issue. The issue of women in ministry (see chap. 25 of this volume) has become an important discussion in the Roman Catholic Church.

The idea of women being ordained to the priesthood would not appear to be a reasonable possibility in the near future of the church but women in ministry is. Celibacy as a condition for priesthood is simply a requirement of Canon Law within the diocesan structure and is one of the legal requirements for becoming a priest in the Roman Catholic Church. On the other hand, for a member of a religious congregation to become a priest, celibacy is not simply a canonical requirement but a part of the vow of chastity, which is essential to the theological and spiritual understanding of what it means to be a 'religious' whether that be a brother, a priest, or a sister.

The radical decline in vocations to the priesthood seems to be caused by several factors. First, in the diocesan structure the necessity of celibacy as a condition of priesthood is questioned by a significant percentage of the lay and clerical population. The necessity for celibacy as a canonical factor only is brought more into question by virtue of the fact that in recent years married priests from other denominations, such as Anglicanism, have been allowed to function in the Roman Catholic diocesan structure. As the personnel pool declines, this aspect of diocesan reality seems to increase.

The emphasis in society on male/female integration as a part of spiritual development is becoming an integral part of theological curriculum of many seminaries. This naturally raises the question of whether celibacy is necessary for the diocesan priest and whether it places a limitation on the spiritual growth of some persons.

Second, the shift in the Roman Catholic Church away from minor seminaries to an emphasis on candidates for ministry being mature adults, insisting most often on the prior completion of undergraduate education, places a much more difficult burden on vocational directors in persuading young men to enter the priesthood.

Third, the secularization of health and education, plus the inability of the church to address a range of moral and sexual issues in a unified manner, has led in part to a decline in parental support for young people to enter the priesthood. An obvious factor is the fact that in the Western world large families are no longer the norm.

An important difference between many of the Protestant denominations and Roman Catholicism is the fact that the ministry of priesthood is seen to be an ontological reality that requires lifetime commitment. The concept of lifelong commitment to a celibate life-style seems incongruous to many young persons today, especially when celibacy is only canonical in nature. We also note that in 1972 a permanent married diaconate was established. The only limitation on this was that candidates must have reached the age of thirty-five to be eligible.

We note that religious orders and congregations in which celibacy is a functional and theological necessity are not receiving new applications to join them. Much of this appears to be related to the fact that many of these congregations provided the man and woman power to serve in many of the human service institutions that are now being managed by the secular society.

The above realities are important factors in the assessment of candidates for the priesthood. In addition, with the radical decline in candidates for the priesthood, many dioceses are moving to lay ministry programs that will enable the laity to perform many tasks previously done by priests.

Anyone assessing a candidate for the priesthood in the Roman Catholic Church must realize that:

1. The Roman Catholic Church is in a crucial state of transition.

2. There is a radical decline in candidates for the priesthood, and this decline is just as radical in religious congregations.

3. A candidate for the priesthood entering a religious order or congregation is confronted with issues different from those facing someone entering the diocesan structure.

The Priesthood and Canon Law

When a candidate is assessed for suitability for the priesthood, the processes that person will be required to go through can be as varied as the number of dioceses and the number of religious congregations that person could join. Canon Law does prescribe minimal requirements that assure some consistency throughout the church as a whole.

Canon 1008 of the Roman Catholic code says:

> By divine institution some among the Christian faithful are constituted sacred ministers through the sacrament of orders by means of the indelible character with which they are marked; accordingly they are consecrated and deputed to shepherd the people of God, each in accord with his own grade of orders. (Coriden et al., 1985, p. 717)

This beginning statement in the code indicates the ontological nature of priesthood within a hierarchical structure of the episcopacy, the presbyterate, and the diaconate.

Canon 1015 notes that the candidate's own bishop is to ordain him "unless he is impeded from doing so by a just cause" (Coriden et al., 1985, p. 720). This paragraph further illustrates what we have addressed above about the hierarchical and institutional nature of the Roman Catholic Church as differentiated from many of the other denominations.

To further differentiate between secular and religious clergy, Canon 1019 states that:

> The major superior of a clerical religious institute of pontifical rite or the major superior of a clerical society of

apostolic life of pontifical right is competent to grant dimissorial letters for the diaconate and for the presbyterate on behalf of the subjects who have become perpetually or definitively members of the institute or society in accord with their constitutions. (Coriden et al., 1985, p. 722)

Persons who are preparing for the priesthood are subject to a common set of requisites for valid ordination. The requisites are that a candidate must:

1. be male and baptized (Canon 1024)

2. have received the sacrament of confirmation

3. have been a formal candidate within a given diocese or religious congregation and considered useful to the ministry of the church and be twenty-five years of age.

Finally, Canon 1029 states:

> After all circumstances have been taken into account in the prudent judgment of the proper bishop or the competent major superior, only those should be promoted to orders who have an integral faith, are motivated by a right intention, possess the required knowledge, and enjoy a good reputation, good morals, and proven virtues, and other physical and psychological qualities which are appropriate to the order to be received. (Coriden et al., 1985, p. 725)

Most of what we see in Canon 1029 converts into specific requirements for candidacy for the priesthood.

The prudent judgment of the proper bishop. This normally translates into a judgment made by the bishop relative to ongoing interviews with the candidate during his seminary period and recommendations from his professors. In other words, the recommendation is really consultative in nature.

An integral faith. The intention here is that the candidate believes in the faith as taught by the church and commits himself to an unending process of conversion. This would translate into recommendations from his parish priest and members of the faith community and his seminary.

Right intention, possessing the required knowledge, good reputation, and good morals and proven virtues. This cluster of issues is getting at the candidate's value system and his potential capacity to be a responsible person who emulates a holiness that makes him a credible figure to the people of God.

Physical and psychological qualities has the following note attached to it in the text and commentary of the code of canon law, which was commissioned by the Canon Law Society of America and published in 1985:

Due to the unfortunate number of priests who have been laicized, the Church has learned to give serious attention to the health of the candidates, especially emotional health. The Church has initiated psychological testing as part of the admissions procedures to seminaries. This practice is the result of laicization indults granted for psychological reasons which antedated ordination but of which the candidate was unaware when he petitioned for orders. This commentator judges that with the consent of the candidate, the results of the admissions testing and interview should be used in the seminary program of human growth and development, which is so important for spiritual growth and so necessary to make a free and informed decision for orders. (Coriden et al., 1985, p. 725)

The Wider Issues: Diocesan and Religious Candidates

One might judge when looking at the section on canon law that the component of "call" to priesthood is on the one hand subjective and received personally and internally by the candidate and on the other hand judged objectively by the community to which the candidate is called. In addition it has become evident in recent years that some candidates who have left the priesthood have not done so because of prior psychological difficulties but because of their difficulty with the institution's state of transition.

This is particularly clear when dealing with candidates for the priesthood who are being called within a religious order or congregation. It could be a priest within the order of the Friars Minor or one within the Society of Jesus. In both cases, a candidate is not only dealing with issues specific to ordination, but is describing his ministry within a community of men who are committed to a particular expression of ministry that is described in the rules, constitutions, and directives of that religious congregation.

The candidate is not only dealing with whether the priesthood is a valuable option for him in the modern world as an expression of ministry, but also with the question of whether or not his values are an expression of the values of the congregation of which he is becoming a part. Most congregations have a very distinct and ordered formation process to enable a candidate to test this out.

This varies in degree and quality, depending on the resources of the particular congregation. Attention has been given in recent years by religious congregations to focusing on their own value systems as expressed in their rules and constitutions and testing this out against the candidate's own journey as an important aspect of the assessment process of one who would be a priest within a religious congregation (see Hall, 1986).

An important part of priesthood for a person who is also a 'religious,' at least theoretically, is learning to live in community (see Arbuckle, 1987). Therefore, a critical issue is the quality of the religious community itself. The same transition period that we have identified above has brought about radical changes in religious life itself, emphasizing ministry and service as arising out of quality community rather than ministry and service as being total functions of what the religious is about.

The emphasis of religious life as service, which dominated until 1960, saw close friendships within a community setting as being a threat. The new definition of service as coming out of quality community, arising out of our new knowledge of the behavioral sciences, has placed religious life into a period of transitional chaos. At present, candidates for the priesthood within the context of a religious vocation are often doing that out of a need for quality community as well as adherence to a particular charism or set of values. The reality of transition and the insecurity it brings is something that a candidate for priesthood to a religious congregation has to take seriously also.

The candidate who is entering the diocesan structure is confronting a situation in which there are an insufficient number of priests to maintain the structures. Often, the priest will find himself living in a rectory either by himself or almost by himself with unreasonable demands being made on his time. Such a candidate must have strength to be independent, in charge of his own sexuality, and have the capacity to cooperate with and delegate to laity, if ministry is to be a creative process. This is especially important to those involved in assessment since they are inevitably confronted with the fact that many who are attracted to the priesthood at this time may not be well balanced in regard to their sexual disposition. The loneliness that confronts the parish priest and the issue of community living that confronts the religious are unique issues for each population.

New Development in Assessment Instrumentation

There was, until recently, an apprehension in the seminary population about the place of psychology in seminary education and the personal development of the seminarian. The preceding discussion illustrates how this has shifted in recent years relative to Canon Law and the stresses on the parish priest during times of transition.

Now seminaries are employing women professors,

and consequently, the whole area of male/female spirituality is opening up. Traditionally, spirituality was seen more as a theological discipline with pastoral dimensions to it. Now there is an awareness of the need to integrate spirituality with the concept of the psychological dimensions of emotional and sexual development.

Although many dioceses have their own candidate assessment programs, it is always done collaboratively with the seminary in which the candidate is being trained. Given the radical transitional state of the church, few vocations, and large dropout rate of candidates after entering seminary, there has been a growing concern to find assessment instrumentation that can aid in predicting a candidate's possibility of success through seminary and ordination.

A number of articles have appeared stressing the need to introduce the human dimension into assessment. Traditionally, psychological testing and psychiatric interviews were to screen out "mentally unhealthy candidates"—that is, a person with obvious abnormalities in mental behavior. Today that is, of course, a continuing concern, but the issues reflected earlier now play a larger part. Susan Stiebe, of the Counseling and Psychological Service Center at the University of Notre Dame, focuses the issues with three questions:

1. How is the applicant's ego-identity related to his motivation for exploring the priesthood and the religious life? [By relating the interview process to Erikson's stages of development, she claims to get at issues of crisis and commitment, so essential to persons understanding of call, more effectively.]
2. What are the strengths and limitations the applicant will bring to community life? [Here she relies on the Minnesota Multiphasic Inventory, the Rotter Sentence Blank, and The Personal Information Form. She uses these and extensive interviewing to get a picture of the candidate's interpersonal functioning.]
3. How will the candidate cope with a celibate life-style? [Here straightforward questions relative to the romantic interludes in the candidate's life are explored to arrive at a profile.]

What she and others write tends to be subjective and does not go beyond the recommendations of an earlier standard work by the Council for Applied Research on the Apostolate (reported in Coville et al., 1968). Two objective instruments that are new and have been validated according to American Psychological Association standards are the Priest Perceiver Interview and the Hall-Tonna Inventory of Values.

The Priest Perceiver Interview

Introduced in 1983, the Priest Perceiver Interview was designed for religious in 1977 and was followed by one for permanent deacons in 1980. The instrument is now available for other professions, such as nursing, school administration, child-care workers, and teachers.

It is a validated structured interview process offered by Selection Research Incorporated (SRI) and is based on the research of Donald Clifton, whose orientation is that ministry talent is not on the decline so much as it needs to be discovered. The instrument looks at the talents of prospective candidates and compares them with the talents of successful priests. As such it claims to be a predictive instrument very much suited to the times of transition presently facing the church.

The concept of talent that it is measuring relates to such things as excellence, yearnings, areas of rapid learning, and areas of satisfaction. Talent, then, is related to the biblical concept of gifts, not simply to learned skills. An original group of twelve persons identified the hallmarks of the successful priest. This emerged into fourteen themes within a seventy-five-question device conducted through an interview format. It covers such issues as motivation themes with an examination of mission, hope, loyalty, and community and themes that are evident in successful priests such as presence, relator, empathy, and enabler. The data collected indicate significant positive correlation between the results of the interview and the firsthand judgments made by persons in leadership positions within the given diocese and by persons who knew the candidate well.

Miller, McCaslin, and Deinlein (1984) note that the instrument is a measure of "social intelligence," which is critical to the character of the celibate priesthood. They add:

Clifton believes that, without a question, persons capable of having the significant effect on people's lives in a society are the spiritual leaders, the kind Catholics call priests. The identification of priestly talent available in our society is an answer to the vocation crisis. It offers us a future of a greater priesthood and an affirmative answer to the question of the ordaining bishop, "Do you know them to be worthy?"

The Hall-Tonna Inventory of Values

Like the Priest Perceiver Interview instrument, the Hall-Tonna Inventory of Values began as one instrument and developed into a family of instruments. It was developed through a joint research venture between Anglican Brian Hall, who was a missionary in Central

America and later a professor at the University of Santa Clara, California, and Roman Catholic priest Benjamin Tonna, who was the communications officer for the Second Vatican Council in Rome. It grew out of an extensive theoretical base that attempted to integrate the fields of spiritual, psychological, and sociological development (Hall and Tonna 1980, 1986).

The first format was a 77-item questionnaire that was released by Paulist Press and Behaviordyne in 1985. The instrument identifies an individual's values based on a comprehensive list of 125 values identified by Hall and Tonna. At this time the languages the instrument is available in are all Western languages, such as English, French, German, Italian, and Spanish.

The results of the questionnaire are printed on approximately twelve pages of profile information that gives the client information on the value patterns inherent in the client's chosen values. The patterns include cycles of development that are correlated with the stages of development designated by Erikson, Fowler, and Kohlberg. Information is given on ethical and faith orientation, gifts, skills, and leadership style.

The majority of results are given in question form. Hall and Tonna think that discernment questions, rather than specific answers, are the key to personal knowledge and growth. As such, the instrument is encouraged as an assessment tool only in relationship to other instrumentation, like the MMPI and Perceiver. It is also an instrument that is used as an ongoing means of growth and development in seminaries and spiritual formation programs. It is rooted in the spiritual tradition of spiritual discernment, which has been historically a threefold process of:

1. Collecting quality (value based) information;
2. Interpreting the information to discover God's plan for an individual, community of system; and
3. Acting on the information. (Ledig, 1986)

New Signs

The radical drop in vocations in North America has led to a new concern about the future of the parish, educational, and health care institutions that can no longer be staffed by priests and sisters. Gerald Arbuckle speaks of the need for "refounding" the church, using the methods of anthropology to discover creative initiating leadership that can transcend the restraints of traditional institutional boundaries and rules. He asks:

What are the causes of the present chaos in religious life today? What should be the goals of religious life today and in the future? How are we to realize these goals? . . . Refounding persons will be the primary agents of this creativity within existing congregations in helping us to face the demands of evangelization in the secular world today and in the future. (Arbuckle, 1987, p. 239)

An international research team led by Brian Hall, Benjamin Tonna, and Barbara Ledig has also developed methods of measuring values in administrative teams and religious documents. The latter uses an electronic scanner and a complete thesaurus program to identify the values (Tonna, 1982; Hall, 1986a; Ledig, 1986).

The importance of the document analysis has been found in the identification of priority values of religious documents, such as the rules and constitutions of a religious congregation. By comparing an individual's profile with the profile of a religious document, invaluable information is gained as to whether a candidate's values are in harmony with the charism of a particular group. This does not necessarily invalidate the call, but may give valuable information about the candidate's ministry development needs. The research group Omega International is developing this methodology with over one hundred religious congregations in Europe and the United States.

One of the most critical movements is the development of lay ministry training programs in North America and Europe. This is evident at the Masters degree level in many universities, but is also becoming an essential part of diocesan lay ministry education programs.

An example is the ministry program in the Archdiocese of Saint Louis, which began in 1986. They are training thirty ministers a year—men and women—to take over 80 percent of the tasks previously carried out by the priest. Since the permanent diaconate is not attracting many candidates, this option is much more attractive to most committed Christians who have families. It is a part-time training course, requiring several evenings per week over a one-year period. A critical issue is screening for the ministry. In this instance, they use the Hall-Tonna Inventory at an individual and group level as a training tool for spiritual development, and as a screening tool.

Conclusions for the Future

35

Assessment in the Future

RICHARD A. HUNT, JOHN E. HINKLE, JR., H. NEWTON MALONY

The issue of assessment of the clergy and of clergy candidates raises many urgent issues for the future of the church. In this volume, thirty-one ecumenical specialists in clergy issues have examined assessment from a wide variety of current perspectives. We see important advances in assessment in the past two decades.

In looking toward the next century and the future, it is sobering to consider our time frame. For example, twenty years prior to 1990 would be 1970, the year of the publication of the Bier (1970) report and four years after the Bier conference was held. If we anticipate twenty years into the future, 2010, or twenty-four years, 2014, will we see any more improvement in assessment than we have seen in the past twenty or twenty-five years? As a basis for considering the future, we will first summarize some of the major findings of the contributors to this volume. (Unless otherwise noted, chapter references are to this volume.)

Assessment in the Contexts of God's Call, Church, Career, Family, and Personal Systems

All Christians are called to minister. Whether a person is called to the ordained ministry and how this call is to be understood and assessed in the context of both theological and technical dimensions are central, as emphasized by Dittes in chapter 2.

Wimberly, in chapter 3, described the steady movement in churches and seminaries toward a more scientific and professional view of the ordained ministry as a profession. Then he emphasized a renewed "formation of ministers professionally and spiritually in the future [that] will take seriously the role of the minister as a bearer of faith," as storyteller, listener to stories of people attempting to live faithful lives, and as enabler to persons who seek a "plot (or structure of meaning) that provides healing, identity, meaning, and direction" in their lives.

For this to happen, clergy and clergy candidates need to see their own lifetime development issues (Gooden, chap. 4) and attend to their own personal strengths and growth areas. Blackmon and Hart (chap. 5) identify five areas of "emotional hazard" for pastors as personal relationships, depression, stress and burnout, sexuality, and assertiveness. Careful attention to assessment, prevention, and treatment of each of these hazardous areas is essential.

In chapter 6, Lee presented a theory of social ecology to provide a conceptual base appropriate to considering the marital and family relationships in which clergy are involved. Social ecology moves the focus from an individual to a relational or system frame. From several types of systems viewpoints, Lee called for a "social ecology" that attends to the interaction of parish congregations with the minister's family systems as they continually influence each other. Then in chapter 7, Hunt addressed specific issues of dual career couples.

There are some promising ways to enable clergy candidates to do their own self-exploration in relation to career, family, marriage, and personal dimensions. Assessing whether a candidate or clergy has the ability to do this may be part of the clinician's assessment assignment. However, the supportive structure and encouragement to do continuing self-assessment and formation must be in the mentoring and formation processes that transcend formal assessment as they are found in the relation of the individual to spouse, to colleagues, and to other support systems, partially described by Hunt in chapter 7.

Research Methodologies and Perspectives

In the section on research methodologies and perspectives, hard-nosed empirical approaches to research methods are combined with exploratory procedures in the development of criteria and the evaluation of instruments and selection procedures. Gorsuch pointed out the pitfalls, as well as the possibilities, of psychometric instrumentation in psychological assessment of candidates for clergy careers (chap. 8).

In chapter 9, Haight and Hinkle addressed issues in criteria development and then presented three models for the identification and development of criteria. Selectors engage in a process of criteria identification, and researchers seek to operationalize the criteria through interview and instrumentation for implementation by clinical service delivery systems. The consensual procedure for criteria identification assures ownership and implementation by selectors. This empirical procedure assists in specification, operationalization, and verification of criteria function in selection procedures.

Hogue (chap. 10) explored the concept of "ministerial satisfaction" through the development of an empirical measure of satisfaction in ministry. His work presents an empirical model for the development of appropriate instrumentation for use in clergy assessment batteries. The developed instrument gives promise of significant potential for use in the measurement of satisfaction in ministry, a highly significant factor in describing effectiveness in ministry.

Comer presented research directed toward evaluating the capacity of selected instruments in the test battery (chap. 11) to predict to what extent clinicians are doing what they say they are doing—that is, making systematic and rational decisions concerning the extent to which information from test data support a candidate's decision of "accept" or "reject." A conclusion was that the clinicians reviewed appear to be making systematic and rational decisions from test data sufficiently well that an empirically documented pattern of decision making is clear. Comer also asked about the other two-thirds of the variance in a test battery, and he speculated that an even higher level of consistency in decision making by clinical reviewers may account for a higher proportion of the test battery variance.

Comer replicated earlier findings on the "severity of record" variable from the MMPI. He added new material to the research effort in studying the fit of self-image with the clinical picture of personality surfaced by reviewers. He found, to his surprise, that reference materials add significantly to the predictive paradigm, while I.Q. equivalency scores from the Shipley-Hartford Institute of Living Scale did not. The most significant impact of the Comer study may well be that it provides a necessary building block in the effort to conduct meaningful longitudinal studies of ministerial effectiveness. In such an effort, one factor is the matter of consistent decisions by reviewers and selectors. Hogue and Comer have each contributed in different, but significant, ways to such a project; Hogue in terms of developing an instrument to measure one of the significant variables, and Comer in establishing as

empirical fact the assumption that the clinicians studied make systematic and criteria relevant decisions.

Adding another significant building block, Holliman, in chapter 12, addressed the question of whether persons who are involved in making selection decisions in a denominational process (United Methodist) understand the purpose and process of psychological assessment. She reviewed seven such units within the denominational system in depth. Both selectors (such as members of committees making decisions about candidates) and candidates are included in the review. The study focused on the "evaluability" of such procedures—that is, are they sufficiently standardized and homogeneous across units that researching their decisions is feasible? The potential contribution to longitudinal research is evident in this study.

To the degree that selection decision making is random, inconsistent, or not criterion relevant, efforts to predict the criteria of ministerial effectiveness will be useless. Holliman found that an unexpectedly high degree of agreement was present across units and between candidates and selectors, concerning the priority to be given to psychological assessment reports in the selection process. It was suggested that sufficient similiarty of decisions exists to make a longitudinal study of psychological fitness issues in ministerial effectiveness worth the effort.

Very high levels of agreement among selectors about the value of the psychological assessment report to the selection decision surfaced in the Holliman study. Approximately 90 percent of selectors using psychological assessment reported satisfaction with the information provided by the report. Candidate responses to the process were quite similar to those of psychotherapy outcome studies. Approximately one-third thought that the clinical assessment interview and the report were most helpful; about one-third thought that they were adequate (affirming what the candidate already knew about himself or herself for the most part), and about one-third felt that they got nothing out of it or that it was a bad idea and was unhelpful, or even destructive. Sufficient variability of conditions was present that a longitudinal predictive study would need to tap into strong patterns rather directly if results are to be empirically significant and programmatically helpful.

O'Neill provided an overview of the many projects that are part of the "Quality of Ministry" program supported by Lilly Endowment, Inc. (chap. 15). As part of this, Stone (chap. 13) describes changes across time on several instruments. In chapter 14, Majovski and Malony described major difficulties in predicting ministerial effectiveness.

Assessment Procedures and Methods

Several issues have characterized procedures used to assess ministerial candidates. Among these are the ways in which expectations, motivations, role performance, predictability, self-evaluation, behavioral ratings, polity differences, and task perceptions and preferences have been emphasized and measured.

The *Profiles of Ministry* project (POM) is the only available procedure whose development was based on congregational expectations (see chap. 16). Both its 1974 and its 1987 surveys of criteria for effective ministry include ratings by laity in the samples. The stability of these ratings over a decade suggests that the nine major clusters of characteristics the POM measures are central to the clergy role. The conclusion that there is considerable agreement among North American churches on negative and positive personal traits expected of ministers suggests that no assessment should ignore concerns for the family, a responsible and caring style, a strong personal faith, and the possibility that a minister might be self-centered. While various denominations emphasize different orientations toward ministry, the POM seems to have encompassed the basic options in its measure of conversionist, social justice, ecclesiastical, and community/congregational emphases.

While the POM is strong on "expectations," the Theological School Inventory (TSI) is equally strong on theological and personal "motivations" for ministry (see chap. 17). The TSI assesses the strength of one's motives in comparison with others who have answered the same instrument. The degree to which candidates perceive themselves as "specially" or "naturally" led, coupled with their definiteness and flexibility, are helpful dimensions to assess and discuss with the candidate. Of equal importance are comparative ratings of the reasons candidates give for wanting to enter ministry, as shown in the AIFLERP scales of the TSI.

"Role performance" is difficult to assess, even by "on-the-job" observers of a pastor's performance across time. The Stage 2 evaluation of the POM includes field observation of ministerial performance, and most candidacy evaluations include ratings by church persons with whom candidates have worked. However, the Structured Assessment Interview (SAI) described by Ridley (chap. 19) attempts to identify the basic factors that enable effective performance of ministry by pastors who start new churches and, by extension, for pastors in other situations. This is done on the basis of job task analyses that are used to structure the interview format in relation to these task demands. Graham also applies a systems approach to personnel selection for church leaders.

The self-evaluations that emerge from Clinical Pastoral Education (CPE) are grounded in reflections on pastoral behavior in a candidate's relationships to superiors, to colleagues, and to parishioners (see chap. 21). Much additional work is needed on linking role performance (criteria) to the various ways of doing candidacy assessment.

Because of polity differences, churches and denominations must adapt assessment methodology to their own unique needs. In chapter 18, Hinkle provided a description and analysis of the example of United Methodism in standardizing a set of procedures to be used throughout the denomination. This process is a significant accomplishment that, we hope, will lead to greater clarity and reliability in the way candidacy decisions are made as well as provide a research data base on which future criteria studies can be developed.

A major predictor of effective role performance is positive interest in doing what the job demands. The Inventory of Religious Activities and Interests (IRAI) provides an extensive survey of interests in ten clusters of church and community work.

The major weakness in most clergy assessment continues to be the low predictive validity for the instruments and procedures used. To date the few studies of the relation between assessment measurements and performance several years after the evaluation usually reach negative conclusions (Malony and Majovski, chap. 14). Since candidates with significantly negative profiles often are screened out, the remaining criterion sample is probably overly homogeneous. As Foster reminds us (chap. 23), we must find ethical ways to balance the need for the various types of validity with the need to select and to nurture candidates, both into and out of the ministry.

At a recent symposium on "Tort and Religion," sponsored by the American Bar Association (1989), another source of assessment liability was strongly emphasized. This was the liability of evaluation for the future behavior of candidates. For example, the courts are now considering such questions as whether assessors, ordination boards, denominations, or churches are legally responsible for the personal injury damages that result from child molestation or sexual abuse (as in adultery). If the legal issues pertain to the question of whether those who approved or hired such ministers explicitly "ruled out" such malbehavioral tendencies along with the affirmation of positive "gifts and graces," the implication is that when an employee misbehaves, the employer could be held responsible for negligence if the employment application process did not directly address background or behavioral tendencies in the offending area. The employer could be accused of malfeasance if the behavior was assessed, a tendency toward misbehavior noted, and the candidate was hired anyway.

It would seem important to identify areas in which ministers seem to be having most difficulty in maintaining appropriate behavior and address them in the evaluation process. Research (Blackmon, 1984) suggests that inappropriate sexual acting out occurs twice as often in ministers as among marriage counselors. Then, it would be wise for every evaluator to assess tendencies toward such maladaptive functioning and either refer candidates where it appears or recommend counseling to remedy the situation. While sexual adjustment can be of all kinds in every situation, the tendency seems to be for the world problem among Roman Catholic clergy to be child molestation and among Protestants, adultery. Although not all those with heterosexual or homosexual orientations act inappropriately, ministry is the type of vocational situation in which the temptation for such behavior is great, and the assessment process should directly address the problem. To do so will not only be professionally responsible, but it will also be legally wise.

Gender and Cultural Issues in Assessment

Huntley (chap. 24) opened this section by narrating a denominational effort to address the issues of culture and gender fairness in psychological assessment by the three merging Lutheran churches in a transitional period. Psychological instruments are embedded in culture and are normed along the lines of culturally relevant criteria. These criteria flow out of cultural understandings of the good person, the good pastor, the good church, the good society, and so on. As cultural values change, or when persons from an alternative culture are being assessed, the issue of culture and gender fairness arises.

The consultations convened by Huntley suggested that when instruments are biased as to culture and gender, the interpretation of results to both candidate and judicatory selection committee should be informed by a representative from the person's own gender and/or culture who either participates in the interpretive conference, in the clinical interview with the candidate, or both. The consultation further proposed that a quality control mechanism be built in at the denominational level so that psychological evaluators and candidates have access to a review board for ongoing vigilance regarding culture and gender fairness. Additionally, in instances where culture and/or gender fairness questions arise in the assessment process, the recommendation was that the candidate have access to a second opinion so that such matters can be settled in any given assessment situation.

Scanlon addressed the matter of gender fairness by presenting a revised theoretical frame for understanding female development (chap. 25). She casts her discussion of assessment in the language of a spiritual discernment of vocation throughout the life cycle as that discernment process would be appropriate to female developmental psychology in contrast with male understandings of developmental psychology, and in particular male psychology as evidenced in the theory and writings of Eric Erikson. She notes that the use of life history as an evaluative tool raises the issue of life course theory and gender differences, which applies to women some of the themes in the first section on contexts of assessment (chaps. 2–7).

Priority themes in female psychology, as seen by Scanlon, are sameness, connection, attachment, and relatedness in the context of identity development. These contrast with differences in competition, autonomy, and isolation in male psychology. The significant developmental factor is that females define themselves in different ways from the way males define themselves.

Scanlon also noted that the assessment of women ministerial candidates, in addition to taking into consideration the feminist critique of personality theory, must also remain open to the contributions of feminist theology and spirituality. The challenge and task of the psychological assessor engaged in a process of discernment with a female candidate for ministry is to be prepared to view the candidate through the lenses of female developmental theory and female and feminist theology and spirituality, and to situate this understanding in the context of the denomination or congregational receiving culture.

Wimberly advocated culturally relevant pastoral assessment for black clergy candidates (chap. 26). He suggests cultural variance as a proper replacement for the notion of cultural deviance, meaning that psychological assessment should be specific to the culture (comparing black candidates to other black candidates) and culture specific—that is, relevant to culturally based criteria. He notes that culturally fair instruments involve standardization, the development of assessment norms based on particular populations, and the utilization of culturally specific and culture fair assessment, rather than abolishing the assessment process altogether for black applicants.

Polischuk (chap. 27) described the diversity of Spanish language groups that make up the Hispanic community. He then reviews psychological assessment instruments in terms of their applicability to Hispanic groups. In particular, he focuses on the several Spanish versions of the MMPI and the IRAI, as these have been used in the assessment of Hispanic clergy candidates.

Polischuk focuses on the translatability of tests in terms of functional equivalence in the translation. Linguistic differences due to background, degree of acculturation, language utilization, and socioeconomic status are difficulties. Polischuk notes that Hispanics recruited and trained in the United States may be assessed with a combination of psychological tests, such as the MMPI, the 16PF, and the IRAI. However, Hispanics have critical attitudes toward mental health issues in general, and toward assessment in particular, so education is needed in these matters. He concluded that instruments that emerge from the cultures of origin as well as in the cultures where clergy will function are needed.

Kim (chap. 28) pointed out that the majority of Asian Americans (Chinese, Filipinos, Japanese, and Koreans) are first generation immigrants who have migrated since 1965. These immigrants live in America with Asian views and values. From the perspective of cross-cultural anthropology, Asian Americans, like Hispanic Americans, are a diverse group. Southeast Asians, Southern Asians, and East Asians comprise major cultural groupings. The Chinese, Japanese, and Korean groups are under the influence of a cultural value system based predominantly on Confucian ethics and conventions. Since major cultural differences exist between the Asian American culture and the dominant cultural value systems of the United States, Kim introduces the reader to some of these differences by adapting a set of cross cultural observations from the Mediterranean world to his purpose and by comparing these with the cultural value system in the United States. Since Kim has focused on recent immigrants, he acknowledges that the degree of cultural assimilation for those who have stayed longer in America will be greater, but their Asian identity and ideas persist. Assessment issues are different and probably less intense for Asians born in the United States.

Concerning Native Americans, Pierce, in chapter 29, pointed to the wide range of indigenous tribal groups in the United States, which includes American Indians, Aleuts, and Eskimos. There is no such thing as "the Native American culture" or the "Indian view" or "the Indian religion," since the hundreds of tribes in North America can be traced to many different cultures, religions, languages, and views. Low education, unemployment, and oral rather than written traditions are important dimensions of many Native American groups. Often feeling unsupported by denominational executives, ordained Native American clergy serving Native American churches have felt that the basis for ordination should be demonstrated competency in the parish rather than school records. For psychological assessment with Native Americans, Pierce emphasizes the critical need for research and norm building.

Applications Among Church Structures

Cardwell (chap. 30) surveyed 202 seminaries to determine empirically how they use assessment. With 157 reporting, she found that in comparison with 1961, in 1988 more seminaries use fewer instruments. Seminaries use assessment for screening, for counseling, for students' self-understanding, and for seminary class or group profiles. Among issues are the relation between seminary and judicatory and whether the seminary, the student, and/or the church is the primary client. The extent of assessment is often related to the availability of seminary faculty, counseling staff, and/or consultants.

In chapter 32, Oswald, focusing on assessment with pastors who are currently in parishes, emphasized the potential damages that poor assessment can cause. He distinguishes between ministerial and administrative types of assessments. The pastor's personal ownership of the process is essential, and often an outside consultant or authority can provide safe support to both pastor and congregation in using assessment for growth and action. Often those most in need of the help that assessment might provide are least able to handle candid feedback. In addition, assessment is more likely to be used only when things are going wrong, which is the worst time to do assessment. Oswald also suggested that functional performance of ministry, like parenting, is much more easily evaluated than the full dimensions of a role. Thus assessment is often unable to consider the full range of ministries of a pastor or congregation.

From the perspective of The United Methodist Division of Ordained Ministry, Kohler (chap. 33) provided a history of the changes in this denominational assessment program as it has moved from being primarily located at seminary levels to the geographical Annual Conference levels as part of the candidacy program for persons at their initial consideration and entry into preparation for the ordained and diaconal ministries.

The Roman Catholic Church, in the context of Vatican II and many historical and contemporary issues concerning priests, orders, and religious vocations in relation to assessment, is summarized by Hall in chapter 34. He describes a group of Priest Perceiver Interview instruments designed for priests, religious, permanent deacons, and for other professions, such as nursing, school administration, child-care workers, and teachers. Hall also described the Hall-Tonna Values Inventory, which samples value priorities and places them in the context of spiritual and human development, ethical and faith orientation, gifts, skills, and leadership style. This instrument is used as an ongoing means of growth and development in seminaries and spiritual formation programs.

Some Advances and Projections

Major technical and conceptual gains in the psychological assessment of clergy candidates and clergy have been described in this volume. There is increased standardization of and research on instruments and procedures, and the renorming of selected widely used assessment instruments for clergy candidate populations. Research and conceptual models have been developed and are now ready for use in areas of criteria development, development and evaluation of assessment instruments and test batteries, evaluation of clinical functioning conjointly with instrument functioning, and evaluations of selection personnel and units. Research on the immediate criteria is encouraging.

In addition to ongoing effort in the foregoing areas, longitudinal studies of the psychological fitness aspect of effectiveness in ministerial functioning are needed. Since many of the necessary building blocks preliminary to such a study are in place, the feasibility of such a longitudinal study is increased.

Adaptations of currently used instruments and procedures to diverse populations is evident. Strategies for assuring gender and cultural fairness in such assessments include (1) renorming current instruments in terms of the population being assessed; (2) translation and renorming of instruments where English is the second language; (3) generation of new instrumentation based on the values of the sending culture; (4) reviewing and revising personality theory in the light of the experience of women and ethnic populations; (5) utilizing clinicians representative of the culture of the candidate; and (6) taking proper account of the culture of the receiving congregation, judicatory, or denomination. Obviously, efforts of this sort need to continue and will need to be evaluated for effectiveness.

Progress with the cultural dimensions of psychological assessment, however, is not adequate when the larger system in which the assessment is nested continues with sexist and racist practices, as is noted by Huntley in chapter 24. Consequently, the effort to develop an inclusive church community at both parochial and para-parochial levels must be continued with vigor and effectiveness.

Assessment Issues for the Future

1. Criteria Issues

If effective ministry depends heavily on the interaction between a pastor and parishioners to accomplish ministries (or produce results), then will it be possible to establish criteria without knowing the parish? Reliable criteria for effective ministries still need to be found. Perhaps the nearest to this is the *Profiles of Ministry (Readiness for Ministry)* project. Reliable criteria are the keys to validity of all predictive or concurrent studies.

Criteria are intertwined in experiential, logical, empirical, and statistical dimensions. Criteria may be logical in the senses of theology, psychology, and sociology—thinking about the minister as person. But, criteria are empirical when they identify persons who do well or poorly in specific ministry situations. Eventually, criteria are self-reports of many persons about ministers according to observers' expectations. We probably must confess our continuing inadequacies to encompass very much of the "variance unaccounted for" in empirical studies.

2. Better Validation of Existing Measures

A common criticism of clergy assessment is the example that Paul would probably have "failed" most current assessment batteries. He saw visions; he was persecuted; and he troubled the established religious hierarchies. In addition, he created dissension, was in trouble with the Roman authorities, and was opinionated and dogmatic. In answer to this type of criticism, we must find ways to make assessment instruments and procedures more theologically informed, more sensitive to potential changes and possibilities in persons, and more closely related to appropriate, useful criteria measures.

"Trend-setters" and "rate busters" may either be screened out by assessment or may become disgusted with bureaucratic procedures, such as assessment batteries. "Fitness" may mean being at the juncture between ability to work in the hierarchy versus ability to work with local congregations, versus balances in personal needs of various kinds.

3. Move Toward Actual and/or Simulated Work Samples Rather Than Self-reports

Work samples are more expensive, but can provide more precise feedback data. Self-reports, such as paper-and-pencil measures, ask persons to report on their impacts on others, which is difficult to do. In contrast, simulated work samples and situations can provide controlled stimulus settings to which a person responds. This technology is now in use in many businesses and industries, including simulations of medical emergency rooms for medical personnel and aircraft for pilots. A step toward this procedure is implicit in the *Profiles of Ministry* casebook procedure (chap. 16).

With increasing availability and lower costs of interactive video and computer technology, simulations of parish and other ministry situations can be presented to a candidate who can respond, with these responses interacting with the simulation to generate additional consequences. This technology can greatly change the way current assessment is done.

4. Prediction May Lock the Future into the Past

Predictive equations depend on past performance of specified criterion groups. As important as longitudinal studies are, the longer the time between measurement and criterion performance, the more the procedure is locked into the past. Some performance criteria may change in the interim. With a changing society, one must determine which qualities will still be needed and which qualities will be increasingly or decreasingly valued in the clergy.

An additional complication occurs if we provide nurture—which we must in good conscience attempt—to the person during this intervening time. It is hoped that the feedback, training, and nurture will improve the clergy's performance, which also changes the predictive equations.

5. Increasing Specialization in Ministries

During the past twenty years, many new career areas in new businesses have resulted from new technology, increased customer demands, and expanding world trade networks. International business positions, travel and leisure related industries, new areas of law, computers, video, world communications, and social services have emerged. A pastor still must be able to do many "old, standard" things well, yet must also learn new specialities. At the same time, the sophistication of the congregation is much higher, thus raising the standards of expectations for ministerial performance. Through television, the local pastor can easily be compared, for good or ill, to televised preachers, public affairs, social service programs, and other televised ministries.

Among clergy, there are more areas for specialization—such as older adult work, homeless, church planting, independent pastoral counseling/psychotherapy, and denominational specialists. Assessment itself is increasingly specialized. In addition, the quasi-ministry careers—such as career counselors, probation officers, marriage and family therapists, psychologists, social workers, and psychiatrists—are better known and

accepted. This means that the church both competes with these for the best candidates for its professional ministry positions and must interact with the widespread dissemination of most of the activities formerly considered to be the sole realm of its pastors.

6. Effects of Major Research Programs

The Lilly Quality of Ministry projects (chap. 15) now being completed is a prime example of what can be accomplished in research on ministry when adequate funding is available. Although the support of Lilly Endowment, Inc., for church related projects is best known, additional foundations do contribute to research projects on ministries and congregations. Adequate research depends on funding to enable personnel time, equipment, and supplies.

If a foundation today were to ask a representative group of church leaders how they would spend a grant of one or two million dollars, what suggestions would be offered? In view of the many competing demands for direct services to the poor, hungry, and needy around the world, clergy assessment, nurture, and training needs are certainly worthy of funding, since this enables the future personnel to continue and expand ministries to all types of needs.

7. Long-term, Stable Research Monitoring Stations

Closely related to the need for dependable, long-term funding is the need to establish "monitoring stations" (agencies or offices) to maintain and improve research on clergy assessment and related issues. Some denominations have maintained budget support for assessment projects. To do this depends heavily on the long-term commitment of key church leaders at the national and regional levels.

The future will see many more competing requests for money to fund, both within the church and in society, many worthwhile programs and ministries. Since gains in clergy assessment will come with long-term, stable funding, we must continue to lift up the needs in these areas as well.

8. Assessment: Selection versus Nurture?

Assessment can be for both nurture and selection. The central question may be more whether and what types of nurture an individual can benefit from. This also affects persons in the candidate's social support network. With changing models of ministry and more dual career couples, churches that have married clergy will need to find ways to balance the use of the minister's spouse and family as one social support network for the minister as a professional versus the needs of the minister and family for autonomy and separation from being engulfed by the demands of the ministry and congregation.

Selection issues also appear in the ethics of assessment. Personal privacy of candidates must be balanced with the church's need or right to know private information about a person that may predict future difficulties. In the absence of other information, past performance tends to be the best predictor of future performance. The church needs to know whether a person has been in trouble in the past because of sexual, addictive, abusive, monetary, or other negative behaviors. At the same time, the person may have received effective treatment and overcome these difficulties.

The danger will continue that formal psychological assessment may be given too much prominence compared to other sources of information about a candidate. Confidentiality in doing assessment will probably be increasingly challenged in a variety of ways in the future.

9. Baselines and Selection Ratio

The acceptance selection ratio for clergy is usually very high, often 90 percent or more. If nearly all candidates are accepted, thus skewing the sample, then predictive validity will be low.

Changes continue to happen to the subject pool. Since the 1960s, the percentage of women in the subject pool has increased from "a few" (perhaps 5 percent) to around 50 percent or more. The percentage of older persons (30+), both men and women, has increased. Yet, the number of applicants for candidacy and seminary has remained rather constant. This means that the percentage of "traditional" younger men has greatly declined. Where have these gone? The available pool of potential candidates is also affected by the potential careers open to persons of all ages, the greater acceptance of career change, both into and out of the ministry, acceptance of singles as ministers, acceptance of divorced pastors, and other changes in both the church and the individuals who may be called to professional ministries.

10. Chemical and Neurological Factors

We are also just beginning to understand the human brain and neurological biochemistry. Already this has made increasingly specific medications available for depression, anxiety, and psychoses. New understandings of "psycho-neuro-immunology" (PNI) suggest new ways in which these biological factors may interact with the "doing of ministry" and its assessment. Ashbrook (1984) has described some linkages already, and clergy assessment must be more aware of future developments in these areas.

11. Commitment and Calling

If all Christians are considered "ministers," what is the special, if any, understanding of the ordained ministry? In the future, will there be any special calling to the ministry, as many clergy in the past described? As Dittes reminds us, we cannot control, and thus predict, how God's Spirit will move among us. We continue to need this reminder lest call and ordination be reduced merely to a confirmation of the church's selecting or assigning a particular person to a given pastorate.

Next Steps . . .

We are doing better clergy and candidate assessment than we have in the past, but compared to what could be done, we still have a long way to go. Many challenges remain, and many goals must yet be reached for us to have assessment procedures that nurture both the candidate and the churches, that enable the types of Christian leadership that are needed in the future, and that fully express God's justice, mercy, and love. May you, as reader, find your part in this important task.

Appendix

REFERENCES

The numbers in bold print at the end of each entry refer to the chapters of this book that make specific use of that reference.

Abel, T. M. (1973). *Psychological Testing in Cultural Contexts*. New Haven: College and University Press. **26.**

Abourezk, J. (1977). American Indian Policy Review Commission. Washington, D.C.: GPO. **29.**

AERA/APA/NCME Joint Committee (1985). *Standards for Educational and Psychological Testing*. Washington, D.C.: American Psychological Association. **8.**

Alberti, R., and M. Emmons (1970). *Your Perfect Right*. San Luis Obispo: Impact Publishers. **5.**

Albright, Lewis E. (1976). "Federal Government Intervention in Psychological Testing: Is It Here?" *Personnel Psychology* (Winter): 29, 519-57. **11.**

ALC/LCA Consultation (1987). *Candidacy and Mobility in the ELCA*. Chicago: Division for Ministry, ELCA. (Available from the Division for Ministry, 8765 W. Higgins Road, Chicago, IL 60631.) **24.**

Aleshire, Daniel (1985). "Readiness for Ministry Instruments: A Five-year Study." Paper presented at the annual meeting of the Religious Research Association. **16.**

Aleshire, Daniel O., M. Brekke, and D. Williams (1986). *Profiles of Ministry Interpretative Manual for Stage 1*. The Association of Theological Schools in the United States and Canada. **16.**

Aleshire, Daniel O., M. Brekke, and D. Schuller (1988). *Profiles of Ministry, Stage 2: Field Observation*. The Association of Theological Schools in the United States and Canada. **16.**

Aleshire, Daniel O., D. Schuller, and D. Williams (1988). *Profiles of Ministry, Stage 2: Interpretive Manual*. The Association of Theological Schools in the United States and Canada. **16.**

Alleman, D. P. (1987). "The Psychosocial Adjustment of Pastors' Wives." Doctoral dissertation, Fuller Theological Seminary, Graduate School of Psychology. **5, 6, 7.**

Aloyse, M. (1961). "Evaluations of Candidates for Religious Life." *Bulletin of the Guild of Catholic Psychiatrists* (8): 199-204. **14.**

American Educational Research Association, American Psychological Association, National Council on Measurement in Education (1985). *Standards for Educational and Psychological Testing*. Washington, D.C.: American Psychological Association. **23.**

American Psychological Association (1981a). *Ethical Principles of Psychologists* (rev. ed.). Washington, D.C.: American Psychological Association. Also published in *American Psychologist* 36 (June 1981): 633-38. **23.**

———— (1981b). *Specialty Guidelines for the Delivery of Services by Clinical Psychologists*. Washington, D.C.: American Psychological Association. **23.**

———— (1981c). *Specialty Guidelines for the Delivery of Services by Industrial/Organizational Psychologists*. Washington, D.C.: American Psychological Association. **23.**

———— (1986). *Guidelines for Computer-based Tests and Interpretations*. Washington, D.C.: American Psychological Association. **23.**

———— (1987). *Casebook on Ethical Principles of Psychologists*. Washington, D.C.: American Psychological Association. **23.**

American Psychological Association: Division of Industrial-Organization Psychology (1975). "Principles for the Validation and Use of Personnel Selection Procedures." *The Industrial-Organizational Psychologist*. Dayton, Ohio. **11.**

Anastasi, A. (1982). *Psychological Testing*, 5th ed. New York: Macmillan. **8.**

Anderson, James and Celia Hahn (1979). "Is Clergy Evaluation Possible?" *Action Information*, 5 (November). **32.**

Anderson, J. D. (1971). "Pastoral Support of Clergy Role Development Within Local Congregations." *Pastoral Psychology*, 22 (March): 9-14. **6.**

Arbuckle, Gerald A. (1987). *Strategies for Growth in Religious Life*. Homebush, NSW: Saint Paul Publications. **34.**

Armstrong, J. S., and P. Soelberg (1968). "On the Interpretation of Factor Analysis." *Psychological Bulletin*, 70, 361-364. **8.**

Arnold, M. B., P. Hispanicus, C. A. Weisgerber, and P. F. D'Arcy, eds. (1962). *Screening Candidates for the Priesthood and Religious Life*. Chicago: Loyola University Press. **14.**

Arvey, R., and J. Campion (1982). "The Employment Interview: A Summary and Review of Recent Research." *Personnel Psychology: A Journal of Applied Research*, 35:281-322. **19.**

Ashbrook, James (1970). "Testing for the Protestant Ministry." In Bier (1970), pp. 87-135. **1, 30.**

———— (1984). *The Human Mind and the Mind of God: Theological Promise in Brain Research*. Landham: University Press of America. **29.**

———— (1988). *The Brain and Belief*. Bristol: Wyndham Hall Press. **29.**

Ashbrook, James B., and Paul W. Walaskay (1979). *Christianity for Pious Skeptics*. Nashville: Abingdon Press. **3.**

Ashbrook, James B., and John E. Hinkle, Jr., eds. (1988). *At the Point of Need*. New York: University Press of America. **30.**

Association for Clinical Pastoral Education (1987). "Guidelines for Admission Interviews to Basic CPE," *The Standards of the Association for Clinical Pastoral Education*. Decatur: Association for Clinical Pastoral Education, Inc., p. iv. **21.**

Association of Theological Schools (1986). *Procedures, Standards, and Criteria for Membership*, Part 3. Vandalia: Association of Theological Schools in the United States and Canada. **30.**

Auerswald, E. H. (1968). "Interdisciplinary Versus Ecological Approach." *Family Process*, 7, 202-215. **6.**

Bader, Golda Elam, ed. (1942). *I Married a Minister*. New York: Abingdon Press. **7.**

Bales, J. (1988). "Integrity Tests: Honest Results?" *The APA Monitor*, 19. **8, 1, 23.**

Baley, S. (1985). "The Legalities of Hiring in the 80s. *Personnel Journal*, 64, 112-15. **11, 23.**

References

Bassett, G. (1965). *Practical Interviewing: A Handbook for Managers.* New York: American Management Association. **19.**

Bassett, W. W. (1986). "Religion and Religious Institutions: The Rising Din of Litigation." *University of San Francisco Law Review,* 20, 775-850. **23.**

Beaver, R. P. "The Churches and the Indians: Consequences of 350 Years of Missions." Unpublished manuscript. **29.**

Beck, A., A. J. Rush, and B. F. Shaw (1979). *Cognitive Therapy of Depression.* New York: The Guilford Press. **5.**

Becker, E. (1973). *The Denial of Death.* New York: Free Press. **4.**

Bemis, S. E., A. H. Belenky, and D. A. Soder (1983). *Job Analysis: An Effective Management Tool.* Washington, D.C.: NBA Books. **20.**

Bernal, A., A. Colon, E. Fernandez, A. Mena, A. Torres, and E. Torres (1959). *Inventaril Multifacetico de la Personalidad (MMPI).* Minneapolis: The University of Minnesota Press. **27.**

Bersoff, D. N. (1981). "Testing and the Law." *American Psychologist,* 26, 1047-56. **23.**

Bersoff, Donald N. M. (1988). "Should Subjective Employment Devices Be Scrutinized?" *American Psychologist,* 44 **(12)**, 1016-18. **8.**

Bertalanffy, L. von (1968). *General System Theory,* rev. ed. New York: George Braziller. **6.**

Bier, W. C. (1948). "A Comparative Study of the Seminary Group and Four Other Groups on the MMPI." *Studies in Psychology and Psychiatry from the Catholic University of America,* 7:107. **14.**

——— (1956). "A Comparative Study of Five Catholic College Groups on the MMPI." In G. W. Welch and W. G. Dahlstrom, eds. *Basic Readings on the MMPI in Psychology and Medicine.* (Minneapolis: University of Minnesota Press), pp. 586-609. **14.**

——— (1970). *Psychological Testing for Ministerial Selection.* New York: Fordham University Press. **1, 6, 30, 35.**

——— (1971). "A Modified Form of the Minnesota Multiphasic Personality Inventory for Religious Personnel." *Theological Education,* 7, 121-34. **8.**

Blackmon, R. (1984). "The Hazards of Ministry." Doctoral dissertation, Fuller Theological Seminary, Graduate School of Psychology. **5.**

Blackwood, Carolyn P. (1951). *The Pastor's Wife.* Philadelphia: Westminster Press. **7.**

Blanchard, Kenneth (1985). *A Situational Approach to Managing People.* Escondido: Blanchard Training and Development. **20.**

Blizzard, S. W. (1956). "The Minister's Dilemma." *The Christian Century* (April 25): 508-510. **6, 14.**

——— (1958a). "The Parish Minister's Self-image of His Master Role." *Pastoral Psychology* (December): 25-32. **1, 6.**

——— (1958b). "The Protestant Parish Minister's Integrating Roles." *Religious Education* 53, 374-80. **1, 6.**

——— (1959). "The Parish Minister's Self-image and Variability in Community Culture." *Pastoral Psychology* 10 (October): 27-36. **6.**

Bloom, J. H. (1971). "Who Become Clergymen?" *Journal of Religion and Health* 10, 50-76. **13.**

Boissevain, Jeremy (1974). *Friends of Friends: Networks, Manipulators and Coalitions.* New York: St. Martin's Press. **28.**

Bradley, David I., Joan A. Hunt, Richard A. Hunt, and Jack T. King (1982). *Celebrating Marriage: Growing in Love.* Nashville: The Upper Room. **7.**

Brekke, M. (1984). "Identification of Criteria for Assessment of Readiness for Ministry." Paper presented at the annual meeting of the American Educational Research Association. **16.**

Brekke, M., D. Schuller, D. Williams, and Daniel O. Aleshire (1986). *Profiles of Ministry Stage Casebook.* Association of Theological Schools in the United States and Canada. **16.**

——— (1988). *Profiles of Ministry Stage 2 Casebook.* The Association of Theological Schools in the United States and Canada. **16.**

Brekke, M., and D. Williams (1986). *Profiles of Ministry Interview.* Association of Theological Schools in the United States and Canada. **16.**

Bronfenbrenner, U. (1979). *The Ecology of Human Development: Experiments by Nature and Design.* Cambridge: Harvard University Press. **6.**

Brooks, L. W. (1986). "Intentional Infliction of Emotional Distress by Spiritual Counselors: Can Outrageous Conduct Be 'Free Exercise'?" *Michigan Law Review* 84, 1296-1325. **23.**

Brown, N. C. (1985). "The Influence of Social Networks on Burnout in the Ministry." Unpublished doctoral dissertation, Graduate School of Psychology, Fuller Theological Seminary, Pasadena, CA. **8.**

Browning, Don S. (1987). *Religious Thought and the Modern Psychologies.* Philadelphia: Fortress Press. **25.**

Butcher, J. N., ed., (1987). *Computerized Psychological Assessment: A Practitioner's Guide.* New York: Basic Books. **23.**

Butcher, J. N., and P. Pancheri (1976). *A Handbook of Cross-national MMPI Research.* Minneapolis: University of Minnesota Press. **27.**

Butcher, J. N., and A. Tellegen (1978). "Common Methodological Problems in MMPI Research." *Journal of Counseling and Clinical Psychology* 46:620-28. **14.**

Butcher, J. N., and L. A. Clark (1979). "Recent Trends in Cross-cultural MMPI Research and Application." In J. N. Butcher, ed., *New Developments in the Use of MMPI.* Minneapolis: University of Minnesota Press. **27.**

Byham, W. C., and M. E. Spitzer (1971). *The Law and Personnel Testing.* New York: American Management Association. **23.**

Campbell, David P. (1971). *Handbook for the SVIB.* Stanford: Stanford University Press. **11.**

——— (1974). *Manual for the SVIB-SCII.* Stanford: Stanford University Press. **11.**

Cardwell, Sue Webb (1967). "The MMPI as a Predictor of Success Among Seminary Students." In Leroy A. Davis, ed., *Ministry Studies* 1:3-20. **14, 27, 30.**

——— (1974) "The Theological School Inventory: Is It Still Valid?" *Theological Education,* 10 **(2)**, 94-103 **(17)**.

——— (1978). "The Development of Persistence Scales Using Items of the Theological School Inventory." Unpublished doctoral dissertation, Indianapolis, Indiana University. **17.**

Carr, Anne E. (1985). "Discussion: Sources of My Theology." *Journal of Feminist Studies in Religion,* 1 **(1)**, 127-31 **(25)**.

——— (1986). "On Feminist Spirituality." In Joann Wolski Conn, ed., *Women's Spirituality.* New York: Paulist Press. **25.**

Cascio, W. (1982). *Applied Psychology in Personnel Management,* 2nd ed. Reston: Reston Publishing Co. **19.**

Cattell, R. B. and IPAT Staff (1949, 1970). *Sixteen Personality Factor Questionnaire (16PF).* Champaign, Ill.: Institute for Personality and Ability Testing. **27**

Cattell, R. B., H. W. Eber, and M. M. Tatsuoka (1970). *Handbook for the Sixteen Personality Factor Questionnaire (16PF).* Champaign: Institute for Personality and Ability Testing. **8.**

——— (1970) *El Cuestionario de 16 Factores de la Personalidad.* Translated by Cristina del Castillo, Raul Mariscal, Luisa Morales, and Armando Velazquez, 1980, Parte 1 and Parte 2. Mexico: Editorial El Manual Moderno, S.A. **27.**

Center on Budget and Policy Priorities (1986). Washington, D. C., News release, September 2. **27.**

Chodorow, Nancy. (1978). *The Reproduction of Mothering: Psychoanalysis and the Sociology of Gender.* Berkeley: The University of California Press. **25.**

Civil Rights Act of 1964; 702, 42 *U.S.C.* 2000e-l. **23.**

Cogan, P. J. (1986). "The Protection of Rights in Hierarchical Churches: An Ecumenical Survey." *Jurist* 46:205-28. **23.**

Coleman, J. L. (1987). *Police Assessment Testing: An Assessment Center Handbook for Law Enforcement Personnel.* Springfield: Charles C. Thomas. **23.**

Comer, Michael P. (1983). "Psychometric Characteristics of a

Ministerial Assessment Battery." Unpublished dissertation, Northwestern University. **9, 11.**

Connolly, Frank J., and John E. Hinkle, Jr., (1979). *Clergy Clusters.* Unpublished workbook, Indianapolis and Chicago. **18.**

Cook, Thomas D., and Donald T. Campbell (1979). *Quasi-experimentation.* Chicago: Rand McNally. **11.**

Corbett, C., and G. Kush (1974). *Mending the Hoop: A Comprehensive Report of the Indian Church Career Research and Planning Project.* Native American Consulting Committee. Available from 708 S. Lindon Avenue, Tempe, AZ 85281. **29.**

Coriden, James A., Thomas J. Green, and Donald E. Heintschel (1985). *The Code of Canon Law: A Text and Commentary.* New York: Paulist Press. (Special attention should be paid to Part I, Title VI: Orders, chapters I-X, pp. 713-34 by Edward J. Gilbert.) **34.**

Costello, R. M., D. W. Tiffany, and R. H. Gier (1972). "Methodological Issues and Racial (Black-White) Comparisons on the MMPI." *Journal of Consulting and Clinical Psychology,* 38:161-68. **26.**

Coville, Walter J., M. M. D'Arcy, Thomas N. McCarthy, and John J. Rooney (1968). *Assessment of Candidates for the Religious Life: Basic Psychological Issues and Procedures.* Washington, D.C.: Center for Applied Research in the Apostolate. **30, 34.**

Cowen, M. A., B. A. Watkins, and W. E. Davis (1975). "Level of Education, Diagnosis and Race Related Differences in MMPI Performance." *Journal of Clinical Psychology* 31:442-44. **26.**

Cronbach, Lee J. (1970). *Essentials of Psychological Testing.* New York: Harper and Row. **26.**

Cronbach, Lee J., and Goldine E. Gleser (1957). *Psychological Tests and Personnel Decisions.* Urbana: University of Illinois Press. **11.**

Cuellar, I., L. C. Harris, and R. Jasso (1980). "An Acculturation Scale for Mexican-American Normal and Clinical Populations." *Hispanic Journal of Behavioral Sciences* 2:199-217. **27.**

Danchi, T. S. (1987). "Church Discipline on Trial: Religious Freedom Versus Individual Privacy." *Valparaiso University Law Review* 21:387-429. **23.**

Daniel, S., and M. Rogers (1982). "Burn-out and the Pastorate: A Critical Review with Implications for Pastors." *Journal of Psychology and Theology,* 9 **(3),** 232-49 **(5).**

D'Arcy, P. F. (1962). "Review of Research on the Vocational Interests of Priest, Brothers, and Sisters." Pages 1-63 in M. B. Arnold et al. (1962). **14.**

Davis, C. E. (1963). *Counseling Prospective Church Workers.* Pittsburgh: Board of Education of the United Presbyterian Church, U.S.A. **14.**

―――― (1967). *Evaluating and Counseling Prospective Church Workers.* Pittsburgh: Board of Education of the United Presbyterian Church, U.S.A. **27.**

Davis, F. B. (1974). *Standards for Educational and Psychological Tests.* Washington, D.C.: American Psychological Association. **14.**

Dawes, Robyn M. (1979). "The Robust Beauty of Improper Linear Models in Decision Making." *American Psychologist* 34:571-82. **11.**

Deming, W. Edwards (1986). *Out of the Crisis.* Cambridge: Center for Advanced Engineering Study, Massachusetts Institute of Technology. **32.**

Denton, W. (1962). *The Role of the Minister's Wife.* Philadelphia: Westminster Press. **6, 7.**

DeWire, Harry A. (1962). "Psychological Testing in Theological Schools." *Ministry Studies Board Newsletter,* 1:2-4. **14.**

―――― (1970). "Conference Recommendations." In Bier (1970), 257-67. **1.**

―――― (1978). *A Survey of Annual Conference Boards of Ordained Ministry on the Use of Psychological Testing in the Process of Candidate Screening and Guidance.* Commissioned by the National Task Force on Psychological Assessment, Exhibit III., # 23. **18.**

―――― (1979). "A Survey of Annual Conference Boards of Ordained Ministry on the Use of Psychological Testing in the

Process of Candidate Screening and Guidance." Unpublished report to the Task Force on Psychological Testing, Division of Ordained Ministry, Board of Higher Education and Ministry, The United Methodist Church, Nashville. **11, 33.**

Directory (1987). *Directory of Asian-American United Methodist Ministers and Churches.* Claremont: Center for Asian-American Ministries, School of Theology at Claremont. **28.**

Dittes, James E. (1962). "Research on Clergymen: Factors Influencing Decisions for Religious Service and Effectiveness in the Vocation." *Religious Education* (research supplement), 57:S141-S165. **2, 14.**

―――― (1964). *Vocational Guidance of Theological Students.* Dayton: Ministry Studies Board. **10, 13, 17.**

―――― (1970a). "Some Basic Questions About Testing Ministerial Candidates." In Bier (1970), 3-45. **1, 2.**

―――― (1970b). *Minister on the Spot.* Philadelphia: Pilgrim Press. **5.**

Division for Professional Leadership (DPL) Management Committee (1983). *Survey Report* (A copy of the written report can be found in the fall 1983 minutes of the DPL Management Committee. These minutes are currently stored in the archives of the LCA at the corporate offices of the Evangelical Lutheran Church in America in Chicago.) **24.**

Doherty, M. A. (1978). "Sexual Bias in Personality Theory." In Lenore W. Harmon et al., eds., *Counseling Women.* Monterey: Brooks/Cole Publishing Company. **25.**

Douglas, W. T. (1957). "Predicting Ministerial Effectiveness." Doctoral dissertation, Harvard University, Boston, MS. **14.**

―――― (1961). Minister and Wife: Growth in Relationship." *Pastoral Psychology* (December): 35-39. **6, 7.**

―――― (1965). *Ministers' Wives.* New York: Harper and Row. **6.**

Drake, J. (1972). *Interviewing for Managers: Signing up People.* New York: American Management Association. **19.**

Ellison, C. W., and W. Mattila (1982). "The Needs of Evangelical Christian Leaders in the United States." *Journal of Psychology and Theology,* 11 **(1),** 28-35 **(5).**

Erikson, Eric H. (1968). *Identity, Youth, and Crisis.* New York: W. W. Norton and Company. **25.**

Esbeck, C. H. (1986). "Tort Claims Against Churches and Ecclesiastical Officers: The First Amendment Considerations." *West Virginia Law Review,* 89:1-114. **23.**

Faber, Heija (1961). *Pastoral Care and Clinical Training in America,* Van Loghum Slaterus. **21.**

Faulkner, B. (1981). *Burnout in Ministry.* Nashville: Broadman Press. **5.**

Fear, R. (1978). *The Evaluation Interview,* rev. 2nd ed. New York: McGraw-Hill. **19.**

Field, P. B., E. D. Maldonado-Sierra, and G. V. Coelho (1963). "A Student TAT Measure of Competence: A Cross-cultural Replication in Puerto Rico." *Perceptual and Motor Skills,* 16:195-98. **27.**

Fielder, D. W. (1964). "A Nomothetic Study of the Southern California School of Theology Seminarian." Th.D. Dissertation, Southern California School of Theology. **14.**

Fitts, W. H., and G. H. Roid (1988). *Tennessee Self-Concept Scale,* revised manual. Los Angeles: Western Psychological Services. **8.**

Flanagan, C. L. (1986). "Legal Issues Between Psychology and Law Enforcement." *Behavioral Sciences and the Law* 4:371-84. **23.**

French, J. R., W. Rodgers, and S. Cobb (1974). "Adjustment as Person-Environment Fit." In G. Coelho, D. Hamburg, and J. Adams, eds. *Coping and Adaptation.* New York: Basic Books, pp. 316-333. **10.**

Friedman, E. H. (1985). *Generation to Generation: Family Process in Church and Synagogue.* New York: Guilford. **6.**

Frohlich, D. (1987). "Will Courts Make Change for a Large Denomination? Problems of Interpretation in an Agency Analysis in Which a Religious Denomination Is Involved in an Ascending Liability Tort Case." *Iowa Law Review* 72:1377-99. **23.**

References

Fuller, C. G. and H. N. Malony (1984). "A Comparison of English and Spanish (Nuñez) Translations of the MMPI." *Journal of Personality Assessment* 48:130-31. **27.**

Gael, Sydney (1983). *Job Analysis: A Guide to Assessing Work Activities.* San Francisco: Jossey Bass. **20.**

Gerkin, Charles V. (1984). *The Living Human Document.* Nashville: Abingdon. **21.**

Gilligan, Carol (1982). *In a Different Voice: Psychological Theory and Women's Development.* Cambridge: Harvard University Press. **25.**

Glatt, K. M. (1969). "An Evaluation of the French, Spanish, and German Translation of the MMPI." *Acta Psicologica* 29:65-84. **27.**

Glock, C. Y., and P. Roos (1961). "Parishioners' Views of How Ministers Spend Their Time." *Review of Religious Research* 2:170-75. **6.**

Godfrey, R. J. (1955). "Predictive Value of MMPI with Candidates for Religious Brotherhood." M.Ed. Thesis, Marquette University, IN. **14.**

Goldberg, Lewis R. (1970). "Man Versus Model of Man: A Rationale Plus Evidence for a Method of Comprising Clinical Inferences." *Psychological Bulletin* 73:422-32. **11.**

Goldberg, Lewis R. (1976). "Man Versus Model of Man: Just How Conflicting Is That Evidence?" *Organizational Behavior and Human Performance* 16:13-22. **11.**

Gonzalez, J. L. (1988). *The Theological Education of Hispanics.* New York: The Fund for Theological Education. **27.**

Gorsuch, R. L., and H. N. Malony (1976). *The Nature of Man: A Social Psychological Perspective.* Springfield: C. C. Thomas. **8.**

Gottfredson, L. S., ed. (1986). "The G Factor in Employment." *Journal of Vocational Behavior,* 29. **3, 8.**

Greene, R. L. (1987). "Ethnicity and MMPI Performance: A Review." *Journal of Consulting and Clinical Psychology* 55:497-512. **27.**

Grissum, G. A. (1986). "Church Employment and the First Amendment: The Protected Employer and the Vulnerable Employee." *Missouri Law Review* 51:911-31. **23.**

Gruneberg, M. M. (1979). *Understanding Job Satisfaction.* London: Macmillan Press. **10.**

Gynther, M. (1972). "White Norms and the Black MMPI's." *Psychological Bulletin* 72:386-402. **26.**

Haight, Emily Demme (1979). "Pastoral Evaluation: Description Prediction, and Selection in Practice and Research." Unpublished paper, Garrett-Evangelical Theological Seminary, Evanston, IL. **11.**

—— (1980) "Psychological Criteria for the Selection of Ministerial Candidates." Unpublished dissertation, Northwestern University. **9, 11, 14.**

Hale, J. (1982). *Black Children: Their Roots, Culture, and Learning Styles.* Provo: Bringham Young University Press. **26.**

Hall, Brian P. (1982). *Shepherds and Lovers.* New York: Paulist Press. **34.**

—— (1986a). "Psychometry, Assessment and Spirituality." *New Catholic World,* 229:100-102. **34.**

—— (1986b). *The Genesis Effect: Personal and Organizational Transformations.* New Jersey: Paulist Press. **34.**

Hall, Brian P., Oren Harari, Barbara D. Ledig, and Murray Tundow (1986). *Manual for the Hall-Tonna Inventory of Values.* New Jersey: Paulist Press. **34.**

Hall, Brian P., and Benjamin Tonna (1980). *God's Plans for Us.* New York: Paulist Press. **34.**

Hall, F. S., and D. T. Hall (1977). *Dual Career Couples.* **7.**

Harrison, R. V. (1978). "Person-environment Fit and Job Stress." In C. L. Cooper and R. Payne, eds. *Stress at Work.* New York: Wiley, pp. 175-205. **10.**

Hart, A. D. (1978). *Feeling Free.* New Jersey: Fleming H. Revell. **5.**

—— (1984). "Understanding Burnout." *Theology, News, and Notes* 31:5-6. **5.**

—— (1987). *The Hidden Link Between Adrenalin and Stress.* Waco: Word Books. **5.**

—— (1988). "Special Report: How Common Is Pastoral Indiscretion?" *Leadership* 9:12-13. **5.**

Hathaway, S. R. and J. C. McKinley (1965). *Minnesota Multiphasic Personality Inventory.* Minneapolis: University of Minnesota Press. **5.**

—— (1967). *The Minnesota Multiphasic Personality Inventory Manual.* New York: Psychological Corporation. **14.**

Heckman, N. A., R. Bryson, and J. B. Bryson (1977). "Problems of Professional Couples: A Content Analysis." *Journal of Marriage and the Family* 39:323-30. **7.**

Hibbs, B., J. Kobos, and J. Gonzalez (1979). "Effects of Ethnicity, Sex, and Age on MMPI Profiles." *Psychological Reports* 45:591-97. **27.**

Hill, A. D., and Chi-Dooh Li (1988). "Discrimination and Religious Institutions." *This World* 23:81-90. **23.**

Hillman, James (1983). *Healing Fiction.* Barrytown: Station Hill. **3.**

Hinkle, John E., Jr. (1979). "Fitness for Ministry." Address delivered at Garrett-Evangelical Theological Seminary at the Consultation on Fitness, February 5. **1, 11.**

—— (1986). "Section II: For the Pastoral Evaluation Specialist." In *Guidebook for Interviewing, Psychological Testing, and Pastoral Evaluation.* Nashville: Division of Ordained Ministry, The United Methodist Church. **30, 33.**

—— (1988). *A Guidebook on Psychological Assessment as Applied to Personnel Selection, Nurture, and Support Decisions in the Ministerial Selection Processes of The United Methodist Church.* Nashville: Division of Ordained Ministry, The United Methodist Church. p. 74. **18, 33.**

Hinkle, J. E., Jr., and Emily Demme Haight (1988). "Personality Assessment in Seminary and Denominational Contexts." In J. Ashbrook and J. Hinkle, eds. *At the Point of Need.* New York: University Press of America. **26.**

—— (1988). "Contributions of Carroll A. Wise to Personality Assessment in Seminary and Denominational Contexts." In J. B. Ashbrook and J. E. Hinkle, Jr., eds. *At the Point of Need.* New York: University Press of America, pp. 227-41. **30.**

Hofmann, H., ed. (1960). *The Ministry and Mental Health.* New York: Association Press. **6.**

Hofstede, Geert (1984). "The Cultural Relativity of the Quality of Life Concept." *Academy of Management Review* 9:389-98. **28.**

Hogan, R., and R. A. Nicholson (1988). "The Meaning of Personality Test Scores." *American Psychologist* 43:621-26. **23.**

Hogue, D. A. (1985). "The Measurement of Job Satisfaction for Clergy." Unpublished dissertation. Northwestern University. **10.**

Hokanson, J. E., and G. Calden (1960). "Negro-White Difference on the MMPI." *Journal of Clinical Psychology* 16:32-33. **26.**

Holland, T. R. (1979). "Ethnic Differences in MMPI Profile Patterns and Factorial Structure Among Adult Male Offenders." *Journal of Personality Assessment* 43:72-77. **27.**

Holliman, Pamela J. (1985). "A Study of Psychological Assessment Procedures as Adjunctive to Personnel Selection Processes in a Religious Organization." Unpublished dissertation, Northwestern University. **12.**

Holmes, Urban T. (1978). *The Priest in Community.* New York: Seabury Press. **30.**

Holroyd, J. C., and A. M. Brodsky (1977). "Psychologists' Attitudes and Practices Regarding Erotic and Nonerotic Contact with Patients." *American Psychologist* 32:843-49.

Hough, Joseph C., Jr., (1984). "The Education of Practical Theologians." *Theological Education* (Spring):66-78. **3.**

209

Hughes-McIntyre, Mary Fran, ed. (1987). *Abstracts of Research in Pastoral Care* and *Counseling, XV*. Richmond: Joint Council on Research, National Clearing House. **30.**

Hulme, W. (1962). *The Pastoral Care of Families*. Nashville: Abingdon. **6.**

Hunt, Richard A. (1974). "Psychological Measurement in Theological Schools." *Theological Education* 10:2. **30.**

——— (1977). *The Christian as Minister*. Nashville: Division of Ordained Ministry of the United Methodist Church. **7.**

——— (1987). *Supervising Pastor's Manual*. Nashville: Board of Higher Education and Ministry, The United Methodist Church. **7.**

Hunt, Richard A., and Joan A. Hunt (1976). *Ministry and Marriage*. Pasadena: Ministry Inventories. **7.**

Hunt, Richard A., S. W. Cardwell, and J. E. Dittes (1976). *Theological School Inventory Manual*. Dallas: Ministry Studies Board. **13, 17, 30.**

——— (1976). *Guide to Interpreting the TSI*. Dallas: Ministry Studies Board. **17.**

Hunt, Richard A., and Robert F. Kohler (1988). *The Candidacy Guidebook*, 2nd. ed. Nashville: Board of Higher Education and Ministry, The United Methodist Church. **7.**

Inclan, J. (1979). "Adjustment to Migration: Family Organization, Acculturation, and Psychological Symptomatology in Puerto Rican Women of Three Socioeconomic Class Groups." Doctoral dissertation, New York University, New York. **27.**

Ingram, L. C. (1981). "Leadership, Democracy, and Religion: Role Ambiguity Among Pastors in Southern Baptist Churches." *Journal for the Scientific Study of Religion* 20:119-29. **6.**

Institute for Social Research (1976). "Experiment in a Juvenile Court: Volunteer Program Proves Ineffective, Researchers Find." *ISR Newsletter* 4:2 and 8. **8.**

James, William (1961). *Varieties of Religious Experience*. New York: Mentor Books. **3.**

Jewett, Paul K. (1980). *The Ordination of Women*. Grand Rapids: Wm. B. Eerdmans Publishing Co. **25.**

Joint Committee on Testing Practices (1988). *Code of Fair Testing Practices in Education*. Washington, D.C.: American Psychological Association. **23.**

Jones, Doris Moreland, ed. (1980). *Guidebook for Pastoral Evaluation Specialists*. Nashville: Division of Ordained Ministry, Board of Higher Education, The United Methodist Church, Nashville, TN. **11, 18, 33.**

Jones, M. (1985). "Memorandum to Chairpersons and Registrars of the Annual Conference Boards of Ministry." Gammon Theological Seminary, Atlanta, GA. **26.**

Jones, R., ed. (1980). *Black Psychology*. New York: Harper & Row. **26.**

The National Task Force on Psychological Testing/Pastoral Evaluation (1981). "Minutes." Division of Ordained Ministry, The United Methodist Church. April 18-19, 1979; June 25-26, 1980; August 2-3, 1981. **26.**

Josselson, Ruthellen (1987). *Finding Herself: Pathways to Identity Development in Women*. San Francisco: Jossey-Bass. **25.**

Jud, G., E. W. Mills, and G. W. Burch (1970). *Ex-pastors: Why Men Leave the Parish Ministry*. Philadelphia: Pilgrim Press. **5.**

Kagan, J. (1988). "The Meanings of Personality Predicates." *American Psychologist* 43:614-20. **23.**

Kanter, R. (1977). *Work and the Family in the United States: A Critical Review and Agenda for Research and Policy*. New York: Sage. **6.**

Kantor, D., and W. Lehr (1975). *Inside the Family: Toward a Theory of Family Process*. San Francisco: Jossey-Bass. **6.**

Kaplan, B. (1955). "Reflections of the Acculturation Process in the Rorschach Test." *Journal of Projective Technique* 19:30-35. **27.**

Kelley, Kathleen E. (1981). "The Priest and Personal Development." *The Priest* (November): 19-28. **34.**

Kieren, D. K., and B. Munro (1988). "Handling Greedy Clergy Roles: A Dual Clergy Example." *Pastoral Psychology* 36:239-48. **6, 7.**

Kim, Bok-Lim (1978). *The Asian Americans: Changing Patterns, Changing Needs*. New York: Association of Korean Christian Scholars in North America. **28.**

Kim, Chan-Hie, et al. (1981). *Opinion Survey on Korea's Unification*. Claremont: Center for Asian-American Ministries, School of Theology at Claremont. **28.**

Kleaver, G. L. and J. E. Dyble (1973). "Effectiveness of Young Pastors." Unpublished manuscript, Office of Research, Support Agency of the General Assembly of the United Presbyterian Church U.S.A. **14.**

Kling, F. R. (1959). "The Motivations of Ministerial Candidates." *Research Bulletin* (Princeton: Educational Testing Service), p. 2. **14.**

——— (1958). "A Study of Testing as Related to the Ministry." *Religious Education* 53:243-248. **14.**

——— (1970). "Discussion: Testing for the Roman Catholic Priesthood." In Bier (1970).

Klopfer, W. G. (1983). "Writing Psychological Reports." In C. E. Walker. *The Handbook of Clinical Psychology*, vol. 1: "Theory, Research, and Practice." Homewood, IL: Dow Jones-Irwin, pp. 501-27. **22.**

Kohler, R. F., ed. (1988). *The Christian as Minister*, 2nd ed. Nashville: Division of Ordained Ministry of The United Methodist Church. **7.**

Kunin, T. (1955). "The Construction of a New Type of Attitude Measure. *Personnel Psychology* 8:65-77. **10.**

Laghi, Archbishop Pio (1982). "The Concern of the Church for the Quality of Priestly Ministry." *Social Justice Review* (July): 123-28. **34.**

Larsen, Ellis L. and James M. Shopshire (1988). "A Profile of Contemporary Seminarians." In *Theological Education*, 21:2. **30.**

Lawler, E. E. (1973). *Motivation in Work Organizations*. Monterey: Wadsworth. **10.**

Ledig, Barbara D. (1986). "Using the Hall-Tonna Inventory of Values." *New Catholic World* 229:128-32. **34.**

Lee, C. (1987). "The Social and Psychological Dynamics of the Minister's Family: An Ecological Model for Research." Unpublished doctoral dissertation, Fuller Theological Seminary. **6.**

——— (1988). "Toward a Social Ecology of the Minister's Family." *Pastoral Psychology* 36:249-59. **6.**

Lee, C., and J. Balswick (1989). *Life in a Glass House*. Grand Rapids: Zondervan. **6.**

Levine, E. S. and A. M. Padilla (1980). *Crossing Cultures in Therapy: Counseling for the Hispanic*. Monterey, Calif.: Brooks/Cole. **27.**

Levinson, D. J., C. N. Darrow, E. B. Klein, M. H. Levinson, and B. McKee (1978). *The Seasons of a Man's Life*. New York: Ballantine Books. **4, 25.**

Likins, William K. (1970). "How Students Decided for the Ministry: A Survey of Methodist Theological Students and Students in Methodist Theological Schools." Nashville: Department of the Ministry, Division of Higher Education, The United Methodist Church. **30.**

Lodahl, T. M., and M. Kejner (1965). "The Definition and Measurement of Job Involvement. *Journal of Applied Psychology* 49:24-33. **10.**

Lupa, I. C. (1987). "Free Exercise Exemption and Religious Institutions: The Case of Employment Discrimination." *Boston University Law Review* 67:391-442. **23.**

McAdams, D. P. (1988). *Power, Intimacy and the Life Story*. New York: Guilford Press. **4.**

McConnell, J. (n.d.). *MCTEST—A Test and Questionnaire Analysis Program*. Northwestern University Computer Center. **10.**

McCord, Joan (1978). "A Thirty-year Follow-up of Treatment Effects." *American Psychologist* 33:284-89. **8.**

McCreary, C. and E. Padilla (1977). "MMPI Differences Among

Blacks, Mexican American, and White Male Offenders." *Journal of Clinical Psychology* 36:147-51. **27.**

Mace, David and Vera Mace (1980). *What's Happening to Clergy Marriages?* Nashville: Abingdon Press. **5, 6, 7.**

McHolland, J. D. (1966). "A Summary of the Influence of Pastoral Care on the Attitudes of Patients in the Rehabilitation Unit of a General Hospital." Unpublished dissertation, Northwestern University. **10.**

McNair, C. (1979). "Progress Report on the Research of Norms on the MMPI for Black Ministerial Candidates." Evanston: Garrett-Evangelical Theological Seminary. **26.**

Maddock, R., C. T. Kinney, and M. Middleton (1973). "Preference for Personality Versus Role-Activity Variables in the Choice of a Pastor." *Journal for the Scientific Study of Religion* 12:449-52. **6.**

Malina, Bruce J. (1981). *The New Testament World: Insights from Cultural Anthropology.* Atlanta: John Knox Press. **28.**

Malina, Bruce J., and Jerome H. Neyrey (1988). *Calling Jesus Names.* Sonoma: Polebridge Press. **28.**

Malony, H. N. (1976). "Current Research on Performance Effectiveness Among Religious Leaders." Paper delivered at the National Evangelical Conference on Research in Mental Health and Religious Behavior, Atlanta, GA. January. **14.**

Malony, H. N., T. L. Needham, and S. Southard (1986). *Clergy Malpractice.* Philadelphia: Westminster Press. **23.**

Malony, H. N., and L. F. Majovski (1986). "The Role of Psychological Assessment in Predicting Ministerial Effectiveness." *Review of Religious Research* 28:29-39. **8.**

Maloney, Michael (in press). "Psychological Evaluation and Diagnosis." *Dictionary of Pastoral Care and Counseling.* Nashville: Abingdon Press. **2.**

Marteau, L. (1982). "Assessment for the Priesthood and Religious Life." *Clergy* 67:31-34. **34.**

Mason, Emanuel J., and William J. Bramble (1978). *Understanding and Conducting Research: Applications in Education and the Behavioral Sciences.* New York: McGraw-Hill.

May, Mark A. (1934). *The Education of American Ministers.* New York: Institute of Social and Religious Research. **1.**

Means, J. Jeffrey (1980a). "An Investigation of an Assessment Model for the Evaluation of the Capacity of Seminary Students to Utilize Clinical Pastoral Education as a Professional Learning Experience." Unpublished dissertation, Northwestern University. **9.**

————— (1980b). "Key Concepts in the Selection and Application of Criteria in the Nature, Preparation, and Selection of Persons for the Ordained Ministry." In Doris M. Jones, ed. *Guidebook for Pastoral Evaluation Specialists.* Nashville: Division of Ordained Ministry, The United Methodist Church. **33.**

————— (1986). "The Nature of Professional Education for the Ministry and the Role of Psychological Assessment." In *Guidebook for Interviewing, Psychological Testing, and Pastoral Evaluation.* The United Methodist Church. **30.**

————— (1987). "The Nature of Professional Education for Ministry and the Role of Psychological Assessment." Chicago: Consultation on Psychological Assessment in Theological Education, Feb. 27-28, 1987. **3.**

Meltzer, J. (1986). "Sex or Sin: Deference to Church Authority Over Secular Employee's Violation of Religious Doctrine." *University of San Francisco Law Review* 20:907-25. **23.**

Menges, Robert J., and James E. Dittes (1965). *Psychological Studies of Clergymen: Abstracts of Research.* New York: Thomas Nelson. **1, 17.**

Mershon, B., and R. L. Gorsuch (1988). "Number of Factors in the Personality Sphere: Does Increase in Factors Increase Predictability of Real-life Criteria?" *Journal of Personality and Social Psychology* 33:675-80. **8.**

Meyer, Herbert H., Emanuel Kay, and John R. P. French, Jr., (1965). "Split Roles in Performance Appraisal." *Harvard Business Review* (Jan.-Feb.): 123. **32.**

Miller, Jo Ann (1986). "Discovering Talent Through the Perceiver Interview." *New Catholic World* 229:133-35. **34.**

Miller, Jo Ann, Patrick McCaslin, and George A. Deinlein (1984). "How to Identify a Future Priest." *America* (February 18): 104-7. **34.**

Mills, E. W., and J. P. Koval (1971). *Stress in the Ministry.* Washington D.C.: Ministry Studies Board. **5.**

Miner, John B., and Mary G. Miner (1973). *Personnel and Industrial Relations,* 2nd ed. New York: Macmillan. **11.**

Miranda, J. C. (1988). "Needed: 2,000 Hispanic Churches." *Action* (July-Aug.): 4-5. **27.**

Mitchell, R. E. (1965). "When Ministers and Their Parishioners Have Different Social Class Positions." *Review of Religious Research* 7:28-41. **6.**

Moberg, D. O. (1970). "Theological Position and Institutional Characteristics of Protestant Congregations: An Exploratory Study." *Journal for the Scientific Study of Religion* 9:53-58. **6.**

Moore, H. W., and P. C. Unsinger, eds. (1987). *The Police Assessment Center.* Springfield: Charles C. Thomas. **23.**

Munger, Edith (1974). "Personality, Motivation, and Experience: Their Effects on Persistence in a Theological Seminary." Unpublished doctoral dissertation, Pasadena, CA, Fuller Theological Seminary. **17, 27.**

Nathan, B. R., and W. F. Cascio (1986). "Introduction, Technical and Legal Standards." In R. A. Berk, ed. *Performance Assessment: Methods and Applications.* Baltimore: Johns Hopkins University Press. **8.**

Native American Theological Association (NATA, 1980). "Toward Culturally Fair Ordination Examinations for Native Americans in the United Presbyterian Church: a Position Paper." **29.**

Nauss, A. (1970). "Development of a Measure of Ministerial Effectiveness: A Preliminary Draft." Mimeographed paper, Concordia Seminary, Springfield, IL. **14.**

————— (1972). "Problems in Measuring Ministerial Effectiveness." *Journal for the Scientific Study of Religion* 11:141-151. **14.**

————— (1973). "The Ministerial Personality: Myth or Reality?" *Journal of Religion and Health* 12:77-96. **6, 13.**

Navarro, R. A. (1971) "El MMPI (Español) aplicado a jóvenes Mexicanos: Influencias del sexo, edad, y nivel de inteligencia." *Revista Interamericana de Psicología* 5:127-37. **27.**

Neal, A. (1981). "Mandatory Drug Testing: Court Weighs Civil Liberties Objections." *American Bar Association Journal* 74:58-63. **23.**

Niebuhr, H. Richard (1956). *The Ministry in Historical Perspectives.* New York: Harper. **1.**

Niebuhr, H. Richard, Daniel D. Williams, and James M. Gustafson (1956). *The Purpose of the Church and Its Ministry.* New York: Harper. **1.**

Nuñez, R. (1967). *Inventario Multifactico de la Personalidad (MMPI)-Español.* Mexico City: El Manual Moderno, S.A. **27.**

————— (1968). *Application of the MMPI to Psychopathology.* Mexico City: El Manual Moderno. **27.**

Nunnally, J. C. (1978). *Psychometric theory,* 2nd ed. New York: McGraw-Hill. **8.**

Oates, W., ed. (1961). *The Minister's Own Mental Health.* Great Neck: Channel Press. **6.**

Okamoto, D. E. (1987). "Religious Discrimination and the Title VII Exemption for Religious Organizations: A Basic Values Analysis for the Proper Allocation of Conflicting Rights." *Southern California Law Review* 60:1375-1427. **23.**

Olmedo, E. L. (1981). "Testing Linguistic Minorities." *American Psychologist* 36:1078-85. **27.**

Olmedo, E. L., J. L. Martinez, and S. R. Martinez (1978). "Measure of Acculturation for Chicano Adolescents," 42:159-70. **27.**

Ostrov, E. (1986). "Police/Law Enforcement and Psychology." *Behavioral Science and the Law* 4:353-70. **23.**

Oswald, R. M. (1982). "How Well Do Clergy Take Care of Themselves?" *Alban Institute Action Information* 8:1-3. **5.**

Pabst, T. L. (1987). "Protection of AIDS Victims from Employment Discrimination Under the Rehabilitation Act." *University of Illinois Law Review* (1987): 355-378. **23.**

Padilla, A. M. (1979). "Critical Factors in the Testing of Hispanic Americans: A Review and Some Suggestions for the Future." In R. Tyler and S. White, eds. *Testing, Teaching and Learning: Report of a Conference on Testing.* Washington, D.C.: National Institute of Education. **27.**

Padilla, E. R., E. L. Olmedo, and F. Loya (1982). "Acculturation and the MMPI Performance of Chicano and Anglo College Students." *Hispanic Journal of Behavioral Sciences* 4:451-66. **27.**

Padilla, A. M., and Ruiz, R. A. (1975). "Personality Assessment and Test Interpretation of Mexican Americans: A Critique." *Journal of Personality Assessment,* 103-109. **27.**

Parsons, Richard D. (1986). "Psychological Testing of Candidates for the Ministry: A Users Guide." *New Catholic World* 229:109-12. **34.**

Patton, John (1981). "Clinical Hermeneutics—Soft Focus in Pastoral Counseling and Theology." *The Journal of Pastoral Care* (September). **21.**

——— (1983). *Pastoral Counseling: A Ministry of the Church.* Nashville: Abingdon Press. **21.**

Pepitone, Rockwell, ed. (1980). *Dual Career Couples.* Beverly Hills: Sage. **7.**

Perkins, N. (1988). "Prohibiting Use of the Human Immunodeficiency Virus Antibody Test by Employer and Insurers." *Harvard Journal on Legislation* 25:275-315. **23.**

Perry, E. L., and D. R. Hoge (1981). "Faith Priorities of Pastor and Laity as a Factor in the Growth or Decline of Presbyterian Congregations." *Review of Religious Research* 22:221-32. **6.**

Peterson, D. J. (1974). "The Impact of Duke Power on Testing." *Personnel* 51:30-37. **11.**

Pietrofesa, John J., and Howard Splete (1975). *Career Development: Theory and Research.* New York: Grune and Stratton. **1.**

Plemons, G. A. (1977). "A Comparison of MMPI Scores of Anglo- and Mexican-American Psychiatric Patients." *Journal of Consulting and Clinical Psychology* 45:149-50. **27.**

Polischuk, P. (1980). "Personality Characteristics and Role Preferences Among Hispanic Religious Ministers." Doctoral dissertation, Fuller Graduate School of Psychology. **27.**

Pope, K. S. (1988). "Avoiding Malpractice in the Area of Diagnosis, Assessment, and Testing." *Independent Practitioner* 8:18-25. **23.**

Potvin, Raymond H., and Antanas Suziedelis (1969). *Seminarians of the Sixties: A National Survey.* Washington, D. C.: Center for Applied Research in the Apostolate (CARA). **30.**

Preparation Committee (1981). *Professional Leadership Handbook: Preparation Committee Edition.* Division for Professional Leadership, Lutheran Church in America, Philadelphia. (Revisions and updates were added in 1983 and 1985.) **24.**

Presnell, W. B. (1977). "The Minister's Own Marriage." *Pastoral Psychology* 25:272-81. **6.**

Pressley, A., E. Haight, and C. McNair (1981). "The MMPI and Black Ministerial Students." Garrett-Evangelical Theological Seminary. **26.**

Prewitt Diaz, J. O., J. A. Nogueras, and J. Draguns (1984). "MMPI (Spanish Translation) in Puerto Rican Adolescents: Preliminary Data on Reliability and Validity." *Hispanic Journal of Behavioral Sciences* 6:179-90. **27.**

Pyburn, K. M., Jr. (1988). "Legal Challenges to Licensing Examinations." Paper presented at the meeting of the American Psychological Association, Atlanta, GA, August, 1988. **23.**

Quirogg, I. (1972). "The Use of Linear Discriminant Function of the MMPI Scores in the Classification of Psychotic and Non-psychotic Mexican Psychiatric Patients." *Dissertation Abstracts International* 33:1B. **27.**

Rallings, E. M., and D. J. Pratto (1984). *Two Clergy Marriages: A Special Case of Dual Careers.* Lanham: University Press of America. **7.**

Reilley, R. R., and G. E. Knight (1970). "MMPI Scores for Mexican-American College Students." *Journal of College Student Personnel* 11:419-22. **27.**

"Research Report to Pastoral Evaluation Specialists" (1980). Evanston: Garrett-Evangelical Theological Seminary, April 22. **30.**

Revelle, R., and T. Rocklin (1979). "Very Simple Structure: An Alternative Procedure for Estimating the Optimal Numbers of Interpretable Factors." *Multivariate Behavioral Research* 14:403-14. **10.**

Ricoeur, Paul (1969). *The Symbolism of Evil.* Boston: Beacon Press. **3.**

——— (1970). *Freud and Philosophy: An Essay in Interpretation,* New Haven: Yale University Press. **21.**

Ridley, C. (1988). *How to Select Church Planters.* Pasadena: Fuller Evangelistic Association. **19.**

Risetti, J. (1981). "Translation and Adaptation of the MMPI in Chile." Cited in Butcher and Clark (1979). **27.**

Ritter, M. I. H. (1982). "The Minister's Wife: An Exploratory Study on Role Conflict and Self-actualization." Doctoral dissertation, The Fielding Institute, 1981. *Dissertation Abstracts International* 43:1265B. **6.**

Rizzuto, Ana-Maria (1979). *The Birth of the Living God: A Psychoanalytic Study.* Chicago: University of Chicago Press. **3.**

Robinson, Herbert L., Jr. (1988). "Hazards of the Ministry for Dual-Clergy Couples." Unpublished doctoral dissertation. Fuller Theological Seminary. **7.**

Rodriguez, M. J. (1986). *Directorio de sacerdotes Hispanos en los Estados Unidos de America.* Forest Hills: Herencia Española. **27.**

Rosinski, Bernard J. (1987). "Priest Perceiver Interview: How Valid Is It?" *The Review for Religious* (July): 533-41. **34.**

Rossi, Peter H., Howard E. Freeman, and Sonia R. Wright (1979). *Evaluation: A Systematic Approach.* Beverly Hills: Sage Publications.

Rothstein, M. A. (1987). "Drug Testing in the Work Place: The Challenge to Employment Relations and Employment Law." *Chicago-Kent Law Review* 63:683-743. **23.**

Rulla, Luigi, France Imoda, and Joyce Riddick (1979). *Psychological Structure and Vocation.* Dublin: Villa Books. **34.**

Rutman, Leonard (1977). *Evaluation Research Methods: A Basic Guide,* Beverly Hills.: Sage Publications.

Samuda, R. J. (1975). *Psychological Testing of American Minorities: Issues and Consequences.* New York: Dodd, Mead, and Co. **26.**

Sawyer, J. (1966). "Measurement and Prediction, Clinical and Statistical." *Psychological Bulletin* 66:178-200. **8.**

Scanlon, Joan (1985). "Life Themes in the Wives of Roman Catholic Deacons." Unpublished dissertation, Northwestern University. **25.**

Scanlon, Joan, and James Zullo (1987). "The Psychological Assessment of Candidates." *Call to Growth/Ministry* (Spring). **25.**

Schnelling, Clarence (in press). "Call to Ministry." *Dictionary of Pastoral Care and Counseling.* Nashville: Abingdon Press. **2.**

Schuller, David S., Merton P. Strommen, and Milo L. Brekke, eds. (1980). *Ministry in America.* New York: Harper & Row. **1, 6, 14, 30, 34.**

——— (1975). *Readiness for Ministry: Volume 1—Criteria.* Vandalia: Association of Theological Schools in the United States and Canada. **16.**

Schuller, D., M. Brekke, M. Strommen, Daniel O. Aleshire, (1976). *Readiness for Ministry: Volume 2—Assessment.* Vandalia: Association of Theological Schools in the United States and Canada. **16.**

References

Schwitzgebel, R. L., and R. K. Schwitzgebel (1980). *Law and Psychological Practice*. New York: John Wiley. **23.**

Silver, M. (1987). "Negligent Hiring Claims Take Off." *American Bar Association Journal* 73:72-78. **23.**

Smith, D. P. (1973). *Clergy in the Cross-fire: Coping with Role Conflict in the Ministry*. Philadelphia: Westminster Press. **5, 6.**

Smith, P. O., L. M. Kendall, and C. L. Hulin (1969). *The Measurement of Satisfaction in Work and Retirement*. Chicago: Rand McNally. **10.**

Southard, Samuel, ed. (1955). *Conference on Motivation for the Ministry*. Louisville: Southern Baptist Seminary. **1.**

Spanier, G. (1976). "Measuring Dyadic Adjustment: New Scales for Assessing the Quality of Marriage and Similar Dyads." *Journal of Marriage and the Family* 38:15-28. **6.**

Speer, D. (1970). "Family Systems: Morphostasis and Morphogenesis, or 'Is Homeostasis Enough?'" *Family Process* 9:259-78. **6.**

Spilka, Bernard, Ralph W. Hood, and Richard L. Gorsuch (1985). *The Psychology of Religion: An Empirical Approach*. Englewood Cliffs: Prentice-Hall. **3.**

Sutherland, J. W. (1973). *A General Systems Philosophy for the Social and Behavioral Sciences*. New York: George Braziller. **6.**

——— (1975). *Statistical Package for the Social Sciences*, 2nd ed. New York: McGraw-Hill. **11.**

Stewart, C. (1961). *The Minister as Marriage Counselor*. New York: Abingdon Press. **6.**

——— (1979). *The Minister as Family Counselor*. Nashville: Abingdon Press. **6.**

Stone, H. (1989a). "A 25-year Study of the Changes in Those Who Enter Ministry." *Journal of Pastoral Psychotherapy*, 2. **13.**

——— (1989b). "Female and Male Called to Ministry." *Journal of Pastoral Psychotherapy*, 2. **13.**

——— (1990a). "Liberals and Conservatives." *Journal of Psychology and Christianity*. (in press) **13.**

——— (1990b). "Predicting Ministerial Effectiveness." *Pastoral Sciences*. (in press) **13.**

Streibe, Susan C. (1986). "Psychological Testing of Candidates for Ministry: A Catholic Psychologists Approach." *New Catholic World* 229:113-16. **34.**

Sullivan, Francis X. (1981). "Preparing for Priestly Ministry in the 'Eighties.'" *The Priest* (June): 19-21. **34.**

Super, Donald E. (1957). *Vocational Development: A Framework for Research*. New York: Columbia University Press. **1.**

Sutherland, J. W. (1973). *A General Systems Philosophy for the Social and Behavioral Sciences*. New York: Braziller. **6.**

Szapocznik, J., M. A. Scopetta, W. Kurtines, and M. A. Arnalde (1978). "Theory and Measurement of Acculturation." *Interamerican Journal of Psychology* 12:113-30. **27.**

Szapocznik, J., and W. Kurtines (1980). "Acculturation, Biculturalism and Adjustment Among Cuban Americans." In A. M. Padilla, ed. *Acculturation: Theory, Models, and Some New Findings*. Boulder: Westview Press. Pp. 139-59. **27.**

Taghvai, N. (1986). "Constitutional Law: Free Exercise Clause Permits Church to Fire Homosexual Employee." *Suffolk University Law Review* 20:19-28. **23.**

Terry, D. R., and R. N. Evans (1973). *Methodological Study for Determining the Task Content of Dental Auxiliary Education Programs*. No. HRP 000-4628. Bethesda: Bureau of Health, Manpower, Education, National Institutes of Health. **20.**

The Book of Discipline of The United Methodist Church (1980). Nashville: The United Methodist Publishing House. **11.**

The Key Reporter (Autumn 1985): 2. **13.**

Tonna, Benjamin (1982). *Gospel for the Cities: A Socio-Theology of Urban Ministry*. Translated by William E. Jerman. New York: Orbis Books. **34.**

Transition Work Group on Ministry (1987). *Report and Recommendations from an ALC/LCA Consultation on Candidate Psychological Assessment*. (Available from the Division for Ministry of the ELCA.) **24.**

Trotter, F. T. (1980). "United Methodist Church." Pages 445-57 in Schuller et al. (1980). **14.**

United Presbyterian Church in the United States of America (1979). "Minutes of the General Assembly of the Presbyterian Church (USA)." Part I: *Journal, One Hundred and Ninety-first General Assembly*. New York: Office of the General Assembly. **29.**

U.S. Equal Employment Opportunity Commission, U.S. Civil Service Commission, U.S. Department of Labor, and U.S. Department of Justice. (1978). "Uniform Guidelines on Employment Selection Procedures." *Federal Register* 43:38290-38309. **8.**

U.S. Department of Health, Education, and Welfare (1984). "A Study of Selected Socio-economic Characteristics of Ethnic Minorities." Washington, D.C. **29.**

U.S. Government Printing Office (1977). *American Indian Policy Review Commission*. Washington, D.C. **29.**

Vaillant, George (1977). *Adaptation to Life*. Boston: Little, Brown and Company. **25.**

Vaugh, R. P. (1963). "A Psychological Assessment Program for Candidates to the Religious Life." *Catholic Psychology Record* 1:65-70. **14.**

Velazquez (1970). Cited in Butcher and Pancheri (1976, pp. 215-217). **27.**

Velez de Para, M. (1967). "Construction of a T Scale for 500 University Students." *Revista de Psicología*, Colombia, 12:41-54. **27.**

Vergote, Antoine, and Alvarv Tamayo (1981). *The Parental Figure and the Representation of God: A Psychological Cross-cultural Study*. New York: Mouton. **3.**

Vetere, A., and A. Gale (1987). *Ecological Studies of Family Life*. New York: John Wiley. **6.**

Waetjen, Herman, ed. (1985). *The Gospel of John in Sociolinguistic Perspective*. Berkeley: Center for Hermeneutical Studies, 48th Colloquy of the Center for Hermeneutical Studies. **28.**

Walker, James T., and Carol J. Sherman (1988). *Marriage in Ministry: An Introductory Manual*. Nashville: Board of Higher Education and Ministry, The United Methodist Church. **7.**

——— (1988). *Marriage in Ministry*. Nashville: Board of Higher Education and Ministry, The United Methodist Church. **7.**

Warner, J., and J. D. Carter (1984). "Loneliness, Marital Adjustment, and Burnout in Pastoral and Lay Persons." *Journal of Psychology and Theology* 12:125-31. **6.**

Watzlawick, P., J. Beavin, and D. Jackson (1967). *Pragmatics of Human Communication*. New York: W. W. Norton. **6.**

Webb, S. C. (1968). *An Inventory of Religious Activities and Interests*. Princeton: Educational Testing Service. **14.**

——— (1970). *Revised Technical Manual: Inventory of Religious Activities and Interests*. Princeton: Educational Testing Service. **17, 27.**

Weisgerber, C. A. (1962). "Survey of a Psychological Screening Program in a Clerical Order." Pages 107-48 in Arnold et al. (1962). **14.**

——— (1971). "The Theological School Inventory and Some Roman Catholic and Protestant Differences." *Journal of Counseling and Values* 16:54-65. **17.**

Wexley, K., and G. Yukl (1984). *Organizational Behavior and Personnel*, rev. ed. Homewood: Richard D. Irwin, Inc. **19.**

Whitehead, Evelyn E., and James D. Whitehead (1982). *Community of Faith*. New York: The Seabury Press. **25.**

Wiggins, Jerry S. (1973). *Personality and Prediction: Principles of Personality Assessment*. Reading: Addison-Wesley Publishing Co., pp. 39, 41. **9, 11.**

Wimberly, C. E. (1981). "Self-actualization and the Minister's Wife." Doctoral dissertation, U.S. International University, 1979. *Dissertation Abstracts International* 42:4280B. **6.**

Appendix

Wimberly, E. (1985). "Minorities." In R. Wicks et al., eds. *Clinical Handbook of Pastoral Counseling*. New York: Paulist Press. **26.**

Wissink, Charles Jay (1975). *Vocational Attitude Changes in First Year Seminary Students*. Dissertation from Princeton Theological Seminary. Ann Arbor: Xerox University Microfilms. **30.**

Wolpe, J. and A. A. Lazarus (1966). *Principles of Behavior Therapy.* Oxford: Pergamon Press. **5.**

Wynn, J. C. (1957). *Pastoral Ministry to Families*. Philadelphia: Westminster Press. **6.**

——— (1960). "Pastors Have Family Problems Too." *Pastoral Psychology* (September): 7-10. **6.**

——— (1982). *Family Therapy in Pastoral Ministry*. San Francisco: Harper & Row. **6.**

York, D. (1982). "Relationship Between Burnout and Assertiveness, Aggressiveness, Styles of Relating, and Marital Adjustment with Pastors." Unpublished dissertation, Biola University. **5.**

Yu, Eui-Young (1982). "Koreans in Los Angeles: Size, Distribution, and Composition." In Eui-Young Yu, ed. *Koreans in Los Angeles: Prospects and Promises*. Los Angeles: Center for Korean-American and Korean Studies, California State University. **28.**

BIOGRAPHICAL PROFILES
OF CONTRIBUTORS

Daniel O. Aleshire

Daniel O. Aleshire has been involved with the *Profiles of Ministry* program, directly or indirectly, since 1975. During part of the early stages of work, he was a research scientist at Search Institute and a member of the *Readiness for Ministry* research team that conducted the initial work on defining criteria and developing instruments. Since 1978, he has been on the faculty of the Southern Baptist Theological Seminary in Louisville, Kentucky, where he is presently professor of psychology and Christian education and seminary director of professional studies. Beginning in 1985, he has worked with David Schuller and other ATS staff to revise the former *Readiness for Ministry* program into the *Profiles of Ministry* format. Aleshire received his M.Div. from Southern Baptist Theological Seminary and his M.A. and Ph.D. from George Peabody College for Teachers.

Richard Blackmon

Richard Blackmon is a founding partner of the Pacific Psychological Resources, a private clinical psychology practice in Pasadena and Simi Valley, California. Blackmon specializes in clergy problems, providing educational resources in the church and church consultation (especially church leadership). In addition, he is an adjunct professor at Fuller Theological Seminary in Pasadena, California, where he teaches personal growth and hazards of the ministry classes for ministers.

Thomas E. Brown

Thomas E. Brown, an ordained minister of the Presbyterian Church (USA), is president of Career Planning Centers of America, Inc., in St. Louis, Missouri. He is a licensed professional counselor and is a national certified counselor and national certified career counselor (National Board for Counselor Certification). He was the first director of Northeast Career Center in Princeton, New Jersey (directed as Northeast Counseling Center by another person for one year), and the first chairperson of the Standards Committee for the Church Career Development Council. He studied at the University of South Carolina, Princeton Theological Seminary, the University of Pennsylvania, and New York University.

Sue Webb Cardwell

Sue Webb Cardwell is professor emeritus of pastoral care and counseling at Christian Theological Seminary, retired as of June 30, 1988. She is a licensed psychologist and has done psychological assessment and interpretations for students at Christian Theological Seminary since 1962. In addition, she has served on the Theological School Inventory Committee since 1971 and participated in its revision in 1972. She has done research, including her Ph.D. dissertation, on seminary students and ministers, using several of the most used tests. She served as associate director of the Pastoral Counseling Service of Christian Theological Seminary from 1976 to 1981 and as director from 1981 to June 30, 1988. She was vice-president of the American Association of Pastoral Counselors from 1984 to 1986 and president from 1986 to 1988.

Michael P. Comer

Michael P. Comer is an ordained United Methodist minister and a member of the North Central New York Conference. His Ph.D. is from Northwestern University. A licensed psychologist in Michigan, he is clinical director of the Samaritan Center in Battle Creek, Michigan. He is a member of the American Psychological Association, Fellow of the American Association of Pastoral Counselors, and is on the faculty of Kellogg Community College.

James E. Dittes

James E. Dittes is professor of pastoral theology and psychology at Yale University, where he is on the faculties of the Divinity School, the psychology department, and the department of religious studies. He has addressed men's concerns in his books *The Male Predicament* (Harper & Row, 1985) and *When Work Goes Sour* (Westminster, 1987). Earlier books have been concerned with the nature of ministry and the self-image of the minister, such as *The Church in the Way* (Scribner's, 1967), *Minister on the Spot* (Pilgrim, 1970), and *When the People Say No* (Harper & Row, 1979). He was a consultant in the development of the Theological School Inventory and the *Readiness for Ministry* projects. Educated at Oberlin College and Yale University, he is a minister in the United Church of Christ.

Leila Merrell Foster

Leila Merrell Foster, J.D., M.Div., Ph.D., is a lawyer, a United Methodist minister, and a clinical psychologist. She has chaired the Chicago Bar Association Committees on Mental Health Law and on Science and Technology and the Law, and the Illinois State Bar Association Committee on the Mentally Disabled. As a minister, she has been pastor of three churches and has served on her Conference Board of Ministerial Training and Qualifications. She is a Fellow of the American Psychological Association and a Fellow and Diplomate of the Board of Medical Psychotherapists. Currently, she is in private practice in Evanston, Illinois.

Winston Gooden

Winston Gooden is associate professor of psychology at Fuller Theological Seminary in the graduate school of psychology. He received his M.Div. and his Ph.D. from Yale University. His research interest area is development in early and middle adulthood.

Richard L. Gorsuch

Richard L. Gorsuch is professor of psychology and director of research/evaluation in the Graduate School of Psychology at Fuller Theological Seminary. He is an ordained minister with a M.Div. from Vanderbilt University and a Ph.D. in psychology from the University of Illinois. He has conducted research, published, consulted, and taught in the area of psychometrics (including scale development and use of assessments). Complementing this technical background is his extensive work in the psychology of religion.

Thomas Graham

Thomas Graham is a consultant specializing in human resource development, personnel selection, leadership training, team building, needs assessment, cross-cultural training, and church growth. He has developed and conducted over thirty assessment centers for organizing pastors for mission agencies and denominational groups. He is president of the Center for Organizational and Ministry Development, a nonprofit organization dedicated to identifying and equipping church planters, providing support services in church growth, and encouraging, training, and nurturing Christian leaders.

Brian P. Hall

Brian P. Hall, Ph.D., is founder of the Omega Institute in Los Gatos, California. He is also on the faculty of the Graduate Humanities Department at the University of Santa Clara, where he specializes in pastoral counseling. Dr. Hall is the author of *Development of Consciousness: A Confluent Theory of Values* and coauthor of the three-volume series *Value Clarification as Learning Process* and coauthor of the Hall-Tonna book *Inventory of Values*.

Emily D. Haight

Emily D. Haight is currently a pastoral psychotherapist and faculty member of the Center for Religion and Psychotherapy of Chicago. Her involvement in pastoral assessment began with her doctoral research, "Psychological Criteria for the Selection of Ministerial Candidates," and includes directing the Assessment and Counseling Services and the Institute for Research in Pastoral Psychology and Counseling while a faculty member at Garrett-Evangelical Theological Seminary from 1979 to 1986. She is a pastoral evaluation specialist for The United Methodist Church, which ordained her an elder in 1978. She received a B.A. in liberal arts and psychology in 1969 from the University of Texas at Austin, an M.Div. from Garrett-Evangelical Theological Seminary in 1974, and a Ph.D. from Garrett and Northwestern University in 1980. She served as a local church pastor for three years.

Archibald D. Hart

Archibald D. Hart is currently professor of psychology and dean of the Graduate School of Psychology at

Fuller Theological Seminary in Pasadena, California. Having trained originally in South Africa, where he is licensed as a clinical psychologist, he first came to the United States in 1971. He is licensed in the state of California as a psychologist and specializes in psychotherapy from a Christian orientation, stress management and the use of biofeedback techniques, neuro-psycho-diagnosis, and cognitive approaches to psychology. He is married and has three daughters. His wife, Kathleen, plays an important part in his professional career, often sharing in his seminars her experience as a woman.

John E. Hinkle, Jr.

John E. Hinkle, Jr., is professor of pastoral psychology and counseling at Garrett-Evangelical Theological Seminary. He is the founder and director of Clergy Candidate Assessment Services. He is a member of the Advisory Committee for Psychological Assessment of the Division of Ordained Ministry of The United Methodist Church. He is the author of *A Guidebook on Psychological Assessment in the Ministerial Selection Process.*

David Allen Hogue

David Allen Hogue holds an A.B. degree from Greenville College, Greenville, Illinois, a M.S. from Indiana State University, Terre Haute, a M.Div. from Christian Theological Seminary, Indianapolis, Indiana, and a Ph.D. from Garrett and Northwestern. He is director of the Christian Center for Effective Living of First Presbyterian Church in Evanston, Illinois, and also served as executive director of the Samaritan Pastoral Counseling Center of Evanston/Wilmette from 1982 to 1985. He served as an associate pastor and hospital chaplain prior to moving to Evanston.

Pamela J. Holliman

Pamela J. Holliman is a pastoral counselor and ordained elder in The United Methodist Church. She completed her doctoral work at Garrett and Northwestern and is certified as a pastoral evaluation specialist by The United Methodist Church. Her chapter in this book is based on her dissertation "A Study of Psychological Assessment Procedures as Adjunctive to Personnel Selection Processes in a Religious Organization," a research project commissioned by The United Methodist Division of Higher Education and Ordained Ministry.

Richard A. Hunt

Richard A. Hunt, Ph.D., is professor of psychology at Fuller Theological Seminary and director of the adult clinic at Pasadena Community Counseling Clinic. He is an ordained elder of The United Methodist Church in the Central Texas Annual Conference. He is licensed as a psychologist in California and Texas, a Diplomate with the American Board of Professional Psychology, Fellow in the American Association of Pastoral Counselors, and member and supervisor with the American Association for Marriage and Family Therapy. He created and wrote The United Methodist Candidacy Studies program and is a member of the Advisory Committee for Psychological Assessment of the Division of Ordained Ministry of The United Methodist Church. He is certified as a pastoral evaluation specialist. He and his wife, Joan, authored *Growing Love in Christian Marriage,* the United Methodist handbook for couples.

Harvey L. Huntley, Jr.

Harvey L. Huntley, Jr., is currently pastor of Messiah Evangelical Lutheran Church (ELCA) in Knoxville, Tennessee. Previously, he served for over five years as associate director for leadership support with the Division for Professional Leadership of the Lutheran Church in America (LCA) in Philadelphia. In that position, he carried portfolio responsibilities for the churchwide candidacy process used by his denomination for church occupations. During nearly ten years as a parish pastor following graduation from seminary, he served for nine years on the preparation (candidacy) committee of his judicatory (the Southeastern Synod) and as chairperson of the committee for seven years. He holds a D.Min. and a M.Th. from the University of Chicago Divinity School. In addition, he is completing a Certificate of Advanced Study in Education in career counseling at the Johns Hopkins University.

Chan-Hie Kim

Chan-Hie Kim is a United Methodist pastor and associate professor of New Testament and Korean studies at the School of Theology at Claremont, California. He was educated at Yonsei University (B.A.) and Vanderbilt University (D.D., Ph.D.), and he has served for the past ten years as the director of the Center of Asian American Ministries at Claremont.

Robert F. Kohler

Robert F. Kohler is a clergy member of the Eastern Pennsylvania Conference of The United Methodist

Appendix

Church. From 1976 to 1979 he was chairperson of the Board of Ordained Ministry of that conference, and since that time has served as the director of the Board of Ordained Ministry Relations in the General Board of Higher Education and Ministry, Division of Ordained Ministry. As a denominational officer, he has been responsible for the development of a system of supervision for ordained ministry candidates, a part of which often involves psychological assessment. His staff responsibility also includes work with the Advisory Committee on Psychological Assessment.

Cameron Lee

Cameron Lee is assistant professor of marriage and family studies at Fuller Theological Seminary in Pasadena, California, where he received both a M.Div. and a Ph.D. He maintains a strong research interest in the dynamics of clergy families and has written and lectured frequently on this topic.

Laura F. Majovski

Laura Fogwell Majovski and her husband are in private practice as psychologists in Pasadena, California. She holds a Ph.D. from the Graduate School of Psychology, Fuller Theological Seminary, and she is a consultant to churches.

H. Newton Malony

H. Newton Malony, Ph.D., is professor and director of programs in the integration of psychology and theology SSP, Fuller Theological Seminary. He is an ordained United Methodist minister in the California-Pacific Annual Conference. He has participated in clergy evaluation for over two decades. He is a licensed psychologist, Diplomate with the American Board of Professional Psychology, and a Fellow of the American Psychological Association. He has authored or edited several books and articles concerning ministry.

Joseph P. O'Neill

Joseph P. O'Neill, former scholar in residence at the Carnegie Foundation, is coordinating the Lilly Endowment's five million dollar program to improve the recruitment and selection of candidates for ordained ministry. He is also a member of the research team at Educational Testing Service in Princeton, New Jersey, which is integrating many major studies of clergy and constructing a profile of entering seminarians for the past twenty-five years.

Roy M. Oswald

Roy M. Oswald, a Lutheran minister, is a senior consultant to the Alban Institute in Washington, D.C., a consulting and training organization that focuses on congregations nationwide. He has served in parish and synod positions and is the author of a dozen books on issues of growth and development for both the clergy and congregations. His book *Personality Type and Religious Leadership,* coauthored with Otto Kroeger, is based on data drawn from Myers-Briggs technology. He is currently engaged in a major study of candidacy processes employed by various denominations.

John Patton

John Patton is the executive director of the Georgia Association for Pastoral Care, a pastoral service and training center accredited by both the Association for Clinical Pastoral Education and the American Association of Pastoral counselors. He also holds a part-time appointment as professor of pastoral theology at Columbia Theological Seminary. He is an A.C.P.E. certified supervisor, a Diplomate with the American Association of Pastoral Counselors, and has a Ph.D. in religion and personality from the University of Chicago. Prior to his present position, he served as a campus minister, parish pastor, hospital chaplain, and was for sixteen years on the editorial committee of *The Journal of Pastoral Care.* He is the author of numerous articles and three books, including *Pastoral Counseling: A Ministry of the Church, Is Human Forgiveness Possible: A Pastoral Perspective,* and *Christian Marriage and Family: Caring for Our Generations,* coauthored with Brian H. Childs.

J. David Pierce

J. David Pierce, Ph.D., is currently an associate professor of pastoral theology and counseling at the University of Dubuque Theological Seminary. He has been involved with the Native American Theological Association and is a representative for his seminary to the Native American Theological Education Consortium. He works closely with the Native American Program at Dubuque Seminary and teaches courses in culture, personality, and religious beliefs. He holds his doctoral degree from Northwestern University in religious and theological studies.

Biographical Profiles

Pablo Polischuk

Pablo Polischuk, a native of Argentina, was engaged in evangelistic/pastoral ministry in his country of origin prior to receiving his Ph.D. at the University of California, Berkeley, and Fuller Graduate School of Psychology. Since 1979, he has been affiliated with Massachusetts General Hospital and Harvard Medical School. At the present, he is the chief psychologist at the Chelsea Memorial Health Center and also director of Willowdale Center for Psychological Services in South Hamilton. He is an ordained minister of the Assemblies of God denomination. He is married to Frances Christine Alexander and has three children, Karen, Kenneth, and Keith.

Charles R. Ridley

Charles R. Ridley received his Ph.D. from the University of Minnesota. He is currently an associate professor at the Graduate School of Psychology, Fuller Theological Seminary in Pasadena, California. Previously, he had been a consulting psychologist in private industry and taught at the University of Maryland and Indiana University. His areas of specialization are cross-cultural psychotherapy, the integration of psychology and theology, organizational consultation, and ministerial assessment.

Joan Scanlon

Joan Scanlon has been a member of Dominican Sisters of Kentucky since 1962. She is an associate graduate faculty member in the master's program in pastoral counseling of the Institute of Pastoral Studies of Loyola University in Chicago and in the doctor of ministry program at St. Mary of the Lake University in Mundelein, Illinois. She is a pastoral counselor with the Christian Brothers Counseling and Consultation Center in Evanston, Illinois. She completed her Ph.D. in pastoral counseling and psychology in the joint program at Garrett-Evangelical Seminary and Northwestern University in 1985.

Howard Stone

Howard W. Stone is professor of pastoral psychology and pastoral care at Brite Divinity School of Texas Christian University. He is a Lutheran minister, a psychologist, and a Diplomate in the American Association of Pastoral Counselors. He has published numerous articles and seven books, including *Crisis Counseling, The Caring Church: A Guide to Lay Pastoral Care Ministry, The Caring Christian: Schleiermacher's Practical Theology,* and *Word of God and Pastoral Care.*

Edward P. Wimberly

Edward P. Wimberly is an associate professor of pastoral care and black church studies at Garrett-Evangelical Theological Seminary. He has served on the Advisory Committee for Psychological Assessment of the Division of Ordained Ministry, The United Methodist Church, since 1978. He is a member of the American Association of Pastoral Counselors and the American Association of Marriage and Family Therapists. He holds a Ph.D. in pastoral psychology and counseling from Boston University. He has published several books and articles in the area of black pastoral care.

INDEX

Academy of Religion and Mental Health, 16-17
Adjective Check List (ACL), 72-73, 75-77, 142, 187
adrenaline, effects on body, 38
adult development in task of minister, 32-35
Advisory Committee on Psychological Assessment (UMC), 187, 188
Alban Institute, 179-83
Allport's Study of Values test, 142
American Association for Counseling and Development, 178
American Baptist Church, 106-7, 164
American Indian Policy Review Commission, 163
Amos vs. Presiding Bishops of the Church of Latter Day Saints, 135-36
Annual Conference (UMC) use of assessment, 184-88
Arbuckle, Gerald A., 195
Archdiocese of Detroit (RCC), 93
Archdiocese of Minneapolis (RCC), 93
Asian Americans, 158-62
Assemblies of God, 106-7, 154, 155-56
assertiveness, ministerial, 41-42
assessment, psychological: applications of, 31, 86-89, 110; in career planning, 86-88, 175-78; development of, 67-71; future of, 198-205; legal liabilities of, 57, 134-35, 137-38; as nurture/selection, 72, 204-5; purposes, 78
Association for Clinical Pastoral Education, 125-26
Association for Religious Values in Counseling, 178
Association of Theological Schools (ATS): and POM, 97, 105, 106; statistics on Hispanics, 154; study of seminary applications, 170-74
authority, value of relations of, 123-25, 127-28

Becker, Ernest, 34
Beck's Depression Inventory, 38
biblical world, sociological studies of, 159-69
Bier, William C., 16, 58, 198
Blackmon, R., on depression, 37
blacks, psychological assessment of, 149-53
Board of Ordained Ministries (UMC), 86
brain chemistry, as factor in assessment, 205
Brite Divinity School study, 94
Bronfenbrenner, Urie, 44-45
Browning, Don, 144
burnout as hazard of ministry, 38-39

California Psychological Inventory, 143

call to ministry: discernment of, 22-23, 90-91, 145, 146, 147, 205; in RCC perspective, 193; value of, 180
Candidacy Assessment Office, 187
career planning centers, 14-15, 175
Carr, Anne E., 146
casebook, in POM project, 102-3
Casebook on Ethical Principles of Psychologists, 136
Cattell, R. B., 155
Center for Asian American Ministry, 159
Center for the Ministry, 176
Center for Professional Development in Ministry, Lancaster Theological Seminary, 175, 176, 178
changing patterns in ministry, 82-85, 174
characteristics of effective ministry, 25
Chinese immigration to U.S., 158
Chodorow, Nancy, 145
Christian Reformed Church, 164
Christian Theological Seminary, 172
church: role in assessment, 21-22, 72; marks of true, 180-81
church career development centers, 175-78
Church of the Brethren, 91
Civil Rights Act, Title VII, 135-36
clergy assessment: definition, 13-16; as diagnosis, 23-24; theoretical issues in, 21-26; basic questions in POM, 97. *See also* assessment, psychological
clergy families, pressures on, 33, 36, 37-43
Clifton, Donald, 194
clinical interview, C.P.E. model, 123, 127-28. *See also* interviews
Clinical Pastoral Education (C.P.E.), 14-15, 123-28
clinical psychologists as evaluators, 14-15
Code of Fair Testing Practices in Education, 137
Combined Model for criterion development, 61, 64-65
Comer, Michael, P., 56, 64, 187
competencies for ministry, definition, 13
Concept Mastery test, 82-83, 84, 85
confidentiality of assessments, 173-74, 176-77
consultants in clergy assessment, 56, 123-25
contract for assessment, 152
Coriden, James A. et al., 192-93
counseling for seminary applicants, 172
countertransference, phenomenon of, 40
criteria: for clergy assessment, 61-66, 67, 97-101, 109; for effective ministry, 23-25; for future, 203

culture-related bias in assessment, 15, 61-62, 140-43, 149, 155-57
culture variant model for bias-free assessment, 149-50, 152-53

Deming, W. Edwards, 180
depression as ministerial hazard, 36, 37-38
DeWire, Harry A., 16, 105, 184-85
diaconal ministers (UMC), assessment of, 188
Diagnostic Reading Tests, 82-83, 84
Diocese of Evansville (RCC), 93
Disciples of Christ, 82-83
discrepancy theories of job satisfaction, 67
disqualification characteristics for ministry, 170
Dittes, James E., 84, 105
Divine Word Missionaries, 92
Division of Ordained Ministry (UMC), 184, 185-86, 187
The Dream, in choice of vocation, 32-33, 34, 35
dual career couples in ministry, 48-51, 176

Educational Testing Service, 94, 105
Edwards Personal Preference Schedule, 143, 151, 185
effectiveness in ministry, 13-14, 67; study by Majovick and Malony, 86, 87-88
emotional hazards of ministry, 36
Episcopal Church, 94, 164
equity theories of job satisfaction, 67
Erikson, Eric, 145, 146
Ethical Principles of Psychologists (APA), 136
Ethnic Leadership Development Centers, 92
evaluation, psychological. See assessment, psychological
evangelistic motivation for ministry, 83-84
exosystem, of social ecological field, 45
extroverts in ministry, 59

Faber, Heija, 124
fair use of psychometric testing, 58-59
Family Education Rights and Privacy Statement, 173
Faulkner, B., 37
Fear, R., 115
Feedback Study of 1970 (TSI), 106-7
feminist critique of psychology. See gender-related considerations for assessment
feminist spirituality/theology, 146, 147
Filipinos in U.S., 158
First Amendment protection, 135-36
Focus Eleven (Archdiocese of Detroit), 93
Freud, Sigmund, gender-related bias of, 145
Friedman, Edwin, 46
fulfillment theories of job satisfaction, 67
Fuller Theological Seminary, 92-93

Garrett-Evangelical Seminary, 64-65, 150-51, 173-74
gender-related considerations for assessment, 15, 61-62, 77, 140-43, 144-48
generativity, nature and effects of, 35
Gilligan, Carol, 145

Gilmore Health Inventory, 151
goals for personnel in ministry (Blanchard), 119
Golden Gate Baptist Seminary, 91-92
Graduate Record Examination (ATS), 171
Gruneberg, M. M., 68
Guide to Interpreting the TSI, 84, 105
The Guidebook for Pastoral Evaluation Specialists (Jones), 187
A Guidebook on Psychological Assessment in a Pastoral Evaluation Process (Hinkle), 186
Guidelines for Computer Based Test and Interpretation (APA), 137
Guilford-Zimmerman test, 171

Haight, Emily, 72-77
Hall, Brian, 194-95
Hall-Tonna Inventory of Values, 142, 194-95
Hart, A. D., 37, 40
Harvard Divinity School, 93
Havighurst, Robert, 166
Hinkle, John E., Jr., 13, 173, 186
Hispanics in U.S., 154-57
holistic approach to assessment, 175, 178
Hough, Joseph, 28
human judgment in assessment, 55-56
Hunt, Richard A., 105-6

Immigration Act of 1965, 159
Incomplete Sentence Blank test, 185
Indian Church Career Research and Planning Project, 164
Indian influence on Asian culture, 158
instruments for clergy assessment, definition, 14
integration in clergy family and congregational relations, 46
intelligence: as predictor of career success, 59-60; tests in assessment, 72-73. See also individual tests
interaction between minister and work environment, 67-68
Interdenominational Theological Center, 150-51
interviews, use in clergy assessment, 102-3, 113-18
introverts in ministry, 59
Inventory of Religious Activities and Interests (IRAI), 16, 85-86, 104, 107-8, 143, 156
itineracy of clergy (UMC), 109

James, William, 29
Japanese in U.S., 158
Jesus as model for ministry, 27-28
job description, instrument for effective ministry, 119-20, 121-22
Job Descriptive Index (JDI), 68, 69, 71
Job-in-General scale, 69
job satisfaction, 67-71
John XXIII (pope), 190
Josephite Fathers, 92
Josselson, Ruthellen, 146

"Key Concepts in the Selection and Application of Criteria . . . " (Means), 187
Kieren, D. K., and B. Munro, 48

Kling, Frederick R., 105
Klopfer, Walter, 129
Kohlberg's moral development theory, 145
Koreans in U.S., 158-59
Kunin "Faces" scale, 69

Latin American Bible Institute of La Puente, 154
Lawler, E. C., 67-68
Lawyer, selection for assessment advice, 137
lay ministry in RCC, 195
Ledig, Barbara, 195
letters of recommendation, in assessment, 56, 72-74, 75-77, 187
Levinson, D. J., 32, 24, 145-46
life histories, use in assessment, 145-47
life satisfaction, 68, 69
life transitions, 33-35
Lilly Endowment, Inc., support of ministerial evaluation projects, 16, 17, 82, 90-94, 105, 107
Lodahl, T. M., and M. Kejner, 68
Lutheran Church in America, 140-43
Lutheran Church Missouri Synod, 106-7

McAdams, D. P., 34-35
McCord, Joan, 57
McTEST program, 69
Mace, David and Vera, 45
macrosystem in social ecology, 45
Marriage in Ministry program (UMC), 50
Maslack Burnout Inventory, 39
Mason, Emanuel J., and William J. Bramble, 78
"Mending the Hoop," 164
Mennonite Church, 91
mesosystem in social ecology, 45
mentoring, process of, 32-33, 92-93
Meyer, Kay, and French (General Electric Study), 180
microsystem in social ecology, 44-45
Midwest Career Center, 176, 177
Miller Analogies test, 82-83, 85, 94
Mills, Edgar W. J., 105
Ministerial Effectiveness Inventory (MEI), 67-88
Ministries Studies Board, 105
ministry as profession, 27-29
Ministry Inventories, scoring service, 105-6, 107, 108, 174
Minnesota Multiphasic Personality Inventory (MMPI): as clergy assessment tool, 58, 72-73. 74, 75-76, 86-87, 88, 171; for criterion development, 64, 65; denominational use of, 142, 185, 187, 195; minority use of, 151-52, 154-55, 156-57, 167; popularity of, 92-93, 94, 111, 112; as psychological indicator, 38, 39, 41, 69, 82-83, 85
"The MMPI and Black Ministerial Students" (Haight and McNair), 151
minorities in ministry, 91-92, 106-7. See also Asian Americans, blacks, Hispanics, Native Americans, women
Moravian Theological Seminary, 90-91
Moses' call to ministry, 21, 22, 24
Multiple Regression Analysis, 70-71, 74-76, 88, 187

Myers-Briggs Temperament Inventory, 143, 171
mythology, in self-image, 29-31

narrative in ministry. See storytelling
National Black Catholic Congress, 92
National Board of Counselor Certification, 177
National Career Development Association, 178
National Conference of Religious Vocation Directors, 92
National Council of Churches, 105, 106
National Institute of Mental Health, 172
national standard core battery of assessment instruments, 109-12
National Task Force on Psychological Testing and Pastoral Education (UMC), 150-52
Native Americans: diversity of, 63; in ministry 164-67
Native American Theological Education Consortium, 164, 165-67
Nazarene churches, 155-56
Network of Pastoral Evaluators, 188
New Testament and clergy assessment, 72, 170
New York Theological Seminary, 91
North Central Career Center, 176
Northeast Career Center, 175, 176, 177
Novaco Anger Scale, 41

occupation, choice of, 32-33
Ohio State Psychological Test, 171
older candidates, impact of, 205
Omega International analysis, 195
Ordination Study by Majovski and Malony, 86-87, 88
Otis Self-Administering Test of Mental Ability, 82-83, 84, 85
outside assessor for clergy, 179, 182

"pastoral," meanings of term, 126
pastors' self-ratings, 89
Paul, apostle, 36, 43
Paul VI (pope), 190
Pearson Product Manual, 73
peer relationships for C.P.E. students, 124-25, 126
performance appraisal of ministers, 121, 179, 181-83
permanent diaconate in RCC, 195
person as key tool for ministry, 36
Personal Data Inventory, 187
personal development in ministry 28-29, 36-42
personnel development in church ministry, 119-22
Phi Beta Kappa members in ministry, 83
Piaget's moral development theory, 145
pluralistic evaluation, 152
Polischuk, Pablo, study of Protestant Hispanics, 155-54
Pope, Kenneth S., 136-37
pre-evaluation study for selection committees, 78-81
Presbyterian churches: career development program, 177; study of Hispanics, 155-56; and TSI, 106-7
Priest-Perceiver Interview, 194, 195
"A Profile of Contemporary Seminarians" (Larsen and Shopshire), 174

Profiles of Ministry (POM): development of, 16, 97-103; wide use of, 92-93, 143, 171
Protestant influence on public life, 93-94
psychiatrists as assessors, 14-15
"Psychological Criteria for the Selection of Ministerial Candidates" (Haight), 187
psychologists as assessors, 21-22, 23-24, 110
psychometric procedures for assessment, 21-22, 55-60, 145-47
Pugh, Thomas J., 150-51

Quality of Ministry Projects, 17, 90-94

Readiness for Ministry, 58, 59, 60, 97, 170. *See also* Profiles of Ministry
Reformed Church in America, 164
regional differences among black ministerial students, 151-52
report writing for clergy evaluation, 129-33
retreats for clergy couples, 50
Ricard, Bishop John, 92
Ricoeur, Paul, 29, 124, 127
Rizzuto, Ana-Maria, 29, 30
Robinson, Herbert L., 48-49
Rochester Divinity School, 92
Roman Catholic Church: Hispanic element in, 154; history in America, 189-90; requirements for priesthood, 191, 192-93; vocations in, 92, 93, 190, 191, 193, 195; women in, 144, 191
Rorshack S-O, 171
Rossi, Peter H., Howard E. Freemen, and Sonia R. Wright, *Evaluation: A Systematic Approach*, 98
Rutman, Leonard, 79-80

St. Francis Seminary (Milwaukee), 94
Satisfaction in Ministry (SIM) as assessment instrument, 67, 68, 69, 70-71
Saunders, David R., 105
Schaller, Lyle, 180
Schuller, D., 170
Schuller, Strommen, Brekke, report on *Readiness in Ministry*, 97
screening, early vocational, 59, 172
second career individuals, impact of, 82, 83-84
selection committees as evaluators, 78-81
Selection Research Incorporated, 194
self-evaluation as C.P.E. process, 123-28
seminary applications as assessment tools, 170-74
Sequential Tests of Educational Progress, 151
severity of record, check for reliability, 74, 75
sexuality and clergy, 39-41, 201
Shipley Institute of Living Scale, 65, 72-73, 75-77, 142, 187
Sixteen Personality Factor test (16PF), 59, 142-43, 155, 171
Smith, D. P., 36
social activism as motivation, 82-83
social ecology of clergy family life, 44-47
Social Network Assessment Profile, 37

social support for clergy, 59
Southern Baptist Church, 91, 106-7
Spanish translations of evaluation instruments, 154-55
Spearman-Brown prophecy formula, 68
Specialty Guidelines for the Delivery of Services by Clinical Psychologiests (APA), 137
Speciality Guidelines for the Delivery of Services by Industrial/Organizational Psychologists (APA), 137
spiritual formation, locale in curriculum, 27-29, 30
Stage I Profile and Interpretative Manual (POM), 102-3
Standard Metropolitan Statistical Areas, studies of Native Americans, 163
Standards for Educational and Psychological Testing, 137
Stiebe, Susan, 194
Story of My Life, for discernment of call to priesthood, 93
storytelling, as function of minister, 28-31
stress as hazard of ministry, 38-39
Strong-Campbell Interest Inventory (SCII): in psychological assessment, 72-73, 74, 171; wide use of, 111, 142, 185, 187
Strong Vocational Interest Blank (SVIB), 72, 74, 75, 171
"A Study of Psychological Assessment Procedures . . ." (Holliman), 187
Study of Values, 151
support groups, usefulness of, 38, 42
"Survey of Resources for Development in Ministry," 178
Sutherland, John, 44
supervision, pastoral in C.P.E., 124-26

Taylor-Johnson Temperament Analysis, 171
technological applications for assessment, 204
Tennessee Self-Concept Scale, 59, 142
theological education, history of, 27-28
theological implication of assessment, 22-23
theological orientation, changes in, 83
Theological School Inventory (TSI): as assessment tool, 8, 58, 59, 60, 69; development of, 16, 68, 90, 105; scales of, 65, 84, 104-7; wide use of, 92-93, 94, 107, 143, 151, 171
TSI Manual, 105
Theoretical/Empirical Model for criterion development, 61, 63-64
Tonna, Benjamin, 195
"Tort and Religion" (ABA), 200
transition as life process, 34-35
Transition Work Group on Ministry (Lutheran), 141-43
transference, phenomenon of, 40

United Church of Christ, 164
United Lutheran Church, 106-7
United Methodist Church: candidacy studies, 49-50, 82-83, 108; decision-making in ordination process, 72, 79-81, 87-88, 109; minorities in, 150-52, 155-56, 164; use of psychological assessment, 62-63, 64, 68, 106-7, 184-88
United Presbyterian Church Vocation Agency, 164
University of Dubuque Theological Seminary, 164

validity of psychological assessment, 22-23, 57-58, 69-70, 203

Index

Valliant, George, 145-46
Vanderbilt Divinity School, 92, 94
Vatican II, impact of, 190
The Very Simple Structure program, for measuring job satisfaction, 68
vocational development approach to assessment, 15-16

Webb, Sam C., 105
Wechsler Adult Intelligence Scale, 151

Wesley, John, "Historic Examination" for clergy, 72
wife of minister, traditional role, 48
Wiggins, Jerry S., 61, 62, 66
Winebrenner Seminary, 90
women in ministry, 82, 83-84, 106-7, 144-48, 205
work samples, use in assessment, 203-4
workshops for assessment professionals, 112
Wynn, J. C., 43